F

A HISTORY OF PSYCHOLOGY
IN AUTOBIOGRAPHY
VOLUME III

A HISTORY OF PSYCHOLOGY
IN AUTOBIOGRAPHY
VOLUME III

By

JAMES ROWLAND ANGELL   O. KLEMM
FREDERIC CHARLES BARTLETT   KARL MARBE
MADISON BENTLEY   CHARLES SAMUEL MYERS
HARVEY A. CARR   E. W. SCRIPTURE
SANTE DE SANCTIS   EDWARD LEE THORNDIKE
JOSEPH FRÖBES   JOHN BROADUS WATSON
                    WILHELM WIRTH

Edited by
CARL MURCHISON

NEW YORK: RUSSELL & RUSSELL

THE INTERNATIONAL UNIVERSITY SERIES
IN PSYCHOLOGY

PREFACE TO THE SERIES*

The author of a recent history of psychology found that it was impossible to get important facts concerning the scientific development of certain individuals except from those individuals themselves. Since a science separated from its history lacks direction and promises a future of uncertain importance, it is a matter of consequence to those who wish to understand psychology for those individuals who have greatly influenced contemporary psychology to put into print as much of their personal histories as bears on their professional careers.

The initial idea, which later developed into the general plan for *A History of Psychology* in *Autobiography,* was contained in a letter of April 10, 1928, from Edwin G. Boring to Carl Murchison. Shortly afterwards, there was a conference in Emerson Hall, participated in by Edwin G. Boring of Harvard University, Karl Bühler of the University of Vienna, and Carl Murchison of Clark University, which resulted in our inviting Herbert S. Langfeld of Princeton University and John B. Watson of New York City to join with us in a committee which would assume responsibility for all invitations extended for inclusion in such a series.

We then proceeded in the following manner in arriving at a tentative list of individuals to whom invitations were to be sent. Without consultation, each member of the Committee compiled a list of one hundred names that he considered eligible for such a series. The five lists of one hundred each were then combined, making a composite list of one hundred eighty-four names. Taking the one hundred eighty-four names as a nomination list, each member of the Committee then voted for sixty names. All chosen unanimously were placed upon a preferred list to whom invitations would be sent as the Series progressed.

Since preparing the original list, the members of the Committee, in conference, have expanded somewhat the principle of selection which originally guided them. We agreed that individuals on the fringe of psychology or even in a neighboring field of science might so influence psychology that they should be included.

It must not be thought that individuals were invited in order of

---

*Reprinted from Volume I.

eminence or of seniority exclusively. There are many factors which determine the order in which autobiographies appear in this Series and it is very probable that some of the most eminent individuals will appear in later volumes rather than in earlier ones. In two or three cases, we decided that certain individuals of the greatest eminence should probably not appear in the first one or two volumes because they are already well known to most psychologists and have recently been discussed at length in other histories, especially in Boring's *A History of Experimental Psychology*. During the next year, perhaps three volumes altogether will have appeared, while a fourth volume will appear in the near future. If our idea proves to be as fruitful as we now believe that it will, it is to be expected that additional volumes will appear at intervals of three or four years.

In this Series, the printing of long and comprehensive bibliographies has been definitely avoided, since these will be accessible in the *Psychological Register*.

CLARK UNIVERSITY
Worcester, Massachusetts
May 22, 1930

CARL MURCHISON, *Chairman*
EDWIN G. BORING
KARL BÜHLER
HERBERT S. LANGFELD
JOHN B. WATSON

PREFACE TO VOLUME III

According to present plans this is the final volume in this Series. The members of the Selecting Committee disband with the publication of this volume.

The Editor wishes to express his deep appreciation for the cooperation of the various authors and the members of the Selecting Committee.

CLARK UNIVERSITY
Worcester, Massachusetts
November 11, 1936

CARL MURCHISON

TABLE OF CONTENTS

JAMES ROWLAND ANGELL

After several years of delay, I am attempting to comply with the request of the editor of this series and set forth something of my life and intellectual history, as I believe it to be, even though I find it difficult to suppose that such a statement will possess any significant value for others.

While I gave some 27 years of my life to teaching and research in the field of psychology, the last 17 years have been almost wholly preoccupied with educational work of an administrative kind, which fact has compelled me to abandon any pretense of active participation in the development of my science. Any account of my life as a psychologist is accordingly already ancient history. If it has any enduring value, it will be for the light it may throw on an interesting and critical period of American psychology with which I was actively identified.

I was born May 8, 1869, in Burlington, Vermont, where my father, James Burrill Angell, was President of the University of Vermont. He had previously been Professor of Modern Languages at Brown University and had also edited the *Providence Journal* for six years. As is well known, he subsequently went to Ann Arbor, where for 38 years he was President of the University of Michigan. It was there that I grew up, went to school and to college. My maternal grandfather, Alexis Caswell, after a brief career as a Baptist minister, was Professor of Mathematics and Astronomy at Brown, later President of the University, and one of the charter members of the National Academy of Sciences. My interest in educational and scientific matters has therefore some possible hereditary background, although in the direct line I do not know of any men prior to my maternal grandfather who had followed the learned professions. Certainly my earlier male ancestry on both sides had for some generations been New England farmers, men of ability and thrift, who enjoyed the confidence and respect of their fellows. On my father's side my first male ancestor, Thomas Angell, came into Rhode Island with Roger Williams in 1636. Like some hundreds of thousands of other American citizens, I am, on my mother's side, a descendant from Mayflower ancestry. Peregrine White, the first white child born of the Mayflower stock, was an ancestor. My only brother, Alexis Caswell Angell, was a highly successful lawyer, for a time a Judge on the Federal Bench, lecturing periodically in the University of Michigan Law School, and for many years widely regarded as the leader of the bar in the City of Detroit. My sister married a Professor of American History, Andrew C. McLaughlin, for some years Chairman of the Department of History in the University of Michigan and for a still longer period head of the corresponding department at the University of Chicago, and sometime President of the American Historical Association. My only son, James Waterhouse Angell, has for some years been Professor of Economics in Columbia University. It thus clearly appears that my domestic environment has been largely academic.

In 1894 I married Marion Isabel Watrous of Des Moines, Iowa, who had been a fellow student at the University of Michigan. A son and a daughter were born to us, both of whom are married and with children of their own. My wife died in 1931 and I subsequently married Katharine Cramer Woodman, who has made my life one of great happiness. Her warm and friendly interest in students and their problems has won her a position of remarkable influence and appreciation in the Yale community.

I was the youngest of three children, my sister being six years my senior and my brother twelve. The home life was very simple and wholesome, although my father's position, coupled with my mother's abounding natural hospitality, resulted in the presence in the house of innumerable guests, many of them members of the faculty who would drop in for luncheon or dinner. Persons of distinction coming to the University on official errands of one kind and another were, in the early years at least, almost certain to be entertained in our home, for the hotels in the town were in those days rather impossible. These circumstances gave me opportunity from early childhood to see and meet many cultivated people from whose conversation I inevitably derived a certain kind of education, and I cherish not a few interesting memories of outstanding figures in the world of letters and public affairs, e.g., Canon Farrar, Mathew Arnold, Andrew White, Grover Cleveland, and many others of equal interest.

Both my parents were devoted Christians and the atmosphere of the home was distinctly religious. Until I was half grown, family prayers were regularly conducted by my father, generally after breakfast, and I grew up accepting religious exercises as a normal part of life. It was therefore a natural thing that in my early adolescence I joined the Congregational Church which my parents attended. Throughout my high school years I was thrown intimately with boys and girls, many of whom were active in the Student Christian Association in which I also took part. In college these religious activities somewhat lessened, as I was not much attracted to the men who directed them, but my interest in religious issues remained definite. While not pious, I was recognized by my mates as being identified with the religious portion of the community.

When I was four, I barely survived an attack of scarlet fever, which cost me the hearing of one ear and seriously sapped my vitality. Some years later, I suffered from recurrent attacks of malaria, so persistent a curse in the early history of southern Michigan. As a result, I suspect, of these mishaps, I was not very robust and the effect upon a rather oversensitive nervous organization was to render me somewhat timid and unassertive. There are tales of my being a mischievous child, but I can verify no episode which suggests more than the normal pranks of a lone youngster in a large household—and I was practically on my own, for my brother and sister were too much my elders to be companions in any intimate sense.

I attended the public schools of Ann Arbor, graduating from the high school in 1886 and proceeding to the state University, where I received my A.B. degree in 1890. Just prior to entering high school, I was for a year and one-half in China, where my father was sent as United States Minister at the head of a Commission appointed to negotiate a treaty, as was successfully done, which should control the immigration of Chinese laborers into the country. This event inevitably broke into my formal schooling, but it resulted in a trip around the world and in innumerable interesting experiences on which I place a very high value for the broadening and enriching of my outlook on life. Not the least of these were concerned with impressions of distinguished persons whom I saw and to whose conversation I listened with attention and interest. For example, Sir Robert Hart, for years the great administrator of the Chinese customs, was a frequent visitor at the Legation in Peking, and, thanks to my friendship with his son, Bruce, a lad of about my own age, he gave me a Korean pony, which I rode all about Peking during my stay.

From the time of my earliest memories, I was absorbingly interested in athletic sports and games of all kinds and, until I was perhaps half through college, there was never a moment when I would not rather play baseball, or football, or tennis, than do anything else whatever. School seemed to me to be a necessary evil whose value was grotesquely overestimated by my parents and other adults. I was a fair student, but rarely worked hard enough to make consistently high grades. In everything having to do with reading and writing, I excelled most of my mates in the earlier grades, perhaps because of superior home surroundings. Geography and spelling were relatively easy for me, because I had an excellent visual memory. Arithmetic bored me profoundly, and I gave it the least possible attention compatible with passing the tests necessary for promotion. I was fond of music and made a feeble attempt to master the piano, but unwillingness to practice faithfully left that achievement seriously incomplete.

When I got into the high school, Orin Cady of the University School of Music Faculty organized a boys' orchestra in which I learned to play a clarinet. Later a band was formed and I greatly enjoyed both experiences, learning a good deal about orchestration and musical construction, which I should otherwise have missed.

In the high school, I followed the conventional classical course, with Latin four years, mathematics three years, and Greek two years as the central core of the curriculum, with history, English, modern languages, and science as fillers. Thanks to egregious loafing the first year, in order to indulge my penchant for sports, I got off to a wretched start in Latin and algebra. The second year was heavily shadowed by the poor record of the first, but then I pulled myself together and by really hard work succeeded in graduating with an "A" diploma, which meant, as I recall it, that for the last two years of the course I succeeded in maintaining on a scale of 100 an average of 90, with no marks below 85. This won me a place on the commencement program and sent me to college without qualifications of any kind.

I came under only one brilliant teacher in the school, though many of the staff were thoroughly competent and, with more earnest students than I, achieved excellent results. Judson Pattengill was a born teacher, and from the first day in his classroom Greek became to me a fascinating study, which I pursued with equal enthusiasm under Walter Miller, later on for many years Professor and Dean of the Graduate School in the University of Missouri. Although I generally received high marks in it, I found the English teaching dull and uninteresting. The modern languages I got nothing of and the only science was a little botany. The time-consumption involved in physics and chemistry made these subjects difficult to combine with the classical curriculum. Unhappily there was no general biology and no earth science.

When I got to college I went on with the classical course, but after my freshman year I began to have opportunity for election and seized the earliest opportunity to get into logic and psychology. The logic which was based on Jevons' well-known little book interested me, though it did not greatly excite me. But the psychology (Dewey's recently published text) instantly opened up a new world, which it seemed to me I had been waiting for, and for the first time I felt a deep and pervasive sense of the intellectual importance of the material I was facing. My previous studies had at times stirred me, notably my Greek, and especially Homer, but I had never before encountered anything which seemed to afford me the sense of grasp, insight, and mastery in a subject intrinsically of crucial significance. With that experience began my real intellectual life, which ultimately led me on into my profession.

I at once started to elect work in the philosophical department— ethics, aesthetics, metaphysics, and Hegel's logic under John Dewey, British philosophy under Williston Hough, general history of philosophy under James H. Tufts, and most rewarding of all in the year following my graduation, which I spent as a graduate student at Michigan, a seminar with Dewey in William James's freshly published *Principles of Psychology*. That book unquestionably affected my thinking for the next 20 years more profoundly than any other.

In the later portion of my college course, I began to think of pursuing medicine, with a view to specializing in problems relating to the brain and nervous system, but weak eyes, from which I had suffered the tortures of the damned from early adolescence (sequelae, as I always believed, of my childhood illnesses, for nowhere else in the family had such a defect appeared), compelled me to forego the arduous microscopic work which was, and still is, an essential feature of medical training. The law did not interest me, the ministry presented intellectual obstacles which were increasingly grave, business was entirely out of my horizon, and I was steadily drawn to the possibility of an academic and scholarly career. My great doubt was whether I had sufficient ability to make a respectable record in that calling. Oddly enough, the economic aspect of the issue, which later cost me so much anxiety, never entered my mind. This fact, perhaps better than any other, shows how little the power and lure of money entered into the serious consideration of the people among whom I grew up. That some of them were very generous and others very stingy was matter of universal small-town knowledge and comment. But there was no great wealth in the place, almost no serious poverty, and money gave no one prestige. The evidences of wealth, when I encountered them in the homes of the rich in other communities, often filled me with a mild contempt and distaste rather than envy. I particularly disliked the flavor of sycophantic domestic service. My father's house was adequately staffed with servants, but I felt that they were all persons and not mere servitors, an attitude which was doubtless stimulated by the violent individualism of the English woman, Kate Martin, who was my nurse throughout my childhood.

With the encouragement of John Dewey, I remained, as I have above remarked, for a year of graduate study at Michigan, taking a master's degree with philosophy as my major and economics and American history as my minors, writing a thesis on imagery, with a study of the varieties of it disclosed in a group of nineteenth-century English poets. During this period, I greatly increased my obligations to Dewey and to Tufts, both later to be my colleagues for many years at the University of Chicago. For my intellectual awakening, for many basic elements in my subsequent habits of thought, and for endless kind and helpful acts in later years, I am under the deepest obligation to John Dewey, whose simplicity of character, originality, and virility of mind brought him the unqualified affection, admiration, and devotion of thousands of students.

On Dewey's recommendation, and with my parents' consent, I went from Michigan in 1891 to study in the Graduate School at Harvard under William James, Josiah Royce, and George Herbert Palmer. Santayana, of whom I had not heard, was there as a young instructor just coming over the philosophical horizon. I had not at the time decided whether to make philosophy or psychology my predominant interest. It so fell out that my year's work was fairly divided between James and Royce, Palmer having no formal courses into which I could expediently enter. A seminar of Royce in Kant was extremely illuminating and very taxing on time and energy. A general lecture course of his on metaphysics I attended as an auditor, with much less profit. I entered a seminar with James devoted to abnormal psychology and gave a large part of my time to miscellaneous work in the newly established laboratory which James, with great relief, had turned over to Herbert Nichols to run. In the seminars I met a number of brilliant and interesting students, with many of whom I established life-long friendships. Charles M. Bakewell, later my colleague at Yale, Alfred L. Hodder, Arthur H. Pierce, Dickinson S. Miller, Sidney E. Mezes, Alfred Buck, later my assistant at Chicago, and many others were in the number. Their presence constituted an invaluable asset in the atmosphere of the place. I enjoyed a peculiarly intimate contact with James by virtue of his turning over to me for study and digest the great mass of documentary material which had come to him in connection with the effort of the American Society for Psychical Research to secure exhaustive and reliable information regarding abnormal psychic experiences of normal individuals—especially so-called veridical hallucinations. This fact not only gave me a first-hand sense of the character of the evidence underlying belief in these phenomena, but it also put me in direct contact with one of the most inspiring and spiritually beautiful human beings I have ever known. If the result was not important for psychic research, it was of the utmost importance for my development and my devotion to a noble person whose friendship was warm and intimate as long as he lived.

Toward the end of the year, the Department suggested that I remain another year as understudy to Dr. Nichols in the laboratory. But I had decided that, if my father would send me, I would more wisely go abroad for further study. At first I considered England, having in mind especially the opportunity of working under Edward Caird in Kant, but closer knowledge of the conditions at the British universities made it clear that an itinerant graduate student would not find it very easy to secure the opportunities desired, and, as I was also eager to work in Wundt's laboratory at Leipzig, I decided to go to Germany. It had furthermore been my desire to study for a time with Hugo Münsterberg in Freiburg, but before my plans were complete, Münsterberg was invited to go to Harvard and that part of my program accordingly came to naught. As a result of my seminar work with James, I was keen to see something of Krafft-Ebing's work in Vienna, Bernheim in Nancy, and Charcot in Paris, where Ribot and Binet also attracted me. Flournoy in Geneva was likewise a man whom I felt a desire to meet. Obviously such an ambitious plan could not be brought to a conclusion in a single year and it was highly uncertain how long I could stay abroad. I was reluctant to submit my parents to further expense and besides I wanted to be married. As so often occurs in human affairs, what finally happened was quite different from what I had thought of.

Early in the summer of 1892, I sailed to Hamburg and went at once to Braunschweig, where more than 40 years earlier my father had gone, and as a member of the household of Pastor Sachs had received instruction in German from his daughter Fräulein Sachs. Arthur Pierce, whom I had come to know well at Harvard, and I found quarters with a Captain Breithaupt and under the teaching of Fräulein Agnes and the kindly ministrations of the Breithaupt family my ear and tongue finally accommodated themselves to the vagaries of the German language, so that when, in the Autumn, I was ready to attend university lectures I found no difficulty in following them and no very serious difficulty in expressing myself, although my conversation on topics other than philosophy and psychology tended to run aground on limitations of vocabulary, which were most exasperating to me and convulsingly amusing to my auditors. I should perhaps add that I had had a couple of years of German in college, but without acquiring any ability to use the language as a spoken tongue.

When I went to Leipzig and called upon Professor Wundt and Professor Külpe, to both of whom I had letters of introduction from my cousin, Frank Angell, who had a few years previously taken his doctor's degree with Wundt, I was most hospitably welcomed, but to my great disappointment confirmed what I had by rumor earlier learned, that the laboratory was full and that I could not secure the advantage of anything but the general lecture courses. As I had already familiarized myself with Wundt's *Grundzüge* which constituted the substance of the general lectures he was then giving, it did not seem to me that I could employ my time to the best advantage by remaining there, especially as there were no lectures being offered in philosophy which appealed to me. Regretfully therefore I turned my steps toward Berlin, where Ebbinghaus and Paulsen were lecturing, the former on the principles of psychology (material which later took form in his admirable book) and the latter on ethics and Spinoza. Dessoir, a young Privatdozent, was beginning his lectures on aesthetics. Dilthey, Lasson, and others were to be heard on general philosophical subjects. I gave my chief attention to Paulsen's courses, reading extensively in psychology, although the eccentricities of the University of Berlin Library made precarious any possibility of confident planning. The collection was grossly defective in contemporary English, French, and American books and periodicals and the method of access to books has too often been lampooned to justify any repetition. It would, however, be difficult to exaggerate its inconvenience.

Paulsen was by far the most finished lecturer I heard in Germany and an altogether charming person to meet. I count my contact with him as one of the particularly bright spots of my year in Germany. Ebbinghaus, for whose work on memory I had great respect, was not so interesting a lecturer and I had no opportunity for the direct contact which I enjoyed with Paulsen. I went occasionally into the lectures of the other eminent scholars then at the University and was especially impressed by Helmholtz, whose monumental works on vision and audition I already knew reasonably well. Between the semesters I travelled rather widely, going to Munich, Nuremberg, Strassburg, Stuttgart, Prague, Vienna, Trieste, Venice, Rome, Naples, Florence, Geneva, and Paris, spending nearly a month in Geneva where I exchanged French and English lessons with a young Swiss student.

I had decided to spend my second semester at Halle, hearing Benno Erdmann on psychology and working with Professor Hans Vaihinger in Kant. I presented myself as a candidate for the doctor's degree and wrote a thesis on the treatment of freedom in Kant's *Critique of Pure Reason* compared with that in the *Critique of Practical Reason*. My thesis was accepted and returned for rendition into more acceptable German, when I received from the University of Minnesota an invitation to come at once as instructor in philosophy and psychology, at a salary of $1500. To accept the post meant leaving almost at once, for the institution opened early in September and, in the fortnight remaining, I could not possibly accomplish the necessary final preparation for my examinations in my major—philosophy—and my two minors—economics and English literature—at the same time revising the form of my thesis. A little earlier President Eliot had offered me again a minor instructional position at Harvard, but at a considerably smaller salary than that proposed at Minnesota.

I was in deep perplexity as to what course to pursue; the prospect of a doctor's degree from a German University of high standing was not lightly to be dismissed. The opportunity to begin my professional career at Harvard had certain obvious advantages, but a living wage in a reputable institution was also not to be cast aside too cavalierly. Having been engaged for four years to Miss Watrous, whom I had much wanted to marry, and having assurance that the Minnesota position would shortly make that possible, I decided to accept their offer and come back at a later date to complete the process of securing my doctorate. This program I was never later able to carry out, and so it happened that, while in after years I was given an honorary degree of Doctor of Philosophy, I never quite completed the formalities for winning it on my merits. In view of the large number of doctor's degrees I have been instrumental in conferring on others, this circumstance has always elicited sardonic reflections whenever I think of it.

It was an agreeable thing to have my first two offers of academic appointment come from Harvard, our oldest university, even though the positions were of minor consequence. As I knew they reflected the confidence which I had won from James and Royce and Palmer, I was perhaps entitled to a little gratification. All three remained my warm friends as long as they lived and two of them, James and Palmer, I am sure considerably overestimated my abilities. Such evaluation is not a bad thing for youth, if it does not confirm a too vigorous natural vanity. I do not know the judgment of my friends, but I have sometimes thought that a larger share of vanity might have contributed to a more aggressive self-confidence which at times in turn might have been helpful. The impressive modesty of my father, however, whose intellectual abilities I well knew to be distinctly superior to my own, undoubtedly influenced me deeply in this respect.

At Minnesota, my old teacher, Williston Hough, was my chief in charge of the Department of Philosophy and Psychology. His kindness and friendly advice were of constant value to me in facing the ordeal of my first teaching. My schedule was extremely heavy. Three successive sections, an hour each in duration, on five days a week devoted to elementary psychology, chiefly patronized by juniors and seniors, with a large twice-a-week lecture course to two or three hundred unchastened sophomores, dealing with fundamental metaphysical ideas, comprised my schedule. In addition, I had to fit out a modest psychological laboratory and in the second half of the year give an introductory course in laboratory methods. Never before and rarely since have I had to work so hard as I did in the effort to carry this load. If I got to bed before two o'clock, I counted myself fortunate, and my first class was at 8:15 in the morning, with a half-hour journey across the city to get from my lodgings to the University. It was a thrilling experience, and my good fortune in almost instantly gaining the interest and confidence of my students made it also a happy one. But I nearly wrecked myself physically and at the end of the year found myself utterly exhausted nervously.

In addition to the hours spent in sheer mastery of the material related to my work, I gave many hours to perfecting a Socratic technique of questioning, the benefits of which remained with me throughout my teaching career. To learn so to phrase lucid questions that they will provoke significant thinking and when answered will open up the next directly related issue and so make the entire class hour one of active thought for every student (and in my classes no student ever knew when he would be drawn in to criticize or assist the student nominally in action) was an objective which I instantly adopted and in reasonable measure achieved. I also, from the first, insisted on the ability of my students to furnish valid and significant illustrations of any proposition they offered. This procedure quickly chastens the glib memorizer and even more the glib phrase-maker and bluffer. On most of my accomplishments I should place a very modest estimate, but I really think I had a genuine flair for stimulating teaching and I certainly gave everything I had to the effort to perfect my knowledge and my technique.

Toward the end of the year, President Harper offered me a position as Assistant Professor of Philosophy at the University of Chicago where John Dewey had gone the preceding year as head of the department. I was to be in charge of the laboratory and the courses in psychology, with an assistant to help me. Simon F. McClellan of the University of Toronto, who later became Professor of

Philosophy at Oberlin, was appointed to this post. Although President Northrop and my friend and colleague, Hough, and others brought heavy pressure on me to remain, it seemed to me that Chicago had the atmosphere of research and advanced study in which I was primarily interested to a greater degree than could be expected for many years at Minnesota, and I accordingly accepted the invitation— a decision which was unquestionably wise and which I never for a moment regretted, genuinely as I had enjoyed and appreciated my life at Minnesota. In the autumn I brought my bride to Chicago, where for the next 26 years we shared together the joys and anxieties of impecunious young people with a growing family.

The faculty at the University of Chicago, when I went there, was made up of a small but extraordinary group of distinguished scholars whom President Harper had drawn by high salaries and the promise of abundant freedom for research to be heads of the departments. Supporting them was a large group of really brilliant young men who have, with few exceptions, attained high distinction. It was therefore a very stimulating place for a young scholar to start in. I found myself housed in the physics laboratory presided over by Albert A. Michelson, who became my warm friend and tennis companion as long as I remained. Robert A. Millikan came the next year and I at once formed a delightful friendship with him, as I did with Henry G. Gale, who came later into the department, having previously been one of my students. My next neighbor was the great physiologist, Jacques Loeb, with whom I instantly established a warm friendship. Another close neighbor was the neurologist, Henry H. Donaldson, with whom I also came into intimate relations of friendship. Eliakim H. Moore in mathematics was another friend and neighbor of the same kind. Laughlin in economics, Shorey and Capps in Greek, Buck in Sanskrit, Abbott and W. G. Hale in Latin, Herrick, Lovett, and somewhat later Manly and the poet, Moody, in English, Small and Thomas in sociology, George E. Hale in astronomy, Breasted in ancient history, Mathews and Goodspeed in theology, Stieglitz in chemistry, were all good friends to whom I owe much. In my own department, Dewey and Tufts and George H. Mead, just brought from Michigan, were my colleagues, and a finer and more delightful group of men it would not be possible to name. Their kindness to me and to my wife was unlimited. She early won a place of importance for herself in the community, identifying herself with many significant social enterprises. Prior to our entrance into the War, she was especially active in the society which cared for the orphan children of French soldiers. She was also an active member of the Fortnightly, a club containing many of the leading women in Chicago, of which she was later President.

To have had some hand in molding the early destinies of a great university in companionship with these men I have mentioned and dozens of others whom I have not named was a thrilling experience for any young man and one which I entered into with the deepest interest.

For seven years I received no promotion in rank and no advance in salary, and to say that I was discouraged and disheartened would be putting it mildly. Finally, as I began to listen more sympathetically to occasional approaches from other institutions, I was in 1901 promoted to be Associate Professor.

In 1903 I was invited to go to Princeton as professor to succeed J. Mark Baldwin, who had accepted a call to Johns Hopkins. This invitation enabled me to discuss my future with the Chicago authorities in a more realistic fashion than before, and, as a result, I was in 1904 promoted to a professorship, with the promise that psychology should be set off from philosophy as a separate department, of which I should be made head. This was done in 1905.

It is always a little uncomfortable to have to wait for such outside recognition before academic advancement is accorded. But, to anyone familiar with the problems and organization of American higher education, the reasons for this are obvious enough. In any case, I felt that I had at length "arrived" professionally. Any man who enters academic life looks forward to a professorial post in an institution of the first class as the highest professional recognition to which he can aspire. The position is indeed one of dignity. Its security of tenure, its assured, even if modest, income, its opportunity for congenial work carried on with much independence and among agreeable surroundings count heavily. Meantime, in 1906 I had received the formal recognition of my psychological colleagues in the country by election to the presidency of the American Psychological Association, a post which I suspect had not previously been held by anyone of my years.

In 1908-1909, upon President Tucker's contemplated retirement, I was, to my profound amazement, invited to become President of Dartmouth College. I had been approached about the presidencies of a number of western universities, which fact had always puzzled me a good deal, as I had had little administrative experience. I suppose it was in part at least attributable to my father's commanding reputation. But until the Dartmouth invitation came, I was never disposed to give very serious consideration to the proposals. I spent several days with President Tucker, who had completely rejuvenated the College and left his imprint upon it in innumerable ways. He was a man of remarkable gifts and outstanding character.

After careful consideration, I decided that, attractive as was the post, its acceptance would involve hazards both for the College and for me which it was not wise to face. Dartmouth was distinctly a college. All my training and experience had been in universities. Its primary obligations must obviously be the teaching of undergraduates. My interests had become increasingly centered in advanced studies and in graduate students. Moreover, Dartmouth was a New England college and, while I had been born in New England and spent my summers among its people, I was nevertheless essentially middlewestern in my sympathies and outlook. For these reasons I declined the appointment and my subsequent experiences at Yale have confirmed my feeling that the decision was eminently wise for all concerned.

This episode having drawn my attention toward administrative work, it was suggested that I try my hand at it and see whether I found it congenial. I was accordingly made Dean of the Senior College and, upon George E. Vincent's acceptance of the Presidency of the University of Minnesota a few years later, I succeeded him in 1911 as Dean of the Faculties, an office which was in effect a vice-presidency, making me next in rank to the President and in his absence Acting President—a position which I had to fill on several subsequent occasions when President Judson was called away on government service or other missions. These latter duties brought me into intimate contact with the Board of Trustees, whose meetings I attended, and thus I became familiar with the entire operation of a great educational organization—financial, administrative, educational. It was splendid training for anyone and I threw myself into it with all my energy. Although I kept up a considerable part of my teaching and continued active supervision of the laboratory and the research program of the department, the division of attention was inevitable and, as so often happens to university men, the administrative work increasingly encroached on the work of the scholar. In many ways I profoundly regret this, although I cannot pretend that I think psychology has suffered any tragic loss by reason of my withdrawal from the field. But no one can give years of his life to a scientific program and then see it fade out of his horizon without genuine regret and a certain sense of frustration. I have only myself to thank for the outcome, as I could at any time, in the earlier years at least, have turned back. The only element of the situation which gives me permanent distress is that so often the controlling motive in the early stages of the change was financial. Salaries were small, the costs of living high, my family growing. The administrative work carried a modest additional stipend which was much needed. Indeed, throughout almost all of my career at Chicago, I was obliged to add to my normal salary by every available means—by teaching in the summer, by teaching university extension courses, by lecturing before clubs, and by teaching in local institutions in the late afternoons, at night, or on Saturdays. All this took a heavy toll of time and energy and left me too little resiliency for my research and writing.

In 1910 I was invited to give the opening series of lectures at Union College on the newly established Spencer Foundation. This led to a delightful friendship with President and Mrs. Charles A. Richmond, and subsequently in 1911 to the publication of the lectures under the title of *Chapters from Modern Psychology*. The work went through several editions and was an effort to present for the lay reader an introduction to the main subdivisions of psychology as it existed at that time. To my surprise, the book was widely used as a text in schools and colleges, where courses were offered designed to acquaint students with the major problems faced by psychology, rather than to offer the basic training necessary to advanced systematic work.

In the Summer of 1917, after the United States had entered the War, I went to Washington as a member of the Committee on Classification of Personnel, which, under the chairmanship of Walter D. Scott, the Army authorities had been induced to accept as an adjunct to the Adjutant General's office. The necessity for the procedure of this Committee, matured in connection with the mobilizing of the huge force which had been called to the colors, was quite beyond question. For example, to determine quickly where 100,000 mechanics of a certain specific degree of skill were to be found in certain cantonments so that they might be sent to France in ten days and not be found wanting when they arrived, required certain techniques for which the Army in peace times had absolutely no need. While certain of the rating scales which were devised for general officers never secured wide acceptance by the regular Army, the general sorting procedures for enlisted personnel were extremely useful and were still undergoing refinement when the War came to an end.

I do not think that I contributed very much to the effectiveness of the Committee's work, but I found it extremely interesting and rather exciting to be connected, in however modest a capacity, with the nation's war machine and I secured from the inside point of view many impressions of the procedure of the government, especially of the Army and Navy, which were most revealing. They left me with a deep respect for many of the men and certain of the regulation I encountered and with an equally profound impatience and almost contempt for others of the rules and procedures, which seemed to me stupid and hopelessly antiquated—far more designed to protect jobs than to produce efficiency.

Some months later I was transferred to the Committee on Education and Special Training, of which Charles Riborg Mann was chairman. Scott accepted a Commission and the first committee was practically assimilated into the regular Army organization. The new committee had as its chief immediate function the effort to knit the civilian institutions into the training mechanism, so that the whole of our national resources would be brought to bear on sending great numbers of men into active service, already specifically trained for their particular jobs. The subsequent record of the Student Army Training Corps, for the creation of which this committee was responsible, was one of a checkered kind. In many institutions it did its work effectively and with a minimum of disturbance to the regular life of the institution. In other cases friction was instant, widespread, and unceasing. As Acting President of the University of Chicago, to which I returned in the Spring of 1918, I was able to see the picture through both ends of the telescope. Where the Army officers—many of them recently converted civilians

—were arrogant, domineering, and unfamiliar with academic methods, where the faculties and executive officers of the institution were uncooperative, unimaginative, and obstinate or pugnacious, chaos reigned. Where reasonableness and tolerance and patience ruled, the infelicities were quickly straightened out and things went ahead peacefully.

Speaking retrospectively, I am sure that the essential idea of the S.A.T.C. was sound and that it represented a wise and economical use of our national facilities, but no venture conducted on such a huge scale and set going in such inevitable haste could possibly avoid grave blunders. The vast relief of the educational institutions when the War ended and the S.A.T.C. disbanded was perfectly natural.

At the close of the War, I was appointed Chairman of the National Research Council, which had rendered invaluable service to the scientific and technical branches of the government, and especially to the Army and Navy, and which, it was rightly thought, might wisely be continued in peace time as an active center of mobilized research in pure and applied science. The University generously granted me leave of absence for the year 1919-1920, and I entered on the work surrounded by a group of extremely able men representing the great branches of modern science, including medicine and engineering. As a child of the National Academy which held a Congressional charter, the Council was available for advisory or other service to any government agency.

During the year I was elected to membership in the Academy, generally regarded as the highest American honor a scientist can receive. Whatever my personal merits, the election gave me peculiar gratification, for, as I have earlier remarked, my grandfather, Alexis Caswell, had been one of the charter members.

This year with the Research Council I regard as one of the most fruitful in my career. It brought me into direct contact with large numbers of distinguished scientists and it allowed me to see how their minds worked, what were the problems peculiar to each of the great natural sciences, as we know them, and what were the vital frontiers of research in our time. It also afforded me most interesting contacts with many of the men at the head of the great industries, especially those in the electrical and chemical fields, where the dependence on the natural sciences was most direct. The difference in the progressive outlook of several of these industries as compared with certain others, notably steel, was very striking.

Largely, I think, through the influence of the astronomer, George E. Hale, Dr. Walcott, head of the Smithsonian, and John C. Merriam, my predecessor as Chairman of the Council, the Carnegie Corporation made a very large gift for the erection of a stately home for the National Academy and the Council, and also for the support of the Council. I had to give a good deal of time to the preparation of the building plans which Bertram G. Goodhue was selected to draft, and with Robert A. Millikan and George Hale I spent some time in inducing a group of generous citizens to contribute $10,000 apiece for the purchase of the site where the building now stands. All this brought me of necessity into some contact with Elihu Root, Henry S. Pritchett, and other members of the Board of Trustees of the Carnegie Corporation. Perhaps as a result, I was in the late Winter of 1920 invited to become President of the Corporation, which, after Mr. Carnegie's death in 1919, had been conducted by a small Board of Trustees under the chairmanship of Mr. Root.

This invitation compelled me to face the most difficult decision I had yet been called upon to make. The Carnegie Corporation, with immense capital resources, had been created by its founder to operate in the United States in the promotion of human welfare, especially on educational lines broadly conceived. To accept the post meant giving up my lifelong connection with university work, it meant breaking up my friendships of more than a quarter of a century at Chicago, and it meant undertaking a kind of responsibility which I had never before faced.

In making my decision, I was inevitably and crucially affected by conditions at the University of Chicago. There I had served as Acting President on several occasions. I had received a good many invitations to university presidencies, that of my own Alma Mater among them, and during the discussions of these calls influential members of the Board of Trustees had more than once expressed the wish that I should remain and, on the retirement of the President, accept the Presidency there—always provided that the clause in the University of Chicago charter, which required the President to be a Baptist, could be abrogated.[1] In any case, however, promotion

---

[1]This was later done and, although President Burton who succeeded President Judson was a Baptist, the legal requirement had been withdrawn, and President Mason and President Hutchins, who successively became President, were not Baptists.

there was, for the time being at least, blocked and my frequent invitations to other positions of consequence kept my status more or less an active subject of comment and discussion in the University community. All this had created a situation which I felt to be a little uncomfortable. Whether President Judson was sensitive to the same situation or not, I have no means of knowing. After rather painful deliberation, I decided to burn my bridges behind me and take over the New York post.

The following year in New York was full of interest. Mr. Root, Mr. Pritchett, Mrs. Carnegie, Mr. Poynton, and others of the Trustees were extremely considerate and helpful in smoothing my path. I was obliged to start pretty well from zero, for there had never been a president other than Mr. Carnegie, and, after his death, the other great Carnegie Foundations tended to look to the Corporation for enlargement of their resources, while those members of the Board who had been Mr. Carnegie's trusted employees, growing up under him in the distribution of his benefactions, tended naturally to follow the beaten path and to look with suspicion, if nothing stronger, upon new faces and new proposals. Accordingly I had first to familiarize myself as well as I could with the history of the Corporation and its relation to these sister institutions, and then to set about determining a wise general policy for the future which could be submitted to my Board. In all this, I had the invaluable assistance of my former student, Beardsley Ruml, who had taken his doctor's degree under me just before we entered the War.

My position brought me into contact with large numbers of the leading people in New York, as well as in other parts of the country, for such persons are typically concerned with the promotion of all kinds of good works, and an organization known to have large resources for expending in similar ways naturally attracts their attention. It was an amusing experience to be sitting at the other end of the telescope from that which I had commonly used for my observations. To be seeking the wisest ways in which to spend money, rather than centering all one's energies on the securing of it, was a novel experience. It gave me a curious insight into the psychology of promoters, which I had not formerly enjoyed. The tearful and sentimental suppliant, the bullying "if-you-don't-see-that-this-is-the-greatest-opportunity-in-the-world-to-use-your-money-wisely,-you-are-a-fool" type, the patient, deprecatory pleader, the optimistic promoter who knows that if you will only hear the whole story you cannot fail to help him—all these and many other varieties passed through the office every day.

I had hardly gotten settled down in my job and matured plans for presentation to my Trustees before I was approached by Otto T. Bannard of the Yale Corporation, to ask if I would be interested to succeed Mr. Hadley as President of the University. Once again I had to go through the rather distressing process of considering whether I should change the essential character of my work. The invitation itself completely staggered me, for of all our great universities Yale had perhaps been most tenacious in recruiting its staff from among its own sons. I was not a Yale man, and, while I had been offered a professorship in psychology by President Hadley after Charles H. Judd went to Chicago (an arrangement for which I was in no small measure responsible) and counted many Yale graduates among my best friends, I had never served on the faculty, nor had I many intimate friends there. To go meant cutting my salary exactly in half, it meant risking a very uncomfortable and unhappy experience in an academic community that might well regard me as a raw western interloper—an attitude which it seemed to me Yale graduates, if not the Yale faculty, would almost certainly take. Furthermore, the institution was organized on a basis of faculty control of appointments and promotions, a system known in only one or two other American institutions, and I saw my ability to assist in building up a powerful faculty thus materially curtailed at the outset. Finally, I knew that the University had just undergone a violent reorganization imposed by the Trustees, with a good deal of vigorous alumni support, to be sure, but entailing wide areas of soreness and discontent which could not quickly be forgotten. And, most unhappy of all, in view of these circumstances, the War had left the institution in grave financial plight.

Looking backward, I think I indulged in far greater risks in hazarding such a change than at the time I had supposed, for the more I have learned of the situation the more unlikely does it seem that an outsider would have been so generously accepted. In any case, I went and, while I have had some dark days, on the whole my life has been very happy. If I have not done all I had hoped, I have at least had fewer obvious failures to regret than I might reasonably have expected.

From the very first the great majority of my colleagues extended to me a hearty and sincere welcome. I am sure they quickly sensed my keen desire to cooperate with them in every possible way to advance the power and prestige of the University and to enable it to fulfill more perfectly its great function in American life. The alumni were also very fine in the support they gave me, many of them at the outset with frank reluctance, which I fully appreciated and completely respected. But their loyalty to Yale presently made them my good friends and, oddly enough, as it seems to me, I apparently won the general confidence of the older group much more rapidly than that of the younger classes. One might perhaps have anticipated that the conservatism of the earlier generation would in this respect have been more tenacious and aggressive, but such was not the case.

The acceptance of the position has at least allowed me to exercise a significant influence in the promotion of psychology and the allied scientific interests. In the Institute of Psychology founded shortly after I went to New Haven and financed by the Rockefeller interests, and later in the Institute of Human Relations, supported by the same group, it has been possible to set up fruitful cooperation between psychology on the one hand and on the other a large group of closely related interests, such as psychiatry, neurology, physiology, biology, anthropology, and the social sciences in general. Any university that counts in its staff psychologists of the calibre of Dodge, Yerkes, Angier, Robinson, Hull, Miles, May, Gesell, with anthropologists like Wissler and Sapir, is fortunate.

With this sketch of the main features of my life considered in its more personal aspects, I turn back to the earlier years of my career as a psychologist and to its trend in scientific convictions and interests.

Dewey's *Psychology,* on which I cut my first psychological teeth, was an interesting combination of fundamental principles and empirical material drawn from a wide reading of German, Scottish, and English scources. There was practically no evidence of contemporary French influence in it. Taking the three fundamental categories of thinking, feeling, and willing, the author had developed a rather subtle and extremely intriguing dialectic which suggested, if it did not actually derive from, Hegel's *Logic.* Accepting, as many other writers had done before him, the irreducible character of these three modes of being conscious, he elaborated the manner in which each not only involved but depended upon the other two to effect the actual achievements of mind and conduct. Reading the book in later years, and in the light of fuller knowledge, it seems here a bit forced and there a bit devoted to special pleading and it all smells of the lamp and the arm chair; but, as the first work of a very young man, it was an extraordinary *tour de force* and its mastery provided an admirable intellectual discipline to all who could survive its rather rigorous and difficult style. I certainly have never seen cause to regret gaining my introduction to psychology and philosophy through so bracing a medium.

Some two or three years later, when I encountered James's *Principles,* I found myself in an entirely different world. The dialectic of Dewey's thinking was utterly alien to the working of James's mind. The great inrush of provocative observation, the wealth of pertinent facts, the ingenious manipulation of data, the wide knowledge of relevant literature, and above all the irresistibly fascinating literary style swept me off my feet. The vital employment of cerebralistic hypotheses to account through habit for the central structure of human conduct and experience together with the radical and, to me at least, revolutionary avenues of approach and points of view contained in such chapters in the *Principles* as the "Stream of Consciousness," "Habit," "Self," "Emotion," and "Will" all left me breathless and excited as one may imagine feeling after coming through a great storm, or an earthquake. Even if somewhat shattering at first, it was extraordinarily stimulating.

To read Wundt, or Bain, or Spencer, or Ladd, after a session with James, was an anticlimax which seriously disturbed one's equilibrium. To a youngster brought up on Dewey, where close-knit, systematic organization was of the essence of the thinking, the complete lack in James of anything which could be instantly recognized as system was highly disturbing.

When I began to teach, I started using James's *Briefer Course* as a text, in which was digested a good deal of the meat of the larger work. From the very first, I found the absence of any systematic articulation which ordinary college students could detect, much less apprehend, a serious obstacle, and this circumstance, perhaps more than any other, led to my writing my own book which now, for reasons which are dark to me, more than thirty years after its first appearance, still sells a few copies. The cordial reception given it was a complete and delightful surprise, for it was not easy reading.

But for many years, it shared with the James the larger part of the college market for psychological texts and at times, I believe, led all college textbooks in its field. After four editions had been published, in response to many requests for a briefer and simpler treatment, I put out an *Introduction,* which had a reasonable success, although of necessity it divided the market with the older book.

Although I had come up to psychology through philosophical channels and was reasonably familiar with the main metaphysical problems and solutions which the European tradition has recognized, I early came to accept the practical wisdom of setting psychology apart as an independent empirical science, a branch of biology, exactly as physics and chemistry had earlier been set off. As part of this process, I followed a then growing tendency and accepted psychophysical parallelism as a device through which to phrase mind-body relationships. I think I never regarded it as anything but a convenient formula, and certainly not as a metaphysical dualism, for, taken as more than this, it involves belief in an incredible and unceasing miracle; but it certainly avoided some of the theoretical difficulties of interactionism, as well as the verbal prestidigitation of some of the forms of monism.

Despite my adoption of parallelism for practical purposes in teaching and writing, I came, first under the influence of James's doctrine of habit, and later under the influence of certain of Dewey's views, in both respects affected by my reading of other men and by my own reflection, to accept as a basic element in my general theory of organic life the conception of mind and body as functional poles in the life of the organism, such that the latter, having as its major task the adjustment of itself to the environment—physical and social —in which it found itself, utilized conscious processes at the point where new sensory-motor coordinations were being established, which later, as they became perfected, permitted the mental aspect of the process gradually to diminish, until, in the limiting case, consciousness had entirely disappeared and the coordination had become completely automatic. It still appears to me that this view was expediently called *functional,* because it obviously disclaimed any dogmatic teaching about the ultimate nature and relation of mind and matter, and contented itself with pointing out the actual living relationship which even a rather superficial observation could verify.

Such a doctrine fits easily and naturally into the further widely held theory, earlier developed, that instinctive and reflex acts, like those exclusively under the control of the autonomic system, may all have originally been acts of the voluntary type which, by some biological means, got themselves deeply enough established to be handed down by heredity from parent organism to offspring. Obviously such a view, defended by not a few psychologists of unquestioned eminence, implies dogma about heredity which in those days of controversy between the disciples of Darwin and Lamarck, to say nothing of the crimp put by Weissmann in nearly all previously accepted notions of the mechanism of heredity, left the matter very much in the air. What bearing the present doctrines of hormones and genes would have on that view, I will not pause to discuss.

Both the functional formulation (as against any existential or metaphysical tenet) of the relation of consciousness to the nervous system and the conceptions of the origin of instinctive and reflex acts have come in for abundant criticism, which it is not my province to review here.

In an article published by the late Addison W. Moore and myself in 1896,[2] we brought our functional view overtly to bear on a specific psychological problem of long standing, to wit: the simple sensory-motor reaction of the voluntary type. Growing out of observations made in a number of laboratories, primarily Wundt's, there had developed a doctrine of reaction types with a widely prevalent persuasion that reactions were more rapid when the attention of the reagent was directed to the movement to be made, rather than to the sensory stimulus serving as the signal for the movement. My friend, Moore, and I showed, as a result of extended experimental studies involving a number of persons, that at the outset of such observations individuals varied appreciably as to the point at which such coordinations required most supervision and discipline. Some persons needed to put their attention on the sensory stimulus to secure the fastest and most regular reactions. More frequently the need was felt to put the attention upon the movement. In either case, by allowing the subject's attention to go to the point where the coordination most required supervision, in other words where it was at the time least automatic, the best results were attained, both in speed and in regularity. The two types would be expected, on our

---

[2]Reaction time: a study in attention and habit. *Psychol. Rev.*, 1896, **3**, 245-258.

Photograph by Bachrach
JAMES ROWLAND ANGELL

FREDERIC CHARLES BARTLETT

MADISON BENTLEY

HARVEY A. CARR

SANTE DE SANCTIS

JOSEPH FRÖBES

O. KLEMM

KARL MARBE

theory, to grow more or less together under practice, and this was exactly what occurred.

The problem is much more complex than this simple statement would imply and there were several variant theories in the field; but at least I trust this statement will make clear how I viewed this conception of the function of consciousness as it applies to a particular concrete set of phenomena.

All of us in the Chicago group had been deeply influenced in coming to the view above presented by ideas which presently were embodied in a brilliant paper which Dewey published at about that time on the reflex arc concept,[3] in which he had elaborated the "circuit" character of all reactions such as those with which Moore and I had been dealing, as contrasted with the notion of an "arc" merely as such, with its termini fixed and final. He showed that the entire organic situation preceding the particular stimulus enters into the picture to determine what the stimulus shall actually be and do, and furthermore that the reaction itself is reflected back into the stimulus and thus conditions the succeeding stimuli. The article incorporated one of Dewey's flashes of insight which in other hands would perhaps have been more patiently developed and consequently led to more fruitful consequences in the area outside the Chicago group.

At about the time I was beginning to write and to organize my own experimental program, there was a considerable controversy abroad about the true objectives of psychology. Whether psychology should remain content to be merely a descriptive science, or should go on to seek valid explanations and, if so, the question as to the nature of such explanations, was much in evidence. In America at least, the general disposition was to seek explanation in terms of nervous activities, the exact character of which was, to be sure, far more obscure than the psychological facts whose explanation was thus sought.

A common view held that psychology should concern itself with the "what" and the "how" of studies of consciousness, but not with the "why." The disposition to reduce all conscious phenomena to elements (patterned after the procedure of chemistry or morphology) was strongly urged, thus producing a kind of psychological atomism, issuing in the hands of one important group of authors in "simple

---

[3]The reflex arc concept in psychology. *Psychol. Rev.*, 1896, **3**, 357.

sensations and simple feelings, or affections," nothing being said about a volitional element. In other instances the tendency postulated a volitional drive, or element, as the basic factor upon which all other psychic qualities were superposed. James, with characteristic independence, had insisted that however correct might be the introspective analyses of the adult consciousness into simple sensations of color, taste, sound, and the like, with their attributes of duration and intensity, the actual genetic beginnings were to be found in "one great, blooming, buzzing, confusion," out of which, little by little, as the infant nervous system matured, emerged first one and then another psychological mass, in its turn to be further disintegrated by the analytic-synthetic effects of experience. He even proposed a plausible account of how analysis, with its ever concomitant synthesis, brought all this to pass.

Closely associated with these issues was a fundamental question of method. Despite abundant criticism, valid in not a few particulars, introspection had been regarded from the beginning as *par excellence* the basic method on which psychology must rest. It remained therefore to refine and compensate for its normal errors, and experimental procedure, largely Germanic in origin, was everywhere welcomed as the savior of the day. Some of this experiment was directed to facilitating introspection under conditions of control. A good deal of it, notably as in Fechner's psychophysical experiments, did not require introspection in any technical sense of the term at all. One simply pronounced a judgment "present," "not present," "heavier," "lighter." The logical extreme of experiment conceived in this second manner came into operation under biological influences with Bechterew's objective psychology and later behaviorism, which my student and assistant, John B. Watson, developed in such an extravagant manner.

In the matter of method I took a broad, and I still think entirely sound, position, i.e., that, as a branch of biological science, psychology should avail itself of any methods which would result in a deeper knowledge of the mind and its relation to the physical organism and its environment. Introspection in one form or another I held to be indispensable as the method from which inevitably derives our original apprehension of the whole field of study—that is to say, the phenomena in question. This too I feel to be a correct position. Exclusive methods, like Watsonian behaviorism, simply beg the question and tacitly assume data which, without essentially introspective processes, performed by their predecessors, if not by the proponents themselves, would be paralyzed and wholly sterile. I may inject in passing that, despite much which seems to me rather ridiculous in its naïveté, I value highly the contribution behaviorism has made both to methodological procedure and to a factual knowledge of both human and animal life.

At the opposite pole from behaviorism were such positions as Miss Calkins' personalism, with which I have great sympathy, and the doctrines of the Gestalt psychologists, which came on the scene somewhat after my active contact with psychology had ceased. As I have followed their writings, the latter group seemed to me to be keeping alive a very important set of considerations which derived logically from much the same source as the a priori metaphysics of German lineage, especially in its Kantian form. But, like the Freudians, they seemed to me to have embalmed their procedure in a rather needlessly repellent terminology.

For myself, to analyze and describe correctly the major aspects of mental experience and to try to bring it into context with the physical organism, to do this in the general atmosphere of recognition of the necessity for adaptive behavior, and to seek at each point to discern what peculiar service conscious processes render in these adaptive acts, both social and physical—that is the essence of what I understood by functionalism and as such set over against a psychological atomism, or a rigid structuralism. The transitory nature of the position never troubled me, and does not now. Changes in viewpoint and method are of the essence of progress in science. If our contribution at Chicago was of material assistance, as I think it was, to the forward movement in psychology which has since taken place on so impressive a front, I am quite content.

My name has been so often connected with the development of the so-called functionalist position in psychology that I feel a somewhat further statement on that subject is warranted, even at the risk of tiresome repetition. Readers who find the matter devoid of interest are advised to omit the next few pages of text.

In an article on "The Province of Functional Psychology," which I presented as my presidential address before the Psychological Association,[4] I pointed out that this variety of psychology is rather def-

---

‘*Psychol. Rev.*, 1907, **14**, 61-91.

initely directed to three objectives. It is concerned first with the identification and description of mental *operations,* rather than with the mere *stuff* of mental experience. In the second place, any description of a mental state, if it is to be at all accurate, must take account of the conditions under which it occurs, the circumstances which evoke it, for it largely depends in its precise quality upon these facts, a portion of which are narrowly physical in nature, a portion social. What the conscious state is doing, biologically speaking, contains the clue to what it really is when descriptively approached and analyzed. In the third place, functional psychology is interested in mental activity as part of the larger stream of biological forces which are constantly at work and constitutive of the most absorbing part of our world. Functional psychology thus desires to understand how the psychical contributes to the furtherance of the sum total of organic activities, considered as adaptive, and not alone the psychical in general, but especially the particular modes in which it appears, e:g., mind as judging, as feeling, etc. It is desired to discover the exact accommodatory service represented by the various great phases of conscious expression. This point of view is well exhibited in studies of animal behavior, where mental adjustments are increasingly in evidence as we move up the scale of organic life. The whole genetic movement, seeking longitudinal, rather than merely transverse, views of life phenomena, is keyed to a functionalism of this sort. Pathological psychology has a similar bearing on the objectives of functionalism. All this leads to, and supports, the theory of consciousness as being that form of organic expression which occurs when adjustment to the novel is involved, and it may therefore be regarded as characteristic of the form taken on by the primary accommodatory process. Selective variation of response to stimulation is its sign. This broad biological ideal of functional psychology may be connected with the problem of discovering the fundamental utilities of consciousness. If mental process is of real value to its possessor, it must be by virtue of something which it does. The functionalist's problem is therefore to discover, describe, and, if possible, classify the great types, or forms, in which these utilities are represented.

Functionalism as a psychophysical psychology is accordingly constantly recognizing and insisting upon the mind-body relation—not as existential, but as functional—as illustrated in the process of habit formation, with the end state one where consciousness has substantially given place to physiological automatism. The dominance of social situations as stimuli, as objects toward which reaction is directed, is always stressed in this point of view.

These three aspects of functional psychology are inseparably interconnected and no one of them can get far without involving the others. If behavior may be regarded as the fundamental category of general biology, so control may be regarded as the basic category of consciousness in a functional psychology. The special expressions of consciousness simply represent particular aspects of the process of control.

In the functionalist view, reflective consciousness and the philosophical disciplines are seen as having a necessary and essentially organic relation to one another. This is hardly true of any other view, and often these disciplines are regarded as quite independent of one another. Thus, when the adaptive functions of conscious processes are seriously followed through to their ultimate implications, one inevitably emerges in the problems with which the realistic logic, ethics, and aesthetics of our day deal, to say nothing of the non-normative philosophical disciplines. These are in fact outcomes of a functional psychology which strives to understand how and why mental process really functions as it does, as well as to find out merely what it is. This is but another way of saying that "value" categories, when treated pragmatically, tend to run instantly over into issues of adaptive function. However it may fare with transcendental values, the values of direct concern in modern ethics, logic, and much of aesthetics are thus colored predominantly with considerations valid in the world of practice. A functional psychology of feeling, for example, cannot keep out of the field of modern aesthetics. Indeed the latter is largely made up of such material. Practical considerations will doubtless always determine where responsibility shall reside for exploration in these fields, where the man who calls himself a psychologist shall cease and the man who would be known as a logician shall begin, but their intrinsic relationship, as here described, can hardly be challenged.

My functional interests naturally made me sensitive to the literature of adaptive behavior and this in turn led me to fairly exhaustive studies of the contribution of Darwin and other naturalists to the whole problem of the evolution of intelligence, with special reference to the history of instinct and emotion. This trend in my thinking is perhaps best exemplified in an article on "The Influence of Darwin on Psychology," appearing in the *Psychological Review,* 1909, Volume 16, pages 152-169. The same influence is also disclosed in the chapter written by me on "The Evolution of Intelligence," in the volume entitled *The Evolution of Man,* published by the Yale University Press in 1922.

I was highly sympathetic to the development of the field of comparative psychology and gave every encouragement to the growth in my laboratory of experimentation on animal behavior. The subsequent excesses of behaviorism as a cult I naturally could not support and my views were frankly set forth in a paper on this subject published in the *Psychological Review.*[5]

At Minnesota, I had barely been able to organize the beginnings of a laboratory and had had no opportunity to make even a beginning at research. At Chicago, I found a considerable amount of apparatus which had been secured at the conclusion of the World's Fair from among the collections that had been brought together there under scientific auspices. I utilized a small appropriation put in my hands to supplement the collections at the points of greatest defect and secured, as a result, sufficient material to conduct effectively an introductory demonstration course covering the simpler sensory processes, such as were chiefly dealt with in the manuals that presently began to appear, the first edition of Sanford's useful little book being already available. As students began to come and ask opportunity for carrying on research, I started them on such elementary problems as their training and the resources of the laboratory made possible. Thus Whitehead's study on auditory and visual memory,[6] the study by Amy Tanner and Kate Anderson in the same volume,[7] and the studies by Mahood, Spray, and Ashley on spacial perception[8] were cases in point where the problems attacked were within the reasonable range of the students' abilities and where the apparatus was either at hand or easily constructed.

Later on, when students reached the point of preparing for the

---

[5]Behavior as a category of psychology. *Psychol. Rev.,* 1913, **20,** 255-270. Although remarkable additions have since been made on the factual side of Pavloff's doctrine of conditioned reflexes, the bearing of this on psychology still seems to me much as it was in 1913.
[6]*Psychol. Rev.,* 1896, **3,** 258.
[7]*Psychol. Rev.,* 1896, **3,** 378.
[8]*Psychol. Rev.,* 1898, **5,** 579.

doctorate, I always encouraged them, if possible, to find their subjects in problems growing out of their own scientific reading and reflection. I soon found that many students expect a thesis subject to be handed out to them, and, for men who wish to utilize such opportunity to set students at work on different phases of a general problem of interest to the professor in charge, the outcome may be valuable for all concerned. It has certainly been found so by not a few scholars in the well-established disciplines, and the fact that some men have rather ruthlessly exploited their students for an appreciable amount of more or less hack-work in this way should not render one oblivious to the compensating benefits.

The variety of subjects chosen for theses by my students in the earlier years of my Chicago teaching shows clearly enough the wide range of interests which they reflect. After Dr. Watson (aided and succeeded by Dr. Carr) had launched our Chicago work in the comparative field, which was done with my enthusiastic sympathy and support, for I had long felt its potential fruitfulness, the tendency for students to choose thesis subjects in the general area of animal learning was pronounced. There were abundant reasons for this, some scientific, some prudential; and the body of work which came forth was highly creditable. To much of it the co-operation of Dr. Donaldson and his assistant Dr. Hardy (and later Dr. Herrick) in neurology was invaluable.

As I always followed closely the progress of my students upon their thesis topics, serving as subject in problems dealing with human processes sufficiently to keep intimate contact with their procedure and the drift of their findings, my own research was doubtless less close knit than otherwise might have been the case. I carried a heavy teaching schedule and, as I have earlier indicated, I was obliged, for financial reasons, to teach a large part of the summer and to find such outside employment as I could in term time. All this invaded both leisure and strength for research. But in this respect my experience was like that of hundreds of other young American scholars.

The fact that I had myself enjoyed a sound philosophical training, and the further fact that I valued highly for psychology the related biological disciplines, especially physiology and neurology, not less than my conviction of the paramount importance for young scholars of direct contact with forceful and productive personalities in other fields, led me to encourage my students to do a considerable part of their work in other departments, particularly philosophy, neurology, and education. This policy was not generally prevalent at the time, but I am sure it was expedient and I think the subsequent careers of many of my doctors demonstrated its wisdom.

Another practice which I believe I developed earlier and more systematically than in other American universities was insistence on a knowledge of the history of the science. This procedure, if well executed, lends background and balance to the young scholar's outlook and often saves him from running after strange gods. Although the library facilities never permitted me to carry out the program in the manner I should have wished, I am sure that my students all profited genuinely by this phase of their training.

I have already cited my work on reaction times with A. W. Moore as an example of the manner in which I tried to bring to bear on experimental problems the general functional conceptions of consciousness, with which I had become intrigued. I may mention another example in the work which I did with Helen B. Thompson as my assistant on the organic accompaniments of conscious processes.[9]

There had been not a little interesting work done abroad, notably by Lehmann, by Binet, and in Wundt's laboratory on the connection between pleasure-displeasure and pain on the conscious side, with cardiac, circulatory, and respiratory phenomena on the physical side. While the findings had by no means been in agreement, the weight of Wundt's authority had been given for a fairly specific correlation in which, for example, pleasure was alleged to be accompanied by deep respiration and by dilation of the peripheral capillaries. Pain and displeasure (not infrequently, though incorrectly, identified) were alleged to have exactly the contrary organic accompaniments, i.e., superficial, broken breathing, and vaso-constriction. The study of blood pressure had not then been brought into the picture. At a slightly earlier period McClennan and I had published a paper[10] on the organic effects of agreeable and disagreeable stimuli, in which we had formulated our failure, on the basis of considerable experimentation on the lines of the authors mentioned above, to demonstrate any constant correlation

[9]*Psychol. Rev.*, 1899, **6**, 32-69.
[10]*Psychol. Rev.*, 1896, **3**, 371-378.

of the kind called for by the theory. We pointed out the complexity of the mental conditions which were supposedly reflected in the particular organic process in question, and urged that a uniform correspondence between any *single element* in the psychic complex with the specific organic activities involved in the experiments could not be reasonably expected.

It should be said at the outset that the apparatus then available for recording these organic reactions was difficult to manage with precision, and, even under the most felicitous conditions, its presence made it difficult to deal with the more delicate and refined forms of stimulation. The ordinary forms of plethysmograph, for example, were cumbrous and difficult to keep functioning without a good deal of disturbing attention from the reagent. It was likewise troublesome to adjust the devices for recording respiration without occasioning a distinct sensory stimulus, which was disturbing to the respiratory cycle. However, the apparatus used by Miss Thompson and myself was essentially like that employed by Binet and distinctly less annoying than that used by the other previous investigators. Agreeing with Binet and with the preceding work of McClennan and myself, we were unable to verify any uniform correlations between such affective conditions as we produced and the organic responses called for on the Lehmann-Wundt hypothesis. Vaso-constriction and disturbed breathing, with accelerated heart beat, were indeed frequent concomitants of painful stimulations, but even here the intensity of the pain and the antecedent circumstances entered in to modify the reactions, and the phenomena called for as the concomitants of pleasure were extremely variable.

The general theoretical prepossessions with which we set out led us to be observant of the action of attention, and we believed that creating experimental conditions where the attention processes would vary in determined directions might exhibit corresponding variation in the organic concomitants with which we were concerned. This expectation was supported by our findings in a manner which seemed to us quite striking. With every allowance for the imperfection of the technique, I am persuaded that we were on a correct trail and that the essence of our findings will stand. If there were subsequently experimental efforts to discredit our observations, they escaped my notice. The work attracted rather less attention than I thought it deserved, perhaps because we did not state our views lucidly enough.

The drift of our discovery was that, regardless of whether we were confronted with vaso-constriction, or vaso-dilation, with acceleration of rate and increase in vigor of the heart beat, or the reverse, with acceleration of respiration, with or without change in its form, or the contrary reactions, we found general dynamic stability in all these processes when the activity of attention was smooth and effective, whereas we met interruption in one or more of them as attention itself became interrupted and disorganized. In other words, the parallelism which we remarked and which seemed to be strikingly uniform was not statable in terms of pleasure-pain and certain sets of organic opposites, but in terms of the smooth and effective functioning of attention, passing from one adjustment to the next without dislocation, correlated with stable or slowly changing conditions in the organic series. Any breakdown in the attention process was accompanied by a shift in one, and often in all, of the organic activities, and these shifts were sudden and violent, roughly in proportion to the disturbance to the adjusting activity of attention.

I may illustrate briefly what is implied. In a situation where arithmetical computations were required, such as continuous adding of columns of figures, as long as the process went forward smoothly and effectively, the breathing and pulse would be quite constant in rate and form and the vaso-motor reactions would show only the slightest change. But let any material disturbance occur in the computations, whether occasioned by external or internal circumstances, and one or all of the organic activities would at once show changes and the more extreme the mental distraction the more pronounced the organic responses.

If conscious processes are, as held, really engaged in facilitating the adjustments of the organism to its surroundings, and if the focal point of conscious process is at attention, as it certainly is under normal conditions, then the changes in the stability of the vital sustaining processes of the organism which we were observing might well reflect exactly the conditions we found. In other words, our findings confirmed in a highly definite (and I may say rather unexpected) degree the requirements of our theory.

In all the researches which I pursued for my own satisfaction, only one of major consequence was devoid of a background of general theoretical interest. That was my study of auditory localization, with the cooperation, in its early stages, of Dr. Warner Fite, whose assistance was of great value by reason of his acute critical qualities.[11]

I had been deaf in one ear from early childhood, a heritage of scarlet fever already mentioned. The hearing in my surviving ear was unusually keen, as repeated tests disclosed. I had always been able to locate sounds with some promptness and accuracy, despite my infirmity, and on the theory then generally accepted regarding the binaural differential as the basis of localization this should have been impossible. The matter seemed well worth examining.

With the use of ingenious apparatus, some of it new, some of it based on improvements in earlier devices, a thoroughgoing study was made of my own powers of localization, and then of four other persons totally deaf in one ear, one having been in this condition for 26 years, one for 14, one for six, and one for one year. The results from these persons were compared with the localizing capacities of normal adults subjected to the same conditions, with the same apparatus. All the known literature was canvassed and advantage taken of any suggestions there to be found.

In general, it was discovered that strictly pure tones cannot be localized in monaural hearing. As the sound stimulus begins to take on acoustic complexity, the ability to localize it grows rapidly. This is at all events the case in the median ranges of pitch. Our experiments did not deal with extremes of the tone scale. With fairly complex tones, such as that of a pitch pipe, the only serious errors occurred in the area immediately opposite the deaf ear. The evidence, which cannot be recited in detail here, makes it quite clear that damping and reenforcements of the partial tones of complex sounds by the pinnae, the meatus, and the bones of the skull produce changes in the sound quality of the stimulus which permit the localizing process to occur. In other words, to illustrate, a complex sound arising to the left and in front of the face of a person deaf in one ear is heard as qualitatively different from the same sound when it arises opposite the right ear. Moreover, practice in such localizing exercises shows marked improvement over a considerable period, even though the reagent is not informed of the correctness, or incorrectness, of his judgments. This circumstance is further reflected in the observation that our monaural deaf subjects in general react more accurately in proportion to the duration of the deafness. The man deaf for one year only was thus much the least accurate.

Later studies of the physics of the sound wave, showing that in normal persons the phase of the wave as it strikes the two end-organs plays an important and possibly decisive part in determining localization, have tended to draw attention away from these psychological monaural studies. Many hypotheses to account for the localizing processes have been offered on the physiological side, e.g., reflexes released by the semicircular canal mechanisms affecting the head and eye muscles, stimulation of the tensor tympani, cutaneous stimulation of the auditory meatus, etc. But none is adequate and most of them encounter obstinate factual difficulties with which they cannot satisfactorily cope. Whatever the final form a successful psychophysical theory may take, I feel convinced that in the field of monaural phenomena my discoveries will stand, and it seems quite improbable that they should not bear fundamentally on binaural theory as well.

From the period of my master's degree, dealing, as before indicated, with a sector of the imagery problem, I have always been interested in this general field and it was therefore inevitable that I should be drawn into the controversy over imageless thought which raged for a time during the first decade of the twentieth century.

I was involved in the issue as early as 1897, as a result of a review which I published of Stout's *Analytic Psychology,* in which I criticized certain statements of his which appeared to defend the existence of meaning devoid of any imaginal, or sensorial bearer. In the subsequent discussion (*Philosophical Review,* 1897-1898), Stout made it clear that his doctrine was essentially like my own, for he said that, in speaking of imageless apprehension, he had in view a partial constituent of a total state, which as another constituent had some sensation or image. A good deal of the subsequent writing in the journals seemed to me to be based on a crude misapprehension of the issue. Stout, Binet, and others were repeatedly quoted in ways evincing the most inexcusable distortion. **My** own views were set forth in an address at Columbia University.[12] After exhaustive canvass of all the experimental findings and of the available literature for discussion and exposition, I came to agree substantially with Wundt that: "The actus purus of the thought experiments is no fact of observation, but simply a consequence of defective observation and false presuppositions."[13] I cannot here repeat all the varied possibilities which are available to explain the radical divergencies of belief and theory as between psychologists presumably equally competent as observers. These are gathered in the article above cited.

The doctrine of voluntary control also raises this question of sensorial and imaginal antecedents, and here again I do not find the views of the defenders of "pure thought" antecedents of such movements convincing as against the older doctrines.

In the *Psychological Monographs* series for 1910[14] I published a study dealing with the various techniques for determining the character and function of imagery. This paper comprised part of a report of a Committee of the American Psychological Association on the standardizing of tests.

Despite my early and sincere interest in abnormal psychology, the Freudian movement with its sundry variants found me driven into an attitude of criticism and hostility, for, while I regarded certain of its contributions as sound and fundamentally significant, not a little appeared to be somewhat romantic and distinctly unscientific. The excesses of its proponents, many of them psychiatrists of the slenderest scientific equipment, compelled me to adopt a position of rather active opposition. It is still too early to appraise its final worth, but it has unquestionably constituted one of the major movements in twentieth-century psychology and one whose impress upon subsequent theory and technique is bound to be of first-rate importance. My impatience was always stirred by the failure of the expounders of the cult to acknowledge adequately the achievements of their predecessors in the psychiatric and psychological field upon whose foundations they were actually building.

The "psychological test" movement was rapidly gaining importance and prestige when I dropped out of psychology, and while

[12]*Psychol. Rev.*, 1911, **18**, 295-323.
[13]*Psychol. Stud.*, 1907, 347.
[14]*Psychol. Monog.*, 1910, **13**, 60-100.

some of my students have made distinguished contributions to its development I myself was entirely on the fringe. Much of it has been shallow and unscientific, and consequently to some extent unwholesome in its effect. It certainly has suffered gravely from premature publicity and from exploitation by the utterly untrained. On the other hand, in its fundamentals, it is essentially sound and, in my judgment, will gain increased significance, both practical and theoretical, as its techniques become more thoroughly established. Already the more radical claims for it in education and in industry have become much chastened.

I am sure that any influence I may have exerted directly on the course of psychological development in my own investigations and publications is less than that which I have exerted indirectly through my students who received their training under me and most of whom matriculated for the doctor's degree. Among the women, Helen Thompson Woolley, June Downey, Florence Richardson Robinson, Kate Gordon, Jessie Allen Charters, Ada Hart Arlitt, Grace and Mabel Fernald, Mary Hayes, Stella B. Vincent, Helen Koch, Jean Weidensall, Dagny Sunne, Edwina Abbott Cowan, to mention only these, have had highly successful careers, while among the men, John B. Watson, Joseph, Harvey, and John Peterson, Walter Hunter, Harvey Carr, Beardsley Ruml, Clarence S. Yoakum, Curt Rosenow, L. L. Thurstone, Joseph Hayes, Myron L. Ashley, Walter V. Bingham, Henry F. Adams, Edward S. Robinson, Harry D. Kitson, Carl Rahn, Conrad L. Kjerstad, Jacob R. Kantor, Louie W. Webb, F. A. C. Perrin, Joseph U. Yarborough, Elmer K. Culler, Rutledge T. Wiltbank, and many others have done fine work and I have watched their careers with deepest sympathy and satisfaction.[15] Five of the members of my doctorate group have held the presidency of the American Psychological Association. To have such young people under one's charge is an extremely rewarding experience. I count my contact with them as among the most precious of my memories. Teaching as a profession has in the United States many drawbacks, but these intimate and friendly relations with strong growing minds are its great rewards.

---

[15]Deeply mourned by all their friends, June E. Downey, Joseph W. Hayes, and Joseph Peterson have unfortunately died.

FREDERIC CHARLES BARTLETT

The first book on psychology that I ever read was Stout's *Manual*. From this it may be gathered that my way into the science was by the philosophy of it. About the same time I read also the same author's *Groundwork* and his *Analytic Psychology*. The third of these books made a particularly great impression on me which remains to this day. I also read Ward's great "Article" in the *Encyclopaedia Britannica,* travelling once a week 18 miles to the nearest public library and bringing back copious notes with me.

Yet even in these early days not all my work was on the philosophical side. I did whatever physiology I could, but this was little and ineffective, for I had no available laboratory then. Soon after its publication I read Myers' *Text-Book of Experimental Psychology*. Much of this fascinated me, but again for lack of a laboratory I gained less than I should have done from my reading. With cardboard, pins, bits of string, and "elastic glue" I fixed up for myself such crude instruments as I could and tried a very prentice hand at experiment. At that time also my interest in political problems was extremely keen, and by the practical prosecution of this I was learning, though I hardly suspected it at the time, some social psychology in the field.

Three years after my introduction to psychology, and with a very predominant philosophical bias in my outlook upon life, I came up to St. John's College in the University of Cambridge. It had a good psychological record. It was the college of G. F. Stout, of William McDougall, and, in my own day, of W. H. R. Rivers. I went to it, in fact, largely because Rivers was there and my interests were turning strongly towards anthropology. However I decided to read moral science first, and that is how it was that I came into the Cambridge Psychological Laboratory. All students reading moral science then did—or were supposed to do—four hours of experimental work weekly in the psychological laboratory. From the first I did my full share, and later a good deal more than my full share, of this work. I started the laboratory courses with little liking and finished them with much. This change was due in the first place to C. S. Myers, and in the second place to Cyril Burt who was then helping Myers with the Cambridge classes. When Burt left for more important work I was asked to take his place and I accepted the offer eagerly. Even then it was in my plan to go for field work in anthropology after a few years' more intensive study of experimental method in the laboratory. The War stopped that. My own war fate was happier than most, though it was not wholly in line with my desires. It gave me much work to do, in which whatever psychology I knew must be harnessed to the solution of some very practical problems.

The War ended and Cambridge slowly struggled back to life again. Psychology, everybody found, had changed. It claimed to stand more by itself. Myers and Rivers had built for dreams that many had considered wide and wild. But their dreams were of the true prophetic order, and the development they designed has proceeded steadily ever since, though it is still far from its complete fulfillment.

*   *   *

Apparently a psychologist must have a descriptive label if people are to take much notice of him. He must be of this "school" or of that, and if his "school" is his own invention thrice blessed is he. There may be something ineffaceably controversial in the typical psychological temperament. This puts me in some difficulty, for, if I am to say what sort of a psychologist I am, I think I can say only that I am a Cambridge psychologist. The trouble about this is that Cambridge psychology of the laboratory type has never committed itself to any hard and fast and settled scheme of psychological explanation. I hope it never will.

To make the matter clear I must say how, what, for want of a better word, I shall continue to call laboratory psychology grew up in Cambridge.

In 1877 Dr. Venn and Dr. James Ward urged the need for founding a laboratory of psychophysics at Cambridge. But they fell foul of certain theologically minded mathematicians who were horrified that anybody should even think of measuring the human soul, and nothing was done. Fourteen years passed by. Other countries had by now definitely gained the lead in the new science of psychology. Ward was still anxious about the matter and in 1891 he succeeded in obtaining a grant from the University of £50 for psychophysical apparatus. If this had been the real start, however, it is difficult to see how experimental psychology could have developed in Cambridge as it has done.

The decisive move came from the physiological side when, in 1893, Sir Michael Foster, then Professor of Physiology, invited Dr. W. H. R. Rivers to come to Cambridge in order to teach the physiology of the special senses. To Rivers, trained largely with Hering and a great friend of Sir Henry Head, the physiology of the special senses was inextricably bound up with their psychology. Four years later a University Lectureship was established in experimental psychology and the physiology of the senses. This was held by Dr. Rivers, and he was given a small room in the Physiological Department as his laboratory.

The work thus begun developed considerably and psychology began to claim independent status. In 1901 a room was acquired in a dark and uncomfortable cottage and in 1903 the "department" was moved to a whole house, equally unsuitable from all points of view, but still a definite advance on the one-room plan. Meanwhile psychology had gained a powerful new recruit in Dr. C. S. Myers. He and Rivers had both joined in the Cambridge Expedition to the Torres Straits and the trip which took Rivers definitely over to anthropology brought Myers permanently within the ranks of the psychologists. This expedition did another thing. It put a social and ethnological stamp upon Cambridge psychology and this has perhaps done more than anything else to make Cambridge psychologists human as well as scientific.

Experimental psychology in Cambridge soon gave promise of breaking out of the bounds of its small house. Helped by the Moral Science Board and by the Cambridge University Association, Dr. C. S. Myers determined to build a laboratory worthy of the place and of times yet to come. The movement began about 1908. Dr. Myers was supported very generously by his family and his friends and with indefatigable energy he got the actual building in hand within some two years. A new physiological laboratory was being constructed about the same time, and, by good fortune and good will, the psychological department, though having an entirely independent administration, was housed in the same large building. Experimental psychology in Cambridge began in the physiological laboratory and it came back to its final home in the most intimate connection with the physiological laboratory.

From this brief sketch it will be seen that laboratory psychology as it exists in Cambridge today is almost wholly the work of two men: of the late W. H. R. Rivers and C. S. Myers, and particularly of Myers. Both were physiologists with wide biological training; both had a profound interest in anthropological and social research; both were medical doctors; both never allowed their love of exact method to override their study of human nature in or out of the laboratory.

It is now easier for me to say what Cambridge psychology is and what it is not. I would like to regard myself simply as a student of Rivers and Myers, carrying further perhaps the views which I have learned from them. They, together with their mutual friend, Sir Henry Head, have influenced my orientation in the subject more profoundly than any others, though I would not wish to underestimate the importance of the philosophical training that I had before I knew them.

I will now attempt to describe that orientation as definitely as I can. In doing so I shall drop the personal style and adopt a dogmatism of expression which I hope in no way represents an equal dogmatism of attitude.

*   *   *

Psychology is a biological science. This means that it definitely restricts its study to the conditions by which any type of animal and human response to stimuli and organization of stimuli is determined. It may, if it so prefers, further restrict itself to a study of those responses which are more complex than tropisms and the simpler reflexes. We agree to give up asking *what* a sensation, or an image, or an idea, or an emotion actually is and we ask under what conditions responses involving these occur. It may be said that we must know what they are before we can study their occurrence. The answer is that all such knowledge that is necessary can be given by the example type of definition.

There is no need that we should artificially restrict ourselves to the study of such conditions of response as can be observed by a second or a third person. Very often the most valuable information can be given in terms possible only to the person himself who responds. Always such information should be sought, and sometimes it may even be the only sort of information possible. When both modes of access are open they continually show such agreement as to warrant belief in first-hand observation as a sound method. For example, the description by the subject himself of the effects of adequate stimulation of the pain sense organs—the slight latency, the "welling up" of pain, the swift adaptation—fits very well the study by physiological methods of the propagation of impulses following upon such stimulation.

Another general point which is of extreme importance is that, whenever stimulation sets up, either immediately or remotely, responses that can be only or best described by the subject's responding himself, these responses may themselves become important conditions determining subsequent reactions. This is by no means to be taken as axiomatic however. Either it must be demonstrated or the whole idea must be discarded.

Since psychology is a biological science, its methods must be as rigorously exact as possible. Here we run into great difficulty. Physics and physiology, to both of which psychology on its experimental side is closely related historically, have their own ways of securing exactness of method. The former rests largely upon constancy of objective conditions. The latter, in order to secure instances suitable for the application of the same ideal, often resorts to the method of simplifying reactions by cutting out other responses than the one that is being experimentally studied. Naturally psychology has imitated these methods, but the results are often disastrous.

Constancy of objective determination is obviously consistent with variety of subjective attitude. Equally, since the human organism has grown up in a very varying environment, variation of objective circumstances is consistent with constancy of subjective orientation. Subjective attitudes or orientations are an important part of every response at the psychological level. It often becomes a matter of nice consideration whether the objective conditions or the orientation of the organism are the predominant determinants of the response. Neither can be neglected, but when the latter takes the lead it is folly for the psychologist to stick to the ideal of constant objective conditions merely because this is formulated and accepted by other scientists.

Again, the ideal of simplifying the response by cutting it off from others with which it is normally combined is all very well in its way, but it is a dangerous and slippery ideal in psychology. A physiologist who is interested in visual functions may isolate a single, or a few, appropriate nerve fibers with their connected sense organs, and observe how impulses are propagated when the sense organs are stimulated. But if a psychologist who is concerned with relatively high-level responses like recall endeavors to isolate the response *by simplifying the stimulus* he has performed a very different operation. This has been the traditional method, as, for example, in the use of so-called meaningless material in the bulk of memory experiments. Though we simplify the stimulus, we leave the responding mechanism as complex as ever and we may merely force it to mobilize all its resources and to adopt unusual and often highly complicated modes of reaction.

The psychologist must refuse to be overawed by the demand for objective constancy and he must treat very carefully and critically the demand for simplification of response. Does it follow that the psychologist must give up every attempt to apply exact method, shut up his laboratory, and relapse into general speculation? This is not the answer that any biologically trained person is likely to give.

We come now to the positive ideas that underly the Cambridge approach to psychology, though no Cambridge psychologist would for a moment wish to maintain that they are his peculiar property.

When any person or animal enters an experimental situation he brings with him certain tendencies to specific response which, in combination with the objective, external conditions, will issue in conduct of one kind rather than of others. Some of these are very deep seated and practically common to all subjects, and we may call them instinctive. Others are almost equally deep seated, are extraordinarily persistent in a given subject even though the external conditions differ widely, and we may call these temperamental. Others again can be shown to come to birth in the course of special training, may often be set up by the play of experimentation itself, and these we may call learned or acquired tendencies. There is a class which demands very special study, for they run through practically all the members of a social group; they may appear as immediate, "simple" and inexplicable as anything can be, and they are also extremely persistent. These we may call socially determined tendencies.

Of whatever class these tendencies, attitudes, and orientations are, they are powerful determinants in all psychological response. The instinctive and the temperamental kind we have to try to pick out, and then make them starting points. We can no doubt raise questions about how they are built up. But if we do, though the problems are extremely interesting, their attempted solution takes us over into general biology and sets an issue at once in terms of heredity and inheritance. We can however take them as we find them and see how, when they are there, they work, and for this we can use both experiment and field observation. Of the other type we can legitimately raise questions both of origin and of results.

In all his work the psychologist must keep his eye upon these reaction tendencies which are not explicable by reference to *immediate* stimuli or situations, or organizations of these. If he does he will speedily come upon another problem of primary importance. Perhaps its nature may best be thrown up by a retort against a current psychological dogma. Everywhere we are being told that the psychologist must study "the whole organism." In actual fact he never does, and the view that utilizes this vague expression can be buttressed only by a relapse into an equally vague philosophy. What he does is to try to find out the order of importance of reactions, of reaction systems, and of partial factors in the objective situation. One subject observing structurally simple forms in the extreme periphery of the visual field will confidently follow the immediate visual or retinal pattern. Another will equally confidently follow some scheme of imagery, of the "primary memory" order or of some other. In each case there is a dominating partial response which sets the stream of his interpretation. Similarly in all other cases: the psychologist is just as concerned with partial responses as is the physiologist, though, by trying to study them in their normal or abnormal settings, he sets himself the task of working out a hierarchy of importance of partial responses in any instance with which he is immediately concerned.

These are the problems of the psychologist: to show the functions of reaction tendencies in combination with the external exciting stimuli, in many cases to show how such tendencies grow up and in all cases how they operate, and to determine the order of importance or dominance of partial reactions and reaction systems in whatever setting they may occur. With these firmly in mind he will use whatever methods he can: psychophysical. statistical, and any others. As all his problems are ultimately problems of conditions and of determination he is throughout scientific, and whenever he judges that the response he wants to study can be produced to order he will use experiment.

Let us now reverse the picture, so to speak. All that has been said so far seems to imply that psychology is through and through functional. So it is. But it appears to be a peculiarity of psychological functions—or at least notably characteristic of them—that the material with which they deal may influence their course of expression; by "material" is here meant psychological material, not mere objective or external conditions. What constitutes psychological material? Sensations, percepts, images, ideas, thoughts, some at least of whatever is present in volition and emotion, and no doubt a good many other things for which the inventive psychologist can find names. Sensations have been roughly manhandled by recent psychologists and we are told that they are a kind of psychological Mrs. Harris— "there ain't no sich person." But a touch, a pain, a light-flash does seem different from perceptions mediated by the same sensorial reactions and in a perfectly understandable sense more primary than these. However that may be, the real point is that this sort of psychological material, once it has occurred, makes a difference to subsequent reactive processes. The presence of a visual scheme may make all the difference between a series of muscular reactions in a dark-room well adapted to secure some practical end and one blundering and ill adapted to the same end. Thus, however "functional" a psychologist may be, he dare not shut his eyes to problems of psychological material. Precisely as a subject has reaction tendencies ready to come into play in every experimental situation, so also he has organized psychological material ready to influence his reactions and to set the course of his interpretations of whatever external conditions may be present.

This psychological material is what an introspectively minded subject will describe if he is asked to say what a given response appears to him to deal with, or, since there is reason to agree that he cannot always arrive at such description, it is of that order of thing. A subject will say that he is perceiving or responding to a tonal field having a certain order of arrangement or certain properties; or he is perceiving a visual pattern possessing boundaries, color, location, and standing against some visual background. In remembering he may say that he is dealing with visual images having temporal and other characters, or with vocally arranged material; or it may be that we can demonstrate in some indirect way that he is utilizing a scheme built upon materials that belong to his past life and so arranged that he can construct from it whatever is needed in the interests of the specific tendency to recall. He is not able to describe this scheme as something that he can find by introspection, but it has a character theoretically the same as other things, e.g., images, sensory patterns, ideas, and so on, that he is able to find in this way. The introspective method gives us psychological material and with it no psychologist can dispense.

The reaction tendencies spoken of already are not in the same position. No direct inspection ever really reveals them or their character. They are hypotheses necessary to account for the varied grouping of psychological material and themselves subject to influence by specific instances and groupings of such material that have already been achieved. They characterize or describe how an individual deals with any psychological material with which he is confronted. Sometimes they are hypotheses made by the experimenter on the basis of the way in which objective facts are selected or grouped by his subjects. For example, two people observe the same landscape. One picks out and describes all the rocks and another all the trees and flowers. The onlooker, finding this markedly different grouping of like materials, infers that the observations are directed by the different tendencies underlying different interests. Sometimes they are hypotheses made by the subject on the basis of how psychological material appears to him. For example, in an experiment on peripheral visual perception with tachistoscopic exposure, a subject finds that one visual pattern, in a whole series of successive exposures, stands out without challenge from others. He can describe this more or less rapidly, without finding that a number of alternative formulations threaten to break in, and he says: "I am confident." Anyway, the tendencies are not of such a nature that they can be set up and directly observed by the subject, whereas psychological material is of that nature. The tendencies are necessary hypotheses which the psychologist must use in order to account for diversities and for diversities of grouping of psychological material.

Since it is demonstrable that psychological material affects the subsequent operation of reaction tendencies, while reaction tendencies account for the grouping and differentiation of psychological material, every bit of psychological observation must be a cooperative effort in which both observer and subject must play their parts. When an observer experiments upon or observes himself, he gains a part of his relevant information directly, as a subject does, and a part by hypothesis, as an outside observer must.

Just the same sort of problems arise about psychological material as about reaction tendencies. From the psychologist's point of view it looks very much as if some organization of such material is as ready made as are instinctive and temperamental tendencies, as liable from the first to influence the course and character of specific reactions. Such, for instance, may be those simple spatial relational references we come to call "above," "below," "right," "left"; such may be the sensory basis of the "light-shade," "sound-silence" differentiations, and such may be some part of the material which is bound up with temperamental reactions. The great part of organized psychological material is, however, built up in the course of experience. We must say how it is built and how, when it is built, it operates.

Undoubtedly, when we turn our investigation upon any instance of psychological material, as it is dealt with by an actual reaction tendency or group of tendencies, we find it both complex in structure and organized. Consequently it may seem necessary to say that in every case this material must be understood to play its part in an indivisible manner—"as a whole." This phrase is just as applicable and as inapplicable as the parallel phrase: "the total organism." For instance, visually presented material will be dealt with by one subject predominantly as colored and by another predominantly as formed. The one does not utterly ignore the form nor the other the color, but different components are dominant in the two cases. It is sometimes said that psychologists must utterly eschew the analytic attitude towards psychological material. This cannot mean that we must refuse to analyze any instance of such material into theoretically simple elements, and regard these as discrete in character and unaffected by any combinations into which they may enter, for hardly anybody ever has done this, and hundreds of psychologists, of all sorts of views, have warned us against doing this. Perhaps it means that we must avoid all theoretical analysis, sticking only to such forms as are found in the actual reactions themselves. Thus a visual pattern may be reacted to as a balance of light and shade with the brighter parts predominating in the responses made. Then the light sensory material and the darker sensory material may be treated as genuine components of the visual pattern content, and in so treating them we literally adopt an analytic attitude, though our analysis is derived from a study of the reaction itself and not from any theoretical division of the whole psychological material into minimum parts. If this is what the contention that we must treat psychological material in the mass or "as a whole" means, then "as a whole" is a strikingly misleading expression to use. Just as we have to study the order of importance of partial reactions and reaction systems in their setting, so we have to try to establish the order of dominance of partial components in their setting, if we are studying psychological material.

Clearly this leaves room for a structural as well as a functional psychology. The view developed here is less interested in questions of structure, but traditionally they have been uppermost in psychological investigation. Moreover, there seems no good reason why a structuralist, if he merely wants to describe completed psychological structure in simple terms, should not push analysis much beyond those distinctions which are made in the course of actual reactions, and so make use of "mental elements," "laws of association," and all the usual stock in trade of traditional psychology. Having done this he must not try to give his results a genetic significance, and he must, of course, recognize that combinations or organizations of "mental elements" may have different properties from the elements themselves.

This rapid and inadequate development of a point of view inevitably leaves many loose ends lying about and raises many points that require far more drastic discussion, but it carries a further important implication. It is merely what it pretends to be: a point of view, an indication of how to use experiment and field observation in psychology, and an expression of a belief that psychology can grow only by the patient use of these methods. It is *not* a scheme of explanation. Just where the psychologist could best have imitated other scientists he has gone his own way all too often. A physiologist, studying peripheral nerves, does not go on to dogmatize about the operations of the central nervous system, or about respiratory or circulatory functions. He looks for working explanations *ad hoc* and not for simple explanatory principles covering all functions of the organism. The psychologist far too often works on perception, or imaging, or emotions, or instinctive reactions and then tires of the effort involved in first-hand observation and gets out of his one bit of real work the clue to everything in mental life. Complete systems and schemes of psychological explanation are the biggest stumbling-block to progress in psychology.

*   *   *

I will drop this dogmatic habit of writing, which I do not like, and resort to a more personal style. A brief exposition of a general point of view is almost sure to be misleading in some places and to satisfy nobody less than its author. Nevertheless I hope what I have written will make it clear that I believe firmly that psychology, regarded as a science, has a great future before it. Whether on its theoretical side, as enabling us to understand the diverse workings of the mental life, or on its applied side, as enabling us to direct and control those workings in the world as we find it, I think that its greatest achievement lies yet ahead.

Perhaps this also is due to the influence of Dr. C. S. Myers, but I am sometimes tempted to think that in a few years it may be found that those who are applying psychology to industry, to medicine, to the organization and training of a nation's fighting services, and to legal procedure have done more than any others to the advance of psychology as a science. The exigencies and nature of the demands in these fields mean that an investigator must hold himself aloof from hard and fast theory, while at the same time he must define his immediate problems clearly. Whether this will be so or not, the method of work in the applied field is, in these respects, the one that has to be adopted by any psychologist who believes his study to be a special branch of biological science.

*   *   *

Is there any royal, best road into psychology? I cannot think there is. Even when it is treated scientifically, and I should be sorry to imply that I think this is the only way in which it can be treated, psychology is a very wide subject, in which there is room for the exploitation of the most varied interests. All I can say on this point is that if I personally had an entirely free hand in the direction of my own training from the beginning I would make it different in certain ways from what it was. Assuming I had reached the stage at which specialization can profitably be begun, I would first have a good practical training in physiology and biology and also in the elements of physical science. Contemporaneously I would read some philosophy and more logic. The positive value of this would, I think, lie in a training in laboratory technique on the one hand and in the technique of thinking on the other. As it is, people who have the first very often lack the second, and people who have the second almost always lack the first. The student whose training is wholly in the field of natural science seems often to lack flexibility when he comes to psychology and to be overmuch in awe of "exact method." The student whose training is wholly in philosophy and logic is generally too prone to rapid speculative generalization and inadequately reactive to the complexity of actual fact. If I had to choose either the one or the other, I should unhesitatingly adopt the scientific training and discard the philosophic and logical, for it is quite certain that scientific advance is never merely a matter of applied logic. But I can never see why the two should not be combined. The negative value of the plan I propose is that this kind of training would do something to prevent that elaboration of physical and physiological speculation which is common among psychologists, and would help to produce a proper skeptical attitude toward universal systems of fixed psychological explanation. After two or three years of this sort of study I think I should be ready to plunge into psychology proper. I would insist upon having laboratory work, and a good deal of it, from the first. A thorough training in psychophysical methods would come early, and so would practice in the use of statistics. Elaborate theory of statistics I would leave out altogether, but I would learn how and when to use statistics as a tool. Outstanding psychological theories I would have presented as history, of value to promote orientation in the learner, but not to be regarded in any single case as dogmatic truth. All the teaching in psychology from the beginning I would have as informal, as conversational, as full of perfectly free discussion as it possibly could be.

The laboratory should be a place to work in, not to live in. I am a firm believer in the great value of dumping a student into a social group that he is not familiar with, for I think that this stimulates observation of genuine human life reactions more than anything else. Further what I learned in social contacts at first hand I would try to bring into the laboratory and test under more exact conditions.

* * *

I will finish with the sort of remark that ought to be perfectly obvious. A psychologist who thinks that his work is done, that all that is now needed is the application of a final scheme to new instances, is dead. Psychology will go on and leave him lamenting. Like the reactions it studies, psychology is living and oriented forward: there can be no end to its achievements.

MADISON BENTLEY

No one knows better than the psychologist the exacting labors of the reporter; for the psychologist reports his own affairs, and no affairs are so difficult of faithful delineation as those in which the witness is himself engaged. First there obtrude the gross obliquities of self-depiction, which both blur and distort the picture. If the skillful biographer succeeds in removing these there still remain quivering velleities and egotistic slips of autography to mar a candid attempt at objective portrayal. Some men have confessed to gloomy discouragement, contending that neither they nor their psychological fellows could ever hope to succeed in the human art of self-report. Instead, they have used the simpler device of prod-and-pantomime, substituting for the cunning hand and the articulated voice the graphic and the photographic arts of the laboratory engineer. Their model is the performing silhouette of the mute and docile rat, galvanized into activity by the prods of the experimenter, who stands *in loco naturae* to his submissively responsive subject. In our present task, it would be convenient to shift the scene to human conduct and to inquire how the psychologizing manikin would itself appear under this clever artistry of pantomime. But here we shall look in vain for patterns and exemplars until the behaviorist has cast into the present work a historical view of himself as responding throughout his mature years to the effective agencies of his environment. While the example of this "objective" portrayal cannot avail his more conservative colleagues, we shall all doubtless profit thereby in our future attempts at writing "intellectual histories." Let us hope that he does not desert his high logic of objectivity and pour his unmellowed wines into the old bottles of tradition.

Of human reports two quite distinct varieties are to be found, the psychological and the journalistic. Out of bare facts the journalist compels a story to emerge. His self-instruction is to be timely and entertaining; but the psychologist instructs himself to be photographic and to be oblivious of the audience. While these reportorial arts are unlike in method and intent, they are alike in that they are difficult. One labors to solicit and to engage the reader, the other to portray simply and with fidelity. In historical writings both sorts appear. One historian reproduces, another weaves his story. Many try to attain both ends, constructing a coherent and engaging narrative out of documented facts.

Where the human organism essays to report its own immediate performance, methodical artifice is called for. Confidences and exhibitions of the journalistic kind are cast aside. They advertise and they console, but they fail to report in the psychological sense. Here the rigors of training, as well as the aids of the laboratory, are invoked. And when the portrayal is extended to the biographic past, only the *animus* of technical control is left. The organism has to rely upon an intent and instruction which will limit it to the relevant and will deliver it from romantic and sentimental interpretations. There coherence, reasonableness, and self-consistency in the object are lesser virtues than a just depiction of those meetings of man and circumstance which must be made to account for the formation and the constant remodeling of a professional career.

After the year 1900, the psychologist who found himself gaining a point of outlook over his field was to be subjected to singular responsibilities. The sturdy central growth of his subject was soon to divide into many branches. Until that time his main allegiance attached him to a man. Soon he was to be asked to choose a school, a banner, and a catch-word. He had been a pupil of Wundt, of Brentano, of Meinong, of Ladd, of James, or of Müller. If his novitiate had fallen a little later, he adhered to an aggressive pupil of one or another of these aggressive masters, pupils who had fortunately migrated to new lands, there to practice their imitative arts without embarrassing competition with their masters. These migrant pioneers exerted a profound influence upon our subject. Their idealization of masters whom they would scarcely have tolerated as colleagues imparted a vivid and romantic tone to the second generation of psychologists in America, as in Europe it granted a new lease of life to a parental stock profiting by advertisement overseas.

Now came a different kind of solicitation. Education was demanding a special brand of psychology to justify it or at least to make it modish. Biology was about to call for a psychological description of her varied forms of life. The medical men, who had wrestled almost without issue with the mentally sick and indisposed, began to spin an account of the human mind out of metaphysics and from shreds of clinical tradition. At first the "new psychologies" so conceived were modest, each dwelling within its own corner of the great field. There was the psychology of animals, the psychology of schooling, and the psychology of the abnormal. But gradually each outgrew its local province, and each became ambitious to occupy wider territories. Their conjunction was only a matter of time, and it is a striking fact that they came together in the child: educational psychology naturally enough; animal psychology because the child had been found at last to be an animal, and a method that had succeeded with the monkey, the cat, and the white rat obviously was appropriate for the human young; medical psychology both because the genetic method was in the air and because certain "psychological" disorders led backward to etiological factors of adolescence and childhood. So the child was set in the midst of the psychological doctors of philosophy. The subsequent flow of gold from the fabulously rich toward Child Welfare has been only an incident in a very decided focusing of interest (especially in America) upon the years of immaturity. Other incidents have been the spread of a eugenic faith, the care of the young defective, the study of the juvenile delinquent, and the new philanthropic cult of mother-and-child. It is interesting to see how powerfully this humane, biological, and pedagogical responsibility for the young has influenced, both directly and indirectly, current trends in psychology. No other fact was more impressive at the recent International Congress at New Haven.

All this is tolerably recent history. To the young psychologist maturing in the first years of the century no single trend appeared to guide his footsteps or to determine in an unequivocal way his professional career. He had rather to decide whether he would be "functionalist," "structuralist," "psychoanalyst," or "educationist" in psychology. And very soon the new and brilliantly lighted doorways of "behaviorism," "phenomenalism," and "configurationism" were to open enticingly at his approach. Here, if ever in the history of the sciences, was a problem in "multiple choice." Observe the behavior of the young psychologist and try to understand it! Is it a case of chance, of tropism, of associative memory, the law of frequency, the stamping in of pleasure, the perfecting of a Gestalt, sublimation, the escape from inferiority, or freedom of the will? The answer depends upon your doctor or your psychological creed; and, since the young psychologue was just then asking himself who was to be his doctor and what was to be his creed, we can scarcely press him for a final answer. There is the possibility, of course, that he sat demurely crouched before the multiple doors of opportunity quietly ratiocinating, dozing, or ruminating (according to his breed), and then neatly choosing that aperture which promised the most succulent of doctrines, the highest of rewards and wages, or the most engaging of nest-mates. But other possibilities also appear to complicate the destinies of our young psychologist. His decision may have been made for him by inertia or indolence, by precept or personal influence, by an ingrained dislike of certain categories or a limitation to preferred terms, by defective knowledge or selective interests, or more probably by the necessities of earning a livelihood and of retaining an academic post. With these complicating factors variously playing upon the decision, what chance had logic or free choice! And when we turn from the general setting of the times and interrogate the individuals actually faced with the momentous occasion, we seem to discover that the youngsters were further shaken into place by the interplay of still more adventitious factors. The tenure of an assistantship, the difficulty of learning a new jargon, commending letters from an instructor, the defense of a doctoral thesis, the complacent bigotry of one's laboratory, imitative mouthings against the basely practical or the uselessly abstract, a hatred of introspectionism or worship of a Wundt or a Galton, stupidity or inaptitude in observation; any one of these could have turned the trick and limited freedom to the floor-plan of the multiple-choice box. "So free we seem, so fettered fast we are." It has always been easier for men to defend the faith after it has been embraced than to embrace it reasonably and without passion.

Our animadversions upon early motives and choices with respect to a career in psychology grow simpler, if not more flattering to self-love, when we recede to the first scientific inducements of all set before the young collegian. The youth was not commonly smitten blind upon his commencement day by the arc light of science calling him to a lifelong service, but at least the terms of choice seemed fewer at that earlier time. Where a scholarship in psychology was offered to the confident graduate, emerging from his four years of elective dissipation, only profound gratitude for the chance to follow a burning predilection would seem to be called for. When the circumstances are inspected more narrowly, however, it may appear that the senior year itself had brought more than a single predilection, that any way out of a hot and dull summer of discontent was allur-

CHARLES SAMUEL MYERS

E. W. SCRIPTURE

EDWARD LEE THORNDIKE

Photograph by Nickolas Muray

JOHN BROADUS WATSON

WILHELM WIRTH

ing, or that the immediate prospect of a long journey to the strange
and enchanted city was, at the moment, far more enticing than the
remoter prospect of a career in psychology. For the adolescent, the
nineties were a parched and deadly decade; otherwise a much more
determined intent to enter the world of business might well have
forestalled such trivial determinations as those just related. Were
we to hunt microscopically for stray specks of dust falling under the
pivot of the wheel of fortune, we should find such meager incidents
as an undergraduate assistantship in physics, an encouraging blue
pencil upon a botany paper, a romantic enthrallment by geology, an
absorbed study of *Sordello, Faust,* and the *Faerie Queene,* and a
minor success in senior dramatics. All mere trivialities, but all
pregnant with causation, any one of them quite capable of setting
the stage for the individual's future.

As for myself, the earlier graduate years proved much less illuminating and absorbing than the collegiate years had been. Left too much
to drift, I allowed philosophical studies to consume too much of
my time, breeding in me, as in my working-mates, a conviction of
superiority over those students who were content to bury themselves
in the narrow details of the arts and the sciences while we examined
with a broader vision the general forms and concepts of existence.
Since that time I have observed the same tendency among other
callow and unseasoned students of the "mother of the sciences."
The very young in learning mistake a superficial acquaintance with
the terms and the thoughts of great writers for a fundamental comprehension of the universe, for a comprehension which really passes
beyond the realm of the verbal and the conceptual only when men
have previously made themselves at home in at least one of the
concrete sciences of nature, and have themselves learned to observe
and to draw responsible deductions from their own observations. It
is a common sight in the sciences to see men who would have been
better balanced and more judicious with philosophical training, but
it is just as common to find a philosophical writer or teacher whose
lack of scientific training has bred in him either a disdain for the
more concrete organizations of knowledge or a half-realized incompetence in his own field.

The indulgence in philosophical studies beyond my meager allot-
ment of time was encouraged by great liking and respect for my
preceptors in those studies, and also by a lack of satisfaction in the

local views and practices within my primary field of research. For a long time I did not recognize the limits of my sympathy for Wundtian doctrines, although I did apprehend, on the negative side, a growing realization of the virtues of my undergraduate introduction to the subject. During the teaching years I have often tried to recover the best things in my own early instruction that I might use them for inspiring junior students. The modes and means of instruction have so greatly changed in the meantime (not to speak of the development of the subject matter) that I am not at all sure of the profit in such recollections; still I set them down for what they may be worth. Interesting exercises in the primitive but resourceful laboratory which I first entered accompanied the lectures and discussions of the initial course. The exercises were impressive and they formed associative nodes. But it was, as I now recover the course, the dissection at first-hand of the sheep's brain which seemed most definitely to put me sympathetically inside psychology. That I was then acquiring sound and relevant knowledge, and not being merely entertained, I have had frequent occasion to realize. And so far from inclining toward a mere anatomy of the brain, those simple but absorbing dissections seem now to have done more than anything else has to form a working conception of the organism which is strictly psychological. The arid discussions of the mind-body problem (as we inelegantly phrased it) were already beginning. No one then realized how long the concepts and the doctrines of idealistic faiths were to preserve an artificial cleavage within the living organism; but I believe that the manual and ocular examination of those organic tissues did more than anything else to preserve us against the vicious notion that somewhere in that mysterious organ of man sat a lofty spirit which accepted a commercial relation with the earthly body only that it might govern and decree. That early teacher—to revert to primary influences—was a very engaging man. It may well be that the experiments and the dissection were impressive and instructive mainly because they were the modes of Wolfe's teaching. One cannot generalize upon such matters, and the facts are too remote in time for a just valuation.

With respect to the influences of the doctoral years, one must not overlook the setting of experimental problems, the opportunities, near the end of the novitiate, for formal assistance in the department, the counsel and intercourse with the director of the laboratory, nor the infectious enthusiasm with which teaching and research were carried out. While the emphasis upon concept and system might well have been less, the air was so charged with topics and problems of research that the logical side of the training was doubtless of great value to the younger men and women, among whom were Pillsbury and Washburn, Gamble and Baird, Bagley and Whipple. Later came the effort at writing and publication, a process which was doubly valuable because it brought also the opportunity to read in manuscript, and to comment upon, practically everything that was on the ways within the department. A staff of two brought possibilities for the intimate discussion of plans and problems, at every stage of maturity, which are quite out of the question in larger groups. For this interchange with Titchener, through many years, the writer is sincerely grateful. In retrospect, he is perhaps most grateful for the following comment upon a cherished manuscript which he had with great enthusiasm submitted for criticism. "Here it is. I don't think that I have ever told you that I thoroughly disliked anything that you had written. I do this. It is decidedly bad. Cut out your figures, and have done with your fine writing." That was a major operation without anaesthetics. Recovery was slow, but it left my organism saner.

The best occasional instruction which we received from the laboratory bore upon perspective. Not many contemporary laboratories laid so great an emphasis upon historical setting. Current men and works cannot be discretely judged save by way of origin and lineage. *Tout comprendre est tout pardonner* cuts too widely, but it suggests an important truth to the young schoolman in psychology. He is a bad representative of his masters and of his scientific faith who has neglected to understand with sympathy and in their historical perspective the tenets and the publications of rival schools and doctrines.

Nevertheless, while we were reading history, there is no doubt that we read it (as who does not?) with a bias. Bias in such matters is not wholly vicious in its effects where it is critically allowed for; but when it makes the youngster doctrinaire, a banner-bearer for a Cause, it saps his efficiency within his group, and it makes him unadaptable, if not ridiculous, when thrown out upon his own resources. The American history of our subject—first, the aggressive migrants bearing a new science to the frontiers, then the zealous followers of these highly individualized pioneers, then the specializing inroads from biology, medicine, and education, then the extreme modes of the iconoclasts and innovators—this history has inevitably encouraged provincialism, partisan differences, and idiosyncratic doctrines. We have seen the inevitable issues of these antecedents in most, if not all, of our primary seats of psychology in this country; and many of the derivative places have imitated a particular tradition without inquiring into its virtues and relative excellencies. But interstate commerce among our men and our laboratories is certainly softening these hard lines and gradually producing a more natural division in terms of problems and interests.

Respect for historical derivations is bound to bring one under outside influences. The result is not always happy. Allegiance to an arrogant leader or system is certain to induce internal conflicts when rival men and principles prove seductive. Such a conflict may well be an indication that the youngster should be transplanted. A change of base is, however, with most of us a serious matter. All sorts of considerations, professional, social, and private, have to be faced. Just when, if ever, the growing psychologist should be transferred to an independent place it is difficult to say. That is a problem which admits of no general solution. Perhaps the best indications are an imitative complacency and a growing sterility in surroundings which have lost their inspiration.

The men who emphasized mental analysis in terms of "process" undoubtedly opened the way to a great many experimental solutions. Those who have not familiarized themselves with the advantages of this mode of approach have missed the significance of a large chapter in our common history during the last half-century. They neither know the Külpe of the earlier period nor can they intelligently estimate the *Tonpsychologie* of Stumpf, the *Physiologische Optik,* and hundreds of experimental articles appearing in *Philosophische Studien,* the *Zeitschrift für Psychologie,* the *American Journal of Psychology,* and elsewhere in our periodicals. The uses of analysis in understanding the detailed functions of the body they do not apprehend, nor do they see the value of defining the qualitative variety in all our experiences. This type of analysis goes wrong only when it attempts solutions for which it is not adapted, or when it limits the problems of psychology to a piecemeal description, as in terms of process. With the present writer, it was the limitation and the inadequacy of this method which were mainly responsible for excursions into the psychology of the animal and of the abnormal, into the problems of integration, into social studies, and later into a general envisagement of the field of the psychologist. These excursions brought to one's attention the new field of animal experimentation, the new proposals in psychiatry, the integrative psychology of Meinong, Ehrenfels, and Witasek, and the wide disparity between the sombre attempts of psychologists to describe the plain facts of socialization and the awkward proposals of sociologists to write their own psychological account of human groups. In the first case, the meager fruits included the early establishment of small animal laboratories at Cornell and Illinois and a manual (never published) for a drill-course in these laboratories. Ill-considered plans to write a "psychology of the abnormal" were checked just in time by the caustic remark of Adolf Meyer, whose counsel had been wisely sought, that he wished he "knew enough to write such a pretentious work." Within the last five years several treatises of this kind have been published by American psychologists to the moderate benefit of the science. A perusal of them reveals the respectable amount of new materials collected within the last two decades. In the immediate future we should become more psychological and less medical, speculative, and anecdotal in this special field. The School of Graz proved to be very stimulating, especially when it was interwoven with those dynamical principles of Wundt which his earlier interpreters had unfortunately overlooked, and with the *Grundzüge* of Ebbinghaus. The first volume of Ebbinghaus, coming near the end of the nineties, was vastly more *grundlich* than the contemporary writings of the American structuralists and functionalists. If Ebbinghaus had had a spokesman in America (Stout sorted out simple bits of him for the English), it would have been fortunate for our subsequent decades. While the present writer is not certain that he owes more to any systematic writings than to those of Ebbinghaus, he does not overlook the great advantage which he derived from the Münsterberg of the middle period that produced the first volume of the *Grundzüge der Psychologie* (1900). Here again I find most copiously annotated in pencil those sections upon the description of psychical objects in which Münsterberg was struggling to free himself from the atomism of the sensationalists. We still want a coherent account of the socialized man which is integral with general psychology.

We have not so much as derived a psychological method for describing and understanding the socialized being which each of us is. Our compromises with the "social sciences" have only deferred the advent of a genuine social psychology, and the fictitious cattle which we find depicted by the behaviorists are superficial caricatures of human actuality.

From the British writers one seems to have derived but little, though without Darwin, Romanes, Huxley, and Spencer one could not have lived as one has; without Spiller's *The Mind of Man* and the McDougall of *Body and Mind* certain vexed problems would have been more vexatious. Ward and Stout have extended the range of vision, but Alexander Bain still stands as the most impressive of a long line. For the filling of the background one could no more do without Charles Bell and Thomas Brown than without Bonnet and Cabanis, Herbart and Lotze, Johannes Müller and E. H. Weber. When one begins upon that long list of worthies, there is no place to stop. More specific mention should be made of Hering and Helmholtz, who have shown us how to attack in an experimental way problems of great intricacy and difficulty, and of Janet and Freud, who have given us glimpses of new worlds and hints of the means for conquering them.

Of our contemporaries we must remain silent. We know them as imperfectly as we know ourselves. Of the present we know but little save that the past leads down into it. As we compare it with the preceding decades, or as we distantly observe it, diminished in the corridors of time, we may apprehend that, so far as the status of psychology is concerned, it is unlike any other time. Much that was important is no longer important. It has its own main problems and its own perspective. As we bring to it the accumulations of past decades, we observe the gift of new methods and of instrumental means, and we observe also the large sheaf of outworn concepts and discarded problems. Possibly this last is the best endowment of the present by the immediate past. It is a relief not to worry about unconscious inference or subliminal sensations, as it must once have been a relief not to be concerned with the relative size of angels and needle-points or of lunar phases and the farmer's seed-time. The body-mind worry is almost dead, and the relative importance of instinct and habit, of heredity and environment, is scarcely a living issue. We are beginning to see that the division of man into an "original" and an "acquired" nature is as sterile a dichotomy as that into "body" and "spirit." We are no longer tortured with the duty of carrying tropisms or reflexes up and up till they embrace the whole conduct of man or of carrying down and down to mammalian forebears our human list of intellectual and temperamental traits. The unconscious is returning to metaphysics and the censor to its home among the abstractions. We see the organism with fewer romantic, philosophical, and traditional encumbrances than ever before, and we come nearer and nearer to seeing it factually and seeing it whole. It remains an object of surprising intricacy and of astonishing functional versatility. Enough then remains to interest the psychologist of every complexion, and sufficient is the endowment of the past to engage us all in the new psychologies of the future.

* * * *

Nearly a decade has passed since these biographies were solicited by the general editor. The intervenient years now call for a comment supplementary to the original sketch. These years have brought not only an incremental change but have also significantly modified both psychology and psychologists. At least three of these modifications call for comment at the beginning of 1937.

In the first place, much that was marginal in the subject in the later twenties has since become fairly central; especially in the applications to business and industry, to delinquency and disorder, to vocation and character. Here technologies have hardened, relations to the arts of practice have been consolidated, and formal associations of men and women in these several special fields have enlarged. These new changes are in part natural outgrowths of two decades when the pressure to extend psychology toward the practical arts came chiefly from those arts themselves and not from a growing abundance of facts and principles within psychology itself. The result is like that which might have been expected had biophysics and biochemistry fashioned themselves within the same last years out of nineteenth-century physics and out of prenuclear chemistry. We accordingly find in these sturdy outgrowths of the physical sciences a state of vigorous health and of thrilling discovery which is not too apparent in most of the "applied psychologies." There are a few notable exceptions in these fields, for which we have to honor a small number of psychologists who have built solidly outward from central and fundamental principles instead of merely translating situations which arise in business, advertising, mental disorder, crime, delinquency, and so on, into terms which possess the flavor instead of the essence of a well-integrated science. To be sure, the flavor has often been tinctured with novel ingredients selected, as a rule, from a popularization of Pavlov's doctrine of "conditioning" and of Freud's doctrine of "unconscious force." The first ingredient is commonly added when the technological context is "learning," and the second in the context of the "abnormal" and the "personal." Since these explanatory devices are still relatively new in general acclaim, though now fairly ancient in sober history, they easily serve in technology. Milder terms, still frequently—albeit illicitly—used to denote causal agents in human behavior, are "memory," "attention," "suggestion," and "will." A large part of the quantitative and statistical methodology now to be found in practical fields is associated rather with its use by certain psychologists and among biometricians than derived through a logical connection with psychology itself.

On the side of engagement and occupation, the recent increase in men and women with some psychological training who are now employed in technological positions in psychiatry, mental hygiene, prisons, courts, industries, advertising, welfare stations, and institutions for delinquents and defectives should not be overlooked. Taken in the aggregate, a notable effect upon psychology and psychologists is already apparent, and it promises—or should we say that it threatens? —to be much more profound within the next generation. The increase here must also be taken with the ending (at least for the present) of a long period of psychological expansion within the universities and colleges. There exists a lively danger that the unequal growth of the technologies and the academies, of the periphery and the center of psychology, will further emphasize the unpleasant connotation of the epithet "academic." Physics and chemistry have successfully passed this danger; but then they have long sanctioned themselves by the effects of their research upon man's practical and comfortable control of "natural forces." The case is not so clear for psychology; nor will it be so long as the layman, the amateur in letters and arts, and the dilettante everywhere are convinced that "anyone can be his own psychologist."

In the second place, no subject so intimately related—at least in popular regard—to the everyday life of man as psychology is could have escaped an impress from the uncertain, harried, and disheartened state of the world since the late twenties. Private, social, economic, and public life have been matters of unusual concern upon which men have come to dwell with a prying and anxious interest. Until something like stability and peace become reasonable expectations, we can scarcely expect that the morbid and the sentimental will disappear from the fringes and margins of psychology. With sobriety and serenity finally attained, the current modes of literature, fine art, and the theatre may, to be sure, still find it difficult to free themselves from the accents commonly called "psychological," but psychology itself may well be expected to resume a more detached and objective course.

Now there can be no doubt that disorder abroad in the world has kindled the psychologist with new problems and has enlarged the range of his professional interests; but the chief and most obvious effect upon our subject has been the hasty acceptance of speculative doctrines and the personal adoption of highly emotional beliefs which have resulted in little good to psychology, however thrilling and comforting to the laity has been the psychological, or pseudopsychological, stamp of approval. It has not been difficult to dress up superficial conceits about the mysterious depths of human nature in the fashion of amateurish dramas of private and family biography which have been readily accepted in the market place and the drawing-room. Here material has been largely taken from the clinic, from sexual aberrations, from the troublesome child, the insane ward, and the bloody narration of crime. The laboratory and its controlled methods have played almost no part in this popular process of psychologizing the seedier and more disturbed and disturbing aspects of living. It is inevitable, therefore, that violent theories should be more exploited and facts and principles less sought out and scrutinized than is common in the established sciences.

A third modification of psychological perspective has come by way of new concepts and new methods in physiology, especially in neural physiology. Neither the anatomist's nor the physiologist's description of the body has been adequate to the uses of psychology. The ancient doctrine of local differentiation of cerebral functions throws little light—even in its current forms—upon the central processes of comprehending, thinking, desiring, and imagining, while the standard conceptions of neural excitation, propagation, and cerebral modification have not greatly helped the psychologist, except as he has forsaken his own problems and turned neurologist. On the other side, those who write physiologically of the body commonly shift to matters psychological in their descriptive chapters on the "special senses" and the "human cortex." Our current physiologies and neurologies would notably shrink in bulk if terms, concepts, and operations illicitly taken from the psychologist were deleted from their pages. The skeptic will find a striking illustration of this borrowing in W. H. Howell's *Textbook of Physiology*. The regrettable confusion of related but distinct fields of inquiry is clearly reflected in so good a volume as *The Foundations of Experimental Psychology* (1929), a book which gives a fair account of the relations of neurology and psychology as they stood at the beginning of the period of which we now speak.

Since the later twenties, new methods have greatly advanced our knowledge of neural excitation, impulse, conduction, and spread. Many believe that this new knowledge is changing the face of psychology. The change most obvious at present is the diversion of young men who have come out of a primary training in psychology toward functional studies in neural physiology. To those who regard psychology as a subdivision of physiology, all advances made here will accrue to the former subject; but to those who look upon psychology as concerned with special activities and issues of the organism (e.g., with "experience," with social living, or with the psychological functions), this new neurological knowledge is not so immediately applicable. It is of the present temper of the writer to follow the new neurological research with the high hope that it will notably aid our understanding of the bodily resources of perceiving, imagining, emoving, elaborative thinking, and other such "psychological" operations. These resources and the government and guidance of the psychological functions he now looks upon as the main problem—after the description of these functions themselves —of the psychologist. It is now apparent that we can expect little from an obsolescent "neurone theory" (still current in most textbooks) which stands primarily for central brain stations, conducting sluiceways, and peripheral reflex arcs, i.e., for the crude "telephone exchange" of nineteenth-century theorizing.

In accordance with this new outlook into physiological and neurological support for psychology, the writer has sought to construct a consistent frame of facts and principles which will forego all mental, mentalistic, and psychoanalytic agents and powers, which may now be finally regarded as *magical* in distinction from accredited or *scientific* means and causes operative within the physical organism. Into this frame he tries to fit older facts and newer researches which describe the distinctively psychological activities of the organism. In the fundamental and more comprehensive field of general psychology he has enumerated and distinguished the basal modes of these functions, their bodily support, their government, and their issues and products in objects, laws, customs, languages, and systems of belief and knowledge (cf. *The New Field of Psychology,* 1934). To a detailed description of these basal modes he is now devoting a fairly long series of major studies from the laboratory. In the special and derivative fields he seeks to relate these same fundamental functions and their issues to comparative, genetic, racial, social, and differential facts and to an account of the disturbed and the disordered. The final aim of this undertaking, still far from complete attainment, is to give in simple and realistic terms a coherent account of man's living which shall serve at once the general and the specific fields and supply also a common basis for the varied applications of psychological fact and principle to business and industry and to the human arts and professions.

HARVEY A. CARR

My early education was obtained in a country district school with all of the advantages and limitations of that type of institution. The community firmly believed in the value of book learning—in so far as its acquisition did not interfere with the serious pursuits of life. In the later years the school was fortunate in securing the services of a few young men who were working their way through college. In this way a few of us supplemented the usual work by obtaining a textbook knowledge of physics and chemistry and a mastery of high school algebra. Likewise we became imbued with the notion that a college education was a distinct possibility for those who desired it.

At 18 I entered the preparatory school of DePauw University. This was a three-year course. On the basis of the extra work in the district school and by taking extra courses, I entered college two years later. I had no particular vocational interests and no knowledge of vocational opportunities. I had no preconceived educational notions and no particular interests except in mathematics. I assumed that a college education was worth while and that it was my privilege to sample what they had to offer. In the preparatory school I began Greek and Latin as a matter of course. The work was interesting and stimulating, but upon entering college I decided that I had sampled these subjects sufficiently for my interests.

Because of my interest and the personality of the instructor, I decided to major in mathematics. It was a subject in which I could become thoroughly absorbed for hours at a time. Its precision and definiteness were fascinating, and I have since felt that it has considerably influenced my modes of thought and expression. No particular difficulty was encountered until I reached differential equations when I began to experience some doubts of my mathematical ability.

I liked physics and had some curiosity about the biological sciences, but little work in these subjects was given, and there was a rumor among the students that the authorities were not well disposed toward biology because of its evolutionary implications. I took two years of German under an extremely effective teacher for which I was later duly thankful. There was a course in medieval history in which there was a minimum of lecturing and a maximum of reading in a small but good departmental library. Here I browsed widely and developed an interest in history that persisted even throughout my later graduate work.

My health was good. I was physically active and interested in sports and games, and I entered with zest all those extra-curricular activities which make up college life in a small town. Life was vital and enjoyable. I adopted the usual attitude toward the grind, an attitude which I have never regretted. I did good work in those subjects in which I was interested, but not so well in those which failed to appeal, though pride sufficiently motivated me to obtain respectable grades in these subjects. The choice of a vocation did not worry me as much as it should have. Law was in the background, but I tacitly assumed that I would need to do some high school teaching in order to finance such an undertaking.

At the beginning of the third year I was stricken with a serious illness, and the rest of the year was devoted to recovery and recuperation. The next year was spent in hard labor on the farm in order to regain my physical vitality. At this time the farming community was afflicted with a period of hard times, and I decided to teach in a country school for a couple of years in order to complete my college education.

The school was located in a nearby community in which I was well known. Much was expected of a person who had gone to college, and my pride motivated me to fulfill their expectations. I had never heard of pedagogy or theories of education and I naturally modelled my procedure upon that to which I had been accustomed in so far as I could remember it. The results were woefully disappointing, and I soon realized that I had a real job on my hands, and one that required considerable patience, reflection, and experimentation. I learned that children—both young and old—will in time respond to enthusiasm, a judicious amount of approval, and a genuine interest in their welfare and development. At the end of the first year, I came across a copy of McMurray's *Method of the Recitation* which made a profound impression and convinced me that teaching is a process that is deserving of serious study. The period is of interest chiefly in the fact that it was primarily responsible for my later specialization in psychology and for the educational slant to my psychological interests.

I was averse to returning to DePauw. There would be a new

student body after four years of absence. The community environment differed but little from that at home, and I needed the stimulative effect of a change of scenery. Futhermore, I had been somewhat repressed and irritated by the distinctly religious tone of the institution.

My grandparents were Scotch and Irish immigrants. My maternal grandparents came from Aberdeen, and I have heard that it was a family tradition for at least one member of each generation to enter the ministry. The tradition was evidently not transported to this side of the Atlantic, for, so far as I know, no member of either side of the American branch of the family has ever been a church member. Whether this attitude toward the church was the cause or the result of the immigration I do not know. My parents were not antireligious. They were indifferent and non-participants. There was no family pressure in respect to religious beliefs and church attendance, and I was free to do and think as I pleased. I frequently attended the churches in the community, but did not join. As a consequence, the continuous social pressure in the college community in respect to beliefs and church attendance was irksome, and the reputed aversion of the college authorities to free inquiry in the biological sciences awakened my distrust. I disliked taboos in the realm of thought.

Through the influence of a friend, I entered the University of Colorado in 1899 at the age of 26, and remained the third year to take a Master's degree. The environment was thoroughly congenial, stimulating, and refreshing, and I look back upon these three years as one of the most enjoyable periods of my life. My only regret is that I did not take the step earlier.

It was my intention to continue my work in mathematics. In a conference I took a dislike to the instructor and at once decided to look elsewhere for a major subject. A few days before the opening of the University I had chanced to meet the Professor of Psychology and Education. My previous teaching experience furnished a background for an extended conversation. I was impressed with his ability, his geniality, and his cordial interest in the mental perplexities of a mere student. I turned to him for advice and, as a result of his interest and encouragement, I decided to turn Psychologist, although I knew practically nothing about the nature of the subject. Mathematics I proceeded to forget with considerable success—a fact which I later came to regret. The incident illustrates a personal peculiarity, viz., that my interest in and willingness to work at a subject have largely been determined by my attitude toward the instructor. The principle of selection has its limitations, but in the main the results have been satisfactory, and I have had no cause to complain.

The completion of a major in two years restricted considerably my choice of related subjects. There was a year of biology which was interesting and profitable. The quiet dignity of the instructor, his modesty and helpfulness, and the clarity and directness of his presentation elicited my respect and admiration and materially influenced my attitude toward science. There was a half year of physics which aroused my interest. The instructor was temperamentally reserved and unapproachable to students, but the lectures were admirably organized. An average student who really listened could hardly fail to pass the course. I was not so well predisposed toward chemistry, and the instructor aroused a mild aversion. As a consequence the educational value of the course was minimal. There were a few courses in history. A minor subject was required for the Master's degree, and I chose American history. There were but three graduate students in the class; the instructor was a young enthusiast, and he decided to give us a taste of the method of historical research. My topic was the Iroquois Confederacy, and I went through a number of volumes of Colonial Documents. I became so interested that I later pursued the topic in my spare hours in the more extensive library at Chicago. It was a time consuming but very effective way of learning history, and I have since been glad of this opportunity of obtaining some contact with the attempt to be scientific in such a diverse field. Perhaps science must be defined in terms of its spirit and method and not on the basis of the subject matter.

Outside of a couple of courses, there was little contact with the conventional type of psychology. The instructor, Arthur Allin, was a young man who majored in philosophy as an undergraduate, took his doctorate in psychology at Berlin, and spent a postdoctoral year at Clark. Because of temperamental affinities, he became a disciple of Hall. He was captivated by Hall's enthusiasm, imagination, and encyclopedic knowledge. Allin took a sympathetic and almost paternal interest in my development, gave me the run of his office and library, continually suggested books to be read, and encouraged me to give an informal report of my reaction to them. This type of erudition was subjected to considerable criticism at Chicago. While I am cognizant of its deficiencies, I still think that such a type of discipline has its values in mental development, and I still have considerable respect and kindly feeling for Hall and his work.

There was no laboratory at Colorado at that time. Allin professed to know nothing of experimental psychology and admitted a distaste for apparatus and machinery. Yet he was continually emphasizing his belief that experimental psychology was the coming field and encouraging me to continue my graduate work and specialize in this line. His attitude, I suppose, was somewhat similar to that of many psychologists—that the key to the solution of all of our difficulties is to be found in some allied field of which we have but little knowledge. In my time psychology put its trust in neurology, but I later found that neurologists had their own difficulties and were but little concerned with the troubles of psychology. We found a few pieces of apparatus in a closet, improvised a few others, and attempted to duplicate some of the experiments in Sanford. Because of the lack of background, this laboratory work was nothing but a series of stunts wholly devoid of psychological significance.

With this equipment I went to Chicago the following year to study experimental psychology. I had not the least notion of what a psychological laboratory was like, and I knew practically nothing of the subject except its name. I was favorably disposed and anxious to learn, but there was a wholesome tinge of skepticism, and I still had to be shown.

In 1902 Psychology and Education were in the Department of Philosophy. The Fellows were distributed among the three fields, and, upon reporting, I found to my keen disappointment that I had been assigned to Education and hence would be required to take a number of educational courses in which I was not particularly interested. There were two in educational administration which were alleviated by the engaging personality of the instructor, but there were others without any such alleviating features.

History of Philosophy was required of all first-year graduate students. I knew little about it, but was somewhat skeptical because of the many disparaging remarks encountered in Hall's writings. However, I had been led to believe that it was an essential part of any well-rounded psychological training. The courses were thorough and effectively taught. First-hand contact with the writings of most of the philosophers studied was required. Those that made the most permanent impression upon me were Plato, Kant, Locke, and Berkeley.

My reaction to Plato's dialogues was peculiar. I previously had had a course in formal logic, and I was thoroughly convinced of the presence of a considerable amount of fallacious reasoning in the argumentation. I first assumed that it was my task to uncover these fallacies, but I soon found that it was impossible to do this and still cover the assigned reading. Moreover it was soon evident that the class was not at all interested in this aspect of the subject. My first reaction was a considerable loss of respect for the author. Why should one devote his time to the serious study of a writer who is guilty of so much faulty though clever reasoning? To my youthful mind an author must possess something more than argumentative cleverness to be adjudged a great philosopher. It then occurred to me that this superior mind might have been thoroughly aware of the fallacies involved, but on this hypothesis the lack of intellectual sincerity was disturbing, and I also experienced some irritation at playing the rôle of a sympathetic auditor and being intellectually kidded by an expert. I have often been amused by my attitude, but I must confess that even yet I find some difficulty in rendering the usual homage to the philosophic genius of Plato. I later found that my teaching was considerably influenced by Plato's example. The Socratic method has its limitations as well as advantages, and I suspect that some of my early students had more reason to be irritated with me than I had with Plato.

I was delighted to learn that I could take a year's work in experimental psychology. Before coming to Chicago I had heard much of Dewey, but nothing of the other men in the department. On reaching Chicago I heard that experimental psychology was taught by an Assistant Professor—a young man by the name of Angell. On the opening day I appeared early so as to have time to locate the laboratory in the maze of Gothic architecture. Imagine my surprise in encountering a small weatherbeaten dilapidated frame structure that had evidently been discarded as unfit for human habitation. I joined a couple of graduate students seated on the front steps and was told that the Professor had not yet arrived. Shortly there appeared a young man with an erect posture, a jaunty walk, a semiquizzical smile, and a hat slightly atilt over one eye. He entered the building and was mentally labelled as another graduate student not socially inclined. On entering the building, I found my graduate student at the lecturer's desk ready for business. Apparently erudition was associated in my mind with age and some degree of pompous dignity. There was nothing to do but make the best of the situation, but I felt much better at the end of the hour, and in a couple of weeks, in common with the other new students, I found myself being completely sold on the Instructor.

It is difficult to characterize this versatile and engaging personality from the standpoint of the students—especially during the period when he was devoting his whole time and energy to the work of the laboratory. There was the keen and incisive intellect, the judicial attitude toward controversial questions, the delightful idiosyncracies of manner and expression, the bubbling humor which ran the gamut from good-natured levity to brilliant wit, and the free and easy flow of choice diction which always seemed so well adapted to the illumination of the topic under discussion. Finally, there was the penchant for long and involved sentences—in the middle of which we would find ourselves in breathless suspense wondering how it would be possible for mere mortal to extricate himself from the bewildering maze of clauses with due conformity to the rules of syntax and grammar. We often compared notes, and were forced to admit that the feat was always achieved—and usually in some unexpected manner. With the beginning of research our relations became more intimate and informal. We found him to be intensely human, stimulating, encouraging, and genuinely interested in our intellectual and scientific development—an interest that continued to manifest itself long after we left the laboratory. Our general reaction was one of admiration, respect, and genuine affection. Due to his influence, the students were a friendly and cooperative group, the laboratory morale was excellent, and there were times when we were even disposed to take some pride in the drabness of our surroundings.

At the end of the first year, Dewey left the University, psychology was made a separate department with Angell as head, and Watson was appointed as an instructor. My fellowship was transferred to psychology, and I felt that the promised land was near at hand.

I had heard of Watson the first year but did not meet him. In my capacity as handy man around the laboratory, there was much contact thereafter. My first reaction was one of slight reserve and suspicion—the basis for which I have never been able to fathom. This initial attitude did not long survive the influence of his genial and friendly spirit, and there soon developed an intellectual and scientific comradeship that persisted many years. I admired his tremendous energy and enthusiasm in both work and play, his irrepressible spirits, his intellectual candor and honesty, and his scorn of verbal camouflage and intellectual pussy-footing. He seemed to be wholly oblivious to the distinction between instructor and student, and regarded us as partners and co-workers in his scientific endeavors. This attitude was an expression of his nature, and it materially strengthened our initiative, confidence, and self-reliance, without exerting any inflationary effect upon the ego. I was thus inducted into the mysteries of animal experimentation, and Watson in turn heartily cooperated in my early experiments in space perception. Watson influenced me in many intangible ways, and his subsequent loss to psychology was a matter of personal regret.

At this time Titchener was used as the laboratory manual. As a matter of method it was followed somewhat literally, and our notebooks contained a series of alleged introspections and opinions about each experiment. Watson as an instructor evinced no hesitation in expressing his opinion of the futility of this material. He was objective minded both by training and temperament, and the appearance of his Behaviorism was no surprise to those who knew him well. He once remarked that it was possible to write a psychology in purely objective terms—starting with the simple reflexes and proceeding to the more complex varieties of mental behavior, and he also added that he intended to write such a book at the first opportunity. Here were the essential features of his Behaviorism long before he heard of the work of Pawlow and Bechterew.

The selection of a thesis topic was as usual a source of worry. The laboratory work on visual sensation and reaction time was interesting but it made no particular appeal to me as a field of research. At the latter part of the course, there were a few lectures on memory and the acquisition of skill, but there were no laboratory experiments. The topic was appealing, but I felt helpless because of lack of knowledge of how to begin. I had done considerable reading in the systematic treatment of attention, and in common with many people at that time I felt that the attentive process was the central and distinctive feature of mental life. On making my decision, I was put to reading the experimental literature but made no headway in formulating a satisfactory problem. While engaged in this task I made a chance observation which excited my interest and curiosity, and with some help and encouragement there soon emerged a thesis problem in the field of visual space perception, a field which has retained my interest ever since. I have since been disposed to feel somewhat grateful for the whims of Lady Luck, for to my mind attention is one of the disappointing chapters in experimental psychology.

There was a year's work with Donaldson in neurology. He elicited my admiration and respect as a man and a scientist, but the subject matter awakened no particular enthusiasm. Like all students of this period we read and studied James with reverence, and I still find him interesting and stimulating. While I was not particularly interested in the topic, his *Varieties of Religious Experience* made a strong impression and considerably broadened my sympathies and outlook. There was a course in Stout's *Analytic Psychology* which was exceedingly interesting. There were many chapters which I read and reread with great avidity. I have always felt that this work exerted a profound influence upon my psychological development, though I have never been able to trace back any of my beliefs to those of Stout. Apparently the work aroused my interest in the problems of systematic psychology and stimulated me to attempt a more satisfying solution.

I took no more formal work in philosophy. Like all graduate students I was greatly impressed with Dewey's ability, his kindliness, and his unassuming modesty. Perhaps the majority of the philosophy students could be classed as "disciples"—a condition which I found rather irritating. I found that I had developed quite an interest in many philosophic problems, and I spent much of my spare time in informal discussion of these questions with philosophy students with whom I was well acquainted. This informal type of educational activity was both enjoyable and stimulating, and I succeeded in attaining some sort of personal orientation toward many philosophical problems, though I was never inclined to take the outcome of these speculative endeavors very seriously. I have since suspected that I was primarily interested in philosophizing and not in philosophies and philosophers.

Upon graduating in 1905, only two positions were open and I failed to land them. It was a discouraging summer, and through a friend I finally secured a high school position in Texas. It was a friendly and hospitable environment in which I found myself, and during the year I gradually became mentally reconciled to a public school career. Two features of the work are of possible interest. This Yankee from the North was assigned two classes in the history of the Civil War. These Southern children proved to be a fine and generous lot, and perhaps they took an interest in my educational development, for we got along quite amicably. There was a small class in geometry composed of girls who could not learn this subject. The class challenged my best efforts and I learned something about teaching. Confidence in my ability was materially strengthened, and I felt that thereafter I could meet any teaching situation with a reasonable degree of success.

I returned to Chicago for the Summer and taught for a few weeks in a State Normal School in Michigan. Late in the Summer I received an appointment at Pratt Institute where I stayed two years. My initial efforts at teaching psychology were woefully disappointing. I might pass a doctoral examination with credit, but certainly there was no mastery of the subject adapted to its effective presentation to beginning students. I worked diligently and faithfully in preparation and experimented much, but it was not until several years thereafter that I attained a content and organization that was approximately satisfying. It is the introductory course that demands teaching skill, and perhaps I could do much better if I should try it again.

In the fall of 1908 I returned to Chicago to take Watson's place. That Summer the department moved into its present quarters—a remodeled three-story double apartment building, and the old laboratory was retained for animal work. The contrast was so great that our new surroundings seemed almost palatial, and they served our needs fairly well until we encountered the post-War influx of students.

I taught the various courses in experimental psychology, and continued the work with animals which Watson had started. The work in learning was extended with the rapid development of this field, and finally a course in space perception was added. The early years were largely devoted to more adequate preparation, and in time there was the supervision of thesis projects as I became established with the students. Life once more was enjoyable and alluring.

The personal contact with the intellectual and scientific development of the graduate students has probably been the most gratifying aspect of my work. One hundred and thirty doctorates have been conferred since my connection with the department, and I have had considerable teaching and conference contact with all of these students. Naturally it was the thesis supervision that was the most stimulating and interesting, and sometimes the most irritating as well. As is well known, interest in animal work rapidly waned after the first outburst of enthusiasm, and it was freely predicted that its possibilities would soon be exhausted. Many of our students expressed an aversion to choosing a thesis topic in this field for fear that they would become known as comparative psychologists, and that this label would be detrimental to their professional placement and advancement. There were eighteen theses in this field, and there is some satisfaction in having kept one center of research going until the remarkable revival of interest in recent years. There was less interest in space perception. This was due in part to the technicalities of the subject, and in part to the fact that the course was usually taken after the thesis topic had been selected. There were five theses in this field, and several others were completed by students who did not take their degree. To my satisfaction, learning proved to be the most attractive, the number of selections being twenty-nine. It was the policy of the department to promote diversity of output by encouraging students to select topics along the lines of their interest, and there were fourteen of this type that were under my supervision. As previously mentioned, this work was extremely enjoyable, and I hope that the students were equally well satisfied.

I had entered the field of experimental psychology with considerable faith, but with little knowledge and an open mind. To what extent were my expectations realized? Quite early in my career, I became impressed with the limitations of the experimental method in the field of human psychology. By experimental I refer to the usual laboratory practice of eliciting certain modes of activity under specified conditions. Any thoroughgoing and extensive control of human activity is a difficult matter. The difficulty of eliciting a genuine fear reaction in a laboratory situation may be mentioned. Industrial psychologists have encountered similar trouble in reproducing genuine test situations. The control of the environment and the entire activity of the subject for an extensive period requisite to the solution of many problems—genetic problems especially—is wholly impossible. The use of drugs is limited, and vivisection is out of the question. This limitation has been responsible in times past for the great interest in "Nature's experiments," and for the extensive use of animals in recent years. Psychologists have turned to animals for the same reason as did physiologists—the inability to experiment with man.

The recognition of this fact involves several corollaries. I have never been able to subscribe to the doctrine that an introductory text should confine itself wholly to experimental material, and to the notion sometimes expressed that a text to be experimental must be one that writes much about experiments. Such positions might be justified if such a course were designed solely for the training of professional psychologists. Perhaps such statements are motivated in part by our well-known inferiority complex and our desire to impress our students with the scientific character of the subject. Again, the validity and value of an experiment are not to be judged on the basis of the amount and complexity of the apparatus employed, nor is the scientific output of a laboratory necessarily proportional to its space and material equipment. Likewise many excellent experiments can be performed without that modern accessory device—the subsidy. But I refrain, for I suspect that my attitude is probably colored to a considerable extent by the fact that I have never had one.

Certainly psychology should be scientific—at least in so far as this is possible. Is the experimental the only scientific method? Geology, astronomy, and mathematics are usually regarded as sciences, but are they experimental in the usual laboratory sense of the term? Do the social sciences have a right to the name? The answer to these questions is obviously a function of the meaning of the two terms, and I shall not define them. However, the two terms must be regarded as synonomous, or we must admit that there are other legitimate ways of studying psychological phenomena.

Perhaps a few expressions of opinion are permissible. I am skeptical of the attempt to define science on the basis of its subject matter. Is psychology a science? I have never been interested in the question. It makes no difference to me. Science is primarily a matter of attitude and method. The important question, to my mind, is: Are psychologists scientists? And I think that most of them are—at times—just like physicists and chemists. Perhaps the essence of the method is the spirit and not the form of the inquiry, and again I shall not define these terms. I am inclined to believe that the form of attack will necessarily vary with the problem, and that in time we will devise modes of attack adapted to psychological problems which at present are not subject to scientific investigation.

I do not think that the experimental method—in the usual sense of that term—is the only scientific method. I am an experimentalist, and expect to remain one, partly because of my training in that technique, but mainly because this mode of attack is so well adapted to those fields which happened to elicit and retain my interest. Are we not all too prone to overestimate the relative importance of our own problems and techniques? We talk much about the desirability of studying basic and fundamental problems, without defining the terms, and I suspect that we all secretly cherish the belief that we are engaged upon such a task. Perhaps all problems are really basic, at least to *something* else, and if this attributive characteristic is a quantitative variable—to use the present scientific jargon—I sometimes wonder if the most basic problems will not of necessity be the last to yield to a solution. Too much specialization seems to be conducive to a loss of perspective and a judicial temper, and yet a catholic attitude is supposed to be one of the essential characteristics of the scientific spirit.

Can all aspects of mind be subjected to scientific attack? The psychoanalysts have been largely responsible for the explicit recognition of the fact that the key to the understanding of many features of mental life is to be found in our developmental history. For example, what were the various reasons that actuated a group of psychologists to write articles such as this? What were the motives that dominated both the selection and omission of material, and the style and manner of writing? What impression did the writer wish to make upon the reader? To the psychoanalyst, the possible interpretations are many and usually not flattering to the writer, and I sometimes wonder at the temerity of a psychologist in thus partially exposing his mind to the psychoanalytic scrutiny of his colleagues.

Like most psychologists, I am extremely skeptical of much of the subterranean mental machinery of the psychoanalysts. Nevertheless the problem is still there, for what we write and the manner thereof

—especially in an article such as this—is an expression of our nature and may reveal much. But which of the various interpretations is correct? Such questions can hardly be decided on the basis of present techniques. Can new techniques be devised that are adequate to the task, and, if not, shall such features of mental life be studiously ignored on the ground of their non-scientific character? Perhaps the scientific attitude is a quantitative variable, and we should attack all problems and be content to be as scientific as the subject will permit. Much depends upon the meaning of the term scientific, and again no definition will be attempted.

Much has happened during my connection with psychology, and it has been extremely interesting. In retrospect, I have been impressed with the unpredictable character of much of this development and the minimal amount of my influence upon it. Likewise I have often wondered how much of this development may be termed progress. What will be the course of future development? Who is so rash as to predict its nature, and why this unpredictability? Is it because we have no commonly accepted system of scientific values and objectives, and hence live a life of simple faith and take the value of our science for granted? Is not this faith often expressed in our tendency to capitalize such terms as Truth and Science? I sometimes wish that I might be vouchsafed a glimpse of the Psychology—or Psychologies—of 1990, but perhaps it is just as well, for I might be woefully disappointed.

SANTE DE SANCTIS*†

The Method of This Autobiography

Autobiography is a literary labor. All novels are autobiographical, whether they be sincere or whether they be full of artifice. But the critic, if he is also a psychologist or a subtle psychoanalyist, uncovers the artifice.

The psychologist cannot be and should not be an autobiographer in the ordinary sense of the term. Under certain conditions he can achieve a substantial reputation in "differential" psychology. The reader ought to demand from the psychologist absolute sincerity, but he cannot demand total sincerity. This is so for two reasons, both very different but apparent: either because many things and precisely those things which ordinarily awaken greater curiosity are common to all average men or because they are things which constitute a truly secret patrimony which imbeciles would be quick to dissipate. It is not a suitable aim for the psychologist, who is not also a man of letters, to make public that which St. Augustine called the "nuptial chamber of the soul," or the most profound and hesitating intuitions which in large part cannot be expressed in ordinary phrases. Hence it is admittedly necessary to keep many things silent; but to write that which is not so would be the same as to lie. The psychologist-autobiographer who would deceive for his own ends would be a false and at the same time an ingenuous person. No one would believe him, and his falsehood would betray itself to keen-minded readers who are acquainted with "differential" psychology and with methods for investigating the subconscious by characteristic expressions, the use of certain words, and the style. I shall say here, therefore, everything that arises in my memory as actually lived reality, even though this should displease me. But, despite the best intentions of the writer, an autobiography is of necessity marred by the great defect of the ignorance of the profound inner impulses of the temperament, of the disposition, of actions accomplished and to be accomplished. Can one expect of a psychologist any keener in-

*Deceased February 20, 1935.
†Submitted in Italian and translated for the Clark University Press by David M. Dougherty.

sight into the sphere of his own subconscious state? I recognize that such inner probing is difficult and may be met with failure; nevertheless, I consider it my rightful duty to make the attempt. On the other hand, it is not permitted to a psychologist to trust his own intuition, even though that were possible. There would be too many fallacies. The more or less conscious aims, the author's own reserve, would falsify the history of any man of high purpose. The biographer, Ludwig, seems to have adopted this method: the psychological method (but not "technical") combined with artistic intuition. But he was the other person (*alter*) in regard to Bismarck, William, and Mussolini. Under such circumstances the man of talent may be successful, although the average of errors will always remain high.

On the other hand, the method of scientific psychology should not be betrayed by the psychologist-autobiographer who has devoted years of constant labor to it. One must know how to divide one's personality; that is the necessary preparation for anyone who is starting to write an autobiography. Then we should keep fixed two perspectives: that of perception and that of memory, that is, to keep patiently and sharply outlined in our minds the characteristic inward situations of the present and those which we believe existed in our past lives. It is not easy to grope in the "cemetery of memory," even when we have the most upright intentions and an ability developed by long experience. But, aside from this, there is no other course worthy of being followed.

In studying personality one should consider its origin, its history, and its psychology. But this is not enough; as I have already pointed out, the attempt should be made to discover the motivating forces in order to give the personality its true meaning. However, I think that the motivating forces should be affirmed by induction and not by deduction. It is not necessary to have recourse to divine providence or to biological prophecy, whatever that may be. I think that from the fruits one should go back not only to the tree but also to the roots, I mean biological roots—an end which may be attained—and also to psychological roots, in any case.

In March, 1932, Professor Spearman of London invited me in a letter to give my reasoned opinion on this subject: "Whether an individual can be described with some hope of adequacy." The Chairman of the American committee for this investigation was Professor Thorndike. I replied with a program from which I select the following premise.

An "adequate knowledge" of an individual may be obtained by using experimental methods (and mathematical elaboration of data). But it is certainly a question of an adequacy which is always "relative." Nevertheless, it is worth while for the psychologist to put a "scientific knowledge of the individual" first, and then complete such knowledge, of psychological-mathematical type, with the addition of intuitive knowledge (Spranger, Jaspers, etc.), which is important not only for itself but also because it should serve for comparison with scientific knowledge. Empirical scientific knowledge concerning an individual will never be adequate unless both the phenomenological and genetic methods are used. The genetic method looks into the race (or the nation), the heredity, the (physical) constitution, and the family. After this inquiry there should follow an investigation into the childhood, the education, the vocation, and the social success of the individual.

In the investigation for Professor Thorndike, I distinguished between primary characteristics and derivative characteristics. There are ten of these in all, as follows: intelligence, habitual orientation of the psychical personality in relation to time, imagination, sexuality, emotional balance, sociability, speed of psychical processes, capacity for work, capacity for selection and determination, and speech and style.

Well then, if I, basing my remarks upon a retrospective glance, that is to say upon the mere observation of my behavior and of the success I have attained, were to carry out the aforementioned scheme, requested by the committee of which Professor Thorndike is Chairman, this is what I should write:

1. Intelligence—good, whether it be a matter of native intelligence or of intelligence applied to technical questions.

2. Habitual psychical orientation generally toward the future.

3. Lively imagination.

4. Sexuality of average intensity and very normal in direction, but with numerous "dismissals" and "repressions," and therefore an inclination towards compensating outbursts and sublimations.

5. Emotional balance—high.

6. Keen instinct for sociability.

7. Speed of psychical processes—above average, especially in writing.

8. Capacity for work—perhaps extraordinary.

9. Capacity for selection—high; I have been and I am an impulsive person.

10. Speech and style—easy, style considered to be somewhat personal.

To whom would it be useful to know such characteristics of one out of so many psychologist-psychiatrists of this world? What advantage would there be from such a summary and assertive application of my scheme? None. If an autobiography may serve some useful purpose in the field of culture, it is only upon this condition: that the judgments be corroborated by the facts which should logically precede and justify them.

One last thought: This autobiography has so modest an importance that I have asked myself, at least a dozen times, *cui prodest?*

I have had to conclude, in order to find time and courage to write it, with this consideration: Even if there be indicated to students the solutions of problems which aid us, which we either do not see or which, even if we do see them, we disregard, it seems to me, nevertheless, that a sincere autobiography can be a small-sized school of life. But for whom? I think that, if satisfaction can come to the writer from writing about himself, this may be hoped for only if the autobiography be turned over to members of his family and to his few friends scattered throughout the world—to the family, because the reading may eventually bring about the solution of some troublesome family "complex"; to his friends, because the reading of the autobiography might change their position for the better, and in any case make them either less deceived or more equitable or kinder to the autobiographer.

I feel that I shall emerge from this autobiography somewhat belittled, in the opinion of a number of men of science, whereas with a few retouches I should have been able to emerge from it considerably magnified. But not on this account shall I lower myself to the extent of making insincere justifications and retouches. I am sure, however, that, if men of science are displeased with my shade, my sons instead will rejoice at it; they will find in this autobiography not desolating dryness, nor intentional contradictions, nor ridiculous self-exaltation, but they will recognize in it their father as he was in the intimacy of the fireside.

BEGINNINGS

Fortunately I can speak of my beginnings with less difficulty than others.

There is in the little village of Parrano, in mountainous Umbria a family which has lived there since the middle of the sixteenth century. The history of this family exists in a collection of old papers, on which the ancestors wrote clearly about their lives and works, always in the third person. This history comes down to the present generation, and my sons are continuing it. There is recorded there the birth, the illnesses, the studies, the career, the economic development, the social success of each member of the family.

I shall transcribe unchanged a passage, taken from old papers, condensed by my son, Charles (a specialist in neuropsychiatry, Chief of Staff at the Ospedale Provinciale, Rome).

The region in which Parrano stands is rich in medieval castles. It is a rough, hilly region; although the altitudes are not very great, the configuration of the soil is nevertheless mountainous. Steep stony slopes, deep little valleys, ravines almost dry in the summer, fierce raging torrents in winter; woods of different species of oak, but, except for the latter, rather scanty vegetation because of the scarcity of water. It is an almost impenetrable massif, having few roads, which must have been even more impenetrable in the Middle Ages, when the castle was built. The region used to be called "the mountain," the allusion being to Mt. Peglia, the highest summit of the range. Parrano is located between Mt. Peglia and Mt. Arale, roosting upon a small and precipitous hill, 440 meters above sea level, overhanging the little valley of the Chiane.

Property in a poor agricultural and grazing section, such as Parrano, was always for the greater part, not to say the whole, in the hands of the feudal lord. (Parrano is a principality.) Very slowly, with the passing of the centuries, there was formed a small property, the greater part of which originated from a long lease. The community administered by a *podestà* or governor, nominated by the feudal lord, assisted and controlled by stewards (*Massari*) or priors, nominated by the people, had rather limited revenue constituted by a tax on flour and on the property of "individual laymen" .... from the proceeds of the sale of salt, from the contracts for the maintenance of the inn and of the slaughter house, and a few other items of revenue of dubious importance.

The De Sanctis family is a genuine plant of Umbria, from the Parrano district. Having sprung from the land, its sons have set their affections and their ambitions upon the land for centuries. From the beginning, in the middle of the sixteenth century, they appear as small country landowners, laborious, honest, and thrifty. For generations they labored intent upon increasing the family patrimony by dint of the most painstaking toil; but from the beginning they were marked by a level of culture higher than the average of their region. They were always middle class: we find doctors, lawyers, nuns, monks, priests, notaries, expert geometricians, and pharmacists there in the early days and at later epochs. No De Sanctis, on the other hand, was ever attracted by the career of arms . . . . they always exerted their activity in the administration of the property of the community, occupying therein the most important offices. The family was always marked by certain traditional characteristics: honesty, mild disposition, although at times quarrelsome, a quick mind, indifference to political contests. In the long genealogical tree there are to be found no insane persons, no imbeciles, no one condemned for crime.

Continuing the story, my son writes:

As far as can be deduced from indirect mention, the smallboned frame and the blond type were common in the De Sanctis family. One member (Guiseppe) was fat and corpulent; others were of the ruddy type and of greater stature, very tall and dark—such as Sante (the writer) and Vittorio, sons of Cesare. There was no semitic infiltration; the marriages were all with Catholic Umbrian-Sabine families . . . . the marriage with the B. . . family is perhaps an exception. The son of Amalia Sante, our father (the writer), considers from numerous and sufficiently concurring indications that the B. . . family, having settled together with the M. . . family, their kinsmen, on the border between the Papal State and Tuscany, were of Jewish origin and had immigrated into our section for the purpose of establishing a small business. This is an hypothesis which Sante drew from a study of the anthropological and psychological type of the B. . . family, of its members' aptitude for business, and of their surname (elsewhere the B. . . and M. . . families are Jewish). It should be added, however, that the ancestral family of Amalia B. . . has been Catholic for at least four generations.

All the De Sanctis' were of healthy constitution; longevity was common among them. None was tubercular, none addicted to the use of alcoholic liquors. But there were occasional unexpected deaths among them (a feudal inheritance?). Their ordinary illnesses were gout, arteriosclerosis, chronic nephritis. Only with the addition of Amalia B. . . to our branch did hereditary cancer show itself in our family . . . . All the De Sanctis' were prolific, and in their offspring females predominate. It is curious that no De Sanctis—except those who entered holy orders—ever remained a bachelor or unmarried lady. Data are lacking to judge the character of those who lived in very remote times. Of a certain Valerio we know that he was "an upright man of excellent habits." Another equally "good man" was his son, Guiseppe, although in deed he appears to have been somewhat ambitious and perhaps rather inept in business dealings. It should be said that from the G. . . family there have come to us some psychological remarks of less sympathetic character . . . . As has been remarked, the De Sanctis' as a matter of principle were always indifferent to political contests. It should be remembered, however, that they remained isolated in their little corner of the world, reached only by very subdued political rumors.

Wishing now to recapitulate in a few words my origins, it is probable that no too serious error would be made if I were to say that there was no semitic racial admixture from 1567 to 1857; at this time it is rather probable that there was Jewish infiltration on my mother's side. No change of social class occurred in 360 years: we were of the land-owning and professional middle class, with few changes in the tenor of life of modest country folk. Professions were the favorite vocations, also those of land-owning farmers, priests, and notaries. People of my region comprise the frontier population between the old Papal State and the ancient Grand Duchy of Tuscany; the heterogeneous character of their customs and commercial relations still exists. A people not heroic, individualistic, superstitious, not mystical, although they are but sixty kilometers from Assisi, the cradle of the cult of St. Francis, with little patriotic feeling and much local loyalty, without aims in life, the work for which is a penalty more than a duty or pleasure. From the point of view of health, hereditary arthritis is common, tuberculosis, uncommon with a tendency toward longevity. More in detail, my father was of medium height, blond, a traditionalist, of mild disposition, and of proverbial uprightness. My mother was tall, dark, intelligent, sentimental, and romantic, possessing marked initiative and a progressive mind.

SPONTANEOUS DEVELOPMENT

By spontaneous development is meant that which is acquired and built up within us, not as a result of a program elaborated at great length but because of temperament, of sudden external tendencies and circumstances, of little validity as far as their future influence is concerned.

When I was born, in 1862, the last echoes of the Roman Republic, and even those of Napoleon, had not died out. I knew two old peasants who had served in the Russian campaign. Then, the memories of the Italy of 1860 and of Garibaldi were very much alive. In fact I was given Camillo (Cavour) as a second name, my brother had Victor Emanuel for a first name, and my sister's second name was Venezia.

My remembrances of childhood extend back until about my fourth or fifth year—not beyond that. I do not remember the care taken of me in infancy. No mishap of sexual nature during my childhood comes to my mind now. I was a boy like all the others of my day. I remember some whippings which I sustained with a feeling of rebellion. Two childhood recollections in particular remain; both are very sad. The horizon of Parrano is limited as that of a cradle; the little town is surrounded on all sides by wooded hills with a few low and dark little tenant houses, scattered here and there with scarcely an opening in the direction of Mt. Cetona. This picture is still as fresh as in my childhood. The second recollection is threefold; the wind whistling and rushing through the fragile shutters of the old house, the flooding torrents which are impossible to cross, and the fear of cold and stormy nights. I read once that Mussolini had expressed, I don't remember when, this thought: "Things, seasons, the country-side have influenced me more than men." Mostly paraphrasing this, I shall say that, as far as I am concerned, the inhabitants of my native village and my familiar surroundings influenced me quite as much as the narrowly limited and cold country-side of my native province.

I should say that, despite my reactions and assertions of independence, I, as a child, accepted everything as a tree accepts wind, rain, or sun, rejoicing or enduring in a state of rebellion but without ever imagining a different kind of season. I possessed a sensitive and reactive temperament, therefore, but imagination of little creative power.

Following ancient traditions and customs, I was sent (as all members of my family) to study the classics in the dioccsan seminary. I have no unhappy memories of that period of my life, but in thinking it over again now, as at other times, I feel myself surrounded by an atmosphere of sadness. I remember with pleasure my success as a student. I do not remember that I suffered from envy, that passion which makes boys and youths suffer so much and which spoils their disposition at the very time it is developing. Thinking the matter over later, I concluded that, if I were not envious as so many others were, it was perhaps due to the conviction that my "sense of inferiority" in one field of endeavor was compensated by the assurance of superiority in other fields. But I am not sure about this. Many years ago I began just such a psychological study of envy, a study which will never be finished. I find the following among the notes (on the subject) collected in my portfolio: "I always recognized readily who was stronger, wiser, better educated, more profound than I." I remember that this particular trait occasioned me later a bit of praise from Antonio Labriola. One day when I told him that I felt the great inferiority of my intelligence in comparison with his and that of Benedetto Croce, whom I met from time to time at the Caffè Aragno (those were the days of the *Lettere a Sorel*, 1896-1898), A. Labriola replied to me: "You are indeed a forthright and courageous man; the only way to win the affection of others is to recognize the superiority of others."

It is remembered that the family, the school, and the community mould the mind in silence as the artist moulds his own clay. There is nothing more academic than that. Even when the educating influence has succeeded in moulding the student according to the established model—a rare occurrence—the daily torment of both is tragic, even if the student has a mental picture of a model which he may substitute for the one imposed upon him. They are open-field skirmishes or masqueraded trench conflicts, never pitched battles. Their result is always a ceaseless struggle between teacher and student, sterile in any case. Rarely is there full awareness of this daily tragedy, a tragedy, furthermore, which is not without its truces and its compensations.

I can admit that, during this "spontaneous" period, my conscience was unawakened, or, better, I had the horizon of my rather limited and brief past and future; nearly like that of a proletarian before the influence of Marxist propaganda, or indeed I was somewhat like the chimpanzees studied by the psychologist, Köhler, at Teneriffa. Those agreeably disposed were intelligent, but mentally their lives revolved within a rather limited segment of time. I lived intensely in the present; I might have been able to see afar, but I did not take the trouble to look. Furthermore, if everything depended upon strength, it would not be possible to endure in the fight. Fortunately, men who conquer adopt instruments of resistance and defense offered by nature and not those made by their own hands. He who is able to know his own remote and recent origins, together with their vicissitudes, and who at the same time knows the psychical condition and the constitution of a goodly share of the members of his own family and the true story of the course of his own "age of evolution," told by an expert and conscientious chronicler and biographer, up to the period of maturity, would be in a position not necessarily of foreseeing his own future behavior but certainly of fairly appraising past conduct in relation to the hereditary family destiny and to the education received. In such a manner he would be able to protect himself against the failures and losses which, without such a conscious appraisal, are certainly inevitable.

There prevails among specialists in biological and natural sciences the conviction that we are nothing more than the victims (portatori) of an inevitable biological destiny. Developing this theory, one would easily succeed in convincing himself that we were nothing more or less than a product (children of our own era) and that, therefore, our behavior within our circle of existence would be only that which would adapt itself more or less plastically to external and social exigencies, strengthened by the immediate satisfaction of biological and personal interests. According to the psychological theory of the "personality," it (i.e., our behavior) would be only the result of component factors which could be treated in mathematical fashion. Indeed, in whatever direction the truth of the aforesaid opinion may lie, nobody can deny it; I have already admitted it, but it is a question of degree. It happens indeed that the more passive and uninformed youth, as early as adolescence, awakens and fights for his "autonomous development," expressed in an ideal. To tell the truth, I was considerably retarded. I could not even specify, really, at what age I became more informed about my past and my future—perhaps at twenty! The struggle and suffering existed, but they impressed themselves upon my consciousness in separate phases, not as a whole. To be more explicit, I did not see the end to which the struggle led. I never tested my will power to attain at any cost a fixed goal. I remember now that, beginning with my student days, I was insensitive and imaginative, but I did not know how to depend upon my own resources and I did not know myself.

My emotional temperament was a propelling force towards individualism. University education and the passive absorption of the predominating political ideas of all countries (I used to read a great deal of Victor Hugo at that time) had "rationalized" my sensibility or, better, had lent my sensibility itself (unsuppressible and inalienable individual patrimony) to a broad political and social justification. But it was only after many years that I became aware of the profound reasons for this. In the matter of politics, for example, I truly *had lived*. I was like my companions, I conformed to the wish expressed in the newspapers and by the authors that I happened to read during the formative period between my twentieth and twenty-fifth years. On the other hand, I have always been an indifferent and ignorant talker about politics: one year as a member of an innocuous republican circle at the age of nineteen and one more year as a member of an equally innocuous liberal party at the age of fifty-three; if I am not mistaken, this is the glorious total of my service. I could not have a deep feeling for politics, however much I felt its formal discipline. As far as I was concerned, acts always appeared to me to be responsibilities of intrinsic value; I could never consider them to be good because they were useful or necessary to a party at one moment of its existence. I was only too much of a historical contradiction. Communal life designed on the Christian model seems to me preferable to that designed on the pagan model, although I recognize that the latter possesses a most particular historical and aesthetic value. Nevertheless, the old spontaneous training explains and vindicates, at least up to a certain point, certain retarded psychical developments or at least the efforts sustained to overcome them.

The War came, despite my neutrality. War is one of those things which are justified by intelligence and history, but denied by the individual temperament and the humanitarian spirit. What is neither wished nor desired little by little becomes absurd, exactly the contrary of other phenomena. When a thing is desired and wished, its coming to pass is almost anticipated; it comes to pass because it has been foretold. It is clear that impressive, strong, and established situations favor the illusions and that the latter act upon logic, substituting for rational logic that of the feelings.

The revolutions came. The Russian Revolution—horrible! If humanity has derived or will derive any profit from it, it is through the ideal and long-planned preparation of the anti-czarist revolution. Nothing good comes from Communism. However that may be, a somewhat romantic individualist could certainly understand or justify Lenin.

The Fascist Revolution—not understood, that is, not sensed as a whole, but only in some of its phases. Especially is its idealistic and stoical significance not understood. After a time the extraordinary man who conceived and led it imposed himself on me as upon everyone. After further reflection, I am convinced that to be attuned to the great innovations (*novatores*) one must be an "extravert" (Jung), as all the great lovers of politics have been. The "introverts" remain more or less at their window, observing, criticizing, admiring, as E. Kant (who was considered to be an "introvert") did from a distance, while the great revolution was pursuing its course in France.

And thus, confronted by a great political event, the psychologist saw only the *personality* of the leader. Professional degeneration? A foreign colleague suggested that I study Mussolini's personality according to our scientific methods. I approved in principle, but I reserved the privilege of working out a program, according to which the project would be carried out by an international committee of five psychologists. I made this proposal but it fell only too well on unsuitable soil and was not followed. Later, Ludwig was more fortunate, but it was then a question of literature, not of psychology in the technical sense. Here I transcribe—*ad memoriam*—a few words that I should have put in the introduction of the proposed psychobiographical study: "The qualities demanded of the head of a small group, such as the family or an institution, are entirely different—I should almost say the very opposite—of those qualities which are indispensable for the heads of a large group, such as a party or a nation. What we men of science consider to be a virtue is weakness in great personalities; therefore, the faith in the superman and the heroic language which our insignificant (*piccola*) psychology and our poor logic do not understand are understood by the imaginative and by the mystics."

But, while I amuse myself with trifling ideas of a purely psychological-differential type, Italy is becoming great and the world is going along the track of new ideas, which we understand but which we do not feel operating within us.

Let us go on to other matters, that is, let us return to the chronicle.

I received the doctorate in medicine by unanimous vote at Rome in 1886, with a thesis on *aphasia*. In 1887 I married an intelligent lady of spasmodic sensibility, very devoutly religious. I had three children—all living and in good health today—three different types of mind, but all superior to the average. The oldest, a doctor (the family historian), has an artistic type of mind; the second, a lawyer, possesses a rational type of intelligence; the third, a girl, has a technical type of mind. In addition, the last-named is gifted with an exquisite sentimentality. First among my friends has been and is my brother, Vittorio Emanuele, a man of superior intelligence, who resembles me in so many ways. I have been living with him for forty years.

I lived in the provinces practicing medicine. In 1891 I was already at Rome, and in 1892 I was assistant at the Psychiatric Clinic of the University of Rome.

My remembrance of my liking for literature, which is clearly outlined in my mind, is worthy of being noted, linked as it was with my liking for medicine and for natural sciences. This trashy mixture lasted (I have a record of date on this matter) from my twenty-eighth to my thirty-fourth year.

At the age of sixteen I had read the plays of Shakespeare, the works of Byron, the voluminous works of Michelet; at twenty-four, Goethe and Leopardi; at twenty-eight, the poems of Heine; at thirty-two, the works of Darwin and of Spencer. I read almost all of these without having chosen them deliberately. I read what circumstances, even the most trivial, offered me. And meanwhile my passion for natural sciences and for medicine was maturing. Many clinical and anthropological-criminal studies, which Cesare Lombroso advised me to undertake, are of this period. At the age of thirty-one I devoted myself to studies of anatomy and psychiatry; with great satisfaction I attended the school of anthropology at Rome, where I became well acquainted with Guiseppe Sergi, a great enthusiast about science, who had considerable influence upon my training. From Guiseppe Sergi I had my first introduction to physiological psychology, just as he instilled into me a love for morphology and ethnography. At about the age of thirty I had enlarged the pattern of my reading, and I remember that then I used to choose the books which most excited my scholar's curiosity.

In 1893 I took my first trip abroad: to Zurich to study hypnotism with Forel; to Paris to carry on advanced studies in psychiatry. In Paris I made the acquaintance of the elderly Falret, Chaslin, Seglas, Arnaud, Christian, and P. Marie. I attended the ceremony commemorating the thirtieth anniversary of the death of Charcot in the church of the Salpétrière (September, 1893).

At that time (as the reading of parts of my literary diary, especially those parts devoted to criticism, has revealed) my convictions were unceasingly occupied with the following ideas. The world, together with life and a certain intermittent pleasure of living, offers stress and sorrow, in their various forms, as a daily food to all men (echoes of *Weltschmerz* and of the reading of *Wurther*). It was, therefore, necessary to combat sorrow. I copy these lines from a page written when I was twenty-five years old: "Eliminate sorrow from the world and you will have solved every religious and economic question." What an illogical program! The following alternative would have been more rational: harden your heart. However, not even in part did this idea present itself during my entire youth. The idea arose in my mind in what I shall call a "philosophical" period of life; but then it was too late either to follow such a program personally or even to preach it to others. It is odd that from none of my teachers or friends did I ever hear words favorable to or, at least, critical of my way of looking at things, or, at the very least, doubts concerning the judiciousness of my thoughts. A sign of the times! Is it not essential to teach youth the optimism of life in any way which would not involve the presenting of more or less pagan precepts? Thus it is that I always remained sensitive, romantic, and individualistic, my attention directed toward the humble and the suffering, and as a logical consequence, on one hand, disposed to relieve myself from spiritual depression by turning my attention to work, while, on the other hand, inclined toward a certain sublimation of exuberant, vital, and psychical energies (Moll and Freud would say *libido*) in favor of an idealistic conception of life.

At this point comment might be necessary to explain how this *libido*, in my case, underwent not only dismissals (*verdrängungen*) but also conscious repressions. But the following word of warning will suffice. I was a youth like many others, but the circumstances of life impelled me more toward romantic love than toward indulgence in unbridled pleasure.

Fortunately this did not produce in me the result of acknowledging myself to be a model of virtue ("professor of virtue," as the followers of Socrates used to say as a jibe at the Sophists). Certainly I was not aware of the ethical nature of certain sentiments! That is why I was able to say later that I had "worked for work's sake" and that I had been directed toward work by motives which I will not call unconscious, but which certainly were not farsighted. I understood later all the difficulty of *nosce te ipsum*.

If being without awareness of one's situation can be humiliating, it can also be very useful. If I was not conscious of struggles, of envy, and of hatred, that very fact fortified me against tragic discouragement which I have never had to endure. This is the customary law of compensation of psychological phenomena.

Self-Knowledge and Self-Criticism

The section which I now begin to develop may be summed up as follows. With the passing of the years, every now and then I directed my thoughts inwardly and asked myself the explanation of the many feelings and ideas which were hammering at my heart and mind. I believe that the miraculous development in me of so pitiless a self-criticism (always incidental, fortunately not continuous) was due to the new orientation of my studies toward experimental psychology and particularly in the direction of individual or differential psychology. There is a beautiful saying that modern psychology is biological, a thing which I again confirm without hesitating. But, in saying *biological psychology,* one gives life to the substantive *psychology*, that is, to a science which treats of extremely complex phenomena, although objectively subjective, for which equivalence and reversibility have not been successfully established with physico-chemical phenomena.

My words tend to show that when one is a psychologist one is more easily inclined to a self-analysis, which is a potent factor in the development of the knowledge of one's self and of the conscious direction of one's own actions, if not of one's own impressionability, the part of us least amenable to discipline.

My knowledge did not go beyond certain limits. I often had to state that I remained an agent—on behalf of third parties. I might relate many anecdotes, for example, that of the great surprise that I experienced in 1920 in going over my bibliography, and then again in 1930, and still again in the last few days while putting in order my publications of the last two years—and so my activity had surpassed any program. But there is something more; that is the gratitude on my part for the aid rendered me by G. C. Ferrari in regard to my "ingenuity" in the *Presentazione* that he composed about me in the October-December, 1930, issue of the *Rivista di psicologia,* which was dedicated to me. The simple problem of the *why* and the *how* I have often encountered and continue to encounter. Why did I work so hard and so rapidly? How did I manage to read and write so much, yet at the same time leading an ordinary human existence, and even with much inner suffering? How was it that I did not realize there was so much opposition and that I believed that life for me would be easy and full of acquiescence? It is hard indeed for me to find justifications. I have not found any which are adequate. Even now I cannot justify my reason for giving up so many things which would have made my life more joyous. Why strive during brief periods of leisure to analyze tortured minds, or to resume my ideas on a question of psychology or of mental pathology, instead of taking that little bit of rest which duty consents that everyone may have, or to yield to the fascination of art? I must always conclude that work for the sake of work has been my demon, as though action were the only thing of importance and were of avail in calming my effort to live, which, however, was not painful.

Notwithstanding this fact, for the last fifty years more light has gradually been shed upon the antecedents of my actions, the individualities of my temperament, the motives of my decisions. With the passing of the years this light has increased, and yet I recognize that I am still in possession of obscure powers which I succeed in dominating only if I reflect at length on my purposes and my decisions.

I believe that I derived a great deal of help in the developing of my knowledge not only from psychological studies but also from my knowledge of psychoanalysis, from reading the works of S. Freud, and from personal acquaintance with Freud himself (which occurred *de visu* only in 1926, but which through correspondence went back to 1900, that is, to the time of the appearance of his work, *Die Traumdeutung*).

Yet it is certain that in recent years I have had awakenings, I have examined myself with my own eyes, I have understood and criticized myself. Such examinings, let me say at once, have made my disposition worse, while they have not cured me from overwork. At any rate, such forthright acknowledgment of one's condition has the advantage of being decisive. At times we feel that we are directing our course where we will. We suffer, we rebel, but the reins remain taut in our hands. And this is liberty. I admitted the objection that liberty was an illusion which belonged to philosophy. But I added to myself: If an illusion belongs to all humanity, it is on this account equivalent to reality. Nor could I think otherwise today. That is why I believed that I was distinguishing clearly in my life the period of spontaneous formation from the next period of conscious and voluntary formation, and therefore either opposed or approved. For determinists such a distinction would be an error, but for us empiricists, no, since there is a great difference between the subconscious, the partly seen, and what is known by intuition, on one hand, and the clearly reflected conscious, on the other. In action it is one thing to follow and quite another to have one's self followed.

The most important characteristic of my knowledge is having understood that one feature of my past life was the *need of certainties,* supported by empirical elements. I was never capable of being absolutely and permanently convinced by a dialectical or metaphysical approach, and rarely by suggestion. For this reason I have always remained a doubting critic, yet never have I known the anxiety of doubt. For fifteen or twenty years of cultural conquests I had dealings with materialists, positivists, rationalists, but they all failed to inculcate into me their philosophical convictions. Those who deny all finality in nature and the universe did not succeed in shaking my belief either at that time or later. I have experienced neither conversion nor repentance. The cultural surroundings made me then what I was to be; nor has anything subsequently taken away or added to what I was. Perhaps I have strong powers of resistance. Later I meditated on these things and in these last twenty years I have consciously determined what I had already spontaneously determined in the first period of my formation. I have always admired those who are convinced. When I saw superior people trifle with atheistic theory and consider men as a better-trained flock of untamed animals, but, indeed, always harassed by trouble, pain, and damnation, without any hope of redemption or of reasonable comfort, I felt a revolt within me, as I do now. Unconscious resistance, without doubt. But are not illusions or dreams preferable to such statements of fact? Is not childhood to be preferred to such maturity of mind? The truth is yes, but *quid est veritas?* Is truth preexistent, or does it come into being? If it comes into being and there is no absolute outside of ourselves, since man creates for himself the Absolute and God, could we not create for ourselves a less discouraging truth? Why wrack poor humanity with such sadistic ardor? Why despoil it of every vestige of hope? They say it is your personal psychology which suggests certain questions to you, but truth is truth. But who, in the name of determinism, could ever free himself from his own psychology? And, if that is so, it is not a question of logic, nor of experience, but rather of statistics. It would be necessary to count the number of men—let us take cultured men, of course—who favor this psychology and the number of those who favor a different one.

I am not willing to deny that the need of certainties was constitutional. The temperament is master of treachery. In mental medicine we say that the psychoasthenic who always bears in mind his personal "responsibility" is a slave of "Duty." But the psychoasthenic is a caricature of the precise individual, and his doubts are painful. I have never had any painful doubts, nor any fear of responsibility, but rather have I been eager to experience these feelings. Yet I always sought certainty in science, for certainty seemed to me to be the ideal of the mathematical type of knowledge. It is not improbable that my enthusiasm for scientific psychology considered empirically, besides other factors, possessed that of conquering certainty in a field in which philosophers were masters with their "pure philosophy."

Certainty for the beginner and for realistic knowledge which is called "ingenuous" is *fact*. "Fact is divine," some positivistic philosopher has said. The cult of fact was strongly felt by me even when the idealists (I read Benedetto Croce very much) evaluated its objectivity.

I remember that Vittorio Benussi, in the presence of very conclusive experimental results, used to answer anyone who asked him for an explanation: "Theory does not matter; experimental demonstration has value in itself." It may be that he was ingenuous in such a belief, but, as a state of mind, it cannot be discounted. I confess that I felt opposed to B. Croce when he republished two articles, "The Sophism of Empirical Philosophy" and "The Empirical Philosophical Method" (1914). It is certain that mental habit could be constructed on the need of objective certainties, that is, of exterior realities, in spite of the awareness of illusions, of fantasies, of suggestions to which men of science, no less than philosophers and poets, are subject. Having admitted this, if speculative orientation in the psychological field were excluded, introspection and self-analysis would not only be admitted but practiced with true zeal; as if the need of objective certainty demanded that the subjective also, that is, the entire inner ferment, should be made objective in a concrete, lucid, expressible thought. I experienced, in fact, a marked inner exaltation, and I always felt the impulse of an urge which came from deep within me. The love of art (especially music), human passions, and less rational hopes could be associated without difficulty with enthusiasm for scientific research.

In recent years I have understood, or it seemed to me that I understood, other things also toward which I had never directed serious consideration. The first is the question of my fervor for work. Yes, it seemed to me that I was obeying an instinct or, better, a most ingenuous tendency. Today, because of the light which has come to me especially from Freudism, I may be precise; work for work's sake is similar to art for art's sake. Both situations, or at least my situation in regard to work for work's sake, were equivalent to a sublimation of *libido*. It might be said that I worked and continue to work with erotic passion. I heard the same sentence pronounced, independently of myself, also by Vittorio Benussi in 1924. It seems to me that the theory of the displacement of energy finds here a clear confirmation. The same inner phenomena occur in insignificant men as in great men; it is only a question of different dimensions and values. Inner resignation is expressed in *Helderleben* with the transformation of the same musical motif, which for Richard Strauss expressed the disdain of his hero. Therefore, one same phenomenon may have or, better, always has several meanings. In my case there are at least two others. Work has been and is the compensating reaction for the persistent occurrence of two ideas which give rise to all sadness, old age, and illness. Work always meant for me forgetfulness, calm, serenity. It bears, therefore, in itself the meaning of "will to live." But there is also a third meaning in it. Enthusiastic work corresponded to the need of possession, satisfaction, and conquest; these are discoveries, not mere academic analogies, because they are endorsed by my profound personal conviction. I later became acquainted with Faust's thought: Research is more valuable because of the result. Activity is a salvation in itself. This thought, very applicable to myself, merited the accurate explanation which I have now made of it.

I have understood my restlessness. I lacked real satisfaction in my work. I never knew the Freudian narcissism. To reread anything that I had written was always uncomfortable for me. I used to say that I had an autophobia. And automatic vengeance followed: other studies and other works.

Was I, then, a virtuoso? Certainly not. Pitiless psychological analysis dims all mirrors, strips all laurels of their leaves! There were always within me vigilant sentinels, a kind of biological "censor" for every attempt at retrogression towards the average and even the inferior type. These were the sentinels: the tyranny of duty, the severity of habit, inner conflicts, the fear of compromising my inner calm and peace of mind, which I always considered the most precious treasure of my existence. Faithful, sworn sentinels, but not virtuous; but rather obliged to fulfill a virtuous office by irresistible and overwhelming forces. If I add that I consider my apparent virtues as defects—and I deplore them—a shadow of doubt falls upon any subsequent merit of mine.

WRITINGS AND WORKS

I began my medical career in small communities, limiting myself to clinical cases which most aroused my curiosity. But very soon I entered the laboratories. Circumstances, not a program, first brought me to anatomical and anatomical-pathological studies in the laboratory of the Insane Hospital of Rome, at that time under the direction of G. Mingazzini. These studies kept me busy for four years. Shortly afterward, I turned my attention to the sick, to clinical observation. In this field my work was persistent. I was most enthusiastic about it. I have mentioned my anatomical works, however, in order to call attention to the fact that they were an indispensable supplement to clinical observation, and constituted the necessary preparation for the study of psychology, considered as a biological science.

Although my extensive work on psychoneurosis and psychopathology may be of little interest to my readers, I must call to mind some of my special works, for the purpose of demonstrating its connection with psychology. In my early years, I explained everything according to the associationist theory; my ideal master was T. Zicheri. Thus, the pathology of attention, the pathology of sleep and of dreams, the classification and pathogenesis of frenzies, tantrums, the psychopathology of negativism, *dementia praecox, mental symptomatology* (two volumes in 1909, of 520 pages, included in the *Trattato di Psicopatologia forense,* by S. De Sanctis and Ottolenghi), the pathology of lucid delirium, motor disturbances, and apathetic, feebleminded children. This study is proceeding at present with the aim of bringing to light the psychology and the type of insufficiency of children who have suffered some mishap (not directly on the cerebral cortex, psychical organ *par excellence*), on the basal ganglia and on some spot on the border region between midbrain and forebrain where the centers of the autonomic nervous system, the endocrine centers, and the centers of muscular tone come together.

The subject fascinates me because I intend to attempt to study the psychopathology of "voluntaryism," and thence the causal pathology of the feebleminded and especially of the "unstable." I consider of interest to psychologists the works on the relations between dreams and madness, on obsessions and musical impulses (first described by me), on the "spiral" type of the visual field (as a sign of exhaustion, described by me in 1894 before Reuss), on the experimental graduation of intellectual insufficiency, on the epileptoid disposition, on *extreme cases* of *dementia praecox* or simple dementia praecox in children (confirmed by Kraepelin and now recognized by all), and, finally, I consider my book, *Neuropsichiatria infantile* (of almost 1000 pages), a collection of thoughts and observations, just as useful to the study of the psychiatry of children as it is to the differential psychologist.

Although readers may prefer to know me as a psychologist, nevertheless they will not be able to ignore completely my work in the field of psychiatry. I shall limit myself, therefore, to a few rapid notes on my studies on *feeblemindedness* and *neuroses*.

The studies on feeblemindedness or phrenasthenia (idiocy, mental weakness) constitute a very considerable mass of work. The subject has been plumbed on every side: on the anatomical-pathological side (infantile cerebral sclerosis, hydrocephalus, progressive myopia with mental weakness), on the clinical side (chief among these are the studies on tantrums and mongolism), and on the psychological, pedagogical, and clinical assistance sides. The organization of a new type of clinical assistance open for children who are feebleminded and unstable in character (1899; school-asylums are still flourishing in 1932) has been the practical result of all these studies. Differential psychology of the feebleminded and "unstable" has been widely developed by me. I received the first impetus for this long series of observations and research from English, French, and Swiss authors; I made wide use of modern findings of American authors in matters of corrective pedagogy and of psychopathology, but the psychoneurotic and clinical assistance part I have constructed on the basis of long years of direct observation (from 1898 on).

Only later did I become familiar with the out-patient clinical institutions for psychical abnormals of Germany, Switzerland, and Austria (a trip to Cologne and Mannheim in 1908, two trips to Brussels in 1910 and 1911, repeated trips to Paris, Zurich, and Geneva).

The evaluation of intellectual deficiency in the feebleminded (and not only of the *mental age* according to the Binet-Simon and American scales) was made by me by means of *mental tests* in 1910; this method, devised and intended for clinical use for the gradation of mental insufficiency, has been for many years in current use everywhere, in Italy, as in Russia, and in North and South America. The little book of 1914-1915, *Educazione dei deficienti*, now out of print, is the only work which does not give me an uncomfortable feeling when I have to consult it at times for bibliographical purposes. Even now, after eighteen years, I find it valid either for what concerns the medical-pedagogical classification of idiotic children or for what concerns the psychology, pedagogy, and free clinical assistance of psychical abnormals.

After this book, various other studies and researches on child psychology and psychiatry appeared. Much of what I observed and experimented on in the ten-year period between 1915 and 1925 is found in the volume, *Neuropsichiatria infantile;* what I tried to build up after 1925 in regard to this subject is found under various words in the *Enciclopedia Italiana* (*Anormali, Scuole per deficienti, Infanzia,* etc.), and was expounded in my lecture at Milan on December 4, 1927 ("I fanciulli differenziati e la Neuropsichiatria infantile"), in *Contributi clinici alla diagnosi e alla prognosi,* etc. (cf. Comun. alla R. Accademia Lancisiana di Roma del 1929), in *Problemi della Educabilità,* 1929, in my report to the National Congress of Medical Pedagogy at Milan in 1930, and in *Alcune forme cliniche neuropsichiche di "deficit,"* 1932.

I have repeatedly discussed neurasthenia and hysteria, as well as genuine epilepsy. A recent systematization of my ideas on neuroses is found in the monograph entitled "Nevrosi," which forms a part of the *Trattato Italiano de Medicina interna* of the Biochemical Institute, Volume II, published in 1931. A point which may be of interest to psychologists is to be noted in the concepts that I defend of malfunctional psychogenesis and of the "psychopathogenesis of neuroses," because they are in harmony with my *proportionalism,* which I shall point out below. Moreover, it contains my theoretical and practical points of view regarding the psychoanalytical cure treatment. This point does not cut into the Freudian doctrine, but the practice of the cure is somewhat independent of it in maintaining that the *moral cure* (psychotherapy) must be complete. This moral cure I have divided into three periods, and my procedure has been sanctioned by success. This, however, in its turn, is conditional on an accurate diagnosis. Psychical cures have a solid, scientific (i.e., psychophysiological) foundation, which I expounded in a brief article in the magazine, *Athena,* in 1932.

Now for a few comments on my more narrowly psychological production. I shall begin with works on general psychology which comprise forty-five publications, including several monographs and six volumes. In this field are outstanding: (1) my concept of the object, aims, and methods of modern experimental psychology, (2) the subject of the dream, to which I devoted a rather numerous series of studies, (3) attention, (4) psychical phenomena in relation to the nervous system, and (5) the law of the cycle or "circular law."

I shall begin with attention. In times when analysis was triumphant, and everyone considered single psychical facts as autonomous in a certain way, I, wholly devoted to experimental methods, determined to consider attention. It is a series of publications in which the attentive phenomenon is studied on all sides and for the most part with experimental methods, for example, perioptometric method, and also from the pathological aspect, as I have stated above. Ebbinghaus introduced the methods and results of my studies on attention to German psychologists. The studies on attention brought to light a new psychopathic symptom, which I called *"paraprosessia,"* by which should be understood a disturbance essentially linked with the fact that, when too much attention is concentrated on an impulse, the impulse becomes inhibited. The phenomenon found widespread confirmation and was later described as a symptom of apraxia (Liepmann), or as *perseveration* (Pick and Liepmann, Kleist), or as *negativism* (Kraepelin).

Together with these studies on attention, another series of studies on the expression of thought was completed about twenty-five years ago. The little book, *La Mimica del Pensiero,* had the honor of a German translation in 1906 *(Die Mimik des Denkens),* because the subject was fairly new and was also interesting to artists. In that little book, I maintain that thought has, in the adult, a specific expression different from that of emotion and that this expression was concentrated in the zone of ocular mimicry, and especially on the action of the thin muscle *corrugator supercilii,* as Charles Bell and Duchenne had pointed out. This muscle, having discharged the philo- and ontogenetic development, its most humble duty as protector of the visual organ and its emotional duty (weeping and wrath), came to assume the most noble office of revealer of the thought (inner attention and prolonged reflection) in the adult man. I made a study of philogenesis and ontogenesis of the mimicry of thought, bringing out the fact that genetically *to pay attention* is to see, and to reflect is to see, i.e., that the mimicry of sensory attention and thought was essentially the mimicry of *visual type*. The interest of such an observation was in the deduction that the development of the senses and especially of the sight has a decisive importance for the development of knowledge.   I concluded that intellectual mimicry was an individual acquisition, as my research on the congenitally blind demonstrated.   In this way, I adhered to Piderit's opinion rather than Darwin's.

Regarding sleep and dreams, I have little more to add, considering the fact that my numerous publications in books, monographs, and memoirs are rather well known.   The first work bears the date of 1896.   This was my thesis for graduate teaching in psychiatry. An experimental work on the curve of the dream was published in the *Psychological Review* in 1902.   For the inquiry into the dream I drew my inspiration from French psychiatric literature and particularly from the *Leçons du Mardi* by Charcot.   I abandoned the subject several times, because the differential psychology of the dream finally seemed to me arid.   But, after the *Traumdeutung* (1900) by Freud, a new horizon was opened before me.

My book on *The Dream* in 1899 was translated into German (*Die Träume*) in 1901.   It precedes the *Traumdeutung*.   Another monograph in German, in 1922, *Psychologie des Traumes,* is a work entirely independent of that of 1901.   In the monograph of 1922, as also in that of 1915, I kept very close to Freud, yet maintained a critical attitude regarding the various points of view of the psychologist.   The last contribution to the psychophysiology of the dream was in 1932 (communication to the International Congress of Psychologists in Copenhagen, August, 1932).   In this recent contribution, I have studied the dream in relation to the *individual cycle of sleep* and to recent views concerning the physiology of the sleep function.   I made a distinction between dreams of *light* sleep and those of *deep* sleep.   The attempt of "experimental dreams" was confirmed.   But I considered the experiment truly important for the study of dream phenomenology after the experimental awakening from the deep-sleep phase; it was this study which led me to the conclusion of the existence of an "undifferentiated psychical energy."   On this occasion I brought out the importance of the *apparent* content (Freud) of the dream for differential psychology and mental pathology.

If opinions in themselves have any importance, I should be inclined to give one on my little publication entitled *La legge del ciclo* (communication to the Philosophy Congress at Turin in 1926). With my report to the Psychology Congress at Rome in 1912, entitled "Psychical Phenomena and the Nervous System," I had solved to my own satisfaction the grave and eternal problem which was concentrated in these four leading directions among psychologists: parallelism (German psychologists and philosophers), interactionism, (Ziehen), monism (Warren), behaviorism (Watson).

The "law of the cycle" composed the dissent of those who did not wish to give importance to subjective fact in applied psychology, and who maintain, for example, that the melancholia victim suffers from a respiratory disturbance or arterial pressure not because of the pain he suffers, nor because of the artificial emotion to which he is occasionally subjected for experiment, but due to the cause which brought about the melancholia in him (for example, because of his constitution or because of some bodily illness: angina pectoris, visceral illness, etc.). Now this evaluation of the psychical subjective fact in favor of bodily cause is untenable and is but the aggressive return of bodily determinism and an epiphenomenon of consciousness.

And all this in order to deny psychical causation, even in a field—the pathological—where no one meant to accept it in the philosophical sense!

Admitting a "proportionalism" between bodily and psychical phenomena, the "reciprocal relationship" (*"circolarità"*—I quote B. Croce), in the opinion of idealists, and the "nervous circle" (Charles Bell)—two very different concepts—seem to me related or at least "relatable." The law of the cycle or of the "circle" I found in ourselves and outside of ourselves, that is to say, in morphology, in physiology, in psychology, in interpsychology, in historiography, and in mental pathology. The universal scheme thus came to be modified—no longer an arc, but a circle. In this way parallelism was rejected and proportionalism was confirmed in all fields, for example, in the relations between thought and word, in the individual psychological problem of genius, in mysticism, and in art.

One of the applications which seems to me most important was that concerning emotion, reported in Volume I of my *Psicologia sperimentale*. The circularity of emotional phenomena coordinated the theory of W. James with that of the centralists and with that of the physiologists (Langley). Dupré had also spoken, in 1920, of circularity in pathology; I stressed this point and enlarged its field. In our organism, continuous spiral and whirling motion takes place, or rather anatomical-physiological and chemical cycles, both invisible and visible; we, ourselves, are included within a larger system of circulation which comprises the world and human society: ". . . the exchange of forces is incessant during the circulation and there is a mutual giving and receiving between the circulating elements" (thus I stated the matter, in 1926).

I have left to the last my contribution to the knowledge of the object, aims, and methods of modern experimental psychology. I have written a great deal, perhaps too much, on this subject. Of particular interest in my studies was the "experimental" determination of what I call "pure psychical energy" ("energy" on the analogy of cosmic energy). I declared my ignorance of the nature and origin of the force which we call "psychical"; I excluded the problem from the psychological domain; but the experiments brought me more than once into the presence of a "psychical experience without content." It was an audacious point compared with more profound explanations, but I was always aware of the fact that it was a question of a boundary-line explanation. Yet I clinched it again recently in my *Psicofisiologia del sogno* (Copenhagen, 1932), when I spoke of *undifferentiated subconsciousness* (we also say "preconsciousness") in regard to dream activity during deep sleep. My concept, several times expounded and defended, of undifferentiated psychical energy *(Psicologia sperimentale,* Volume I, pp. 75 ff.), or basic situation, happened to coincide with analogous concepts expounded by mystics and by various psychologists, and now proved experimentally. Thus, the *pure feeling* of English authors, the *Bewunstheit* of Marbe, Ach, etc., the "purely emotional state" of V. Benussi, found in me a supporter convinced by direct experience.

I come to the writings in the field of applied psychology. Of fifteen works on the applications of psychology to the *science of work* I consider those on the psychology of *vocation* (1919) and another on the application of the "reading method" to be of some importance. In 1926, I summarized my concepts in an article in *The Pedagogical Seminary and Journal of Genetic Psychology*. Several times I have dealt with the applications of the laws of work in the education of abnormals. But the conclusions regarding the technique for the study of mental work and regarding possible applications to daily practice were expounded by me in a documented report at the Congress of the Medicine of Work at Milan, in April 1932 (my report is published at length in the *Archivio di Psicologia,* last issue, 1932). This report gave rise to controversies; but I supported, as I do here support, my "reading" method and my "curve of mental work," purified by the curve of concomitant muscular work (by Donders' process of elimination). While recognizing all the uncertainties regarding the replacement of nervous tissue and regarding nervous and mental fatigue, with the elements of sensory and muscular fatigue removed, I maintained, in my report, that it was possible, however, to derive some directive practice from the "psychoergographic curve," stripped of non-essentials by my method.

I am certain that my method will yet find more or less benevolent commentators; but of one thing we may be sure: that the laws of mental work are not entirely identical with those of muscular work and of the work of single groups of motor nerve cells; and that the problem of pure mental fatigue is now the order of the day and cannot be solved by the methods, however excellent, of Kraepelin and of Patrizi.

My twenty works on psychology applied to *Criminology,* as also the chapter on judiciary and criminal psychology in *Psicologia sperimentale,* Volume II, have been the result and at the same time the cause of nearly twenty years' teaching of Judicial and Criminal Psychology at the School of Juridico-criminal Application, founded by E. Ferri, later replaced by the course on the Perfecting of Penal Law at the University of Rome. It treats principally of demonstrations in the presence of the biological and characterological component in delinquents. The contributions which I consider most important in this series of my works have to do with the relations between crime and mental weakness (a question treated at length by the Englishman, Goring, and by Americans) and between psychiatry and criminology. In recent years I have developed the concept of "latent criminality" and of criminal dreams (dream-crimes, conceived, initiated, completed, and evaluated during the dream).

I have come to the conclusion—and here I confirm the conclusion—that the "apparent" content of the dream is an excellent test of the latent criminality of the dreamer.

Far more numerous are my writings on psychology applied to the *science of education.* The subjects that I treated are expounded in *Psicologia sperimentale,* Volume II. These comprise forty-four publications in volumes and memoirs, among which many concern the practice of clinical assistance of "feebleminded" and "unstable" children. The entire value of this vast work lies in the actual practice, that is, in the organization of clinical assistance outside of the hospital of psychically abnormal minors, according to the dictates of differential psychology and mental hygiene.

Narrowly scientific publications on the subject of pedagogical psychology concern my tests for the measurement of mental insufficiency; my book, *Educazione dei deficienti,* summarized the results of many physiological, psychological, and pathological researches on abnormal minors, the feebleminded, and the delinquent. And, finally, in a little publication of 1929, entitled "Il problema della educabilità," and in another, in 1930 (published by the *League of Nations Bulletin,* No. 17), entitled "Il cinematografo e organizzazione scientifica del lavoro," I expounded the practical method for the evaluation of the educability and of the capacity for learning in abnormal minors. I consider these works useful for those concerned with pedagogical psychology.

It would not be surprising if, in my entire production of the last thirty years, on the subjects of child psychology, psychopathology, and mental pathology, the influence of S. Freud were apparent. I must call attention to the fact, however, that, in my works on psychoneurosis in children and in the technique of corrective pedagogy, German and American thought is dominant.

The Freudian influence is evident to me in everyday practice and in the study of criminal minors. I declare with pleasure that from S. Freud I learned to complete my knowledge of the child mind, of nervous individuals, and of intimate interpsychology. Freud had a great influence on me, not so much in the matter of psychoanalysis as regards the method of cure, and almost not at all as a bearer of enlightenment concerning the history of religion, language, or custom, but rather by his extraordinary contribution to the knowledge of the human mind, the principal object of my studies during the last decade. So I may say that I owe to Freud that small degree of penetration into mental illness, beyond that of ordinary mental symptomatology, which has since increased my enthusiasm for psychopathology.

In brief, outstanding in my production are the applications to the science of application, to the science of work, and to criminology.

The applications to religion concerned me especially for teaching reasons between 1921 and 1928. About 1920, however, I was in touch with Antonio Fogazzaro (who was sent to me by Her Majesty, Queen Marguerite, who knew of my studies in the field of religious psychology). I had a long, interesting conversation with Fogazzaro, but it is appropriate neither to summarize it nor to comment upon it here. The volume, *La conversione religiosa* (1923), which was translated into English, gave a summary of my studies. This work, however, represents an illustration and a conformation of some views of Freud, in a field up to that time unexplored. The book originated from a series of lessons on the subject, a subject I had learned to appreciate from reading Flournois, James, and other books by American authors. My book met with perhaps more criticism than endorsement. A rather curious thing: I received the harshest criticism from Anglo-Saxon Protestants and more kindly criticism from Hebrew writers. Catholic writers were almost all opposed to me; however, I had in my favor two profound critical studies, one by a Spanish medical psychologist, Barbado, and the other by the famous German writer, H. Ball, both of them Catholics.

My studies on supernormal psychology left no traces on my mind or on my writings. In an old study on a somnambulist I applied the pathological explanation.

On the whole, today there remain, as living witnesses of my enthusiasm for psychology, three portfolios: one on the psychology of the dream, a second on child psychology, and a third on work. "Work" was a subject very dear to me from 1911 to 1930. And that is easy to understand. Did I perhaps devote myself to that study in order better to know myself, an unceasing worker? The same hypothesis in another field: Is my enthusiasm for the psychology of the dream and for the psychology of adolescence perhaps due to the fact that I am a dreamer and still somewhat a child? The self-analyzing psychologist must use certain interrogatives.

A rapid note about my university teaching. I confess that I

was very enthusiastic about teaching. I began my classes in the University of Rome as a graduate teacher of Psychiatry in 1896; I continued them as a *chargé de cours* in Physiological Psychology in 1902-1905, and then as Associate Professor and Professor of Experimental Psychology from 1907 to 1930. In 1930 I became Director of the Neuropsychiatric Clinic, where I have been teaching since 1930. I put the same enthusiasm into each subject taught, as much in the official courses of Psychology and Clinical Psychoneurosis as in the supplementary courses, such as that in Pedagogical Psychology, which lasted about ten years, and that in Judiciary and Criminal Psychology, which is still going on after nineteen years.

For two years, however, all my best efforts have been concentrated on the organization of the Neuropsychiatric Clinic of Rome and on the new teaching program. I have been able to organize there a special Department for Neuropsychopathic Minors and Neurological Invalids, equipped with two specialized laboratories (morphological and psychophysiological), for the study of the constitution and for the determination of degrees of mental development and of psychical disabilities. Moreover, to the laboratories already existing in the clinic I have added two others, a biological and a psychopathological laboratory.

THE CONCLUSION OF A MEDICAL PSYCHOLOGIST'S LIFE

I have been above all and essentially a physician. I have not been nor am I now a philosopher. I deny myself any right to philosophize. The philosopher explains the basis of things, since he gives the general doctrine of knowledge, treats the fundamental norms of thought (as A. Labriola used to say), and has no doubt. On the other hand, the psychologist dwells upon phenomenology and on empirical genesis. From a certain point of view, I could say that I am a thinker, but certainly not a philosopher. I have been, above all, a pragmatist in my life—a pragmatist with moderate scientific preparation, but a unilateral pragmatist, for, because of concentration on some particular points, I have neglected great practical considerations, for example, business and politics. I have been particularly absorbed by action. I confess that I have accomplished a great deal. This is perhaps the only praise that I deserve. And it is not pride, I need hardly add, without hypocrisy, in having done a great deal, for fundamentally all my accomplishments have been small.

Certainty: Is it the crystallization of an illusion which, experienced by several individuals, becomes reality? Is it the halt of a fleeting moment or of a dream? Unamuno asks himself this question in *Nebbia,* as many philosophers have asked themselves. What does it matter to us? Certainty is an enlightened condition of our minds. This is an interesting point. But every certainty implies the coexistence of a measure of reality which can be known, but which is unknown, and therefore uncertain, even when one believes and hopes that what is uncertain today will become certain tomorrow. It was the need of certainty that made me more and more a psychologist. Even in my early years, I perceived that scientific psychology could give me certainties in a field invaded by suggestion, imitation, philosophy, and religion. The certainties of medicine always seemed to me insufficient. And so I cultivated my orientation towards science, but I gave up the greatest problems. Although I have always had the tendency to widen the boundaries of empirical psychology, as my ideas on the applications of psychology in the field of ethics and aesthetics prove, yet I have always recognized the existence of a "residue" beyond the thing demonstrated. To leave liberty confronted with the "residue" seems to me to be a wise policy on the part of a scientist and pragmatist, who, likewise, regarded himself as incapable of elaborating the "residues" left by empirical research by combining them into a rational system.

To be able to separate the scientific from the artistic and from the ethical is already a concession. After all, as there has been naturalism in art—and will be again—there could be, with equal right, art in naturalism. Freudism is perhaps the new attempt. Yet I have always claimed, and still do claim, for my part, the separation between science and art, even if it should cost painful renunciation. For the present, and perhaps for many long years, divorce is better than dissention within the union. But I consider the union inevitable. The unitary concept is making strides in all branches of learning and living.

I have always felt that I had no wings to fly, but I have always believed in and still believe in the possibility of flying—whether they were wings of fancy, of faith in logic, of faith in experience, or of faith in the invisible and unknowable. *Faith*: another enlightened condition of the mind! In 1918 and again in 1921, I gave lectures on the subject, "the believing state of the mind." In my book published in 1923, *La conversione religiosa,* I recapitulated my thought. After that, one can understand how I have always marvelled at all those who made philosophical or religious declarations with full conviction. With the same interest I read *El castillo interior,* of Saint Theresa, *The Religious Conscience,* of William James, and *La Philosophie biologique,* of Le Dantec. I detested only those who manufactured for themselves comfortable convictions. Nor have I ever changed my mind since. The Spanish proverb, *"De las cosas más seguras la más segura es dudar"* ("Of all sure things the surest is to doubt"), I learned as a student from Moleschott. I recall that the master did not hesitate to declare materialism to be a faith for him. Meanwhile, I perceived that science everywhere was descending from the Olympus of the greatest problems which men asked each other in every epoch, without being able to solve them through experience, and was hovering low, ready to come down to earth. I followed this movement and loved scientific psychology more than ever.

But there came Neo-Hegelism. In Italy, empiricism was in disrepute; it was loudly denied that psychology could be an "empirical science" (I was as convinced as Benedetto Croce that there was no "empirical philosophy"). He was called little less than a charlatan, certainly a deluded person, a person to whom was assigned in 1907 the first appointment in graduate teaching in experimental psychology (by ministerial decree, in spite of the opposing opinion of the Kantian Cantoni, a member of the teaching staff itself and its coordinating representative on the Higher Council of Public Instruction).

At the International Psychological Congress in 1905, an opposition was made (a posthumous opposition, for the Congress had adjourned) by a few philosophers who had taken part in it. These opponents did not win. The official university teaching of experimental psychology was decided upon by Minister L. Bianchi, and today there exist six chairs of experimental psychology, occupied by full or assistant professors. For this also I take credit. There followed, however, endless debates on the specific program of experimental psychology. I have been forced for a quarter of a century to delineate its aim and method. It is not important that my thought was not followed by everyone.

It may be well for me to be very explicit on this point. In psychology I *always* recognized one same end: the practical one. A medical psychologist could not escape such evidence. Except that in the first period of my studies it was an "implicit" end, which, by rereading old memoirs and old lessons, is easy to recognize. Later, and even now, the aim has become "explicit" and verified in all its various directions.

To work in psychology and in psychopathology on biological bases has always been my principle and ideal. But at the same time I have never feared extra- or ultra-biological premises or hypotheses. To arrive at "value," either by the biological method or by means of the analytical elaboration of one's own feelings and judgments, seemed to me the same thing. I maintained that the most fruitful hypotheses were those advanced by artists, by people with imagination, who so often become forerunners of knowledge. It was, therefore, not necessary to follow the biological path to the point where it is no longer discernible, because in the darkness one loses the evidence, the only characteristic for the sake of which so much labor is endured. At this point, intuition and the concept of value are better. I have always borne in mind a bit of advice of Professor Cuboni, illustrious naturalist of the University of Rome, who honored me with his friendship: "Hold fast in the scientific field, but seek liberty without it." This was the conclusion of a long conversation with him in Geneva in 1903, speaking of spiritualism (we really say *medianism*) to which, at that time, two masters of positivistic philosophy, Cesare Lombroso and Enrico Morselli, seemed to adhere, following the example of Charles Richet.

Just as I kept aloof from the enthusiasm for Eusapia Palladino, I could not subsequently follow Monakow, who had introduced a metaphysical notion, with his *hormé* and *valore,* into the neurobiological field. Monakow insisted upon being bigoted on biological thought to the degree of supposing even metaphysics to be good biology. I used to say the *objective* neurobiological method reaches this point; later, if ever, I shall avail myself of other instruments. I always thought that he who has formulated a naturalistic philosophy without "residues" and resisting every objection has solved a problem of will (*will to believe*), not one of knowledge. On the other hand, there is certainty of a naturalistic type in the sciences and, in my opinion, also in those inspired by biological psychology, even admitting in psychology the existence of a "residue," ultimately to be evaluated by intuition and not by figures. I used to say that a question of methodological limits is a question of the difference between theory and hypothesis. On the limit-line of its competence, psychology formulates hypotheses and not theories. At this point a line of Goethe comes to my mind: *"An der Beschränkung zeigt erst der Meister"* ("The master first reveals himself by restricting his endeavors"). I consider myself to be an inspiring master.

However, notwithstanding so many conflicting ideas, experimental psychology was alive in Italy, and applied experimental psychology found skilled cultivators. I did not aspire to anything more, I who was the first graduate teacher of that subject. I remained a psychologist and I resisted in the renunciation of treatment of problems properly called philosophical.

I come now to the explicit aim of modern psychology, which today, at the sunset of my life's journey, constitutes more than ever an ideal.

The aim, let us even say the mythical goal, of psychology is the *knowledge,* I should almost say the *technique of men,* obtained and obtainable by all the methods and procedures which science has at its disposal. Differentiable somato-psychical knowledge of the sexes? Knowledge of the newborn, of the child, of the adolescent, of the adult, of the aged? Yes, of course. But this is not enough. To know man, woman, child, the aged in the abstract? Very well. This is a separate "secondary" task, as they say in psychology, in the manner of Külpe. But new research must be at the same time in two directions: Know the individual, but know him also as one of the members of the family, of the group, put on a common basis by a need, an aspiration, a contract, or a social system. Interpsychology and social psychology are indispensable for the knowledge of men. The laws of ability and competition, of predominance, of responsibility, are makers of men, whereas the laws themselves were formulated and developed, thanks to the psychology of men (the law of the circle).

I wished especially to know the small human groups: the family, the community, the school. And it was there that I found the truths proclaimed by Freud. I found the proofs of conscious and subconscious progenital erotics, the Œdipus complex, the Cain complex (S. De Sanctis), and the inferiority complex (Adler). I wished to know healthy and sick babies, then those who are suffering, and finally myself—which was and is the most difficult task.

The American Committee, as Carl Murchison states in his invitation to write my autobiography, desires to know from psychologists who write their autobiographies what the most important problem in psychology is. Well, I do not hesitate to answer that the most important general problem is the perfecting of *the means for the knowledge of men and of human groups*. Coming down to details, I hold as problems, in the direction of which psychology is and must always be moving, the following: the study of verbal expression, of facial and gesticular mimicry, of automatic motions, of style of writing, the study of instinctive and temperamental activities, exploration of the subconcious, and intimate and group interpsychology as a foundation of custom and politics.

Moreover, knowledge is a step in the direction of foresight; it therefore opens the way for the correction of evil and of all that we call antisocial. Thus psychology comes to the very threshold of ethical aims. In fact, any foresight into an undesirable destiny implies the search for an instrument of struggle against the destiny itself. In this way the cycle of the aims of psychological investigation is completed, according to my concepts and practice. The last tie, therefore, is the ethical one: individual ethics and social ethics.

But the posing, and indeed the evaluation of the aforementioned problems and programs of study, does not at all imply contradiction regarding the "renunciation" of those major problems on which philosophy constantly labors during the development of the history of culture. The renunciation remains.

Meanwhile, in spite of the ethical aim of psychological investigation, there remains the individual psychology of the investigating psychologist. Does not the very psychologist who works to attain a moral goal work perhaps for an earned reward? This is not an idle question. We are here on the subject of autobiography. Why have I pursued those ends? Such lack of ethical sense in the renunciation would be incomprehensibly hypocritical. I realized this many years ago. Even the psychologist works for personal enjoyment. The psychologist dominates what he succeeds in knowing. In him the will to power operates, as in the artist, the politician, and the war-hero. The psychologist who knows always generalizes, foresees, also marks out and modifies, up to a certain point, the destiny of an individual or of a group; in this way he makes himself victorious and predominant. Antiquity would have called him a "magician."

And yet I felt a perpetual dissatisfaction within myself! Of one thing I have been and am now more and more convinced. Whatever stable and consoling factor remains in us is only the good we scattered along the road of others, even of those who scorned us, or who invented harmful stories about us, formulating bitter criticism and placing obstacles in our path. For this reason I considered it an *opus divinum* to mitigate the pain of the flesh or spirit in others. Meditating upon this subject, I spoke of "active goodness" in at least three lectures (the last in Milan, in 1932, on "Educative Torture"; cf. *Rivista di Pedagogia Credaro,* Rome, 1932), and I wrote about it in an article on clinical assistance ("The Psychology of Clinical Assistance," in the *Giornale della Lega d'Igiene e Profilassi Mentale,* 1931). Why did I do so? Was it for rhetoric? I do not believe so. It was an ingenuous feeling, which however does not satisfy, despite its appearance of virtue, as I have already stated. Is it not always a question of egotism? I am convinced that it is. For that small amount of good that I scattered about me, I confess I never asked gratitude. But not on this account was my work less egotistical.

This is very curious; I had, and still have today more than ever, a thought which often comes to my mind: What will they say of me after I am gone? There is no denying the fact that this idea, which is almost an obsession, is not the result of egotism. It is a kind of sense of immortality which pales with the cold contact of reason, but which, however, persists unchanged; it is the displacement of values toward the shadow of the unknown, but it is still a value which may be contemplated. Is it a hereditary sense of immortality, or is it childish, or is it involuntary defense against personal evaluation and in favor of pride? Reflecting upon it, one understands that this tormenting question becomes legitimate because of an antecedent for the most part subconscious; and that is because of the hope that all that one does may constitute a bill of credit with an unknown creditor. This result of my personal investigation must not surprise my readers. I recall that one of my colleagues at the University of Rome, Federico Garlanda, Professor of English Literature, used to say to me: "You have two faces; in one I see Mephistopheles, in the other, Saint Francis."

My condition is easily justified by the little provincial world in which my youth developed—spontaneous development! At that time we all lived in harmony with the ethical and intellectual atmosphere of pure Hebraic-Christian stamp, which for centuries formed the background of the historiography of large and small nations.

And so I am justified. But there is something more: There are within me mystical "resistances" which I never tried to overcome during the period of my "voluntary development." These were favorable to me. Moreover, modern critics certainly do not misrepresent the restless soul of Faust in attributing to it mystical experiences, nor do they misrepresent the soul of Goethe when they disclose the clear lines of the Christian model amid the meanderings of his paganism.

One cannot escape certain psychological requirements. "Voluntaryism" may direct the behavior but it cannot inhibit the inner tumult with its consequences. Reason and sentiment form in the personality two worlds, distinct, although related in many ways. The encounter and interpenetration of these two worlds occur within the individual, who for this reason *becomes unified,* but this fusion is not always permanent. The general rule is the continual wavering, even in the most firmly balanced minds, of the relations between reason and feeling. And this is well. The rupture between these, that is, the permanent dissociation between idea and affection (as we call it in psychology), becoming specific, gives us in fact two antithetical characterological types: the cynic type and the cenesthopatho-emotional type, both undesirable. Harmony between the two worlds would seem ideal, but in reality it is almost never a question of harmony; it is, rather, a question of compromise.

At the end of my work I reread the introduction and wonder whether, beyond the personal satisfaction or dissatisfaction, any generic importance can be attributed to such autobiographies. I believe that sincere autobiographies, even if anonymous, would constitute excellent material for bringing to light the biological and psychological sources of the historiography of human thought. If the study of the evolvent and regressive variations of human thought, through time and schools, is a great thing, then it would not be too small a thing if autobiographical psychology should reveal to us a part of that biopsychological determinism which certainly influences the thought and social behavior of men.

JOSEPH FRÖBES*

The story of my intellectual life, which has been requested of me, falls naturally into three groups: my life experiences as preparation for scientific psychological work, my achievements in experimental psychology, and my work in philosophical psychology.

I

My home is in the Rhineland. I was born in 1866 in Betzdorf on the Sieg. My parents, however, came from the neighborhood of Bonn; my father, Anton Fröbes, of peasant stock from Godesberg on the Rhine, near the Siebengebirge; my mother, Josepha Westphal, from Eitorf on the Seig. My maternal grandfather was an emigrant Protestant from Saxony, who in his new home had come to know the Catholic Church more intimately, and, finally, in the twilight of his earthly sojourn, had returned to it for refuge. My mother had been informed that members of his family had made their mark in the world of science, although no more precise knowledge of their activities has come to my notice. Through the exigencies of his vocation as engineer on the Cologne-Giessen Railroad, my father was forced to move to my birthplace, Betzdorf, later to Siegen, and shortly thereupon to Giessen on the Lahn. My earliest memories take me back to that town—to the narrow strip of ground between the lofty railroad embankment and the Lahn, the marvels of the neighboring mill, the distant but oft-visited garden, and, beyond that, the church. Somewhat more definitely I remember the public school, which I entered at the age of five, and where I received a world of new impressions.

Despite their very modest circumstances, my parents decided to educate me, and consequently cast about for a school with Catholic atmosphere. They moved to a little town in the neighborhood of Darmstadt, which boasted a grammar school managed by the Catholic clergy. I entered this seminary at the age of eight and one-half years; but the following year this institution was suppressed because of the current religious antagonisms (Kultur Kampf). Finally, as a reward of extensive inquiry, which lasted the entire period of my

---

*Submitted in German and translated for the Clark University Press by Susanne Langer.

grammar school years, I was placed in a Jesuit boarding school near Feldkirch in Austria. Here I continued my studies.

The five school years that followed (1877-1882) now appear to me as the most beautiful memory of my life. The demands upon my powers of learning were by no means slight, as the school prepared for entrance examinations of higher institutions of learning. Futhermore, the hours of recreation with their compulsory English games (soccer and rounders), which were at that time almost unknown in Germany, and the regular tramps in the mountains taxed my strength heavily.

Religion permeated our entire existence, not as one of the multitudinous duties, but as something that imbued everything with motive and enthusiastic life. At the same time, there was no dearth of pleasures which one could not fail to miss during vacations: sleigh rides in winter, days of leisure in summer, musical and theatrical productions, church festivals, and tramps through the mountains, which contrived to lend to the life a gay background. Small wonder it is that the fledgings of this nest in later life often returned to visit this scene of their youthful joys.

Since the studies gave me little trouble, I should hardly have received the necessary training in will power had it not been for the strenuous games and walking tours. With especial ease and pleasure did I embrace the study of mathematics. Of the electives, English appealed to me most strongly, although I had not the least idea of what a rôle this language would play in my future. In our second year of English our instructor was a born Englishman, who accustomed our ears and tongues to the correct pronunciation of the language. In the third year we launched on the undertaking of reading, rapidly and without translation, a novel by Lady Fullerton.

Since the school was a private institution, its graduates were not considered eligible for the State Examinations. For this reason it was necessary to shift, in the last years, to an officially recognized State *Gymnasium*. Now I stood confronted by the problem of choosing a profession. The religious training at home, its entirely complete and satisfactory continuation in school, and admiration for my teachers, with whom we came in closest contact, gradually swelled my desire to emulate them, to be a priest and a member of their order, which I had learned through many lessons and experiences to respect and love. In the 50 years of my subsequent life I have never once regretted this step; rather has my profession filled me with undiminished enthusiasm and thankfulness to God, who has bestowed on me this precious gift.

After the first two years, which were set aside for religious study, and do not have bearing on our theme of preparation for scientific work, there followed two years in which I completed my humanistic studies. The greatest stress I laid on poetry and rhetoric, which are indeed the very foundation of higher Latin and Greek literature. In rhetoric my own attempts, which I repeated year after year, helped me more than anything else to reach a real working knowledge and facility, at least as far as was possible in default of actual contact with audiences.

The higher academic curriculum of the Society of Jesus embraces seven years, three of philosophy and four of theology. The three-year course (1886-1889) I began when I was just 20 years of age. The first year of philosophy included the fundamental subjects: logic, critique of reason, and ontology or metaphysics, with nine lectures a week. The doctrines here presented were then reiterated by the students in class and in addition debated in scholastic form three hours a week.

The philosophy which we were taught was that scholastic philosophy which in Kant's day still held the favor of German universities. The content of this philosophy as taught at that time may be found more or less completely in Lehmen's textbook. It is not the work of one individual thinker, but might be called a general philosophy in which the achievements of the greatest philosophers are gathered together, sifted and synthesized into that total thought which seems our closest approximation to Truth; yielding gradually that cumulative effort of successive generations which characterizes any sound and progressive science. The thinkers of the early Christian era approved it, since its foundation, resting on the works of the great Greek thinkers, in no way contradicted the revealed teachings of Christianity.

Naturally there was in this scholastic philosophy no lack of moot questions, which were championed by the great schools of the orders: the Franciscans, who retained much of the Augustinian doctrine of Christian antiquity, the Dominicans, among whom we find Thomas Aquinas, that master system-builder, and the Nomilastists, more or less independent of any particular order, many of whom already showed strong tendencies toward modernism, etc. At the beginning of the modern era, Suarez, the most outstanding philosopher of the Jesuits, contrived a happy combination of all the best elements of the scholastic tradition. His work of unification found great favor for hundreds of years, even in non-Catholic universities. The other subjects of the first year of philosophy, besides some natural history, consisted of intensive mathematical study, a review of arithmetic, and a continuation of algebra. An elective course in higher mathematics continued through all of the three years.

In the second year of philosophy I studied the physical sciences and the elements of philosophical psychology together, five hours a week and two weekly seminars. Most emphasis was placed upon the natural sciences, physics and chemistry, which required two hours a day. At that time the *Gymnasium* laid less stress upon these subjects than it does at present. The third year of philosophy finally yielded a review of psychology and philosophical theology, and, aside from this, general and special theory of ethics, ten hours a week inclusive of four hours' seminar. Each year terminated in a final examination, the third year closing with a one-hour examination covering the total field of philosophy. The examinations consisted of essays written on prescribed themes and, especially, the rebuttals offered by the student to the criticism of the examiner.

In contrast to the elementary courses, these philosophical studies were the first to require of the student definite independent opinions and personal convictions. Of such independent thought I first felt myself totally incapable. I felt distinctively that I was playing the part of the so-called "good pupil" who has learned his lesson well, and knows how to defend his contentions along orthodox lines, but who is far from capable of attacking moot questions with independent speculation. In my secondary courses, I felt more security. My instructor in mathematics was a famous mathematician, P. Epping, who had made a name for himself in Babylonian Discoveries in Astronomy. In his elective course he expanded the principles of analytical and synthetic geometry and infinitesimal calculus, which to me was all very new and fascinating. But most impressive of all were the lectures of the eminent physicist, P. Dressel, whose further development of the theory of physics, appearing at a later date in a voluminous textbook, was highly esteemed. My preference for these studies, in which I could easily note my own rapid progress, gave me the necessary incentive for the undertaking of my first independent endeavor in the realm of more complex literature. The first work which I studied was Secchi's abridged *Einheit der Natur Krafte,* in which in my youthful enthusiasm I believed myself to have found the ultimate explanation of our universe. But my critical faculties were still undeveloped. Nevertheless, this labor gave me a method of thought which was fundamental to my later work. During this period of study I continued to pursue the hobby of my undergraduate days, namely, the study of modern languages. A few of these later became very useful to me, especially Italian and Spanish. My success in the natural sciences at this time compensated me in part for my incomplete mastery of my philosophical studies. Little did I realize at the time that these sciences would later pave the way for my achievements in philosophy. At the time, I had one definite conviction, namely, that I was still too young for the latter study. Many years later I found, to my great joy, in the works of that ancient master Aristotle, the partial justification for that conviction. "Young men may be competent mathematicians, but they cannot be good philosophers, for they lack the ground-work of life's experience." Thus, the growth which I sought so anxiously and yet so vainly was to come much later in my life.

Following the custom of my order, I now interrupted my studies in theology and served five years as pedagogue. The subjects of mathematics, physics, and chemistry I taught in practically every class in the *Gymnasium.* It would be impossible for me to stress too heavily the importance of the influence that this period exercised on my life's work. What it brought me directly was a thorough and sure knowledge of those subjects which the process of teaching made it imperative for me to repeat constantly, *docendo discimus.* And, what was of even greater importance, these subjects formed a prodigious part of the groundwork of many of the practical sciences I was later to practice. In addition to these came a technical victory which was to help me immeasurably in my literary career, the faculty of making a point clear to the pupil. If the written explanation does not suffice, which is often the case, the teacher must try again and again to drive home his point with a variety of methods until success reveals to him the correct one. It may be easily seen that this practice will turn the light of reason and self-criticism on many things which one has held unimpeachable, in oral teaching as well as in pedagogical writing.

After the first period of adaptation I found increasing hours of leisure, which I now devoted to independent study. This study I carefully confined within the bounds of the pedagogical sciences in order that my field of endeavor should not become too greatly diffused. Thus, the five years became school years for me in the truest sense of the word; lectures were replaced by the study of books, which is the life-work of any scholar. In this manner I soon passed through the stage of undergraduate mathematics. The chief subjects were analytical geometry, algebraic analysis, and, most important of all, differential and integral calculus. In this last subject I worked through an immense collection of problems in order to fix indelibly in my memory this important material. Other mathematical sciences gradually linked themselves to these above mentioned: synthetic geometry, number theory, theory of expansions. In later years I filled a gap in my preparatory work, namely, the theory of probability, so important in practice. Although the study of physics and chemistry, due to the large amount of laboratory work required, demanded much of my time, I found time to study through the works of Pfaundler, Wüllner, Weinhold, Reis, and many others. The *Classic and Analytic Mechanics* of Poisson, who makes the spirit of scientific physics to shine in unparalleled fashion from the printed page, was to me a star of the first magnitude.

Since higher mathematics and the law of probability are the very foundations of psychophysics, morphology, and correlation-theory, the immediate usefulness of these studies became very apparent to me. Likewise did my knowledge of experimental physics prove indispensable in my psychological experiments. But still more highly do I rate its influence on my inner growth. Thus, analytical mechanics gave me some insight into the vertiginous sense of knowledge which came over the philosophers of the Enlightenment, whose standpoint seems so strange when approached by the path of pure philosophical procedure. Furthermore, the study of advanced physics showed me how one may, even in more complicated subjects than the transparent mathematical ones, arrive at well-founded and definite opinions. My success in these studies gave me confidence in my ability to achieve the same in other sciences.

The four-year course in theology which followed (1894-1899) was based upon the scholastic philosophy. In some matters the philosophical foundations were continued, only on a higher plane, as, for example, in theological morality, which may be compared to our former philosophical ethics. This is the reason why the study of theology often throws light upon philosophical problems. Strictly speaking, of course, neither theology nor the following years of ascetics falls directly within the pale of my preparation for later psychological activity.

After this 17-year period of preparation in Orders, I began my real life's work, the teaching of philosophy. On an initial three-year appointment I taught all the systematic subjects (with the exception of ethics, which had its own permanently appointed professor) in the following order: logic, critique of reason, ontology, cosmology, psychology, and theodicy. But at the same time it was my task as a teacher to keep philosophy abreast of the times, to study all the newest systems, glean and absorb that which was new in the practical sciences, and replace insufficient evidences and opinions with new and better ones.

The new duties I had not undertaken of my volition, and I approached them with great misgivings. Would I marshall the necessary force and clarity of exposition so indispensable to the teacher? Would I be able to contribute anything to my science? The first practical test allayed my fears, for my long preparation had lent me confidence. The first year had scarcely passed when I already perceived the shortcomings of the material I was teaching. Most of all did psychology seem to require a thorough revision. Here was a newly discovered science which no one as yet had found time to combine with the old philosophy. A casual examination of Wundt's textbook and periodical showed conclusively that here was a new realm which could not be conquered without technical study; with this in mind I sought and received permission to interrupt my teaching activities and to seek sources for my research at the University.

Up to this time I had thought only of Wundt, to whose laboratory students gravitated from all corners of the earth. But as two of my brothers were then studying at Göttingen, I learned that there, too, the new science was well represented. The convenience of living with them there influenced me to cast my lot temporarily for Göttingen, and what at that time seemed to be a mere measure of necessity later proved to be a kind dispensation of Fate. George Elias Müller, the first and most profound critic of Fechner's *Psychophys-*

ics, the classic of the new psychology, who was never equalled in exactness and method, was at that time at the height of his influence. With great kindness he took a personal interest in my work, a thing which Wundt, despite the best intentions, would never have had time to do. Especially, he arranged my program of lectures so as to give me the greatest possible help in my psychological studies. As a foundation he recommended the one-year course in physiology by Verworn, including the required laboratory practice, the regular course of the medical students. In psychology there were Müller's major lecture course (which subsequently appeared in a pamphlet) and a series of his secondary lectures and exercises on psychophysics, on reaction-experiments, and on color-sense. I also learned much in the rôle of subject for experimentation. Directly upon my entry into his classes, Müller outlined for me a plan for some original research in which I was to supervise the whole experimental work. Its theme was psychophysical: the superceptible Sensory Differences in the Fields of Sight and Weight Perception. I was to study the literature according to his direction. He planned the experiments and ran through them, using himself as subject. Later, in the next semester, I was called upon to develop these experiments, using others as well as Müller as subjects. This work, for which, of course, credit must be given entirely to the master, has this advantage: the student learns the procedure in detail. Müller laid the greatest stress on the development of my thesis, and criticized my presentation heartlessly in all its details. Many long digressions he struck out completely. Once, when he was criticizing every single sentence, I finally begged him first to read the passage in its entirety in order that he might pass judgment on its possible usefulness. To this he consented and thereupon felt satisfied. "There are really some facts in that passage; there is nothing I can do about it." The final revision, for the sake of safety, he took upon himself.

At that time, N. Ach, then Müller's assistant and now his successor in Göttingen, offered selected topics in educational psychology. Futhermore, with him as well as with Müller, I was allowed to act as subject. Here I gained considerable insight into practical experiment and self-analysis.

As more or less preparatory courses I might count my laboratory work in physics, conducted by Rieke, and some lectures on applied mathematics, such as infinitesimal quadratics and mathematical statistics. In the field of applied psychology I derived the most profit from a course in psychiatry with Kramer, with clinical demonstrations; the connection with general psychology has been well presented by Störring. Later I treated of this psychiatry in my general psychology at much greater length than was customary, for which I received the applause of the psychiatrists. I profited further by lecture courses on general philosophy, such as G. E. Müller's natural philosophy, a combination of various old and new doctrines, Husserl's history of modern philosophy, and a lecture by the latter on the Freedom of the Will. The physical chemistry of Nernst, which is the foundation of Müller's theory of colors, had important implications for psychology. The most impressive address I ever heard at Göttingen was Reichenbach's lecture on hygiene, with its superabundance of experiments and its pregnant conciseness, which offered a maximum volume of material in a minimum of space.

What the student, if he is reasonably well prepared, learns at a university is not so much the detail of the lectures, for this usually has already appeared in print and is easy to review; rather it is the multitude of demonstrations which he has witnessed, better still, often executed himself; most important of all are the studies under the immediate supervision of the instructor, the intimate discussions of pertinent questions, and the advice of the instructor on the choice of books. I remember especially one instance of a so-called "famous book" of which I spoke to the professor, intimating that I did not expect to be able to read it profitaby until I was more advanced, and his laconic reply, "You will never be able to profit by the study of that book!" Furthermore, I was greatly interested in the different emphasis that was given to various subjects; in matters of experiment every possibility was exhausted, every result tested to the utmost, but when it came to purely philosophical questions, such as the substantiality of the soul, the discussion rarely went beyond more or less probable guesses.

The fourth semester of my two years of leave I used for a pilgrimage to Leipzig, the birthplace of the new psychology. By far the most important offering in this University was Wundt's major lectures in psychology. Despite his 70 years, he handled his material with astonishing freshness of outlook; his lectures were accompanied by demonstrations, a thing that was not possible in Göttingen at that time. An introductory course by Wirth initiated me into the technical resources of the Leipzig laboratory. Since the time of my sojourn in Leipzig was limited, I could hardly participate actively in the work; only in Spearman's experimentations in tactual illusions I acted as subject. Of the remaining subjects the one I liked best was a course in phonetics by Siever, who covered the field in its entirety, and by virtue of a magnificent technique drove home its contents in unparalleled style. The study of harmony with Oettingen also proved to be fascinating. For both these subjects I later had good use.

II

My program of work for the years immediately following developed naturally as a summation of all these studies. My aim was the exposition of the whole field of psychology, the experimental as well as the philosophical. Circumstances conspired to hasten the completion of this work, for since 1904 I had been lecturing annually on experimental psychology, and the necessity of a systematic guide was becoming ever more apparent to me; since I was also teaching a greater part of speculative psychology, and later, in fact, was to cover the whole field, I felt that in this subject, too, a textbook was becoming indispensable, especially so since speculative psychology had become a major philosophical department commanding five hours a week with constant reviews by the pupils, weekly seminars, and a final examination at the end of the year. The constant repetition of the material in the lectures, together with the assimilation of the literature pertaining to the course, gave me an ever increasing comprehension and called for many a mental rearrangement of the field. The ideal constantly before my eyes was a compromise between Ziehen's *Guide* and Wundt's three-volume work, similar to that which the physiologists had already found years ago in Tigerstedt. Should I succeed in writing such a book, one which should be recognized as a peer of Wundt's and Ziehen's, I felt that I should be qualified as an authority in the new science. This would also give me an opportunity to combine what was substantial in the old psychology with the salient points of the new material into truly modern synthesis.

The slow and painstaking method of gathering source material, which I had cultivated for years, now stood me in good stead. In my files I had gathered every piece of current literature and made an abstract of its contents; this material was now at my disposal for synthesis in any form I pleased. The two textbooks progressed simultaneously; but, since empirical study is the more fundamental and must first stand the test of public criticism, my *Experimental Psychology* appeared long before the *Philosophical Psychology*. For this reason we shall deal first with the former, the history and contents of the textbook of experimental psychology.

The first autographed edition of the *Experimental Psychology* of 1905 was a small guide of 220 pages. It already shows the large lines of the later arrangement, but is very different in its relative allotments of space. The discussion of spatio-temporal perceptions follows that of association; the chapters concerning the higher realms of consciousness (comprising only memory and imagination), higher emotions, and the will are condensed in a small space. Psychophysics alone monopolizes 22 pages, occupying as much space as higher emotional and volitional functions together. Diseases of the mind are allotted one page. Obviously this text still limited itself entirely to the purely experimental work thus far investigated. This, of course, is all materially changed in the second expanded edition of 540 pages (1908-1910). All that is lacking in this second edition, as compared with the third, are the chapters on general perception, the ego, and most of those in the ninth part. After further extensive gathering of source material, and rearrangement, there appeared in print the first volume of 1915-1917. The second volume followed in 1920, and, as the completion of both volumes had come in a relatively short period of time, I undertook to revise the first in 1923. The second was sent to the printer in its original form, and it was not until 1929 that it appeared fully revised, the product of four years' labor. In the course of time several prospective translators appeared, but they all lacked the necessary tenacity of purpose, with the solitary exception of the Spanish, in which language Volume I appeared in print, and Volume II is now in the process of translation. An English one was repeatedly offered, but the translators evidently failed to marshal the energy of the Spaniards; the monumental proportions of the labor confronting them invariably put them to rout. Translations into various other tongues failed because no publisher could be found.

The style of the textbook, as might be expected, sought to imitate in clarity of terminology, completeness of material, and discrimination between the important and the unimportant that of the best current textbooks. That I could not equal the objectivity and fluency of Ebbinghaus I realized from the start, so I contented myself with the simple expository methods I had learned in the course of my training in mathematics and physics. At the same time it occurred to me that my readers would demand certain new requirements which my predecessors had not fulfilled. The first was a broader conception of the scope of psychology. It would not do to deal exclusively with psychological experimentation; the new work demanded the treatment of the mental existence as a whole, including reason, creative imagination, emotional reactions of all sorts, and so forth. The objection may be advanced that this is empirical rather than experimental psychology. In the present incomplete state of our science that is probably true, but not decisive. All the sciences of the mind have long demanded a psychology of the higher realms of consciousness, if only with the shallow degree of exactitude which ordinary observation can offer, and of such observations there is no dearth. Even Aristotle, in his *Poetry, Rhetoric, and Ethics,* had already made a multitude of scientific observations which underwent much elaboration as time went on. Besides, experimental psychology has succeeded in working its way slowly upward into the more complex funtions of the mind, including research in the fallibility of the description of impressions, the measure of intelligence, the investigations of emotional reactions, and the processes of volition. Yes, even aesthetics, morality, and religion in this age undergo the process of experimental analysis. Furthermore, it falls to our share to bridge the gap between psychology and the neighboring sciences; that is to say, psychology must borrow all those teachings of the other sciences which are instructive in the knowledge of the entire intellectual life and include them in its general theory. In this way aesthetic experiences illustrate the higher emotions in an ideal form, and thereby much of that which concerns the emotional life becomes more lucid. In a similar manner it will aid us in the study of the psychology of languages and social psychology. A particularly valuable addition to most of the chapters on the psychology of the higher emotions is psychiatry, for it exhibits the lowest forms of mental reactions, and also the effect on our general intellectual life of those disturbances resulting from either deficiency or exaggeration of certain functions of the system.

A second desirable trait of the textbook appeared to lie in the exposition of experimental psychology as a purely empirical and positive science, and the omission of all speculations concerning philosophical matters which the empiricists cannot treat successfully. Just as physics treats only of fundamental laws and facts and their immediate explanations, denying itself all philosophical speculation, so psychology must also limit its field, if it would hold a place with the other empirical sciences. This consideration was not observed by the authors of many early works on psychology, for example, Ebbinghaus, who opens his dissertation with the exposition of his opinions on the nature of the soul, actualism, and parallelism. Such an introduction makes the false impression that these doctrines are the necessary premises for his experimental psychology, and that the latter is just as vulnerable as his philosophical suppositions. For the same reason I exclude from the textbook any discussion of ultimate questions which occasionally confront the student in psychology, such as telepathic visions and the nature of mysticism. However, when a metaphysical opinion is supported or contradicted with empirical evidence, it cannot always be evaded. But even in this case we are dealing with ultimate conjectures from which no further empirical consequences follow, and not with the foundations of our science.

The further problem as to how much detailed research should be presented had a subjective aspect, being more or less arbitrary, and an objective one based on the relation of such researches to the purpose of the textbook. The scope of the work was also a matter of the author's choice, i.e., whether it was to become a short guide or a voluminous textbook. Here there was no guiding precedent. Even in the firmly established science of physics, both types (large and small) are represented. External circumstance played an important part in dictating the quantitative nature of the work, especially the element of the time allotted for gathering the necessary material. As a result of these forces, the little guide grew to the maturity of a two-volume textbook in the course of the years, almost automatically. But there was also an objective reason for this expansion. The textbook is not primarily designed as a reference book for professional psychologists, but rather as a compendium of all the accepted material for the use of the student. Biography differs from the so-called Psychogram in that it seeks to glean from the bare collection of data (the Psychogram) the material for a unity in which the impertinent is neglected, the pertinent combined, and isolated paradoxical items even discarded entirely. In the same manner I sought, by the employment of my broad outlook born of long study of all details, to further the comprehensiveness of all parts of the system. To what degree I have succeeded in this task of synthesis remains for others to judge. In my own estimation the successive editions show an advance in this respect. At first I succeeded only in the case of disagreements among scholars on fundamental problems, which long have been the food of scientific discussion; for example, the problem of nativism or empiricism in the psychology of perception, the problems of the nature of thought, the nature of associations, intelligence, and the character of volition. In other cases I contented myself with an objective exposition of both sides of the conflicting arguments. But deeper and deeper reflection and the ever onrushing flood of new material led me finally to a definite stand on the best solution of many moot problems.

What actual contributions does the textbook offer? The answer must, of course, be formed from consideration of the subject in its present state. It would be impossible for me to go into detail; I must be content with a consideration of fundamentals.

The first sections, those dealing with the theory of sensations, contain material common to psychology and physiology. Both sciences treat of the dependence of sensations upon external and internal conditions; the objective, however, differs in each case. Physiology of the sense organs seeks to establish the dependence of the physiological processes, especially in the case of certain brain functions, upon their conditions, the stimuli. Only, because these processes are almost totally unexplained, physiology uses, instead of brain functions, their immediate results, namely, sensations, which consciousness reveals to us. Psychology, on the other hand, seeks to describe the special character of these sensations and to establish their relations with their immediate sources. And, since the immediate physiological sources are not known, we substitute for them the more remote external stimuli. For this reason, the emphasis of the two sciences lies in different directions. The special problems, of course, reappear in practically every textbook. Of the color theories I have favored that of G. E. Müller, not because of personal feeling and memory, but because from a purely objective standpoint it seems to me the most profound, in the use of scientific evidence after the manner of Hering, as well as in its physiochemical explanations. In the treatment of tone sensations, the musical element was stressed somewhat more. In all discussions of sensations, an attempt is made to arrive at quantitative notions. The chief value of the chapter on erotic sensations lies in its psychological descriptions, for, in regard to their physiological concomitant phenomena, which formerly received most attention, it is becoming increasingly uncertain as to what psychical contents are really to be measured by means of them.

The most comprehensive part (Chapter 3) treats of imagination and perceptions. The fundamental question of the psychology of imagination, whether imagination differs from perception in kind or only in degree, has found a recognized solution. Here Jaensch's theory of visual images and the theory of localization of images, which has been developed chiefly by Müller, appear for the first time. More exact statistics on the intensity of ordinary images, such as Goldschmitt established for after-images, would at this point be welcome. In the passages concerning tone-combinations certain questions of musical theory are further pursued.

The long third chapter culminates in theories of the perception of surfaces and of depth, and reaches a final solution of the fundamental problems in this field. In the perception of depth it seems to me that we cannot get away from some innate element which establishes a foundation for the analysis of the empirical criteria of depth. The numerical measurement of visual space in paragraph 10 I may claim as my own idea. The evident paradox startled me even in childhood. At that time the vault of the heavens appeared to be so very near that we children accepted the illusion as reality. In the same manner it terminated visual space in all directions, like a hood. It always surprised me that when we travelled on the train we did not need to pass through a tunnel into the next "hood territory" (*glockengebiet*), but always seemed to remain in the same one. It was many years later that I learned that we do not see distant objects at their true distances, but at a much smaller one; but the question "How far away do we really see them?" remained for a long time unanswered. I found the answer at last in an excellent investigation by v. Sterneck, who compared the visual distances and magnitudes of the firmament directly with corresponding figures at close range, which could be assumed to be seen in true proportion, and so established the appearance of the heavens under different conditions. Strangely enough v. Sterneck did not risk the next step, that of declaring those distances as the ones actually perceived, and ascribed materially larger values to them on the ground of certain other premises. It must have startled him to find the apparent distance of the sun at the zenith 10 m. For this reason he refers to these values as *imaginary perceptions* which the mind creates that it may more easily compare such immeasurable sizes (reference planes). This fear seemed to me unfounded. I induced one of my students to apply experiments, which had hitherto been conducted solely in connection with the heavenly bodies, to distant terrestrial objects (Ph. Schmitt, "In welcher Entfernung sehen Wir die Koerper?" in *Natur und Offenbahrung,* 1910, **56**), which yielded not the much greater values of v. Sterneck, but values on exactly the same order of magnitude, under 100 m., just as in the case of celestial objects.

Investigation into the perception of motion is today in full swing. The sixth chapter, on thought, could have come under the head of perception only if thought had indeed resolved itself into sensations and images. This had to be decided here. The careful comparison of the respective arguments on both sides and of the experimental investigations speak unanimously for the irreducible nature of thought. In the chapter on perception, the greatest emphasis in the light of modern investigations is given to the apprehension of "Gestalt" and to the process of comparison. The exposition of the former topic in the second edition was judged satisfactory by Köhler himself. A new edition will have to bring much supplementary material in this field.

Perhaps the exhaustive treatment of psychophysics is a personal preference of my own, since my work at the University was focused upon it and my studies in mathematics brought it into prominence. On occasion, French scholars have mentioned this hobby of mine with a certain degree of friendly humor. At the present writing, I should say that the formulae in the first chapter could have been given much shorter treatment, because we now have various psychological handbooks and compendia which handle these matters with sufficient thoroughness for the purposes of the scholar. In Chapter 2, the formulae of Weber and Fechner are indeed of no great practical use, but for theoretical purposes they retain their importance. The answer to the question of possibility of psychical measurements is nowhere better illustrated than in the matter of the intensity of the sensations. When certain of Fechner's errors have been corrected, which can be effected without impairing fundamental values, the deduction may be drawn, which is the valuable theoretical one, that relative intensities may be measured. Furthermore, Fechner's formula for the measurement of approach shows how physical stimuli in the process of translation into a perceptual image undergo a logarithmic foreshortening, which certainly must be in the interest of better apprehension.

The fifth part introduces the laws of the normal origin of associations; their value for psychological explanation is incontestable. Association reactions, of course, did not yield all that they seemed at first to promise, in spite of various valuable partial results.

The second volume of the textbook marches steadily forward toward the present time. The psychopathology of association leads us into a discussion of the interaction of body and mind. Here many a viewpoint has been modified in a conservative fashion by the study of war literature. Disturbances of speech are compared with normal phenomena, in the interests of psychology. Reflection upon inhibitions of memory lets us weigh the current theories of the material foundation not only of the senses but of images as well. The result is a demonstration that purely mechanical theories do not suffice, but, instead, that psychical inclining dispositions are necessary for the determination of physiological processes.

Part 7 summarizes all the higher cognitive processes. In the field of attention, psychological theory had a better chance. The true significance of the concept of intelligence has won much clarity in contemporary literature. On the subject of the formation of judgments, our war experiences of mass convictions have furnished us with material of the finest sort. Before this time, the discussion of intelligence testing was confined chiefly to methodology. In this regard, English literature has effected a great change. Burt, Terman, and Spearman have given us a wealth of new information quite eclipsing the old; for example, the distribution of the intelligence quotients in the population, the development of intelligence in the individual and its limitations, characteristics of high talent, the nature of the *general factor,* and its part in various special achievements. There have lately been added to these works the impressive studies of Piaget.

The eighth chapter on the emotional reactions profited greatly from the fact that I now had access to the English psychologists, especially the classical work of Shand. Here the theoretical question of the irreducible nature of the higher emotions is very important and is brought to solution. This same discussion I subsequently expanded and justified in an article of my own. The evidence lies in the nature of their origins, which could otherwise have no explanation. Shand attributed too much independence to the sentiments. It is not until one considers their common core, the personality, that they assume their true significance. The psychological analysis of the separate emotions was really introduced only by Shand and was a valuable complement to the exclusively physiological descriptions that had preceded it. In the chapter on aesthetic emotions several valuable experimental researches concerning the effect of poetry and music were introduced. I may add that this work has gone on since that time and promises to yield a complete explanation. In the case of volitional actions the main revision was in the discussion of mental and physical work. The theory of acquired skills has been clarified by some excellent experimental researches; most of all, the laws of physical labor have been advanced by the new principles of work (economy, monotony, etc.). For the study of mental work Thorndike's *Critique* has accomplished most, especially in clearing away the exaggerations of Kroepel. In all probability even Thorndike's work will not be final, but will merely pave the way for a future synthesis. The irreducible nature of volition has found new support. In view of the attempt to disprove the freedom of the will through actual experiment, it was no longer possible to circumvent the inclusion of a brief exposition of the theory and its foundations. In the classification of psychological types, Jung's introvert-extrovert dichotomy had received the greatest notice. The part on morality, in spite of its promising experiments in the qualitative determination of moral dispositions, when compared with our intelligence tests, still leaves much to be desired.

The problem of psychic development was divided, for the sake of lucidity, into two chapters: the first being on individual and the second on social development. In the former, our study of child psychology has taken a noticeably new turn. Experiments are no longer confined to a few socially privileged children, since the Viennese school of Charlotte Bühler has carried out mass investigations where separate steps in age and occupation are statistically established. In the chapter on mental derangements, which cannot be given any exhaustive treatment in my book because they belong to the field of applied psychology, the material changes concern only those researches whereby the psychiatrists have delved more deeply into psychology. The milder forms of insanity, for instance, bear out the hope of its explanation in psychological terms. Hysteria and compulsion, especially, have psychological import; in regard to the former, Kretschmer has explained many phenomena psychologically. In the recently developed science of psychotherapy it is often possible to make counter-experiments, testing the psychically conditioned origin of such abnormalities.

A direct personal consequence of my occupation with this textbook was the greater frequency with which I attended the Philosophical Congresses. Such a congress serves, above all, to further the acquaintance of philosophers with one another. It is very interesting to meet in person those whose mental physiognomy one has already studied in literature, and everyone is noticeably pleased if one knows his work and can discuss the same. The value of the lectures varies with the individual. For the lecturers themselves it is the chance to present a new research, for their colleagues in the field it lies in the discussion of those investigations, and for the neutral listener, who follows the progress of philosophy with consuming interest, the lecture is important chiefly as an index to the direction of general interest; thus for me the Recognitions of Thought Psychology in Leipzig was a real experience.

The completion of the textbook brought with it an invitation to give a course of several months in experimental psychology at the university of our order in Rome, the Università Gregoriana. This course has been continued ever since, on the same general line, by other persons. On the trip to Rome I met Gemelli, the Franciscan, Rector of the Catholic University in Milan, and gained some insight into his remarkable organizing activities; and later, upon reaching my destination, I made the acquaintance of that most cordial psychologist of the State University, Sante De Sanctis.

III

Philosophical psychology is not the antithesis of empirical psychology; on the contrary, both are departments of general psychology and mutually benefit each other. Many recognized leaders in the practical sciences, Helmholtz, Hering, Ostwald, and Driesch, show a tendency to delve into the philosophical element of their sciences. With especial zeal did Wundt apply himself in this direction; his many philosophical works bear witness thereof. Ebbinghaus tried, at least, to give his experimental psychology a philosophical groundwork. Despite the fact that his method of combining the two departments seems to me unfortunate, this is not because it means the unification of both sciences in the same spirit, but because this combination carries the strife over *Welt-Anschauung,* with all its implications, into territory from which, in the interests of mutual practical scientific endeavor, it should be excluded. Experimental psychology should, like physics, be a field where all those engaged in research could work in harmony to achieve the same ideal. That the one-sided use of either of these sciences has its dangers may be easily understood. If the pure philosopher regards empirical psychology as small potatoes, he will find that his account of the spiritual life will be deficient in part and ofttimes inaccurate. In any case, he is tempted to withdraw from the rich fields of reality into generality and thereby lose contact with what is vital in science. In the same way the pure empiricist, who contents himself with superficial philosophical premises, will find himself confronted with many a contradiction, which may extend even into his profoundest scientific explanations.

It is not a matter of indifference to our conception of the spiritual life whether we base it on the notion of a soul-substance which is enriched by its accidental proper acts, retains them in memory, and is responsible for all its past acts, or whether we conceive it in the empirical manner of Hume, who has at his command only the causal chain of separate acts which enriches no personality, has no memory, and above all carries no responsibility for past acts.

The philosophy which I learned and later taught was not the evanescent inspiration of a single scholar; instead, it was the synthesis of the philosophies of antiquity to which were added the contributions of later generations. Of course, not even scholastic philosophy is a perfect unity in all its details. There is no dearth of dissenting schools which centered about famous names such as Thomas Aquinas, Scotus, Occam, and, later, Suarez. But this dissension does not affect fundamentals. The same realism which all the practical sciences hold indispensable is recognized by all these schools. The reality of matter and its functional properties which physics requires, the truths of reason, whose purest examples are logic and mathematics, and their applicability to the real world form the major assumptions of this realism. On these two rests the structure of the old metaphysics, which was valid for the fundamental relations of beings, substance, modes, relations, and causes. Here, as in the natural sciences, men trusted in the power of reason, asked questions, found hypothetical solutions for them, and debated these to and fro, until the most probable or at least generally accepted was universally adopted, just as in the sciences. In the scholastic philosophy there is such a thing as tradition, and there are criteria for reason and belief, by which one can find one's way.

With the growth of science in the beginning of the modern era, an entirely new situation arose. The philosophers no longer could hope to absorb all that the sciences offered. It is easy to see that they often yielded to the temptation to withdraw from that which they could not hope to conquer and to retreat into the abstract, which was not yet touched by scientific investigation. It was hundreds of years later that the idea began to dawn on them that philosophy must be divided into many departments, every one including its empirical foundations. The first branch to feel the change was ethics, which was combined with the rational sciences of law, sociology, national economy, etc. Gradually, too, the natural sciences merged with the knowledge of modern physics, and the philosophical teaching of life with natural history.

The division of psychology from the philosophical parent-stem came relatively late, as that of the experimental sciences had come. Among the neo-scholastics who attempted the above-mentioned synthesis, Gutberlet, who had already undertaken the same task in behalf of many other sciences, deserves mention, although, because of the gigantic proportions of the work he had undertaken, the effect was not of a lasting nature. At that time Michael Maher attempted in his psychology, in the Stonyhearst Series, to combine the English psychology, then in vogue, with philosophy; German psychology, which was just in its infancy, he could not include in his system. The School of Lyons, under the leadership of Mercier, had undertaken the division of philosophy into its various departments and the combination of those parts with the special sciences; Mercier took an active interest in psychology, although he had in mind biology rather than the true experimental psychology. The nearest approach to the ideal was the excellent *Psychology* of Geyser. My objective lay in the same direction.

My philosophical text developed out of the needs of pedagogy. *Sensory Psychology* (the conscious life of animals) was first autographed in 1906 and later often revised. *The Psychology of Reason,* which deals with the soul-life peculiar to man, was first added in 1911. In 1927 these two works appeared in print under the title of *Psychologia Speculativa* in two small volumes of 250 and 350 pages, respectively. Their main characteristic is the scholastic form of exposition as it has gradually been developed in the later scholasticism. At the beginning of every passage the conclusion is stated in the form of a thesis to be established. Thereupon comes the *status quaestionis,* the explanation of the terms and the enumeration of conflicting opinions among the ancient and modern authors. Then the proof is rendered in syllogistic form and justified in detail. According to the circumstances, this may be followed by immediate inferences (*corrolaria*), and relevant questions are discussed (*scholia*). The book closes with a consideration of some objections to the hypothesis, with brief rebuttals as an exercise in debate. Any part of this scholastic method, though perhaps in a freer form, may be found in modern treatise.

The method of instruction, more precisely, is this: The theses are explained with the help of the book, then the students are required to prepare a brief account of the thesis and the most important proof material in their own words, in order that the whole thesis may be read in about ten minutes. In class these theses are read by the students and the questions of the teacher answered in brief scholastic form, a first test of the students' comprehension of the material. Still more highly does the scholastic method prize the many seminars, in which one student delivers his thesis and then defends it against the criticisms of his colleagues, which are prepared preferably to anticipate the defenses. The professor functions as guide in the discussions wherever it seems necessary, and presents the solution. These exercises of repetition and well-prepared material discussions both pro and con, eventually, in the course of years, give the pupil a growing sense of security in his knowledge of the doctrines and of his own powers of comprehension, so that this education is no mere memorizing process, but a personal mastery of the materials. The student knows what he understands and to what degree.

I assume that even those scholars who differ on certain individual questions would be interested to know how far the ultimate problems of psychology may be answered with more or less certainty as a result of the combination of the old and the new psychology. Therefore I will now attempt to give a comprehensive survey of the main ideas of my speculative psychology. The psychology of sensation is divided into a general theory (*Psychologia Sensitiva Generalis*) and a special theory (*Psychologia Sensitiva Specialis*). The first part deals in the manner of a summary with the functions of animal life and deduces directly their significance for the nature of the sensory soul. The large second part treats each sensory function in detail and explains it, in so far as is possible in the present stage of our science. In this part the new psychology is best represented, and the combination of both branches is furthest advanced.

The *Psychologia Generalis* includes the whole class of sensory creatures. Animals are not robots or purely vegetative beings. They are endowed with sense perceptions, emotions, and desires. This is proved conclusively by the perfect analogy with the sense-life of man, and still more directly by the impossibility of explaining the everyday actions of the domestic animals by the exclusive assumption of mere reflexes. The new zoölogy has even been able to trace the development of sense endowments in the animal hierarchy, for example, whether bees are color-blind, or color-sensitive, like human beings. The sense endowment of animals is by no means limited to their sense impressions. There is also a central process of employing the sense impressions to arrive at a perception of objects. In scholastic language these actions are subdivided into four different inner senses: *sensus communis* (the modern "Gestalt" perception), phantasy or the ability to form images, the power of evaluation (*vis estimativa*) or instinct, and sensory memory, by which the recalled perceptions are correctly placed in the past. At this point the baffling instinct of animals is treated in great detail in order to establish a boundary for the true capabilities of animals. A survey, taken from the modern literature, discloses an enormous wealth of these processes in the animal kingdom, and presents them in their order. Probably the most acute observations are those offered in the classic investigations of W. Köhler.

The theory of purely mechanical reflexes as well as that of actual powers of reason must definitely not be applied in the explanation of this problem. The solution can lie only in the realm of sensations, and points to something like memory grooves, except that they are present at birth; there are native tendencies toward certain feelings and processes which appear consistently when the correct stimulus is applied.

The upper border, which the animal does not attain, the Rubicon between Man and Beast, is, according to the old theory, the intelligence. But one must not regard this word in its everyday ambiguous meaning; instead, it must be used in the sense of logic, that is, restricted to purely abstract thought, especially in regard to general concepts such as form the premises of geometry, the apprehensions of relations as such, and notions of cause and purpose, in contrast to mere apperception of "Gestalt," which today has been proved valid even for animals. Only according to this sharp philosophical definition is animal intelligence denied. The proof lies in the utter lack of rational language in the animal kingdom, lack of progress in science, art, and morality, which is to be explained by the absence of abstract thought and of any understanding of relations.

The outline of the sense-life of animals supports the conclusions in regard to the principle to which the animal owes its powers, that is, the *animal soul*. Here one must meet the issue of materialism. Here the best contributions have been made by certain philosophers, especially Busse, in his classic work on *Mind and Body*. The moderns also analyzed the fundamental distinction between reason in any form and physical phenomena; the unity of consciousness makes an explanation by means of the extensional functions of matter impossible. How do body and soul cooperate in the sense functions? The Platonic theory, which found many adherents, saw in sense perception an exclusive soul function, for which the organism at most supplied the conditions. Aristotle opposed this viewpoint with his theory of a substantial connection of body and soul which unites both in a single substance that manifests itself as something unique, especially in the lower functions of life. If I am not mistaken, a certain psychophysical parallelism, which may be assumed within limits, offers new justification for this view. Further characteristics of the animal soul are its identity with the vegetative principle and its simplicity.

On this basis, psychology of the special senses treats in detail of the separate physical acts, the first being taken from the human sense experience, which is given to us directly by introspection. To prove that it is pure sense experience, we must constantly compare it with its parallel in the animal kingdom. In this part it is clearly apparent that the results of the new psychology are not by-products of the old science, but that it is they that breathe new life into the old problems.

The simplest form of cognition is pure sensation, which, however, must not be compared with anything of a physical nature; it shows the dual characteristic of ontological and modal determinations,[1] which are completely distinct and yet are both necessary. The general characteristics of sensation include specific sense energy and the laws of sense intensity, such as Weber's law. For extension and duration, a simple relation of similarity with the stimulus suffices within certain limits. Sensation is no mere passive reception of physical effects, but is a living reaction, since only the presence of a soul can explain the super-physical characteristics of sense. Does the object of our sensation first become our mental property in a subjective sense, so that another act is necessary to establish it outside? Or is the object with its true characteristics immediately before us? Self-observation confirms the latter hypothesis. In this immediate perception of objects the recognition of the content of the perceptual image certainly is inherent. The extreme sense organs are no longer regarded as the place where the sensory images are formed, but instead this function is generally ascribed to the cerebrum; even the specific centers of the various senses in the cerebrum are known today. The many facts which the new psychology has revealed have greatly ramified our knowledge of the senses.

Scholasticism, as I have said above, subsumes the higher sense functions under its system of the four internal senses. This sometimes includes even the bare sensory perception of the ego *(sensus intimus)*. Naturally this involves no abstraction of the ego, but, on the contrary, is the concrete perception of it, inseparable from its concomitants, as, in the case of a moving object, the movement is perceived as a part of the object. The ego given sense is a part of every sense function, just as extension is the common ingredient of all tactual and visual sensations. The first true internal sense *(sensus communis)*

---

[1]Seinsbestimmungen und Objektsbestimmungen.

embraces two activities: (1) the combination of sensations of different types of unity of location, as when one finds the white lumps of sugar to have a sweet taste, and (2) the perception of proximity, of shape and movement, to whose differences an animal can be taught to react.   In this activity lies a part of the phenomenon which "Gestalt" psychology is at present investigating.

The second inner sense, imagination, postulates merely that images can appear without concomitant outside stimulus, that is to say, on a basis of disposition left by former perceptions.   Included under this head are the formation of associations and their later reproduction. Today we are in a better position to prove that images do not differ radically from perceptions, but that, rather, there is a very gradual transition from one to the other.   Philosophically the most significant question is that concerning the nature of memory traces.   Are they something purely mental, as Lotze still thought, or something purely material, as is generally accepted today, or something psychophysical, a disposition of the soul, which depends on its cooperation with matter, a theory which Becher has defended with great energy? In behalf of this last-mentioned theory one might quote the fact that the reproduction is independent of the location on the retina where the stimulus appeared; it is also independent of the size of the image of the physical characteristics of the separate parts of the new percep- tion, if only essential similarity is maintained.   This view I have not taken from Becher; I have long been convinced of it for philosophical reasons, but Becher's powerful handling of the evidence by means of relevant experiments gave me no slight confirmation.

Instinct had already been treated under animal psychology. There remained only its application to man, for which the English psycholog- ical literature had furnished much valuable material.   The fourth inner sense, the sense memory, contains no real contention that the present situation has been experienced before, but demands only that the present experience be included in a temporal series, which regresses from the present moment, possibly with a certain evaluation of the interim, such as we have of spatial distances. The new psycho- logy permits the explanation of many perceptions hitherto regarded as mysteries, especially the perception of space.   For planes, the per- ception of adjacency is absolutely necessary, in contrast to the third dimension, where the empiricists' interpretation holds.   Locali- zation on one's own body and outside is to be grasped as a unity to facilitate its corporation in one system of ideas of the space relations. As a result of all this, perception proves to be a complicated network of different processes, its most essential characteristic being the unification of sensation in the unity of the object and the segregation of this object from others, in short, the function of the *sensus communis*.

The nature of the other fundamental properties of sense experience, of the affections and impulses, was already known to the ancients; only, today, by systematic introspection, the nature of these acts may be more clearly contrasted with cognition. Aristotle had already separated the various emotions under the name of "passions." The division of the emotions into the component elements of feeling and striving marks a step in the progress of philosophy. The question— Which are the ultimate elements in this system?—could, of course, be raised only by the moderns. This discussion led to a disagreement between the Wundtians and most other psychologists. According to the latter there remain only three elements which cannot be further reduced: pleasure, displeasure, and striving. This solution seems best to suit our evidence. In the new psychology one often finds the faculties of the mind divided into three ultimate elements: reason, feeling, and striving, in contrast to the Aristotelian system of two elements. At the same time it is difficult to deny that the similarity between the two subjective elements of feeling and striving is much greater than that between them and reason. According to this a compromise seems advisable, an initial dichotomy of mental powers into the objective faculty of cognition and the subjective one of attitude, and then a subdivision of the latter into feeling and striving.

For the ancient philosophers the problem of the power of thought and volition over our limbs was insoluble. The moderns have solved it by assuming an association of the motor-innervation from which certain body movement springs, with the following consciousness of movement. A position mediant between the permanent ability and the transient act is properly assigned to the acquired disposition of habit (*habitus*). The theory of the ancients finds confirmation in the new psychology point for point and occasionally even receives a further development. This last applies especially to the laws of imagery which have received a much richer content through our association-psychology. Even this short outline, especially its second part, shows what is meant by the incorporation of the modern in the old psychology.

For the psychology of the higher faculties, treated in the second volume, the combination had not yet borne so much fruit. Most of its questions were neglected if not denied by most psychologists. Moreover, experimentation was limited chiefly to the lower mental processes, which are more easily isolated. Kulpe's school was the first to attack the higher problems. The psychology of the higher faculties embraces the theories of reason, will, and the soul. In the theory of reason the fundamental problem is the distinguishing characteristic of the intelligence function, as contrasted to all sensory cognition, even the highest, the perception of Gestalt. Philosophy has favored this contrast unanimously, from the ancients down to Kant, and so, for the most part, has the logic of the moderns. Sensationism arose in opposition to this doctrine and immediately dominated experimental psychology. The proof here, as in logic, was based upon the special character of general and abstract concepts, the apprehension of non-physical entities, realization of the absolute necessity of mathematical principles, etc. The scope of rational consciousness transcends incomparably the sensory consciousness of animals, for, by the employment of general concepts, it inaugurates scientific procedure, and in this way becomes capable of unlimited expansion; one has but to consider geometry, which is utterly inaccessible to animals. The transition to intellectual knowledge does not in any way require innate ideas. The mere capacity of abstraction makes it possible to draw conceptual elements from the existing sense material and by comparison of these elements to derive conceptual principles which suffice for the development of the entire field of mathematics. Further positive concepts of intellectual content are furnished by reflection upon one's own intellectual processes: the concepts, judgments, inferences, voluntary acts by which the concepts of intellect acquire a positive objective content. Logic divides all rational knowledge into conception, judgment, and inference. Modern logic and psychology have made some additions, such as the development of the comprehension of the spoken word and a number of refinements in regard to comparison and judgment. In the case of judgment either of the forces may play an important rôle, especially the emotions and the will as one could see clearly in certain mass convictions during the War. Judgment is not a voluntary act, but is a special intellectual experience, a taking possession (literally an apprehension) of Truth (*Besitzergreifen der Wahreheidt*). To the theory of inference, too, thought psychology has made various contributions, such as the researches of Störring, Selz, and Lindworsky. Newman's somewhat earlier disquisitions on the Logic of everyday life are also well worth notice. The rational functions are intimately connected with language. Even though the French traditionalism, which maintains that all thought is a matter of tradition, is a gross exaggeration, we should not be blinded by the immense importance of tradition for the development of rationality in the individual. Another exaggerated system, ontologism, despairs of the capability or reason to cope with any of the higher rational knowledge, and sees in all insight a divine revelation. In a scholastic exposition of the rational consciousness, the famous Aristotelian system of the formation of concepts, which the scholastic later elaborated, may not be ignored. The permanent gain from this controversy was the establishment of a true intellectual memory which has found recognition and experimental proof in the new thought psychology (Bühler, Selz).

The second large part, the theory of Will, must prove that there is a volition and feeling proper to the rational soul, over and above all sensuous striving and feeling. Proof of the rational Will is easy, for the act of volition includes its apprehended object; thus, an act of volition cannot possibly have an abstract objective, e.g., science, art, morality, if it is a purely sensory act. For the higher feelings the proof is indirect. This proof I first executed in the latest edition of the textbook, and later expanded it in an article on Scholasticism. A philosophical question arises as to the mutual influences of the several faculties of the soul: reason, emotion, and striving. This influence may be direct, indirect, conscious or unconscious, physical or moral. Many of the philosophers encounter difficulties because they unwittingly regard each faculty of the soul as a separate identity which acts independently, instead of recognizing that the soul acts as a unit.

The explanation is simplified if the various functions of the faculties are treated as being modes of certain proper functions of the soul, through which the soul adapts itself internally and thus becomes capable of performing other acts. For example, the consciousness of a valuable object is a condition of the soul, through which it may now pass into the relevant emotional condition. The exact description of all acts which precede and follow the decision of the will has been already described very conscientiously even by the ancients. Modern experimental investigation of the will has traced statistically the components through their actual occurrences and has also approached the solution of the problem of volition more closely in introspection.

The central problem in the theory of the Will is the Problem of Freedom. Not every act of will may be regarded as free; certain conditions must be fulfilled, especially the recognition of sufficient motives for and against the act. It is not contended that motives have no influence over the will, but that their influence is not insurmountable. Practically without exception the determinists attack a conception of the Freedom of the Will which is defended by nobody. Here the classical proofs of free will are set forth in consecutive order. In what sense can one use the consciousness of freedom as a proof of the actual Freedom of the Will? It can be used only in so far as we are convinced of any of our other faculties when we have repeatedly used them under similar conditions. Great weight is generally accorded to the moralistic argument that otherwise all responsibility in its true sense ceases.

If the Freedom of the Will is established, the consequences are manifold. It must then be untrue that every voluntary act is unambiguously determined by the mandate of an unfree cognition; likewise it is impossible that the will necessarily follows that which is recognized to be the better course. From the philosophical point of view it is especially important to general problems of mental faculties whether or not these faculties of the soul are as separate entities differing in nature from the soul itself. The decision on this subject is not without importance for the conception of substance.

At present, the most vehement attacks are likely to be launched against this third part of the *Psychology of Reason,* which treats of soul-substance and its basic characteristics; the empiricism, popular since Hume, so sharply repudiates every analogy with other functions and conditions, and also the basic fact of the identity of the ego in the regular chain of subjective experiences, that one must suspect some other source of this opposition. The fact is that this lies in the vulgar conception of substance as an unknown X, a carrier in the form of a salver on which letters are borne, an absolute and in every respect unchangeable unity, etc. For this reason the concept of substance needs to be clarified and elaborated, especially in regard to its inner relation to its conditions. If this is effected, soul-substance reveals itself as something which despite its numerical identity is capable of various modes of manifestation, exactly like the accidentally alterable body; it is recognized precisely by its permanent and transitive characteristics; verily, no body is so well known to us as our own soul and its history. The absolute characteristics of the soul offer little difficulty to him who recognizes the soul itself as a necessity. These are its essential singleness, which was already evident in the animal soul, and its identity with the sensory and vegetative principle.

For every philosopher the question of a hereafter of the soul, in which it reaches its objective, is paramount. The significance of this question for morality and religion is obvious. Here it is mandatory that all the traditional proofs be enumerated and their validity tested. The so-called metaphysical argument proves immortality as a conclusion drawn from the summation of all previous philosophies. The teleological argument investigates the natural yearnings of the human soul, that is, its capacitation. This points to the infinity of a being endowed with reason, and only of such a one, and to its unlimited progression toward perfection in reason and morality. Naturally many objections are at hand which must be conscientiously examined. The moral argument, that otherwise there would be no sufficient *sanction,* which for most people is an indispensable premise of morality, has always been regarded as the most formidable. The ethnological argument, based on the agreement of independent convictions of the several civilizations, has gained new adherents through the discoveries of Andrew Lang.

The final question is: What is the relation of the soul to the animate body? Parallelism, widely disseminated since Spinoza, has assumed in recent times many varying forms. Among these are the idealistic, the materialistic, and the theory of identity, all of which seek to escape in various ways from the unreasonable parallelity of two independent series. Busse has examined in exemplary style this fashionable theory in all its ramifications and has demonstrated its untenability. But how, then, is an interaction between body and soul metaphysically conceivable? The famous Aristotelian doctrine of entelechy, which is also accepted by the scholasticists, finds the solution in a synthesized substance, as has already been demonstrated in the case of the animal soul. The proof of this assumption rests upon the elimination of all other possibilities.

This is the extent of my work up to the present. What remains to be accomplished in this direction? If we peruse the works of other outstanding psychologists, we find that one desire for a complete philosophical basis of general psychology has led them to delve even into the remoter principles of the science, especially logic and epistemology. I call to the attention of the reader the three-volume work of Wundt (Logik), Külpe, Störring, v. Kries, Ziehen, Driesch, and their predecessor, Lotze. The material connection may readily be perceived, since the main concepts of logic, idea, judgment, inference, etc., are common to both empirical and philosophical psychology. To turn the revelations of psychology to the uses of logic is an obvious step, although logic is not merely psychology, but a separate science, which seeks to reach its objective by methods of its own. On the other hand, epistemology is the foundation of all practical and philosophical sciences. For this reason I believe that, if God gives me the necessary time and energy, I shall prepare an exposition of these philosophical foundations, probably in the form of a continuation of the scholastic philosophy.

A prognostication of the future of experimental psychology I should consider ill-advised, for all too often in the past has prediction on the strength of probability been given the lie. This is one of the greatest temptations of the successful investigator.

OTTO KLEMM*

I. Nature of the Retrospect

Within the compass of human life there are always two possible ways of viewing matters: we look at the attainments of the present moment either in a forward direction, from the beginning to the goal, or, retrospectively, from the result to the beginning. Individual experience, too, may be seen in either of these two perspectives. Our mental development has a goal of its own. Its searchlights penetrate the general dusk of possibilities, and search the horizon for that which is to become its special purpose. But a retrospective view of our actual accomplishments is apt to present a very different picture. In people of our stamp, who have devoted themselves to the service of science, retrospection is focussed upon actually recorded experience, upon actual products of teaching and demonstration, as its objective credentials. But such records are largely a matter of chance. What we happen to have brought to expression and completion is only a sample of what we have actually lived. Moreover, experimental work is almost always performed in conjunction with others, and is linked with problems which are not the exclusive property of any individual. The individual mind in the course of its development absorbs all sorts of foreign inspirations, and at the same time takes part in the work of other minds, especially of younger persons, so that a good deal of its output appears as that of somebody else. I can look back upon many a study that has issued from the Psychological Institute at Leipzig, and is now preserved in the pages of the *Psychological Studies,* and feel this sort of close relationship.

This background of life, and the way it is mirrored in the total experience of the individual, belongs to the content of our personal destiny, just as much as the endeavor which is not recorded in any objective form and is perhaps even unaccomplished. Here is the place where a few of these things may be spoken. There are certain personal matters of this sort that will go through one's mind again and again, as one takes the homeward path after a hard day's work, and one's thoughts are no longer bound absolutely by theoretical demands. What has life profited us in an unprofessional sense,

*Submitted in German and translated for the Clark University Press by Susanne Langer.

what has remained as a positive gain of a personal sort? The winter landscape has given us days of freedom. The ocean dunes have cradled us. Children look at us. Bitter necessity demands the fulfillment of some duty. All that is temporal falls away, no human frailty stands between us and our furthest horizon. And what, through all this wealth of experience, persists as the actual content of life? Certainly not anything that can be reckoned as a balance of successes and failures. I used to keep a book about my experimental labors, a book of possibilities and impossibilities. Under the first head I classed my experiences of feasible methods, little professional tricks and other devices; under the second head I listed my failures, vain efforts and unsuccessful results. Certainly the book of impossibilities grew to be much greater and more varied than the book of possibilities. But the point is not to play up the one against the other. That does not tell the whole story; far more important than all this is the gratifying consciousness that part of our ability was devoted to theoretical problems, the value of which can no longer be challenged by any exigencies of external circumstance. And, finally, the deciding factors are not the contents which we discovered in this or that way, but the fact that there was such a way for us to go. And, even if we had only once encountered the noble joy of insight, this would have been enough to produce a transfiguration. The fact that such a glimpse of heaven was given to us, just one view of the stars, or one such moment of reverence for the human soul, aside from any extraneous purposes, is a matter of eternal value.

II. EARLY ANTICIPATORY EXPERIENCES

As a psychologist I have often enough reflected upon myself, yet this is a different sort of reflection. Now I am about to contemplate past experiences not in order to apprehend them in themselves, but for the sake of fitting them into the total picture of an individual life. What I have thought out in my own way within the psychological field does not lack connection with remote anticipatory experiences. One of my earliest childhood recollections enshrines an experience, well authenticated by the details of a concrete situation, wherein I tried to formulate the idea that the world as a whole was not necessarily existent. At the same time I absorbed the notion that possibly the non-existent was merely crowded out by the existent, and toyed with the mental transition from one to the other. External evidence enables me to place this experience somewhere in the fourth year of my life, i.e., in 1887. How the indicated content of this experience was expressed at that time I am unable to describe, since the experience did not remain isolated but was repeated and gradually enriched. The chief vehicle by which the sense of that experimental content is brought back to me from earliest times is certain motor reactions and a feeling of complete, overwhelmingly beautiful self-surrender.

Closely connected with this, later on, was a state of mind wherein somehow the dependence of the external world upon the mode of our perception was adumbrated. I can well remember the first walks I took without escort, the walk to school for example, during which I conceived the fantastic notion that trees, horses, or buildings always came into existence just as I passed by them. This, too, remained a game which the maturing boy discarded.

The first connected realm of facts that presented itself to me was the kingdom of stars. The boy's phantastic thoughts, kindled no less by the infinity of space and time than by the unattainable and supramundane, rose upward through the silent winter nights. The contradictions of religious dogma were challenged and experienced over and over again with a peculiarly sweet tension. When I was 15 I received a gift of a three-inch spyglass with a lense of 80x magnifying power, and with the help of wood and paper constructed a telescope. Armed with the physics of the ninth school year I began to make observations and concoct theories. I was happy when a semi-popular astronomical journal printed some of my productions.[1] Pure and unbroken was my experience of scientific research, as it can be only for a youth.[2] I may call it this because it was in no wise mixed with any professional ambition. I was free as yet from any dealings with the powers of real life, and tasted to the full, as my birthright, that which in later years, retrospectively, we call the prerogative of youth.

But from this astronomical hobby arose a decisive turn of mind. The joy which I had found in scientific insight was perturbed by the philosophical deductions especially of the materialistic school of

---

[1]Über die Enstehung der Sonnenflecke und Lichtfackeln. *Sirius,* 1899, **32,** 265-268.

[2]Bewegungstheorie der Sonnenflecke. Gäa, 1900. S. 1-14.

thinkers. In disgust—and flying to the contrary extreme, as is usually the case in such adolescent phases of development—I broke off my astronomical observations. The critical philosophy made a profound impression on me.[3] Now it was no longer just philosophy of nature that confronted me, but from my inmost nature a philosophical passion broke forth. Filled with higher expectations than I have ever known in later life, I enrolled at the University at the age of 19.

III. STUDENT YEARS

Did I choose the study of philosophy? No—certainly not—rather I was never faced with a moment's doubt of the fact that I must pursue it. Although I realized by that time that I would afterwards have to take up a profession, I left that matter entirely out of account. I did not evade the question; it simply did not exist for me. In a soul that was so completely possessed by the treasures of philosophical thought, so deeply affected by everything that youthful enthusiasm can cherish and adore, from Heraclitus the Obscure to Neitzsche's *Cycle of Eternal Recurrence,* how could there have been any room for questions of a vocation planned along economic lines?

At Munich, in my first semester in 1903, I came in contact with Th. Lipps, and for the first time the word psychology acquired a definite meaning for me. At Munich those who had registered as students of philosophy were obliged also to name their special subject. I felt somewhat disconcerted. For me, philosophy was a special study. Some older friends advised me to name psychology. So now I was a student of psychology. From Lipps I learned the method of self-observation and followed him from his theory of perception even to his doctrine of the cosmic Self. Most respectfully we read his *Leitfaden der Psychologie* which had just appeared. But a more powerful influence upon us was his self-confession, his uncompromising spirit, his defiant *yes* and *no,* his pure devotion to truth. "When I was a student," he once remarked, "and my father died, I was poor as a church mouse." This human utterance I have never forgotten. Whole nights long we sat in the Psychological Club and discussed the concepts of similarity and dissimilarity, the distinction between acts and non-acts, and other pairs of concepts that occur in phenomen-

---

[3]Von den Voraussetzungen der Naturphilosophie. Gäa, 1902. S. 1-10.

ological psychology, and carried on Lipps's dream of carrying out a reform of German psychology with headquarters at Munich.

One thing struck my attention: the small collection of apparatus for experimental psychology, which stood unused and somewhat dust-covered in a corner of the seminar room. My scientifically trained eye kept turning to it. Here I felt the presence of a gap; through this gap I passed to another great field, that of experimental psychology as W. Wundt in Leipzig had conceived it. I read his *Grundzüge der physiologischen Psychologie* with a degree of care and attention such as I have rarely bestowed on any other book, and was at that time particularly receptive to the general, fundamental problems, to his psychophysical analysis of higher mental functions, to his principle of creative synthesis, and his complementary principle of the heterogeneity of ends. When, in 1904, I became a member of the Psychological Institute at Leipzig, I soon became aware of the long road that led from experimental details to those far theoretical horizons. About Wundt there was an atmosphere of vast spaces—unexplored regions, to which the new method promised to give access.

During my second semester at Leipzig, in the year 1905, I started an experimental research of my own. Is it surprising, in the light of what I have told above, that I was working on certain complication-experiments, i.e., on a subject suggested by certain fallacies in as-tronomical observation?[4] At the same time I was engaged in writing a prize essay for the Faculty of Arts and Sciences, on the history of late Renaissance philosophy. Studies in this field took me to Naples in 1905. Many long days I sat around in libraries reading manuscripts left unpublished by G. B. Vico, whose history of philosophy and social psychology I was dealing with. In this way a little bit of source-work became one of my memorable experiences. Warm, bright May days dawned for me, the shadows of the palms outside fell into the high interior of the library at Rome, while the ab-sorbed reader dwelled with his thoughts far in the distant past.[5]

In connection with this work I visited the Fifth International Congress at Rome. Here I saw for the first time, clearly and strik-ingly, the confusing dichotomy of theoretical standpoints. James had talked about the Self, and the Leipzig psychiatrist, Flechsig,

---

[4]Versuche mit dem Komplikationspendel. *Psychol. Stud.*, 1907, 2, 324-357.
[5]G. B. Vico als Geschichtsphilosoph und Völkerpsychologie. Leipzig: Engelmann, 1906. S. 235.

whom I esteemed as the most astute specialist on human brain-structure, replied to him, "If I but slice away a little strip of your cerebrum, that is the end of all your Self." Both men now are dead. I suffered from such animosities; likewise from certain sharp, critical words from Lipps. F. Krueger read, in hearty tone, a message to the Congress from Wundt, and it seemed to me that now I understood why Wundt was wont to declare to his most intimate friends that he never attended a Congress. Thus the impression I received was, all in all, not homogeneous. There was no lack of external recognition. Brilliant receptions, gracious gestures from the ministers at the capitol, lent a festive air to the occasion, but I was more excited over the conflict of theories than anything else.

The end of my studies was approaching. I had made good use of our academic freedom of choice, though it was clear to me from the beginning that physics and mathematics were going to be my minor topics. When finally the question of finding a position actually stared me in the face, Wundt offered me an assistantship at his Institute. Joyfully I accepted. That solved, for the present, my economic problems. Moreover, I felt henceforth my firm connection with contemporary psychology.

IV. The Law of Generation

In this I always see an exemplification of the idea that haunts me whenever I think of my own advancing age. At first sight, indeed, it seems as though the specious present were hurrying through Time, gradually overtaking the particular positions which previously were viewed as the future; but that is an external point of view. In spiritual reality there is no such overtaking. A youth sees his elders before him, and in psychology the novice sees the wisdom of older generations, the sureness of their methods, the clarity of their conceptions, perhaps the closed confines of their systems, as something that lies before him. But just as he begins to ascend to that higher level, step by step, the plane inclines itself toward him. I feel no older now than I did then, but I observe that now—in the psychological profession—there are far more youngsters about me than before. More precisely: I have not yet attained the mental attitude that I used to suppose in my student years must be that of an older, independent, recognized scholar toward a novice, but am still the same person, only amid a new coming generation. That is not a play with words, but a fundamental trait of mental development. We would not be the older generation today if it were not for the younger one that is arising. And therewith my relation to my own elders has remained just what it was, as also my former fellow students still appear to me to remain at about the same youthful age as before. Thus the vision of contemporary psychology which I entertained expresses this purely personal perspective. Although it includes several psychologists who have won recognition in much the same way as the leading men at the beginning of our century, they are distinguished in my mind from those—discounting entirely my objective opinion of their work—simply through the fact that they are members of my own generation. This angle of vision dates for me from the time just after I had finished my training, when I was 21 years old. I find it much harder to fit the achievements of my contemporaries into an objective development of ideas than those of my forerunners. With the latter's concepts we must take issue. They stand before us authoritatively, or invite our critique. But what my own generation accomplishes is always clothed for me with the enterprise of one's student years; it is something unfinished, something growing, more personally experienced. In accordance with this distinction between generations, certain stratifications and other correlations take place. Here it is especially relevant what personalities were given to a young man as the first representatives of the old generation and what sort of influence these exerted upon him. For by these factors his development is determined, just on account of that gradual fusion of generations, far beyond his student years.

Whoever realizes this fact must be most keenly aware of his duty and responsibility toward that younger generation, the guidance of which is intrusted to him. Fundamental traits of character may remain perfectly unchanged through life and yet be welded into a certain line of development by reason of this influence of the generations: the enduring, individual form of each human being stands in mysterious relation with the tendency of his time.

V. My Entry upon an Academic Career

What was it that agitated my spirit toward the end of my student years? Was it still metaphysical problems? Had the question of the freedom of the will been settled? What about Kant's *thing in itself?* Where did the propositions of logic really originate? How far did consciousness go, and what was its real nature? Finally, how much of the sense of all world-process had revealed itself to me? I will not continue the array of these questions, with which the young mind had burdened itself. Certainly, I know much more now than formerly about the approaches to a solution. But a youthful spirit is not content merely to discover directions of thought, and to acquire a systematic ordering of previous theories; it wants a glowing *yes* or *no*. What will not bend may go and break. All or none—that has ever been the demand of youth, and will always remain so. One thing is certain: a youthful mind approaches its studies with far more desire for insight into the subject matter than for any critique of existing theories. It is actually obsessed by a thirst for wholeness, and too much critical contemplation serves only to abrogate such a desire. Thus Wundt, the positive man of psychological theories, impressed me far more than Wundt the critic, who repudiated practically all other tendencies in psychology.

My *History of Psychology*[6] was an attempt to relieve all these tensions. I organized it as a history of psychological tendencies, psychological basic concepts, and psychological theories. This division was conceived in a perfectly systematic spirit. For once I wanted to see the iridescent manifold of completed ideas before me in its objective structural wholeness and at the same time in its fruition. At the same time I was in a receptive mood for all philosophical implications. I took pride in viewing on a grand scale the heritage of the century, and in being able to call the whole field my own, unhampered by any experimental details. In the matter of the "tendencies" I felt least independent; there, indeed, the main lines of division have long been established for the history of psychology; my chief concern was to collect within a small compass the most important features. The "basic concepts" involved an explicit attitude toward theory of knowledge and a description of various methods. The most important part seemed to me, at that time, to be the "history of psychological theories." In this field I felt most keenly the real development of psychological thought. The status of a theory seemed to me to be, above all, the surest index to psychological development. All our knowledge about a thing is brought

---

[6]Geschichte der Psychologie. Leipzig: Teubner, 1911. S. 388. Eng., Jap., Span. Übersetzung, 1914; Ital., 1922.

together in a theory. Even in experimentation the point at issue is always a decision for or against some theory. I entertained the notion of calling my book not *History of Psychology,* but *A History of Psychological Thought,* and leaving out all mention of individual thinkers. Whether such a vista across the centuries would let us see beyond the personal representatives of intellectual evolution, I am not able to say even now. At the same time, history shone for me as something between a burden and a redemption. "Thoughts for which great hearts have been broken in the past, we breathe today like pure air." This feeling was alive in me and guided me.

In the meantime, in 1908, external circumstances forced me to business activities in the book trade. I feel that I ought to make some brief mention of this. These years were not devoid of significance for my attitude toward scientific matters. In the first place I owe to this experience a sense for economic achievement and a great respect for the man who labors indefatigably for a small remuneration without doing it for the love of the work; but at the same time it caused me to appreciate the gulf between such economically determined work and free, voluntary activity. In the second place, I was faced once more with the possibility of a different career, not as a mere play of ideas, but with the full weight of stern reality. I evaded it, and in 1908 achieved my habilitation at the University of Leipzig, where I have remained to this day. Certainly such decisions have nothing to do with any psychological theory. They concern only the subject of such experiences. What were the moving forces that actuated it? Not, indeed, any evaluation of the style of life that was associated with the one occupation or the other; the central problem for me was my inward relationship to the respective fields of activity. Since then I have frequently recalled the matter-of-fact way in which I then preferred scientific occupations to all others, and have taken comfort in the fact: for in youth the human heart does not err, and the dignity of a thinker's career will not fail him who has elected it. Although at that time my business activities seemed to me like an obstacle, in retrospect I would not dispense with them, and could really wish everyone who follows the call of science the experience of some such decision.

VI. Experimental Researches

The following years were full of special studies in experimental psychology.[7, 8, 9] I was attracted particularly to experiments by which general principles were to be fortified with exact laboratory proofs. I harked back to my old idea concerning Lipps's theory of space, and thought that in this connection I might be able to carry on my former problem in complications. In complication experiments we inquire into the temporal correlations of impressions in various sensory fields which stand in some sort of spatial relation. My problem at present was whether contemporaneousness or non-contemporaneousness played any part in the apperception of spatial relations. And I believe that I have indeed demonstrated the fact that there is such a "law of spacial induction."[10]

Such experiments led me quite naturally beyond experimental psychology into other branches, especially into what Wundt had called by the name of racial psychology *(Völkerpsychologie)*. Once I attempted, in the light of the principle of the heterogeneity of ends, to thread my way through all the special fields of psychology. I was tempted by the idea of taking this principle, as a transformation of yet more general principle of creative synthesis, for my guiding light, and to employ in its full scope the postulate of experimental psychology, that the whole is always more than the sum of its parts.[11]

My researches on the oscillations of attention rested on the conception that the course of mental processes can be traced by the oscillations of achievement in the various sensory fields. I thought to established the oscillations of difference-perceptions as an index, or, to speak more carefully, as a symptom, of the process of attention. I carried on these experiments together with my trusty friend of student years, G. F. Arps, inducing oscillations of attention artificially, as for instance by rhythmic influences upon the experimental subject. Thereby I discovered that our sensitivity to variations in

---

[7]Vold, Untersuchungen über den Traum. Bearb. 1910-1912. Leipzig: Barth, 1910-1912. S. 897.

[8]Ein nordamerikanisches Lehrbuch der Psychologie. *Zsch. f. päd. Psychol.,* 1910, **9**, 205-219.

[9]Zusammen mit Wirth, W. Über den Anstieg der inneren Tastempfindung. *Psychol. Stud.,* 1913, **8**, 485-496.

[10]Lokalisation von Sinneseindrücken bei disparaten Nebenreizen. *Psychol. Stud.,* 1910, **5**, 73-162.

[11]Die Heterogonie der Zwecke. In *Festschrift zu Volkelts 70. Geburtstag.* München: Beck, 1918. S. 173-186.

the separate parts of such a rhythm, as for instance a dactyl, is keener for the accented than for the unaccented portions, and at the time I took the differences of firmness among the separate parts of such a rhythm to indicate variations of attention.[12] Since then we have grown more cautious with regard to the concept of attention, and the Gestalt psychology of our day sees these details in a much more general complex. Yet this may be taken as an illustration of the fact that although experimentally-acquired observations change their meaning with the mutations of theoretical viewpoints, they still retain their value as facts.

In a general exposition on illusions of sense, which, I must add, was not published until after the War, in 1919, I took stock of all sorts of common regularities.[13] Through the various theories about sensory illusions one can trace a good many lines of development of the fundamental psychological concepts. At that time I employed chiefly the conceptions of Wundt, and therefore distinguished the peripherally conditioned illusions from those which were centrally conditioned, and paid attention to the relationship between the parts productive of illusion and those affected by illusion within such a structure. Likewise the distinction between the associative and the apperceptive conditions for an illusion were expected to give rise to some systematic organization. Today it might be said to have resolved itself for us into a pattern of attitudes, one voluntary and the other involuntary. Certainly one can already elaborate some of the earlier concepts with later refinements and interpretations. But the fact that such a retrospect is possible must not blind us to the new and individual character of such a progressive conceptual formulation, let alone cause us to question it. In my books on sensory illusions I recalled the important pointer which the discoverer of the Müller-Lyer illusion had given us in his principle of "Confluxion," namely, that the part appeared in the character of the whole: the introverted figure is smaller *in toto,* and therefore a part of it, namely, the central line, also appears smaller. In the case of the extroverted figure the opposite holds. It is not fair to try with such details to steal the thunder of the Gestalt psychologists. For there remains a distinct difference between a

[12]Zusammen mit Arps, G. F. Der Verlauf der Aufmerksamkeit bei rhythmischen Reizen. *Psychol. Stud.,* 1909, **4**, 505-529.
[13]Sinnestäuschungen. Leipzig: Dürr, 1919. S. 107.

correctly apprehended detail and the conception and exposition of a general principle. Whoever sees bits of his own work in the light of such principles is just in position to have a very lively feeling toward those matters wherein the new science is superseding the old. I quote an example from my study in illusions of sense. At that time I was looking for the conditions under which—in the sense of the above-mentioned principle—the part appears with the characteristics of the whole as in the Müller-Lyer illusion, and under which —so to speak, on the defensive against these influences—it assumes just the opposite character. This is the case in certain illusions of contrast. The greater of two equally heavy volumes does not appear as heavier, too, but on the contrary seems lighter. Several formulations of that time I should not feel called upon to alter now. Yet it must be admitted that then the background of my thinking was always the separation of the material into its constituent factors, whereas now I take even that idea quite differently and resolve it into a psychology of the whole. But is not such a transformation of meaning-relations the mark of all intellectual development?

These preoccupations with sense perceptions found their continuation in my account of perception-analysis for Abderhalden's *Handbook*.[14] I wrote this in 1919—after the War—basing it generally on my own pre-War work. Since it concerned a methodology, I was led to a division into quantitative, qualitative, and temporal analysis of perception. My chief concern at the time was the exposition of experimental methods. A good deal of it has remained valid in spite of the changes of theoretical outlook which the influence of Gestalt psychology has since brought about. It is precisely the exact application of such methods to newly propounded, and above all newly perceived, problems that has led to important solutions in Gestalt psychology. A good example of this from the field of sensation-analysis is the relation between the agreeableness of right angles and their susceptibility to variation; from qualitative analysis, the impression of curvature; from temporal analysis, the perception of configurations under unfavorable conditions for apprehension. He who sees these methodological connections is especially qualified to perceive the new light which the concept of the totality, in contrast to that of the element, has cast for us. It

---

[14]*Wahrnehmungsanalyse. Abderhaldens Hdbh. d. biol. Arbeitsmeth.*, 1921, Abt. VI, T.B, H.1, 1-106.

is not a question of new methods or a new technique, but of a new meaning that has been bestowed upon the fact.

VII. THE WAR YEARS

Then came the great common fate of our generation, the War. On the day of the Sarajevo assassination, I was with a friend from Edmonton, Canada, whither I had received a call; and he made the significant remark, "Now you will never come to Edmonton." What these years have meant to us—spread out between overwhelming eventfulness and unspeakable emptiness—between most poignant value-experiences and a descent well-nigh to the beast— that goes far beyond the attitude of any individual toward scientific matters. A new and independent feeling was born for the intrinsic value of intellectual things, to which we looked up and whose consolation really never fails us in any circumstances of life.

Besides this, however, I came upon an unexpected application of psychological methods, in connection with my earlier work on the localization of sounds. Starting with certain peculiar illusions of sound-localization, I had formerly worked on the influence of intensity,[15] had discovered that there is also a strictly monotic sort of localization,[16] and had then become aware of the joint functioning of the two organs of hearing.[17] In this connection I had even managed, by a sort of analogy to Stratton's experiments with the inverting glasses, to alter the localization cues for the right and left ear temporarily to such an extent that a crisscross localization took place. In the course of preparatory studies for a survey lecture to be given at the Fourth Psychological Congress at Göttingen in 1914,[18] I had come across numerous previously advanced suggestions for refining the localization of sound by artificial means, thus making it available for nautical purposes. Now the problem was to apply such methods of acoustical triangulation to the purpose of artilleristic intelligence service, and herewith I had my first experience of genuine applied

---

[15]Untersuchungen über die Lokalisation von Schallreizen. 1. Der Einfluss der Intensität auf die Tiefenlokalisation. *Psychol. Stud.*, 1913, **8**, 226-270.
[16]Untersuchungen über die Lokalisation von Schallreizen. 2. Versuche mit einem monotischen Beobachter. *Psychol. Stud.*, 1913, **8**, 497-565.
[17]Untersuchungen über die Lokalisation von Schallreizen. 3. Über den Anteil des Beidohrigen Hörens. *Arch. f. d. ges. Psychol.*, 1918, **38**, 71-114.
[18]Über die Lokalisation von Schallreizen. *Ber. d. VI. Kong. f. exper. Psychol.*, Leipzig, 1914, 169-258.

psychology.   In order to select suitable persons for this purpose and for other phases of artilleristic observation, certain fitness tests were instated, which, although they often had to operate by abbreviated methods, yet presented the psychologist with many interesting problems.   I wrote an account of the results for Abderhalden's book after the War, in 1919; unfortunately it did not appear until 1928, when it was published in its original form.[18]   Those were the first tests for individual fitness, which I made at that time according to my own lights.   They were directed partly toward the achievement of an elementary analysis, but in part also they tried to establish connected forms of behavior.   I have since made a special study of such connections by the method of correlation, and have found, for instance, a fairly high degree of correlation between the scope of apprehension for unorganized groups of points and for the amount directly remembered, as well as the certainty of reproduction of irregular groups of rhythmic beats.   These were just the symptoms of such common foundations of the various special talents.

The above-mentioned practical problems in acoustic localization led me on in another direction.   In working on my survey lecture I had come across Mallock's supposition that the sense of sound direction was based upon the minute difference in the time of arrival of the two waves of sound upon the right and left ears, respectively. The difference, easily computed, seemed to me to make the absolute amount of this discrepancy something so far below any known threshold that I could not utilize it in any way.   But after important experiences and experimentations from other quarters during the War had spoken in favor of this theory, I undertook in 1919 to clear up the point, by effecting such temporal discrepancies between the right and left ear as the theory called for, up to $30\sigma\sigma$ with the aid of a Helmholtz pendulum.[19]   And, in fact, the theory proved to be correct. At a single stroke the efficacy of minute time-intervals was revealed, which formerly could have been credited only for some purely imaginary world.   I was able to demonstrate similar effects in the realm of touch, and the recollection of this experiment always comes back to me most vividly when I am looking for an example

---

[18]Über die Lokalisation von Schallreizen.   *Ber. d. VI. Kong. f. exper. Psychol.*, Leipzig, 1914, 169-258.

[19]Untersuchungen über die Lokalisation von Schallreizen.   4. Über den Einfluss des binauralen Zeitunterschiedes.   *Arch. f. d. ges. Psychol.*, 1920, **40**, 117-146.

of the sort of surprise that may occur in the course of laboratory work.[20, 21] At the same time, experiments of this sort teach us how very guarded should be our statement of any supposition concerning such effects in the border regions. Here I believe that I have before me a new field of microchronic effects, of which only a very small part is known to us at present. Here too, of course, we tend to assume a thesis which by this time amounts to a commonsense assumption, namely, that the nervous impulse travels at a measurable speed and that the temporal discrepancy is realized at some ultimate center. But it seems almost as though our assumption would fail us here. Not only are the differences of time too small for its purposes, but, most important of all, further experiments taught me that the retardation of reaction-time by means of a considerable intervening piece of physical exertion is not coupled with a corresponding attitude in the reception of temporal stimuli to various parts of the body. The unfathomable problem of Time is forever shimmering through, and perhaps some theoretical vista will open for us, some reorientation of the psychological conception of time, which may be related to certain lines of thought mapped out by the theory of relativity.

VIII. Studies in Applied Psychology

Besides all these ideas, certain problems of applied psychology, upon which I had touched for the first time during the War period, remained in the focus of my thinking. The Leipzig Institute, which had passed into Krueger's hands in 1917, expanded the scope of its activities in several directions, and the pursuit of applied psychology fell to my especial share. It brought me into touch with various practical sides of life.[22] I became interested in the psychology of human work[23] starting with an examination of the external

[20]Über die Wirksamkeit kleinster Zeitunterschiede auf verschiedenen Sinnesgebieten. *Ber. d. VII. Kong. f. exper. Psychol.,* Jena, 1921, 137-139.
[21]Über die Wirksamkeit kleinster Zeitunterschiede im Gebiete des Tastsinnes. *Arch. f. d. ges. Psychol.,* 1925, **50**, 205-220.
[22]Der Rundfunk als neues Hilfsmittel für massenpsychologische Versuche. *Radio-Umschau,* 1924, 991-993.
[23]Die angewandte Psychologie in der Landwirtschaft. *Vortragsfol. d. Leipzig Ökonom. Soz.,* 1927, 109-119.

aids and devices[24, 25, 26] and the typical processes of mental work,[27] gained a fairly close acquaintance with educational psychology,[28] became directly interested in the problems of ability-tests[29, 30] and public vocational guidance,[31] and, finally, collected all sorts of experiences from the realm of problems summarized under the heading of court-room psychology (gerichtliche Psychologie).[32, 33, 34] Such problems in the field of applied psychology not infrequently arise from external needs and chance incentives. Therefore a survey of them all presents, casually, a rather motley conglomeration. Yet I might indicate certain points at which, quite apart from the practical successes and failures of such methods, general connections dawned upon me.

I will paint in the foreground what I had a high opportunity to observe. The problems of applied psychology in Germany had been completely altered after the War. The stress of the time required decisions. The tremendous upheavals had disturbed alignments. A new generation was crowding in. Slogans rang through the air. Political passions rent our nation. The demon of Labor lifted its ominous head, and the fight for the rights to the returns of work flared up. The spirit of the time shimmered with many colors and shadings and was as susceptible to a strict, purely economically oriented rationalization as to the temptations of an occult psycholo-

---

[24]Zusammen mit Sander, F.   Experimentelle Untersuchungen über die Form des Handgriffes an Drehkurbeln. *Prakt. Psychol.*, 1923, **4**, 300-302.

[25]Arbeitspsychologische Untersuchungen. *Ber. d. VIII. Kong. f. exper. Psychol.*, Jena, 1924, 188.

[26]Zusammen mit Sander, F. Arbeitspsychologische Untersuchungen an der Häckselmaschine. Leipzig: Barth, 1924. S. 20.

[27]Über Pausenwirkung bei hochwertiger geistiger Berufsarbeit. *Psychotechn. Zsch.*, 1927, **2**, 144-145.

[28]Zusammen mit Olsson, E.   Über den Einfluss mechanischer und sinnvoller Hilfen bei Gedächtnisleistungen. *Zsch. f. päd. Psychol.*, 1925, **26**, 188-194.

[29]Ein Streckenregistrierhobel. *Indus. Psychotechn.*, 1924, **1**, 118-120.

[30]Beiträge zur Eignungsprüfung für den Lenkerberuf. *Psychotechn. Zsch.*, 1926, **1**, 195-198.

[31]Psychologie und Berufsberatung. (*Berufsleitung, No. 5.*) Leipzig: Arbeitsamt, 1927.

[32]Atmungsdiagnotische Erfahrungen an Untersuchungsgefangenen. *Comptes rendus de la IV conf. int. de psychotechnique.* Paris, 1928.

[33]Erfahrungen bei einer Eignungsprüfung an Kriminalbeamten. *Neue psychol Stud.*, 1929, **5**, 1-22.

[34]Über die Atmungssymptomatik bei Untersuchungsgefangenen. *Neue psychol. Stud.*, 1929, **5**, 111-132.

gy. In the miracle-mongering of a profoundly shattered and disrupted age, pseudo-psychology found a fertile soil.

And therewithal, the crisis of psychology arose in the intellectual sphere itself. Rational psychology of the older school tried to maintain its distinction from experimental psychology as from a purely empirical science. With brilliantly tempting hypotheses, psychoanalysis and individual psychology competed for the claim to a new interpretation of mental life, and promised to yield, in addition to such an interpretation, mental cures and education.

I met with these new trends in psychology chiefly through their consequences for applied psychology. It was from this angle that I took issue with their fundamental theses and antitheses. At the same time I gained a great deal from my admission to the faculty of the Leipzig Institute, which came to me as a promotion after I had declined an offer of a different position in 1923. I believe the psychologist can never give too much attention to the work of other scientists. Hereby he is able not only to practice his insight into the reason and commendability of other methods of work but also to test or correct by these whatever concepts he is himself in the habit of using, or whatever categories seem familiar to him. The idea of an integrational psychology *(Ganzheitspsychologie)*, which Krueger had firmly established, gave direction to the further development of my Leipzig work. Undoubtedly there is no psychology current in Germany now which is not in some sense integrational psychology. But the special characteristics are the recognition of the prime significance of feelings, the distinction of *Gestalten* as a special type of whole, the derivation of everything from structure, and finally the conviction of necessary development.[35]

I remember how such ideas in turn grew into an experienced and authenticated whole within my own work. Ultimately the part of applied psychology which has some connection with such fundamental principles reaches up into the higher plane of my own intellectual development and the evolution of theoretical notions. The sense of doing something that has practical effects, from the mere formation of a suitable hand motion up to the judgment of human beings and the disclosure of criminals, brings with it a certain satisfaction of its own. The office of an expert who submits his opinion

[35]Meaning and symbolism in psychology. *Proc. and Papers 9th Int. Cong. Psychol.*, New Haven, 1930, 260-261.

under oath to the courts of law bestows a dignity and carries with it a special distinction to which I have never been indifferent. And it seems to me that the applied psychologist should uphold his practical work in his own estimation and that of others, and should gain satisfaction from his connection with the real demands of life. All this does not alter the fact that only the connection with theoretical ideas really ranges applied psychology in the line of intellectual developments.

IX. Connections with Theoretical Ideas

If one really takes the implications for pure theory seriously, then applied psychology widens out far beyond mere considerations of utility. I was often puzzled by the problem of just in what the real profit of such applications might lie. Especially in educational psychology I frequently asked myself this question, and often it seemed to me that the real gain must lie on an entirely different level from that of the mere application of laws for the purpose of gaining certain effects. The real purpose is to gain, with the aid of psychology, an insight into the mental process that takes place in the course of educational activity. The end is not merely the improvement of some method of teaching. I will give a single example. In elementary writing exercises, a six-year-old child might well write "in" instead of "im," and maintain, "There is an i, and there is an m" (because it counts the three downstrokes again as a unity). This "error," as we call it, is a typically childish one; it is based on a childish integration experience, which has not yet been dissected into our conception of parts. In the total form "in" the child sees both the i-form and the m-form. To engross oneself in the process by which such an error arises has a value of its own quite apart from the dydactic measures which it might prescribe for the teaching of penmanship. And from such easily apprehended cases we arrive at more serious ones: the duress under which the youthful mind must grow into new spheres of life, and gain not only an attitude of sympathy but of understanding. To prepare the way for this gain is one of the beautiful tasks of applied psychology, for hereby the technique of application is transformed into an ethics of application.

Various studies brought me in contact with the psychology of bodily exercise. In this splendid realm one could see with special clarity how far we have already transcended the formulation of mere achievement tests, especially of fatigue tests in the old style. Particularly, our observations on bodily movements teach us to recognize the influence of volitional total attitudes, which completely explodes the old mechanistic conception of an alternately depleted and regenerated store of energy. They lend themselves especially to the study of integral forms of action. It is always quite apparent that in these higher forms of bodily movement mental functions gain the upper hand.[36]

X. Vocational Guidance

My responsible office as collaborator in public vocational guidance led me repeatedly into questions of talent. Here I met with greater success the more I acquired the habit of treating such consistent foundations for special achievements as integrally constructed. I assume intellectual total levels which form the background for related special achievements. We do not get any further by dissecting intellectual accomplishments forever into parts and then coordinating the alleged factors with particular traits. Of course one can talk about differences in the acuteness or excellence of combinations in special fields of interest, or about differences in the achievements of memory, etc., but it is far more important to remember that in the end human accomplishment is not put together out of such separate elements, but is built up on an integral foundation of general achievement. It depends on the level of the person as a whole. Such a level—in the case of intelligence, the receptivity of the subject for connections of sense and the power of concentration with which they can be produced—is the deciding factor.[37]

In matters of detail the method of correlation goes further. With reference to some success and failure experiments with female textile-workers, I have given considerable attention to the problem of how the separate items of a fitness test may be integrated to form a general characterization of a person. The correlation of the total with actual practice—erected upon the averages of a fitness test—is higher than the average of these separate correlations with practice. As I became absorbed in the mathematical conditions of such a computation, I saw new and significant features of true wholeness beginning to dawn; the calculation of such correlations gives one an insight

---

[36]Gedanken über Leibesübungen. *Neue psychol. Stud.*, 1930, **5**, 145-168.
[37]Wer ist intelligent? *Westermann's Monatshefte*, 1929, **146**, 245-248.

into the characteristic factors determining the total attitude in practice and corroborates the theory of general levels of capability.

Under the title of *Streifzüge durch die Psychotechnik* I have recounted a number of experiences with tests used at the Leipzig Bureau of Vocational Guidance, not in order to supplement the existing collection of psychotechnic methods, but in order to delimit the characteristics of fitness tests and their place in the total process of vocational guidance, quite apart from the interests of my colleagues in this special field.[38] Once the idea of fitness tests had found a footing in economic thought, expectations were in part pitched too high; in part—especially outside the psychological profession—the tasks of a fitness test were apt to be deemed much simpler than in fact they are. I do not see the real and important differences between human beings—even with reference to vocational demands—as they often appear in fitness tests, as such isolated individual functions as "pure eye-measure" or "simple reaction-time," but on the more fundamental level of a formulated activity. Perhaps a test for eye-measure really reveals patience, precision, and general reaction to a visually conceived task rather than actual excellence of an eye function, a faculty as constant and objective as, for instance, clearness of vision. But above all I was often troubled over the decisions as to fitness or unfitness for a trade. Personality and vocation need not fit each other like form and counterform. Both are still entangled in the meshes of a much subtler network. Misfits, too, may become effective: the vocational advisor must always be receptive to the prevailing mood of the personality in question, which cannot be rated in the numerical results of a fitness test.

XI. Points of Contact with General Psychology

I have occasionally had the audacity to let directly practical decisions follow from tenets of general psychology. Years ago I pointed out in the course of a court proceeding that a peculiar illusion of speed to which an otherwise reliable automobile driver had been subject was in keeping with his personal equation, to which I habitually gave attention by virtue of my early experiments with complications.[39] In the same way the relations of the Ranchburg phenome-

---

[38]Streifzüge durch die Psychotechnik. In *Aus der Praxis der Berufsberatung*. Leipzig, 1930. S. 269-310.
[39]Die Bedeutung der persönlichen Gleichung im Lenkerberuf. *Ber. d. Int. Kong. d. Psychol.*, Groningen, 1927, 320-322.

non or of the Aubert-Foerster phenomenon could be considered with respect to the activities of a chauffeur. On the other hand, I found ever new illustrations of the peculiar nature of integral processes in the interpretation of practical experience. From this conviction grew the gradual modification of the fitness tests from isolated elementary performance tests to work samples.[40] The fact is simply that the decisive differences among human beings do not lie in their elementary faculties. Of course I am not talking about pathological deviations, but about the scope of variation within normal mental life. Careful measurement here leads us back invariably to the psychological constants that were current in the philosophical psychology of W. Wundt. But the decisive differences of ability are lodged in the integral undivided processes of work, in that which a man can do, or cannot do. I am growing more and more into the habit of taking such fundamental views even in matters of the smallest detail. In this way a study of chance and skill, undertaken with a view to censorship of automatic gambling machines, became the basis of a theory of human skillful acts in general.[41] I found such integrated acts as, for instance, hurling things at a goal to be as much superior in precision to any of their constituents taken singly (analogous to the relation of whole to part in perceptions) as, in turn, this activity itself exceeded the limits which one would set for it on a basis of one's own experience with the course of such acts.[42] From this I could derive characteristic laws for bodily action which may have implications far beyond any recorded details.[43] Even in such little traits, the properties of the soul *in toto* may be traced. He who keeps his eyes open may find miracle upon miracle even here. He becomes modest in his demands upon knowledge, but, at the same time, he repudiates, from his inmost heart, the trickeries of an occult psychology. In my youth I had occasionally—under the influence of older companions—met with occult manifestations; rumored experiences with spiritists seemed to promise a realm to which I must gain access. But how great was

---

[40]Zur Berufsversorgung von Hilfsschülern und Taubstummen. *Ber. d. IV. Kong. f. Heilpäd.*, Berlin, 1929, 323-329.
[41]Zufall oder Geschicklichkeit? *Neue psychol. Stud.*, 1929, **5**, 23-64.
[42]Ansätze zu einer Theorie des körperlichen Tuns. *Proc. and Papers 9th Int. Cong. Psychol.*, New Haven, 1930, 258-260.
[43]Über Eigengesetzlichkeiten körperlichen Tuns. *Ber. d. X. Kong. f. Psychol.*, Jena, 1930, 100-104.

the discrepancy between such expectations and the impressions which I was later to receive in the sanctum of the spiritists! My own experiences in occult experiments, so far perfectly negative throughout, may be taken for what they are worth.[44] A purely personal and irremediable necessity constrains me to reject this type of thinking. Whoever dares to grope along by the guiding thread of things as they are, and to draw a breath somewhere beyond the intuitions of time and space, no longer fettered by the laws of sensory appearances, is breathing a different air from that which fills the secret chambers of the spiritists. This I know from experience.

XII. PHILOSOPHICAL REFLECTION

This account would be incomplete were I not to mention how I have settled in my own mind certain problems within the realm of philosophy. The striving for philosophical insight which had marked my early years continued through later life. Ever and anon I found myself caught in those paradoxes to which every philosophical thought must lead if one pursues it to the limit. This constrained me to think of the final configuration of the world which is at all accessible for us as one which progressively falls into contradictions for human thought, and to postulate the principle of necessary contradiction. Since the world may just as well not be, as be, every notion that would fathom its inmost reality must become enmeshed in this antithesis. The order of our cognitive functions, which Kant has erstwhile demonstrated, may be permuted in any way whatever, without altering any aspect of its relation to metaphysical reality. Thus Kant's antinomies could be taken to signify essentially the necessary contradictions which are manifested in them. The task of philosophy seemed to me no longer to lie in the solution of these contradictions, nor in relating the contents of experience without contradiction, but rather in setting forth these necessary inconsistencies and in realizing the essential inconceivability of these matters. In this spirit I undertook an attempt at a non-Kantian philosophy, and applied the suggested principle to many special philosophical problems. I sought to re-experience these essential contradictions, not in order to silence them with principles and postulates, but in order to think of them as the basic character of all things; thus, I thought, I had found the only form in which it is possible for human

---

[44]Dunkels beim Hellsehen. *Neue psychol. Stud.*, 1929, **5**, 133-142.

beings to grasp such borderland thoughts. I had all sorts of material at hand for such a non-Kantian philosophy, but always maintained it merely as a possibility. Just because it was never published, it was to me a particularly personal possession, and many a time this reversal of the Kantian standpoint has proved a great asset. The world, in which we find ourselves among other things, can only be intelligible for us so long as its rationale remains unintelligible. This produces a mental attitude which no longer seeks to climb up by the separate rungs of scientific law only in order to catch metaphysical truth from the topmost step, but which finds every step just as near or far as any other. Our conceptions of the nature of the soul can never have any finality because they involve just such essential contradictions. Computable and incomputable elements are interwoven in the fabric of the soul, and the more its secrets are unveiled for scientific inquiry the greater grows the realm of the Unknown. For behind it lies the vast ocean of the Undiscoverable, alternating between storm and peace, unfathomable in its possibilities. Wherever the little bark may happen to float, to which we have intrusted ourselves, it is always equally far from the boundaries beyond which man cannot explore.

XIII. Prospects

To foretell what developments await us in the future is always a difficult undertaking, since everyone can see such prospects only from his own point of view. Titchener once declared that future psychology textbooks would be as full of formulae as the physics books of today. Future developments did not corroborate his statement, yet the remark remains significant just because it expresses the expectations of a scientist and characterizes his way of thinking. In trying to formulate my own expectations of further developments I break the confines of that narrow field in which my own work happens to have put me. I should like to open my mind much more to the future significance of the special branches of psychology, and the work which I myself have done now enables me to understand these divergent lines and see them in their proper relations. I hope to progress further by starting, for once, not with familiar matters, but with the unfamiliar. I propose the questions: What more does psychology owe us? What is there yet to be discovered? No one will demand the impossible: the peripheral problems everywhere reach out into the philosophical realm and lead to the Un-answerable. But, if we remain within the limits of the knowable world, I would venture to say that no special field, from the analy-sis of perceptions up to the interpretation of personality, is inacces-sible to scientific discovery, provided we do not limit ourselves to any one-sided view of things or to any single method of approach. Just as the experimental method is inadequate for revealing person-ality, so is mere preoccupation with personalities unable to teach us anything relevant about those simple, yet no less impressive, facts of mental life. In this connection it is easy to say that the various branches of psychology deal with the same process from different points of view. But actually it is in this that the whole secret lies. Certainly I can regard any object in the external world from various points of view: a signpost may be viewed with regard to the wood of which it is made, or in relation to the person who built it, or to the place it points to, etc. These are easy distinctions. Human beings can simply regard the signpost under its various aspects. Mental life, however, is the only realm in the world for which this does not hold. Here the object of observation and the observer are fused in a way that defies all further description. The various relationships wherein the mind happens to stand are not produced, as in the case of the signpost, by the fact that different observers see it from different points of view and different interests, but lie in the object itself. It is essential to the nature of experience to have such a variety of meanings. Now we are distinguishing between general human traits and a particular personal mode, then, between the actual mental processes and the meanings which they convey, or, again, we are distinguishing between the members of an evolutionary process and the process itself, and likewise between individual mental traits, and such as have sprung from contact with other people.

My own orientation along contemporary lines of development in psychology arises from the fact that I regard this ambiguity of mental life as one of its essential characters. From this point of view it no longer seems important to pit one method against another, but rather one's task seems to be to become so absorbed in the nature of mental life that its characteristic ambiguity becomes evident. Here I link my psychology with my philosophical views, according to which such inconsistencies become the more significant the closer one ap-proaches to the last level of the Knowable. I do not believe that any method is destined to crowd the others off the map; on the contrary, the more precisely we develop our experimental technique the more daring will be our interpretations of personality, and the more clearly the innumerable delicate shadings of mental life will figure in our psychological insight.

And, in the same measure, theoretical psychology will gain in fruitful contacts with other interests of life that concern the soul. What doctors and judges, educators and economists expect of psychology is, of course, partly determined by their own special fields. Now psychology will never divide into component parts according to its bearing upon such special disciplines, which in the end would be a division on extra-psychological grounds, but, for its part, it will be guided by the idea that the peculiarly ambiguous nature of mental life can be apprehended only through a study of all its expressions and effects. I do not believe that this demand upon psychology will ever be obscured again. The history of the subject shows us under how many and various forms, in the course of centuries, the problems of psychology have evolved. The short but crowded period which we may review as beginning with the advent of experimental psychology was inspired by a transformation of fundamental concepts. But, in spite of such variations of method, we can still see a basic unity, and it is this that supports our belief in a fruitful future development.

XIV. To the Beginners of Today

Undoubtedly the position of a beginner in psychology today is very different from what it was at the beginning of our century. The new ideas which have shattered the realm of classical experimental psychology flash brilliantly indeed—but where can we find a real psychology in their light? The overwhelming influence of Wundt's *Outlines of Physiological Psychology* which extended well into the beginning of our century did indeed bind the student to a certain outlook and direction, but it also gave him an astounding wealth of detail and positive knowledge.[45] Today the beginner himself has almost the greater part of the responsibility for the type of psychology to which he shall devote himself. Here, too, the general rule is probably applicable, that only serious reflective experience

---

[45]*Zur Geschichte des Leipziger psychologischen Instituts.* In 2 Aufl., *Wilhelm Wundt, eine Würdigung.* Erfurt: Stenger, 1924. S. 92-101.

and independent activity can lead to a profitable relationship with those problems. Views which seem to us erroneous in retrospect are not necessarily wasted and worthless for our inner development. In them, too, something genuine and original may have played its part. Therefore the quick exhaustion of psychological theories which have scarcely survived the span of one generation need not be regarded so tragically. Past errors prepare the way for the future. The content of theories that are no longer valid must be repudiated, but the way in which it was once acquired and experienced may be retained and may survive: that is a consolation for him who fears that our fundamental conceptions, too, will some day be of mere historical interest.

What things would I tackle quite differently, were I to begin over again today? I see a wealth of possibilities before me and could mention many things that I have missed. Neither would I shrink from confessing to this, and from indicating the many domains of mental life that I have not explored. And yet I hesitate to make the answer which rises to my lips. Psychology has undergone such profound changes since 1900 that many wishes of today would have been impossible of fulfillment if not actually meaningless in those days. And most of all I realize that my present wishes have arisen just on the basis of the earlier work I have done. I will quote an example. Today, in individual psychology, we have a dynamic theory of ability, which contrasts quite consciously with the classical, static theory. It teaches us that the original tendencies of man are much more uniform than his subsequently acquired permanent differences of ability. A person determines his abilities—usually in early youth—largely by his own efforts. It is obvious enough how such theories must react upon any educator in the future, in that they augment the field of his possible effectiveness in the most spectacular way. If this theory were correct, an individual would feel himself responsible for his own heights and failures of ability. It is not easy to test one's own level of ability under this aspect. But in so far as one takes the idea underlying this theory at all seriously, evidence for or against it might be derived even from introspection. Owing to my previous work I was particularly receptive for the new theory of individual talent, and often wished I knew a great deal more about the actual development of human abilities in order to be able to appreciate it.

But the older static theory derived from experimental psychology had to be fully known to anyone who would assume a critical attitude toward it. I cannot make up my mind to advise any student— no matter how greatly he may feel attracted by that inexhaustibly interesting subject "human personality"—to begin his training with the study of individual psychology.

But on the other hand I can say something very positive. The importance of personal initiative and independent experience seems to me to be beyond dispute. Of course no one can afford to neglect the psychological literature. But the main thing seems to me to be that one must live some part of it, must find it through personal experience. Anyone who has ever staged even a single experiment may have suddenly gained, through this bit of shop-work, a great deal of insight into the real meaning of experimental psychology. I remember vividly the sense of responsibility and the high tension that accompanied my first experiments. Our own work remains forever an unchangeable and inalienable possession. And this does not necessarily apply only within the psychological laboratory. A visit to an insane asylum under the guidance of a wise and practiced psychiatrist may reveal to a novice the worlds which he wants to explore. And in no lesser degree, a single living impression of the art of pedagogy, one glimpse of an anthropological museum, with its countless evidences of primitive mind, or a chance participation in a single inquiry behind the bars of a prison cell—any of these things may suddenly enlighten a young person as to the particular phase of mental life that appeals especially to him. If I have any wish, it is just this—that I might have had more experiences of this sort. For the most important thing is always to distinguish truly personal experience from that which has been but indirectly known. Young people have a particularly keen sense of what really personally concerns them, quite independently of mere fads and fashions of the time. Today the tendency of the times is not favorable to experimental psychology. It is opposed equally by rational psychology, on the one hand, and individual psychology, on the other, which, springing from the realm of psychoanalysis, tries to supersede it with new demands for insight and interpretation. At the same time, the experimental psychologists may claim in all fairness that it was just their methodology which forced us to break away from our older theoretical concepts. Integral psychology finds its strongest support in experimental data. Does not the very fact that those old concepts could be reforged in the fire of new ideas, the older notion of elements reshaped into the new notion of the whole, speak for the excellence of the original material out of which they were fashioned?[46]

To pay no heed to the tendencies of the age, but rather to make one's decisions according to one's own nature, has ever been the prerogative of youth.

XV. EPILOGUE

While crossing the Atlantic, I have written down the things that rose before my mind's eye. Days of rest are the lot of the traveller. Willingly he yields himself to the majestic rhythms of the sea, his senses filled with rushing of waters and with sunlight, stars rise and set, and in this remoteness from all human activity the soul lies open to the Eternal.

I am finishing this epilogue on the return trip from the Ninth Congress of Psychologists at New Haven. Almost exactly a quarter of a century has passed since that Congress at Rome, when I myself was a student of psychology. The meeting at New Haven showed me once more how vastly psychology has grown, especially in the New World, of which I have just had my first experience. How small, by contrast with this great wealth, appears the compass of my own researches!

And how about the answers to those riddles of the Sphynx which ensnared the boy of 20? The hands of the maturer man of today no longer reach for the unattainable; they grasp more firmly that which has become spiritually his own. But his eyes are still fixed upon the stars, which are just as far away now as they were of yore.

---

[46]Wandlungen der experimentellen Psychologie. In *Zur Psychologie der werktätigen Jugend*. Berlin: Hilger, 1926. S. 14-17.

KARL MARBE*

I. Work in Commercial High Schools and Practical Attitude

The reason why I am only now responding to the very friendly and complimentary request which came a few years ago from Professor Carl Murchison, that I write my biography for this collection, lies in the fact that precisely in the last few years I have been carrying a particularly heavy load of work, from which I am only now beginning to recover somewhat. In addition to conducting my scientific work and my professorship at Würzburg I taught for five and one-half years (up to October 1, 1931) in the Commercial High School in Nürnberg (High School for Social and Industrial Science) where, as in Würzburg, I represented the subjects of psychology, pedagogy, and philosophy, also belonging to the Senate of the high school. In Nürnberg I was furthermore in charge of the Psychological Institute of the Commercial High School.

Although the Nürnberg position became more and more exacting, I enjoyed my work in it. Although in general a university can certainly give a psychologist and philosopher much more stimulation than a commercial high school can, yet my working in such a high school did have certain special advantages for me.

Immediately after the War I had begun to be interested in the psychology of advertising, which arose in the United States and which, like industrial psychology as a whole, was first made known in my country by Hugo Münsterberg. Already in 1924 there appeared a book on the psychology of advertising by Theodor König, then one of my students, which, as the first German book on this subject, had a large circulation, went through three editions, and had been written originally as a doctor's thesis in my Würzburg Institute. Already in the year 1925 I had written for the journal, *Die Reklame,* an article entitled "Die psychologische Beratung bei der Reklame," and before and after this I had been called upon many times by the most varied concerns for expert opinion in the field of advertising. I had been interested from the start in the aptitude tests from America. And even before the War I had

---

*Submitted in German and translated for the Clark University Press by E. Marion Pilpel.

been concerned with the practical significance and utilization of psychology. My essay, "Theorie der kinematographischen Projektionen" (Leipzig, 1910), already aimed at a practical application of psychology. As long ago as 1912, at the Fifth Congress of the German Society for Psychology, in Berlin, I presented an extensive summary of discussions of the significance of psychology for the other sciences and in practical life.

It is plain that this practical attitude of mine, which revealed itself in the above-mentioned activities and also in many other writings, some of which are to be mentioned later, necessarily made work in a commercial high school appear desirable. Also, there were many fields of industrial psychology—as, for instance, the question of aptitude for being a merchant and of the psychological analysis of industrial markets—in which, inevitably, commercial high schools were more interested than universities. In Nürnberg I worked particularly on the psychology of advertising, often lecturing there in conjunction with the Professor of Industrial Management, Dr. Alfred Isaac Kurse, on the psychology and technique of advertising.

It is also quite plain, however, that all my efforts in the field of industrial psychology were necessarily much deepened by association with my Nürnberg colleagues. While my book, *Psychologie der Werbung* (Stuttgart, 1927), was still written primarily during a time when I was not working in Nürnberg, my work on the *Psychologie der Wertreklame* and two essays on the psychology of command and obedience come within my Nürnberg period.

Furthermore, I had already worked once before for a time in a commercial high school, namely, while I was at the Akademie für Sozial- und Handelswissenschaften in Frankfort a. Main, where I taught from 1905 to 1910. During the first semester of 1909-1910 I worked simultaneously in Frankfort and as regular Professor at the University of Würzburg, where, even before moving to Frankfort, I had been for nine years, first as a Privatdozent, then as an externe professor, and finally as Vice-President of the Psychological Institute and for a year also as the official representative for pedagogy.

In my time the Frankfurter Akademie was at the same time a commercial high school, and even today, although it has become a university, it still counts the tasks of a commercial high school among its most important functions. My interest in questions of industrial science had already been aroused in Frankfort, although of course industrial psychology did not exist at that time. The practical attitude which I have mentioned showed itself also in the invention, development, and application of my "Russmethode" (method using smoke of flame for direct recording of voice), to which I devoted a considerable number of articles in the *Physikalische Zeitschrift,* the *Zeitschrift für Psychologie,* and other journals, and which falls within my Frankfort period, although this invention itself originated in purely theoretical considerations. During my earliest activity in Würzburg I had been interested, among other things, in the psychology of lanugage. This interest was perhaps particularly stimulated by a friend who died all too young, the well-known linguist, Albert Thumb, with whom I had published, in Leipzig in 1901, the essay, "Experimentelle Untersuchungen über die psychologischen Grundlagen der sprachlichen Analogiebildung." Later I had published my work, *Ueber den Rhythmus der Prosa* (Giessen, 1907), in which I was able to show, among other things, that the aesthetic impression of a prose work depends essentially upon the rhythm of the work, that this rhythm is different in different works and authors, etc. It seemed a logical step to me then to subject the melody of speech to experiments similar to those relating to dynamic rhythm and to find a technique which suited me for the graphic registration of the melody of speech. In this way I came upon the now generally known "Russmethode," which I at once had Eggert, my student at the time, apply to the melody of speech (*Zeitschrift für Psychologie,* 1908, 49, 218-237), and which later led Thom and me to the plan of investigating the melody of dialects by this "soot method"—a plan which was, of course, frustrated by Thom's death (1915).

I also treated the "soot method" from the theoretical point of view (cf. Marbe, K. and Seddig, M.: Untersuchungen schwingender Flammen. *Annalen der Physik,* 1909, 30, Series 4, pp. 579 ff.), and it has also been applied to phonetics. Its invention likewise led me to the most varied practical applications, which were far remote from the field of language. Thus I have shown that it can also be applied to the graphic registration of heart sounds and pathological heart noises, a fact which lead to the book, *Klinische Untersuchungen über die Schallerscheinungen des Herzens* (Leipzig, 1911), by my friend the internist Ernst Roos, who, alas, has also died.

Further testimony to my practical attitude is borne by my articles, "Ueber Psychologie und Eisenbahnwesen" (*Archiv für Eisenbahnwesen,* 1924, pp. 729 ff.), "Psychologie und Versicherungswesen" (*Zeitschrift für die gesammte Versicherungswissenschaft,* 1925, **25,** 337 ff.), and "Ueber Strafanstalt und Psychologie" (*Zeitschrift für Psychologie,* 1926, **99,** 375-382). Evidence of this attitude is also given by my actual psychotechnical investigations, such as, for example, the one on aptitude for surgery and dentistry (*Deutsche Zeitschrift für Chirurgie,* 1928, **208,** 289-317; *Deutsche Zahnärztliche Wochenschrift,* 1928, **31,** No. 6) and also my little essay on "Psychotechnische und faktische Eignung" (*Industrielle Psychotechnik,* 1928, **5,** 16-20). This attitude likewise explains my wish, which is continually being reactivated, to obtain practical recognition and practical significance for psychology as extensively as possible in the most varied fields of life and science.

Perhaps my largest accomplishment in this respect has been attained through my effort to bring psychology and jurisprudence into closer contact with each other. The first German psychological legal expert opinion was my testimony in a case of sexual assault in Würzburg in 1911, in which I had to discuss the question of the testimony of children. Soon afterwards came my testimony in the suit resulting from the big railroad accident at Müllheim in Baden, which was argued before the Provincial Court of Freiburg i. Br. At that time I was able to utilize not only the psychology of alcohol but also, and especially, the theory of reaction times, which has been brought up so many times since, and must be brought up, in the psychology of accidents. This case was argued in 1912. Since that time, through my agency and that of others, a mass of psychological expert testimony has been submitted, bearing continually upon new circumstances. Thus, for example, in 1930, as an expert witness in a case in Elberfelde, I was able to treat experimentally, among other matters, the question of whether or not certain impostures and deceptions are possible.

My successful activity in the railroad case which I have mentioned, which led to many other similar juridical activities on my part, I owe, incidentally, to pure chance. The district attorney in the case of the Müllheim railroad accident, who is now Reichsgerichtsrat Justus Bender, is one of my friends. When I heard of the accident I addressed myself to him personally and pointed out that psychology was in a good position for explaining much in this connection; I was then named as the medical expert in this case.

My first general publication on legal psychology was my *Grundzüge der forensichen Psychologie* (München, 1913); my most recent work in this field is my little book on the Halsmann case (Leipzig, 1932), in which I discussed in detail the essential significance of the psychological expert, of which I had already frequently spoken. In my work, *Der Psycholog als Gerichtsgutachter im Straf- und Zivilprozess* (Stuttgart, 1926), I presented a survey of the legal activity of psychologists to date.

I attach particular value to my work on the psychology of accidents, to which I have devoted several essays. This work is perhaps best known through my little book, *Praktische Psychologie der Unfälle und Betriebsschäden* (Munich and Berlin, 1926), and again reveals my practical point of view. On the basis of the data of a large insurance company I was able to show that the probability that a given person will have an accident varies directly with the number of accidents he has already had within a given time. Furthermore, on the basis of data from the German railways I was able to show that the probability that a given workman will cause damage will likewise vary directly with the number of times he has already caused damage within a certain period of time in the past. It was also possible to show that those people who frequently suffer accidents are the same ones who repeatedly cause them. Psychological analyses and experiments showed that the psychological prerequisites for the causation of damage and for special liability to accident are, on the whole, one and the same. These facts led me to the concept of the *"Unfäller"* ("accidenter") and to the recognition of the deep significance of the psychology of personality in the avoidance of industrial damage and accidents of all kinds.

Naturally, however, in my book on accidents, the psychology of personality in general also had to be discussed. I had already devoted attention to this subject in my essay in the *Festschrift für Robert Sommer* in the year 1925 (*Zeitschrift für die gesamte Neurologie und Psychiatrie, 1925, 94, pp. 359 ff.*) and later treated it again and again, as in my detailed review, "Persönlichkeit und Aussage," given at a congress of the *Kriminalbiologische Gesellschaft* in Munich (*Mitteilungen der Kriminalbiologischen Gesellschaft, 1931, 3, pp. 89 ff.*) I attach particular value to the concept of the momentary personality (*momentane Persönlichkeit*) and to the fact that, in spite of the great significance of the congenital factor and of the deeper levels of personality, the individual is nevertheless a different person, as it were, each moment. The theory of modifiability (*Umstellbarkeit*), which is of great practical significance, which can be treated experimentally, and which is of importance to the psychology of accidents, among other subjects, my associates and I have discussed again and again. Individuals vary very widely in their ability to adapt themselves to new situations. To many people repeated adjustment of the personality seems desirable and pleasant. To others it is unbearable. I reckon among the more important results of my researches the establishment of the theory of modification (*Umstellung*), which I was able to use, among other places, in an article on homesickness (*Archiv für die gesamte Psychologie*, 1925, **50**, 512-524).

My practical attitude is again shown in my pamphlet, "Eignungsprüfungen für Rutengänger (Munich, 1927), and also found expression in the invention of various pieces of apparatus and series of experiments, of which my apparatus for shifting sectors (*Sektorenverschiebungsapparat*) has probably come to be best known. This apparatus, which I invented as a young physician during my stay in the Leipziger Institut of Wilhelm Wundt, and which I discussed in 1894 in the *Zentralblatt für Psychologie,* Volume 25, pp. 811 ff., makes it possible to change the sectors of a rotating disc during the rotation. I had heard that the Physikalisch-technische Reichsanstalt in Berlin was working on the solution to this problem, so I plunged into the question and completed my apparatus and published it considerably sooner than the Reichsanstalt finished its efforts. Today both sets of apparatus, which, incidentally, are based upon quite different principles, are widely used.

Always, however, my practical efforts have been closely related to my interests bearing on theoretical psychology. This connection, to my mind, is necessary. "The psychologist who stops his studies when they lead him to practical attitudes and practical measures incurs the just reproach of narrow-mindedness. But one who aims only at practical results lapses into a wretched technicalistic psychology (*Laboranten psychologie*)." This was approximately what I said at the Kongress der Deutschen Gesellschaft für Psychologie (at that time the Gesellschaft für experimentelle Psychologie) in Munich (1925), amid the general approval of my auditors.

II. Basic Attitude on Pure Theory. Student Period. Entrance into the Faculty of the University of Würzburg

The practical attitude which I have strongly emphasized so far, and which, of course, was associated with pleasure in practical results, developed very slowly in me and at present seems to be receding again. When, at the age of 18, I passed my matriculation examination in my native city of Freiburg i. Br. and then served there as a volunteer for one year, during which I was registered as a student but could not study, my orientation was at first a purely theoretical one. Pure science was my ideal. At that time all practical activity seemed to me inferior. At first I had intended to study Germanistics and modern German literature, and during my first semester in Freiburg after my period of military service I attended lectures primarily in philology, literature, and philosophy. At that time I was interested particularly in Old Norse, Middle High German, and Sanskrit. I was introduced to philosophy by the famous philosopher, Alois Riehl, who was then teaching in Freiburg and with whom I had a two-hour seminar on basic philosophies of life. With the newer psychology, then only little known in general circles, I was occupied only incidentally in that I made the personal acquaintance of Hugo Münsterberg, who was at that time active as a Privatdozent in Freiburg, and also attended his one-hour lecture course on hypnotism. Incidentally, it was something quite new to have university lectures on this subject, and Münsterberg was probably one of the first to lecture on hypnosis in an institution for higher education.

Toward the end of my student period in Freiburg I asked my instructor in Germanistics, the philologist, Hermann Paul, who was also then working in Freiburg and who later became very famous, where I ought to go to continue my studies, as I had no desire to go on studying at home indefinitely. Paul advised me quite decidedly to go to Halle, where the professorship in Germanistics was held by Sievers, whom he esteemed very highly and who later became known to the psychologists through his investigations (to my mind entirely erroneous), or rather his assertions, on the psychology of language and of music.

Sievers and his students taught that every author is characterized by a special voice quality (*Stimmqualität*) and that absolutely every work created by man in the field of sound, whether language or music, is dominated by certain sound constants (*klangliche Konstanten*) which are of basic importance in the character and effect of the sound product (*Klangwerk*) and show large individual variations. Sievers claimed that it was possible, on the basis of difference in voice quality alone, to decide whether a given piece of prose or poetry was to be ascribed to one author or two different authors. Never, however, did Sievers conduct real experiments with which he might support this theory, which at first found many adherents but then decidedly lost in interest. At the Kongress für Aesthetik und allgemeine Kunstwissenschaft in Berlin in 1914 I first made Sievers' acquaintance. Not only I but also the Berlin psychologist, Carl Stumpf, and others opposed his theory at that time.

I did not follow Paul's suggestion that I transfer my studies to Halle. I wanted not only to study but also to enjoy the world and life, and therefore, at the end of April, 1890, I went for one semester to Bonn, which had been described to me as one of the loveliest of the German university towns. Here I continued my studies in philology, but also came in touch with Götz Martius, a student of Wundt's, who was a Privatdozent at Bonn at that time and who had been mentioned to me by Münsterberg. At that time Martius was making all sorts of reaction experiments, in which I helped him and which increased my interest in modern psychology. I also attended his seminar on Spinoza, which deepened my philosophical interests. I also began at that time to read other philosophical classics besides Spinoza, and I continued this reading during the subsequent vacation and during my whole student period.

During the following Winter Semester, 1890-1891, I studied in Berlin, having meanwhile decided to become not a germanicist or a literary historian but a philosopher. I still remember quite definitely that, upon my arrival in Berlin, I wrote to a friend that I had now decided to devote myself entirely to philosophy, which had always interested me. How I came to this decision, however, is hard to state in a few words. Certainly I did not make it in the course of a few days or weeks. Rather it undoubtedly matured quite gradually. At that time I considered myself a young man who was rich or at least very well-to-do, and in a certain sense I really was.

For being rich consists not in having an income of $30,000 or more but in having an income which exceeds one's needs. At that time not a soul dreamed of the losses of income which we Germans were to incur as a result of the War and inflation. And the thought that I would ever have to or wish to live on the income of a professor was quite foreign to me. The reason why I turned first to the study of philology and literature lay in the fact that one of my teachers at the Gymnasium at Freiburg had especially aroused my enthusiasm for these things. Philosophy, in which another teacher had interested me, I had regarded only as absolutely necessary to the intensive study of literature. It gradually interested me more and more, however, and all other scientific interests receded proportionately into the background. Thus my subsequent intention of becoming a philosopher did not represent a real transfer to another field, but rather only a gradual redirection of my interests. Also, when I came to Berlin, I naturally was not thinking of choosing psychology as my special subject. At that time in Germany there was probably no one who held the view, which I stressed strongly later on, especially at the Congress of Psychologists in Marburg in 1921, that psychology should be separated from philosophy as a distinct field. And when, in Berlin as previously in Freiburg and Bonn, I did do some work in the new psychology, which at that time we called experimental or even physiological psychology, I did this only because, in my opinion, this, too, belonged to philosophy.

My Berlin psychological studies were conducted under the guidance of Hermann Ebbinghaus, who was at that time Professor Extraordinary in Berlin. I studied philosophy under the famous historian of ancient philosophy, Eduard Zeller. I also attended additional lectures, in part regularly and in part as an auditor, in order to further my general culture, which I regarded from the first as fundamental for a philosopher.

In the summer of 1881 I returned to Bonn, where I studied mainly with the three regular professors of philosophy, the Kantian Jürgen Bona Meyer, J. Neuhäuser, the authority on Aristotle, and Wilhelm Bender. Bender was an evangelical theologian who had been moved out of the evangelical-theological into the philosophical faculty because of his very advanced views. Through Neuhäuser, who, incidentally, was a scholasticist and thoroughly clerical in his orientation, and through student friends of mine in the field of classical philology I was stimulated to extend my philosophical reading to ancient philosophy and to do it more in the original. I cannot say that, except in this one respect, I received very much stimulation from the three teachers named above. It would be more accurate if I said that the fact that I did not allow them to frighten me away from the study of philosophy shows that my interest in philosophy was very active at that time.

At that same time in Bonn I also attended the big laboratory course in physics under Heinrich Hertz, the discoverer of the electric wave, and his assistant at that time, Philipp Lenard, later the famous Heidelberger physicist, while I frequently used my vacations, which I usually spent in Freiburg, to work in a private chemistry laboratory there. In Bonn I also attended the lectures in physics and chemistry by Hertz and Kekulé. It was thus not until this second Bonn period, which lasted up to the time of my doctorate examination (1893), that I began to study the natural sciences.

During this period I again worked with Martius, under whose guidance I had, as a student, already written an article on the fluctuations in visual sensations (*Philosophische Studien,* 1893, **8,** 615-637) and in whose private institute I also wrote my doctor's thesis, "Zur Lehre von Gesichtsempfindungen, welche aus successiven Reizen resultieren" (*Philosophische Studien,* 1894, **9,** pp. 384 ff.).

The article on the fluctuations of visual sensations bore upon a problem treated several times by students of Wundt under the head of fluctuations of attention. I was able to show experimentally that these fluctuations are not really fluctuations of attention, but rather fluctuations in sensation. That a philosopher should hand in as his dissertation an experimental study of successive stimuli and visual sensations at that time caused some surprise and shaking of heads. It did not do me any harm, or at least not much, in connection with my receiving the degree, for I received it with the designation *"insigni cum laude,"* not frequently given in Bonn at that time. I was examined for an hour each by Jürgen Bona Meyer and Neuhäuser in philosophy. Just before this examination I had to take the *Magisterexamen* (master's examination) in mathematics, natural sciences, history, and classical philology, each for one-half hour. This utterly senseless Bonn arrangement, which kept many people from taking their degrees in Bonn, and by which of course any half-way thorough knowledge of the subjects was not to be expected, has meanwhile been quite abolished. In classical philology I was examined by the famous philologist, Bücheler, who put before me the *Ethics* of Aristotle, which I was easily able to master, as I had read more difficult writings of Aristotle.

Perhaps I would have handed in, in Bonn, not an experimental but a purely philosophical piece of work as a dissertation if I had been more strongly attracted to the teaching of the three regular professors of philosophy mentioned above. Perhaps I might not have remained in Bonn at all if I had not been held by certain personal relationships to which I will revert further on.

During my second stay in Bonn I also studied more closely the writings of W. Wundt, to whose *Grundzüge der physiologischen Psychologie* my attention had already been directed by Münsterberg in Freiburg. Wundt's combination of medical and specifically physiological, psychological, and general philosophical interests, and his great literary productivity impressed me tremendously at the time. I read many other modern philosophical authors also during my student period in Bonn. It was always, however, the association of universality with specific scientific achievement which I valued particularly then. A comprehensive view over the whole realm of science and considerable positive research and achievement in special fields seemed to me to be the distinguishing marks of a great philosopher. I was not yet capable then, since I still lacked independent judgment, of reaching my later opinion that W. Wundt frequently erred as a positive investigator. Another whom I counted among the most universal and important thinkers of the new era was Eugen Dühring, whose writings I have probably read *in toto,* who was active in political economy, mathematics, and natural science, and of whose weaknesses I was likewise not aware at that time. That I was still woefully lacking in universality I did recognize, however. To acquire it more fully than I had yet been able to do and to work first of all in the field of modern psychology in a scientific way was my next plan.

I therefore went for a year to Leipzig, where I found much stimulation in Wundt's Psychological Institute, in which I prepared many problems for my future research, and where, incidentally, I was inscribed as a medical student and now also studied anatomy and zoölogy.

Returning to Bonn for a third stay, I worked there in the Zoölogical Institute. I also wrote my faculty habilitation thesis (*Habilitationsschrift*), to the contents of which I had already given much thought in Leipzig. My two Bonn studies and the little Leipzig article, already mentioned, on the apparatus for shifting sectors (*Sektorenverschiebungsapparat*) were related to more comprehensive studies in the field of physiological and psychological optics. In connection with these studies and especially with my dissertation I developed my habilitation thesis, "Theorie des Talbotschen Gesetzes," which was later published in *Philosophische Studien* (Volume 12, pp. 279 ff.), and whose contents were again utilized later in the article, "Theorie der kinematographischen Projektionen," likewise mentioned above. I showed that Talbot's law and all the facts connected with it can be deduced from very simple physical and mathematical considerations.

With this piece of work I entered the faculty in Würzburg as a Privatdozent in the entire field of philosophy. In order to enter I had to discourse upon a purely philosophical theme, the Freedom of the Will, assigned to me three days in advance, and to defend twelve theses, proposed by me, which belonged almost exclusively to philosophy proper, and which, I must admit, make a very childish impression upon me when I read them through again today.

The reasons why I chose to teach in Würzburg were personal. In Berlin and Leipzig I had made the acquaintance of a group of young, active psychologists and philosophers to whom I was indebted for much stimulation. Among my fellow students in Berlin were Arthur Wreschner and William Stern, who are at present working in the Universities of Zurich and Hamburg, respectively. Among those studying in Leipzig at that time, with many others whose acquaintance I made, were the present Professor of Pedagogics and Philosophy in Freiburg i. Br., Jonas Cohn, the present Professor of Psychology in Turin, Friedrich Kiesow, and also the Pedagogical Therapeutist, Theodor Heller of Vienna, famous today. I also established a very stimulating relationship with Ernst Meumann, who at his death was professor in Hamburg and who, in my Leipzig period, was Wundt's second assistant. I owed most, however, to my association with the young Privatdozent, Oswald Külpe, who in my time was acting as first assistant in the Leipzig Institute.

Külpe had uncanny industry and was, even then, better read than I have ever become. The fullness of his reading, which he was continually extending, spread not only over psychology and philosophy but also over the most varied other scientific fields. Külpe, with whom I ate lunch regularly in Leipzig and whom I also saw much of otherwise, both inside and outside of the Institute, was always accessible for all questions I asked and for the explanation of all problems I attacked. The appreciation which I accordingly and inevitably felt for Külpe soon showed itself to be mutual, although I realized even then that he and I were quite different sorts of people and represented quite different types of young scholars with scientific interests.

During my third sojourn in Bonn, Külpe had been called to Würzburg as a regular professor (*Ordinarius*). And in view of our friendly relations and of everything which I owed him it was of course natural that I should seek my field of activity in the place in which he had gained a decisive influence upon instruction and investigation. Also, in view of our relationship and the lack of another private instructor, it was quite agreeable to Külpe that I should come to Würzburg, especially since he was making an attempt (in which he also succeeded) to establish a psychological institute in Würzburg and since he knew that he could be sure of my help and practical collaboration in this.

It should be clear from the details of this chapter that the practical attitude was really quite foreign to me at first. At most, one might see certain modest beginnings of a practical point of view in the fact that I helped Martius in a practical way to build his apparatus for the investigation of reaction time to sounds—a fact which he explicitly emphasized (Martius G., *Philosophische Studien,* 1891, 6, 403) and in the fact that I invented in Leipzig my apparatus for shifting sectors.

III. Later Life and Work up to the Present Time

My first period of work in Würzburg, lasting for nine years, was the most pleasant period of my academic career. The teaching went very well. During the first semester (the Summer Semester of 1896) I gave a one-hour public course on Arthur Schopenhauer and, during the second semester, a private colloquium on the general history of philosophy. The next semester I taught Ethics. It was only gradually that I undertook the teaching of psychology also. The teaching and my successes gave me much pleasure. At that time, already, as I do today, I attached particular importance to expressing myself clearly and understandably, while at the same time presenting as much material as possible. Külpe, who was himself a popular and respected teacher, was far from envying me my effectiveness; on the contrary, he seemed to rejoice in it almost more than I did.

Already, during my third stay in Bonn, I had devoted myself to a certain type of teaching with great pleasure. I not only helped Martius in his work in his private institute but also prepared many friends and other students who were working toward their degrees in Bonn for the doctor's examination. The situation was that everyone whose main subject was not philosophy (and it was but rarely that a philosophy major came to Bonn at that time!) had to be examined for half an hour in philosophy during the doctor's examination. Philologists, chemists, in short, everyone who wished to obtain the doctorate, thus also had to undergo an examination in philosophy. Since many students were naturally not at all suited to this field and since most of them had not attended philosophical lectures and moreover had not even covered the field, a philosophical coach for the philosophical portion of the doctor's examination was much in demand at that time. Since it was already pretty well known what the three regular professors of philosophy usually asked in the doctor's examination, and since they were also willing to have the students take a special, not too large field as the subject in which they wished to be examined, I did not find the coaching, which I regarded as a sort of sport and for which I never accepted pay, too hard.

Today, also, teaching has undeniable attraction for me, but my manifold scientific interests and other tasks somewhat limited the pleasure of instructing. My lecture courses today I usually enjoy only while I am on the platform, though I am as enthusiastic about teaching in the Institute and in seminars as I was before.

My scientific activity during my first stay in Würzburg was expressed in a series of publications on psychological optics, in which I entered partly into opposition with Götz Martius. I also pointed out at this time in an essay in Pflüger's *Archiv für die gesamte Psychologie* (1903, 100, pp. 551 ff.) that Talbot's law and all facts connected with it are valid and must be valid in the field of acoustics also. That during my first stay in Würzburg I also did research in the psychology and the esthetics of language I have already stated above.

In my work, *Naturphilosophische Untersuchungen zur Wahrscheinlichkeitslehre* (Leipzig, 1899), I approached a very different field. In school I had already become familiar with the elements of the calculation of probability. In the work mentioned above, I treated, as d'Alembert had done before me, the problem of the agreement of experience with the expectations to be cherished on the basis of the so-called a priori consideration of the probabilities. These studies I resumed in my two-volume work to be mentioned later, *Die Gleichformigkeit in der Welt* (München, 1916-1919), in which I was also able to utilize my work with Thumb, *Experimentelle Untersuchungen über die psychologischen Grundlagen der sprachlichen Analogiebildung* (Leipzig, 1901), mentioned above, and other later publications of mine connected with it.

In my work with Thumb, belonging in my first Würzburg period, it was shown for the first time that the association reactions of a rather large number of subjects in response to the same stimulus word were to a large degree the same. There are always the most preferred, next preferred, etc., reactions, and finally some which are purely idiosyncratic (*auseinanderfallend*). There was also revealed the law of familiarity (*Geläufigkeitsgesetz*) according to which, on the average, the more familiar a reaction is, i.e., the large the number of subjects, relatively, in whom it occurs, the more rapidly it occurs. These and allied facts have found their way into many other writings and have also led to the so-called association test, since it has been found that it is possible to draw certain conclusions from the fact of whether a subject does or does not conform to the general regularity of the process of association. Linguistically the work showed that the words which in the history of language have influenced each other in the direction of linguistic analogy formation are at the same time those which show themselves to belong together on the basis of the association experiments.

My strongest influence, however, during my first stay in Würzburg was probably exercised through my work, *Experimentellpsychologische Untersuchungen über das Urteil* (*Eine Einleitung in die Logik*) (Leipzig, 1901). Studies in logic had shown me that the logicians have widely varying opinions on the psychological nature of judgment. I therefore determined to investigate the nature of judgment from a purely psychological point of view. I requested several trained subjects, under quite definite conditions set by myself, to make judgments and to give accounts of the conscious processes which occurred while they were judging. The large amount of material which I obtained in this way showed that all the prevailing psychological theories of judgment, including W. Wundt's—that it is an analysis of a total concept into its parts—were erroneous. In fact, I came to the conclusion that no psychological criterion of judgment existed. Many judgments of the utmost practical importance seem to take place quite reflexly, as it were, or automatically. The merchant or the mathematician who adds 2 and 7 and obtains the answer 9 carries out this judgment process without the presence, or need for the presence, of experiences particularly characterizing judgment. Many psychological considerations and experiments which had paved the way for this work also led me at that time to the concept of "conscious set" (*Bewusstseinslage*). It appeared that a reduction of the whole conscious life to sense perceptions, memory images, and feelings of pleasantness and unpleasantness, such as was the rule at the time, was entirely inadequate, and that quite different experiences exist which are not, or are not yet, accessible to analysis, and which I designated as conscious sets. In my work at that time I discussed the conscious set of doubt, of uncertainty, of expectation, of surprise, of agreement, of recognition, and many other conscious sets. The "feelings" of tension and relaxation and other experiences described by Wundt as feelings were accordingly classed in my work under the head of conscious sets. More obvious conscious sets, too, such as the recollection of conversations, were deduced by me from my experimental records. Others have subsequently used the expressions "consciousness" (*Bewusstheit*) and "thoughts" (*Gedanken*) for the whole or parts of what I designated as conscious sets.

This essay, in which the consciousness of understanding, also, was explicitly discussed on the basis of experiments and which dates the beginning of my opposition to Wundt, who until then had always been very fond of me, is the first work in which the psychology of thinking is systematically and experimentally treated. That its results are by no means all negative, as someone recently stated them to be, is already shown by my theory of conscious sets.

My methodological procedure was likewise entirely new. That there cannot, however, be a positive criterion of judgment follows from the fact that the concept of judgment must be conceived as a logical and not as a psychological one. As I have explicitly shown in the essay referred to, whether conscious phenomena should or should not be treated as judgments depends upon the meaning (*Sinn*) we attribute to them, but not upon their psychological structure. This meaning may be but is not necessarily given in consciousness in the form of conscious states (*Beswusstseinslagen*). Also, the value of a judgment for science and for practical life is in no way dependent upon the conscious processes which represent the judgment, but solely upon whatever we wish to express through the judgment, although of course this desire for expression need not necessarily be really conscious at every moment. The merchant into whose calculation the proposition "twice two is four" blends quite automatically is, of course, making a judgment just as truly as is the A-B-C-scout (*Abc-Schütze*—first grader) who painfully works out this proposition.

This essay led Külpe to assign to Mr. H. J. Watt and Mr. A. Messer further subjects in the field of the psychology of thought. I was somewhat vexed by this, perhaps somewhat unjustly, and did not like to see the psychology of thought, which at the time lay very close to my heart, being led into fields in which I could not make my full influence felt. When, in the Spring of 1905, before Watt and Messer had yet completed their work, I responded to a call to Frankfort, K. Bühler, too, came to Würzburg, and worked on the psychology of thought afresh, entirely under Külpe. Also, Külpe assigned his students still further studies in the psychology of thought. Finally he, too, first in the Fifth Congress of the *Gesellschaft für experimentelle Psychologie* (1912) in Berlin, then in the *Internationale Monatschrift für Wissenschaft, Kunst, und Technik* (also in 1912), and finally in his philosophical book, *Die Realisierung* (Leipzig, 1912), took a stand in regard to the psychology of thought. He finally spoke of the "monarchistic arrangement" of our consciousness and said: "The Ego sits upon the throne and carries out governmental acts. It observes, perceives, and ascertains." Although I had previously intended to do so, I did not work specifically any more on the psychology of thought, but in an essay (*Fortschritte der Psychologie und ihrer Anwendung-*

en, 1915, 3, 27) I did reject, sharply and on the basis of explicit reasons, the course which the psychology of thought was taking under, after having previously repeatedly expressed my concern to him verbally, without success even though without actual contradiction on Külpe's part.   For this essay, which had been directly stimulated by the avowed performances of Külpe and which appeared shortly before his death (1915), Külpe never forgave me.

In this essay I also emphasized my independence of Külpe in this field.   Much as I owe him, I have never been his student.   I never attended a single lecture of his and never took part in the laboratory work which he directed.   I was never his assistant and never worked in fields which he had suggested to me or in which he had previously worked himself.   And if I have ever been independent in anything it has been in having arrived independently at the idea of applying the method of systematic introspection (*Selbstwahrnehmung*) to the study of logical thought.   Although Külpe acted as a subject in my experiments on the psychology of thought, this fact showed only that he was interested in this work, as in all my work at that time.

Taking over ideas from other people to develop them has never been my interest.   It is only in independent work that I really feel at ease; from the start I have emphasized the attainment of new facts, trying at the same time to pursue the study of psychology in as exact a way as possible.   I was animated by this striving when I tried to place the psychology of thought upon an experimental basis. When a younger psychologist wrote that the striving after precision was the weakness of my school, I gladly accepted this reproach, since I regard it as the highest praise by which our work can be distinguished.   I necessarily disapproved, however, when another psychologist, in the course of a scientific discussion, attempted to disparage the direction of my researches by using the expression "fact finding" (*Tatsachenforschung*).   In my opinion, theories have a place in science only in so far as they explain facts or have a heuristic significance for the obtainment of new facts.

I naturally regret very much that I displeased Külpe in the essay I have mentioned in the *Fortschritte der Psychologie und ihrer Anwendungen.*   Perhaps after all I should have been more cautious in my choice of words, although, before having it printed, I had the essay read through by my wife and by a professional psychologist who now holds a regular professorship, and although I took into account, to a large extent even though not completely, the mitigations of expression which were suggested to me. For the rest, Külpe, when I read him the most important parts of the manuscript of my essay, *Experimentelle-psychologische Untersuchungen über das Urteil*, with which I desired to found a systematic psychology of logical thought, was at first very enthusiastic. The fact that he then turned aside from me with his school was undoubtedly due to the circumstance that, when Külpe was further developing the psychology of thought, I was no longer in Würzburg but in Frankfort, and that he now yielded to other influences than mine.

One of the reasons why I found my first stay in Würzburg very satisfying was that, in agreement with Külpe, I was able to stimulate independently some work by students, to guide it, and to lead it to conclusion. The fact that the number of auditors at my lectures declined after a few semesters and only gradually increased again I cannot regard as evidence against my statement that I was a successful teacher.

This decline is to be explained as follows. I was baptized and brought up as a Catholic and bore a name which had a very good sound in Catholic-ecclesiastical circles. An uncle of mine was a Central representative in the Reichstag and in the Bavarian Diet. I myself had gone beyond any Catholic or even generally religious attitude, since my school days. My name, however, attracted at first a large number of incipient Catholic theologians to my lecture room. These soon perceived, however, that I was not, as they had probably at first expected I would be, a representative of the Catholic attitude toward the world.

My leaning toward complete freedom also became known far and wide through an occurrence which is not without interest. In a public lecture on the problem of causality, I had occasion to discuss in great detail the cosmological evidence of God, and also to characterize briefly the other arguments for God. In this connection I contested the stringency of these arguments (in the Kantian manner) without otherwise entering into the question of the existence of God. In March, 1898, one of the many rural and priestly representatives then belonging to the Diet made a long, spready speech culminating in the assertion that a teacher in one of the Bavarian upper schools had said before his class, "We do not need to discuss the evidence for the existence of God, for there is no God." This reputed statement was discussed in detail everywhere by the speaker himself and by several of his colleagues. It was said that evidence of the existence of God had been suppressed, and that there had been dishonesty, pedagogical tactlessness, and other nice things. Only v. Landmann, the minister of public worship and education, who likewise was close to the centrist party, maintained that such debates never led anywhere. Since the aforementioned attacks of the representatives bore upon my person and my lecture on the problem of causality, he then had me make a written report on the occurrence. At the same time, all available students of mine were questioned on the content of that lecture. This questioning led to the finding that neither this statement nor any statement of similar meaning had been made in my lecture. Thus, all the gossip in the Diet resolved itself into idle talk at the cost of the Bavarian taxpayers, and the instigator of it, after being sharply reprimanded, was obliged to make a public acknowledgment of his mistake. One of my auditors had told a clergyman about the content of the lecture in question, and then, through the spreading of gossip (according to the well-known facts of the psychology of rumor), there developed a statement which was entirely nonsensical and almost the opposite of what I had said. Although the matter was thus settled very favorably to me, I was nevertheless branded in the eyes of many who had originally been well disposed toward me. Auditors with Catholic tendencies all removed themselves from me at first. They were replaced by others, and in the course of the following semesters confirmed Catholics also again appeared at my lectures.

During my first stay in Würzburg, I also began to work into the field of pedagogy. Even in Leipzig my attention had been called, through talks with Meumann, to the possibility of applying modern psychology to pedagogy. Also, Külpe had suggested to a student by the name of Johann Freidrich a thesis on the effects of duration of work and pauses in work on the mental achievement of schoolchildren. This study later appeared in Volume 13 of the *Zeitschrift für Psychologie und Physiologie der Sinnesorgane* (1897, pp. 1 ff.). I had also obtained some information from other experimental-pedagogical studies. At that time I still knew very little about these matters, however. It was not until I came under the influence of Meumann's book (*Vorlesungen zur Einführung in die experi-*

mentelle Pedagogik und ihre psychologischen Grundlagen, 1st ed., Leipzig, 1907) that I acquired a stronger interest in psychological questions in the field of education and instruction. And later I not only assigned to my students many dissertation topics relating to psychological pedagogics but I also worked in this field again and again. Thus, in the study already mentioned on psychotechnical and practical ability, I showed to what a great extent the achievements of children in the same grade at school depend upon their chronological age. Finally, in association with Ludwig Sell (*Zeitschrift für Psychologie,* 1931, 122, pp. 177 ff. and pp. 188 ff.), I also studied the dependence of school achievements upon the environment and upon the occupation of the parents of the children.

Still less did I understand, during my first teaching period in Würzburg, of the history of pedagogy, which I had not yet studied at all. The historical study of pedagogy and with it my general pedagogical interest were well set on the road, however, by an external circumstance. The Würzburg professor of pedagogy, Lorenz Grassberger, who has become known through his work on education in ancient times, had retired from his teaching in the year 1901. The position could not immediately be filled. The history of pedagogy absolutely had to be given, however, at least for one semester of the year. At the end of the Winter Semester of 1901-1902, Professor Martin Schanz, then rector, known through his studies on Plato and through his history of Roman literature, came to me and urgently requested me to give a course in the history of pedagogy. My objection, that I knew nothing about the subject, was not allowed to prevail, and finally I consented. Immediately and during the subsequent vacation and during the Summer Semester of 1902 I read pedagogical classics and textbooks almost day and night, and in the same Summer Semester I gave a four-hour course in the history of pedagogy which, while certainly not the work of a trained professional, was nevertheless quite adequate.

In Frankfort, to which I moved, as stated, in the year 1905, I had the opportunity, with large means placed at my disposal, to establish a Psychological Institute and a notable philosophical seminar. In addition to working on my soot method (*Russmethode*) I was busy with quite different problems there too. Specifically, I began in Frankfort to work on my philosophical essays, which I published under the title of "Beiträge zur Logik und ihren Grenzwissenschaften" in the years 1906-1912 in the *Vierteljahrschrift für wissenschaftliche Philosophie und Soziologie.*

During my stay in Frankfort, where I also took a very active part in the upper-school affairs of the Academy, which was then evolving into a university, and where, as already stated, I was planning many practical applications of my soot method, my practical tendencies began, for the first time, to develop strongly—tendencies which subsequently, during my second stay in Würzburg, were even more strongly brought out through my legal involvement, the influence of American industrial psychology, and other agencies.

In Frankfort, too, I stimulated various scientific studies by students. Here, too, I found satisfaction in teaching, although the satisfaction was not as strong as it had been during my first, and was again during my second, stay in Würzburg. The auditors of the new Frankfort upper school (*Hochschule*) consisted of young commercial high school students, high school teachers, high school superintendents, physicians, society ladies, and people from many other circles. Although I was able to be effective through my suggestions in the Institute, it was nevertheless very diffcult to offer in the lectures something which should be equally satisfying to all the different elements of which my audience consisted.

I must not neglect to state that, in Frankfort, at the age of 38, I married the painter, Milly Fries, the daughter of a Frankfort manufacturer, who has very zealously continued her activity to this day, and who since her marriage has been exhibiting under the name of Milly Marbe-Fries. Although my marriage has remained childless, it has nevertheless been a very happy one.

Having returned to Würzburg in the year 1908, I worked (besides doing much other writing of which I have already spoken in part) particularly on my two-volume work, *Die Gleichformigkeit in der Welt* (Munich, 1916-1919), in which I discussed from the most varied points of view the problem of uniformity, to which I had been led by the consideration of probability and by studies on association. It had already been shown in my essay with Thumb that, the reactions of subjects in association experiments are concordant to a very large extent, and now I was able to show in addition that the behavior of human beings, when they are subjected to similar conditions, reveals striking similarities or uniformities to a greater extent than it was previously assumed to do.

During my second stay in Würzburg I also wrote my essay on animal psychology, "Die Rechenkunst der Schimpansin Basso im Frankfurter Zoologischen Garten" (*Fortschritte der Psychologie und ihrer Anwendungen*, 1917, 4, 135-186). This animal had brought thousands and hundreds of thousands of people into the Frankfort zoo to admire its arithmetical skill. Before her lay a pile of little tablets upon which the numbers from 1 to 10 had been written. Then the caretaker said, for example, "Basso, how much is 10 minus 8?" whereupon the chimpanzee took a tablet into her hand upon which stood the number 2. The caretaker thought that he had systematically instructed Basso in arithmetic, but then became convinced that, after all, her achievements were due not to instruction but rather to thought transference. The superintendent of the zoo was not able to account for the behavior of the chimpanzee. And when, while I was temporarily staying in Frankfort, I had occasion to see Basso at work, I too was completely at a loss. Through systematic investigations which the superintendent of the zoo permitted me to conduct, I was finally easily able to show, however, that with his questions the keeper combined involuntary and unconscious movements, on the basis of which Basso figured correctly. Thus what was here revealed was essentially the same as what had been established previously by Pfungst when he was studying Clever Hans, the calculating horse of Mr. von Osten in Berlin.

Subsequently I have used this study, in which I also treated more general questions in animal psychology, again and again as a point of departure of the emphatic statement that it is only through systematic experiments and not through mere observation that apparently mysterious performances of human beings and animals can be solved.

I have tried in many other writings, also, to reduce occultistic statements to their proper scope by means of an exact scientific attitude. I treated in this way the problem of the wishing rod (*Wünschelrute*), among other problems. Unfortunately, however, I cannot maintain that I have achieved anything in a practical way by my fight against occultism. The mob's craving for sensation, especially in periods of economic depression such as we have had to experience in Germany since the War, is far too strong to be shaken by the sober expositions of a scholar. I found out, inevitably, in this as in other fields, that faith is much stronger than science.

It was not until the time of my second stay in Würzburg that I attained a following on a larger scale. A large number of studies of the most varied kinds issued from my Institute here. Slips of the pen, the problem of instruction in languages, the testimony of witnesses, the psychology of lying, musicalness, the psychology of the deaf and dumb, and many other quite different matters were investigated by my students under my direction. Some of these studies have appeared in the five volumes of my *Fortschritte der Psychologie und ihrer Anwendungen* (1913-1922). Other studies have been printed in other journals, mainly in the *Archiv für die gesamte Psychologie,* in the *Zeitschrift für Psychologie,* and in the *Psychotechnische Zeitschrift.* About 90 doctors' theses and other publications by my collaborators have come out of my Würzburger Institute, not including the many studies by my assistants. My own studies have been published in psychological, philosophical, natural science, legal, and medical journals. Many studies by me which are not mentioned in the present article have been listed under "Marbe" in the "Psychological Register," edited by Professor Carl Murchison. Many have not been mentioned there either.

I have certainly come to realize more and more clearly that fame is not an advantage, but rather a disadvantage, and that in particular to flirt with the practical calls forth a mass of inquiries, correspondence, and studies which one would often be very glad to do without. Therefore, as already indicated above, my practical ambitions have gradually been receding. At present I am again turning toward philosophical problems, so far as other unavoidable tasks permit.

IV. Supplementary Remarks. Personality. Youth

We may make acknowledgment when, as I have done, a scholar continually turns toward new questions and when he inspires efforts here and there and works on a great variety of problems. This type of activity can undoubtedly also be criticized, however.

A professor on the staff of one of the three high schools in which I was working once criticized a habilitation essay before us because it gave the impression of being a piece of occasional writing rather than a study resulting from systematic work. In a certain sense, I can say that all my writing has been occasional writing (*Gelegenheitsschriften*). Almost always I have been guided by certain notions or ideas which I obtained in the course of my reading, conversation with scholars or men of practical life, or other experiences, and I have never been able to decide to study a field for the sake of writing an essay or a book about it.   If some few of my writings have resulted from stimulation by a third person, I have responded to this stimulus only when I believed that these writings offered me the opportunity of expressing in action, or at least of publishing, ideas that were in my mind.

It is clear that I cannot treat a subject successfully unless it interests me strongly, and I have no talent for what Herbart calls an even distribution of interest over everything such as is involved in large systematic studies.   Today I have even reached the point of basing my study of scientific literature almost solely upon my own ideas and investigations and, of course, also upon the requirements of my teaching.   Clearly, the urge to investigation, the wish to have an effective influence upon science and life, and the aim of being able to offer my students the material they need have become the exclusive, or almost the exclusive, deciding factors in my work.

I mentioned above that, as a student, I regarded universality and achievement in special fields as the principal earmarks of the great philosopher.   Undoubtedly, I have achieved a certain modest universality in that I have extended my studies, more than it is customary to do, over the most varied fields.   To deepen and broaden this universality, however, as Herbert Spencer and Wilhelm Wundt did, for example, and on the basis of this to progress to systematic works on a grand scale was not granted me, because I lacked this even distribution of interest.   The wish, too, to bury myself in subjects which held my interest, even when they were not of general interest, hindered my development into a universal philosophical author. When I had once set myself a problem, my desire was to exhaust it to the extent of my ability, and to touch upon a thousand questions, gaining only a literary mastery over them, has never appealed to me. And, lastly, I have also recognized that the authors of large systematic works have hardly ever been able to avoid superficialities in detail which I have always personally strenuously repelled, although I do not on this account reject work of a more encyclopedic trend.

When Külpe saw, in Leipzig, that I kept on working again and again on the construction of the apparatus for shifting sectors (*Sektorenverschiebungsapparat*) and the outlines of my theory of Talbot's law, he remarked, without meaning to reprove me, shaking his head, that that type of activity was impossible to him.   And indeed he and I were quite different scientific personalities.

I ultimately noticed that I was much too critically minded by nature to make a universal writer on philosophical subjects. In the early period of my activity I wrote a large number of reviews and also some very sharp critical essays. As I have already stated above, my critical attitude brought me into opposition with Martius, Wundt, and also Külpe. Other oppositions, too, have arisen through my critical attitude. Although today I avoid polemics and no longer enjoy the writing of criticisms, I undoubtedly still have, even now, a very critical attitude toward others, and also, if I am not very much mistaken, toward myself. This critical attitude, too, was a hindrance to the writing of large systematic philosophical works.

And, in conclusion, writing itself, even to this day, has never come as easily to me as it does, and must, come to the productive writer on philosophical subjects. Rather, I am still inclined, even now, to reflect on almost every word which I write down or dictate.

In speaking of my critical manner, I am far from regarding it as a pure asset. "You always emphasize only what separates us and never what unites us," the philosopher, Heinrich Rickert, once said to me when I had personal association with him for a time and had explicitly criticized his book, *Die Grenzen der Naturwissenschaftlichen Begriffsbildung* (*Part I*), in the *Zeitschrift für Philosophie und philosophische Kritik,* and had taken a critical attitude toward his views in other places also. He was not far wrong in his observation, and in it he showed, perhaps unintentionally, that critical endowment also constitutes a weakness to a certain extent.

Just as I could not manage to write large systematic philosophical works, I could not manage to write philosophical textbooks or other kinds of textbooks, although I consider the writing of good texts, which, in the subjects I have taught, are decidedly lacking, in my opinion, as exceedingly meritorious work. To begin with, in view of my personality, I would find the writing of a textbook much too tedious. Historical problems, too, and also historical researches, have never fascinated me, although I have done much teaching of the history of philosophy and of pedagogy.

My desire was always to do concrete research, and, after attaining my practical attitude, to influence not only science but also practical life. When I had once made a subject the object of my research, however, I never ceased my investigation when my research led me beyond the borders of the subjects I officially taught in the high school. Thus I took particular pleasure in making my soot method (*Russmethode*) useful in as many ways as possible. And thus also my studies in uniformity have led me far beyond psychology and philosophy proper and have made it possible for me to be influential in many varied fields, as for example in sociology. And it is solely because of my urge to keep on investigating when I was possessed by ideas on uniformity that my two-volume work, *Die Gleichformigkeit in der Welt,* which is, of course, neither a systematic philosophical structure nor a textbook, became so enormous. In this I was also led into the field of mathematics. That I influenced several great mathematicians through this work could easily be proven. But that here, precisely in connection with mathematics, I was frequently guilty of errors should not be concealed but rather emphasized. In my latest essay, *Der Strafprozess gegen Philipp Halsmann* (Leipzig, 1932), I did not hesitate to use legal questions also, particularly in connection with Austrian jurisprudence, as subjects of my discussions.

It is possible to advance the cause of philosophy by large systematic works and by textbooks, but also, of course, by criticisms and by attacking special problems, as I tried to do particularly in my book on uniformity in the world and in my essays in logic and kindred sciences. If, however, I compare my philosophical writing with everything else that I have written, it occupies only a modest space, especially in comparison with psychology. That I have applied myself so extensively to psychology is not due, any more than was my transition from the history of literature to philosophy, previously discussed, to very definite resolutions. Psychological questions simply gradually came to interest me more than the actual philosophical ones. And the more I worked myself into the field of psychology the stronger my interest in this subject became.

Naturally, however, the form of my activity was determined not only by my innate personality but also by the stimulation that I received from all sorts of directions and which I obtained particularly from scholars with psychological interests. In addition to those cited above, I must mention here Alfred Binet, in whose Institute I worked immediately after my doctorate examination during a long vacation in Paris, and with whom I came into friendly relation. Incidentally, even today I regard myself as a psychologist only in that I have worked primarily in the field of psychology. Just at present, as I have already stated, I am again engaged in philosophical studies. That I may ultimately adopt quite different subjects as the object of my interest, however, is by no means out of question on principle so far as I am concerned. I have long recognized, however, not only through scientific psychology but also on the basis of ordinary common sense, that my capacities are not as many sided as, in the frenzy of youth and in my first enthusiasm for science, I had foolishly taken quite for granted that they were. When I began to study, I did not even consider the question of capacity at all, and at that time I overvalued the importance of the will in relation to achievement to an almost unbelievable extent.

There are many other things, too, done or not done in the past, which I am compelled to criticize today. Although I certainly made my studies cover many fields, I nevertheless omitted important matters. Thus, for instance, I regret today that I did not study psychiatry more thoroughly from the start. While I was a student in Bonn, the well-known psychiatrist, C. Pelmann, was giving well-liked lectures on borderline states, which he also discussed in his book *Über die Grenzen zwischen psychischer Gesundheit und Geistesstörung*. It did not occur to me, however, to attend either these or other lectures on psychiatry. It was not until later that I made myself familiar with psychiatric topics, utilizing for this familiarization (not until a few years ago, either) a rather long period of study in an asylum for the insane. Undoubtedly, it would have been much better for my development if I had earlier occupied myself more with psychiatry. It is true, however, that in my time other young psychologists were not thinking either of the importance of psychiatry for our field. I have also regretted very much that during my entire student period I did not come closer to jurisprudence, with which I did not come into more intimate touch until the time of my expert testimony in the Müllheim railroad accident case and in which, since then, mainly under the guidance of my highly esteemed Würzburg colleague, the criminologist, Friedrich Oetker, I have done considerable work. While I was studying, my opinion of jurisprudence, Heaven knows why, was much too low. Today I do not doubt that this important field would have held me spellbound if I had turned to it in the beginning, and that I might very well have found fulfillment in the study of jurisprudence too.

So far, I have spoken only of my studies and my scientific work and never of *not* studying and *not* working. The reader would receive an entirely false picture of my personality, however, if I did not also bring out that I have not been, and am not, oriented toward science as exclusively as might appear from the discussion thus far. Just as, when a student, I chose the University of Bonn not for scientific reasons but because I wished to live by the beautiful Rhine, so during my student period and later I also had a great many other extra-scientific interests. For decades I was particularly absorbed in hunting. Even as a schoolboy I was sometimes taken along by hunters and later I spent a large part of my life in hunting. Apart from the fact that I followed hunts and accepted invitations here and there, I rented, sometimes alone and sometimes with other hunters, lovely hunting grounds (especially on the upper Rhine), in which I felt extremely happy, since unhindered wandering in the midst of beautiful nature, but above all the passion for hunting, had a strong hold upon me. For months I lived on the hunting grounds, where I thought almost exclusively about game and dogs. Here I often used practically to forget that I was also a scholar and a professor, and it was a great annoyance to me to receive letters and packages here which reminded me of my profession. Temporarily, to shoot well seemed much more important to me than to do good scientific work. And often, when in the Fall I returned with my guide from the hunt and we were both so laden with partridges, pheasants, and wild ducks that our upper bodies had become almost invisible, or when I had shot a fine buck or a rare piece of game, I was prouder than I could have felt if I had invented perpetual motion. But a strange thing happened. About ten years ago I had so many professional duties for a time that I did not have a chance to hunt, and all at once I had lost all of my great interest in hunting. And yet formerly I would never have thought it possible that I would be doing scientific work and even giving lectures longer than I would be hunting.

I had the same experience with many other interests. As a schoolboy I did a good deal with music. I learned to play the piano and at the age of 16 began to play the violin too. Toward the end of my school period I also took courses in the theory of music, in harmony, and in counterpoint. Then and later I hardly missed a concert which seemed to me at all important. But these music interests too, although they have certainly not been completely lost, have given place, in the main, to others. For a few years I was very enthusiastic about difficult mountain and glacier climbing, which I later regarded as superfluous. Toward the end of my schooltime I felt very sympathetic toward the drinking customs, the societies, and other practices of German students, and my school work at that time was much less important to me than the imitation of these things, which at that time were current among the pupils of the upper high school classes in university towns. But by the time I had finished my military service I was no longer enthusiastic about these student activities. In Bonn, it is true, I joined the so-called Bonner Kreis, in which I established many relations of personal value, but this club was not a student society in the usual sense. It was rather a club with many decades of existence, officially quite unknown and externally quite inconspicuous, made up of young people with serious scientific interests, particularly classical philologists, who were held together solely by a certain tradition and not by any sort of statutes or regulations of that kind, and who, within the widest limits, permitted each individual to pursue happiness in his own way. The very advantageous scientific stimulation which I received here and the friendly relationships which I established, and which, as I indicated above, partly were influential in directing my studies into the field of ancient philosophy, have led me back to Bonn again and again.

I cannot, of course, name here all the places and persons to whom I owe scientific inspiration. I have already mentioned my colleagues in Nürnberg and Frankfort. Other sources have also been cited. By far the largest debt, however, is the one I owe to the University of Würzburg, in which to this day, in all the faculties, I have found men who were interested in my problems and from whom I have learned much. Many advantageous relationships have been established by correspondence and in national and international congresses. My students and assistants, too, have encouraged me again and again. Among the latter may be cited Mr. F. E. Schultze, now regular professor in Königsberg, Mr. W. Peters, who migrated with me from Frankfort to Würzburg and who is now regular professor in Jena, Kurt Koffka, well known in America too, who was my assistant in Würzburg while I was teaching simultaneously in Frankfort and in Würzburg, O. Sterzinger, now professor in Gratz, my Nürnberg assistant, Ludwig Sell, and my present excellent assistant in Würz-

burg, the instructress (*Privatdozentin*), Maria Schorn. I must not
forget, either, my technician, Joos, who has been with me for many
years, who helped me particularly with the apparatus for the soot
method, and who also migrated with me from Frankfort to Würzburg.

When I was speaking of hunting and other matters, just now, I
mentioned that my interests have often changed. This is not a
striking fact in and for itself. I do believe, however, that this
tendency to shift is stronger in me than in most other scholars.
Clearly, I do not come as close to being all of one piece as do some
of my colleagues, and I am ruled more strongly than they are by a
certain restlessness, as is shown in my manifold activity, always
attacking new problems, and in my disinclination to write large
systematic treatises covering entire fields. It cannot be said, however, that I easily abandon views or experimental findings which I
regard as correct, or that in general I am particularly inclined to
vacillation in judgment. Clearly the changes in question relate
particularly to personal values, which I assign sometimes to one and
and sometimes to another scientific or extra-scientific activity. That
the frequent change in my interests was and is accompanied by a
change in my knowledge is obvious. While during the first part
of my academic career I took great pleasure in often conducting
practice classes in the translation of Greek authors, I have now, because of the regression in my knowledge of the Greek language, long
felt myself incapable of this, and while as a student in Bonn, as the
only pupil of the well-known Sanskritist, Jakobi, I had to translate
a text from German into Sanskrit once a week, I have now forgotten
even the letters of the Sanskrit alphabet. I do not see any special
disadvantage in these and similar instances of forgetting. We do
not learn and work in order to retain everything. But the personality which is ours at a given time is essentially dependent upon
those earlier experiences which have long sunk into the subconscious,
as I have stated again and again in my writings on personality.

Although, of course, the history of populations runs a strictly logical
(*kausal*) course, yet nevertheless historical development is also dependent upon what we call chance occurrences. Who would deny
that the World War and misfortune that it has brought to Germany
was caused to a large extent by the politicians and other persons who
then happened to be at the helm in Germany and elsewhere? Who

would deny that, in all the great decisions in history, accidents, that is, factors which in themselves seemed to be unimportant, have played a rôle? The same thing happens in the life of the small individual human being. And thus it has been with me, too. For, although my development was surely determined essentially by my innate personality, yet other factors, such as are called accidents, have also been decisive.

I was born in Paris on August 31, 1869, as the only child of my parents. My father, like my mother, was of German descent and was conducting in France a business which consisted primarily of the exportation of French merchandise into Germany and other countries. A few years after my birth, however, my father became ill. A few years later he found himself compelled to give up his Paris business activity and to move to his home city of Freiburg i. Br. to rest. And a few years after that, when he was only 37 years old and I was only eight, my father died in Freiburg. If he had stayed well as long as I, we would not have moved to Germany for decades, if at all, and my whole development would thus have been different. My father said to my mother before he died that he thought I ought not to become a merchant, but that I ought to study. Well-educated people, he said, had a much lovelier life than business people, who were compelled to struggle day and night. Thus it came about that, after I had spent a few years in the Freiburg elementary public school, I was sent to the Bertholdsgymnasium there, which, except for the public continuation school (*höhere Bürgerschule*) was the only upper school in Freiburg. I was well pleased with this arrangement, since other people, though not my mother, had suggested to me that the high school student, the university student, and the member of a learned profession was a much higher being than a business man. When I had entered the "Gymnasium," however, I was told that I must work hard, or I would be sent to the continuation school. I am not able to judge today whether it was so especially fortunate for me that my father expressed that wish and that during my upper-school life I was not so careless or lazy that I was not immediately taken out of the "Gymnasium" and transferred to the continuation school. But I am definitely convinced that my entire development hinged essentially upon the type of education which I was given. This type, that is, the humanistic, undoubtedly tended to turn me away from practical life and to develop the theoretical attitude of which I spoke above and which was balanced only to a certain extent later on. A more detailed discussion of the course of my school life and adolescence is not likely to be of interest here. The only thing I would still like to emphasize here is the idea that my tendency to go my own way in science and not to attach any special value, in general, to the treatment of topics of the day has probably also been favored by the fact that I never had any brothers or sisters and that hence an essential basis has been lacking for adapting myself to others.

I have also failed in such adaptation in that I have failed to read the autobiographies of other psychologists that are already available before starting to write my own. It did occur to me, however, that in his valuable work, for which he deserves many thanks, Professor Murchison was not only collecting biographies but also seeking to further the psychology of personality, a thing which can certainly be done most successfully if each author proceeds quite independently. I shall study the remaining sections of the book with all the more pleasure on this account after my lines have been printed.

CHARLES SAMUEL MYERS

INHERITED AND EARLY INTERESTS

I was born in London on the confines of Bayswater and Notting Hill on March 13th, 1873. My father (one of nine brothers and sisters), both my grandfathers, and my four great-grandfathers were all business men in or near London. My mother (one of 15 brothers and sisters) was wonderfully sociable and had exceptional powers of musical expression and pianoforte technique; one of her brothers was attracted in an amateur way to philosophical and historical studies; a third, who founded a successful firm of solicitors, gathered in his leisure hours a celebrated (the Montagu) collection of coins. Two of my father's brothers spent their later bachelor life in travelling, one of them devoting himself to Egyptology.

Thus perhaps I can account for my interests in organizing and in humanity, my love of music, my enjoyment of travelling, and my attraction to archaeology. But I can find little hereditary basis for my early attraction either to literary composition or to chemistry—a subject then taught to all pupils save in the lowest forms of the City of London School, which I entered at 11 years of age. I remember buying for myself pieces of phosphorus and sodium at about the age of 12, throwing the latter into water and the former into a vessel of oxygen in the basement kitchen of my London home, and nearly injuring the cook and myself by the accidental explosion of a hydrogen-making apparatus which I had made from purchased parts. At 13 I constructed a cylindrical frictional electrical machine out of a wine-bottle. Meanwhile at school I kept to a mainly classical curriculum, gaining prizes in English composition and showing such promise in Latin prose and verse that my classical composition master bade me hesitate, when at the age of 16 my candidature for a Cambridge entrance scholarship came under consideration, whether I should offer classics or natural science.

Indeed, my first hard conflict arose at this juncture. As his eldest son, I knew that my father would have liked me to enter his business. But as a wise father, he bade me to consider myself at full liberty to make my own choice. I decided to try for a scholarship in natural science at Gonville and Caius College in 1891. But my science master at school knew little biology and less physiology, and in the private tuition which he gave me I used to find him reading my textbook in physiology (Michael Foster's) so as to keep just ahead of me. I left school in 1890 and joined a year's course in elementary biology, chemistry, and physics at St. Bartholomew's Hospital. Thus, hurriedly and poorly equipped, I gained an entrance exhibition, and soon after a foundation scholarship at Caius.

UNDERGRADUATE DAYS

My idea when I entered Cambridge University in 1891 was to prepare for the medical profession. I spent my first two years there in working at chemistry, physics, botany, zoölogy, and physiology, becoming especially attracted to botany (in which I gained a College prize) and most of all to physiology. In my second two years (1893-1895) of undergraduate life, I specialized in physiology and human anatomy. The latter, as then taught for the second part of the Natural Sciences Tripos, was a subject of remarkably wide scope. As Sir Michael Foster once said, "The whole subject of comparative religion forms but a small part of Cambridge human anatomy!" Fired by my teacher Dr. A. C. Haddon's enthusiasm, I became specially interested in physical and racial anthropology. Before I took my B.A. degree in 1895, I had already begun investigations (published in 1897 in the *Journal of the Anthropological Institute*) on a recent find of ancient skulls in a field near Brandon in Suffolk. I also remember deducing, in my undergraduate days, from a table of angles of torsion of the humerus set out in an American publication on certain ancient Mexican skeletons, that this particular people must have been left-handed—only a few years later to find that, from an examination of certain Mexican pottery, the supposition had been entertained that it had been made by a left-handed people.

The first piece of organization for which I remember myself responsible was concerned with amateur theatricals at the age of about 15. At Cambridge much of my undergraduate leisure time was spent in reorganizing the University Musical Club devoted to the amateur performance of chamber music, in which, as violinist, I took a prominent part. I had already dipped into epistemology and the history of philosophy during and even before my undergraduate years at Cambridge. I had read Buckle's *History of Civilization* and Huxley's philosophical essays; I had purchased Lewes's *History of Philosophy* and I had chosen Herbert Spencer's works for a College prize.

THE ORIGIN OF EXPERIMENTAL PSYCHOLOGY AT CAMBRIDGE

On leaving Cambridge, I had no idea as to my future career. Certainly I felt disinclined to medical practice. My main interests were by then divided between anthropology and experimental psychology. My introduction to the latter subject had come about in the following way. In 1893, Sir Michael Foster, Professor of Physiology, realized the need for more expert university teaching in the special senses and also in physiological psychology. But, as long ago as 1877, Dr. Venn and Professor James Ward, from the philosophical side, had tried (but failed) to establish a laboratory of experimental psychology at Cambridge. Had this effort been successful, Cambridge, instead of Leipzig, could have boasted of being the first University to found such a laboratory. In 1882, and again in 1886, further fruitless attempts had been made in this direction. But in 1891 the Special Board for Moral Science was more helpful, and a grant of £50 was obtained from the University for psychological apparatus in connection with Professor Ward's lectures. About this time, too, Professor McKeen Cattell, from New York City, spent a short period at Cambridge, where he gave some informal instruction in the subject, resident as a fellow-commoner at St. John's College. Finally, in 1923, Sir Michael Foster's choice, in his search for a teacher in the physiology of the special senses, fell on Dr. W. H. R. Rivers. He was officially attached to the Special Board for Moral Science, and gave lectures at the University both on the senses and on experimental psychology, holding a practical course in both subjects in a small room lent him by Sir Michael Foster in the physiological laboratory. I attended Dr. Rivers' first course.

ANTHROPOLOGICAL FIELD WORK

Soon after I left Cambridge in 1895, Dr. Haddon began to plan his Cambridge Anthropological Expedition to Torres Straits (New Guinea) and Sarawak (Borneo), and asked me if I would join it. He proposed that it should leave England in March, 1898, and I realized that by that time I could have just managed to obtain a medical degree at Cambridge and at the College of Physicians and Surgeons. My interests in anthropology and psychology, my keen desire for travel, and my ready acquisition of foreign languages bade me accept this invitation. Dr. Rivers was also able to be a member of this expedition, and at my suggestion my contemporaries, William McDougall, of St. John's College, and C. G. Seligman, of London University, were invited (and agreed) to join it. My leisure time in my student days at the hospital was partly spent in orchestral playing in the hospital orchestra and in the Royal Amateur Orchestral Society.

As I have said, I had already decided not to become a medical practitioner, but largely through my intimate friendship with the late Professor A. A. Kanthack, begun at St. Bartholomew's Hospital, I was becoming strongly drawn to research in pathology. Had it not been for his premature and grievous death in 1899, I might have returned to a study of the subject. But his death and the experiences of the expedition left me in little doubt as to my future career. In Torres Straits I assisted Dr. Haddon in investigating native rites and customs. But my main work lay in cooperation with Dr. Rivers, and I devoted myself chiefly to a study of the hearing, smell, taste, reaction times, rhythm, and music of the peoples in Torres Straits and Borneo among whom I spent the following 12 months.

I returned from the Cambridge Anthropological Expedition in March, 1899, just in time to take up the appointment of House Physician at St. Bartholomew's Hospital promised to me before I left England. A few weeks before the termination of this office, in March, 1900, a breakdown in health forced me to Egypt, where I wintered at the end of this year and also in the following year. During the latter half of 1900 I wrote a criticism of Ward's *Gifford Lectures on Naturalism and Agnosticism,* which was published in 1901 in the *Philosophical Review.* While in Egypt I studied hieroglyphics, stayed with excavators of antiquities, and journeyed on camel to the Great Oasis. In 1901 I prepared an M.D. thesis on *myasthenia gravis* and I carried out a study of native tattooing and an extensive piece of anthropometrical work in Cairo and Khartum among the soldiers of the Egyptian and Sudanese Armies, which were later published in a series of papers in the *Journal of the Royal Anthropological Institute,* 1903-1908. I had to decline an invitation from the late Sir William Garstin in 1901 to accompany him on a visit to Abyssinia.

PSYCHOLOGICAL WORK IN CAMBRIDGE AND LONDON

In the Spring of 1902, thoroughly restored to health, I resumed residence in Cambridge, where I remained for the next 20 years, save for the period of the Great War. I was at first engaged in working out my Torres Straits, Sarawak, and Egyptian psychological and anthropometric data and in carrying out research on the upper limits of audible pitch. In 1903 I was offered a lectureship in Liverpool under Sir Charles Sherrington, but I declined it as he could offer me no assurance of his retention of the Professorship of Physiology at that University.

By this time I had begun helping Dr. Rivers in the conduct of his practical classes in experimental psychology at Cambridge. He had become University lecturer in experimental psychology and physiology after some years and was using as his laboratory three rooms in a dilapidated building in St. Tibbs Row, unwanted by the Pathological Department for which the building was then serving as its temporary premises. In 1903 the Psychological Laboratory was transferred to 16 Mill Lane, a cottage belonging to the University Press, of late used, but now vacated, by the Department of Surgery. In this year Dr. Rivers secured from the University the munificent grant of £50 for the purchase of instruments and a promise of £50 annually for the maintenance expenses of his laboratory.

In 1904, the year of my marriage, I was offered but declined the paid Secretaryship of the British Association, and I was appointed University Demonstrator in Experimental Psychology at Cambridge, shortly after I had begun part-time teaching work in the subject at King's College, London. Here a Professorship was created for me in 1906 and I carried out research with Professor H. A. Wilson, now of the Rice Institute, Texas, on the influence of binaural phase differences on the localization of sounds. Although our explanation of this influence (in terms of intensity differences) has not gained general acceptance, no other hypothesis has since been proposed which does not, to my mind, present equal or greater difficulties.

During this period I was also engaged in making observations on the color sense of my eldest infant, and I was largely occupied in preparing my *Text-book of Experimental Psychology,* the first edition of which appeared in 1909. The sole books on the subject in the English language hitherto available were the purely laboratory manuals of Titchener and Sanford. None of the existing textbooks on psychology devoted adequate space to describing the results which had been reached by experimental methods. About this time my attention had been directed to the importance of some knowledge of statistical methods; and so, for the first time in any scientific textbook, a chapter on this subject was included in my book. Through Dr. Rivers' teaching I had become impressed also with the importance of a thorough training in the psychophysical methods, no other natural science possessing so refined and delicate a system of experimental procedure. I believe that the several "schools" into which psychology is now so unfortunately divided, and to none of which I have ever been able to give undivided allegiance, owe their existence largely to lack of training in these methods and to the undisciplined conduct of research, the rash generalizations, the prejudice, and the influence of suggestion thus engendered.

It was partly in order to insure adequate knowledge of the psychophysical methods that I began my textbook with a study of the sensations, although I made it clear in my introductory chapter that sensations must not be considered as the simple, original elements of experience but are to be regarded rather as the outcome of ultimate differentiation and analysis in psychology. I recall, by the way, with what pleasure in later years I received the intimation from one of the leaders of the Gestalt school (who had undertaken the translation of my book into German, which was interrupted by the Great War and finally abandoned) that he had been largely influenced in his extreme insistence on context, configuration, and structure by the just-mentioned views which he had read in the first chapter of my textbook. In 1911 I published a briefer, more popular *Introduction to Experimental Psychology* with the object of informing the general public concerning the scope of psychological experiment.

I resigned my London work in 1909, when I was forced to take a six months' rest, and was then appointed University Lecturer in Experimental Psychology at Cambridge, Dr. Rivers now dividing with me his former joint lectureship in this subject and in the physiology of the senses.

In 1910 I was appointed by Cambridge University to a syndicate instructed to arrange for and to report on the provision of a suitable laboratory for experimental psychology, in place of the "damp, dark, and ill-ventilated cottage" (as it was publicly described) which then did duty for the purpose. The cottage was at that time being used by 14 elementary students, by two others doing advanced work, and by three research workers, as well as by the lecturer and demonstrator. It was hopelessly overcrowded. In 1912 the new laboratory was opened, which I had planned after holiday visits to American and German universities. It contained on three floors a lecture-room, mechanic's room, animal room, library, experimental classrooms, dark-room, sound-proof room, and research rooms. My father had died just before this time and I devoted anonymously part of the money which he had left me to defraying most of the cost of the building in his memory. It remains, I think, the finest psychological laboratory in Great Britain and one of the best planned of any elsewhere. In the same year I was appointed Director of the Laboratory and in the following year was granted an Assistant paid by the University, in addition to a Demonstrator who was paid out of the fees received.

Meanwhile, I was endeavoring to improve the university status of the subject and to promote a wider interest in it. I was largely concerned in establishing in 1912 the University Diploma in Psychological Medicine which was unique in requiring written and practical examinations both in psychology and in neurology—two most important adjuncts to the equipment of the thoroughly trained psychiatrist. Unfortunately another diploma in the subject was later established elsewhere in England, in which these needs were not thus recognized, and, being more readily obtained, it attracted a greater flow of candidates. For this reason, when economic considerations pressed heavily on Cambridge after the Great War, and also through lack of sympathy from a quarter in which fuller cooperation might have been expected, the Diploma was subsequently abandoned.

I was also responsible for getting an examination in psychology included at Cambridge in the choice of so-called special examinations in the curriculum for the Ordinary (pass) Degree for B.A. In this examination, established in 1911, animal and educational psychology could be offered as additional optional subjects. In 1914, a Tripos in Anthropology was established, which I likewise initiated. I was further closely concerned in the foundation of the *British*

Journal of Psychology in 1904, which in 1914 became the organ of the British Psychological Society. It was edited at first by Professor James Ward and Dr. Rivers, and from 1911-1913 by Dr. Rivers and me, when I became the sole responsible editor, continuing to act in that capacity (save while on active service during the War) until 1924. Thus I started on a life of article-reading, manuscript-revision, and proof-correction, from which I have never since been free. My research at this time related mainly to primitive music, synaesthesia, the influence of timbre and loudness on auditory localization, individual differences in the attitudes of listeners to musical sounds, and visual contrast. The research rooms of my laboratory at Cambridge were in such demand that it was already becoming difficult to accommodate my research students and staff. Through it passed F. C. Bartlett (now my successor at Cambridge), Cyril Burt (now of London), Eric Farmer and H. Hartridge (London), John Laird (Aberdeen), E. O. Lewis (London), J. P. Lowson (Brisbane), C. A. Mace (St. Andrews), B. Muscio (Sydney), W. Sprott (Nottingham), Frank Smith (Newcastle), R. H. Thouless (Glasgow), C. W. Valentine (Birmingham), and others who have since obtained University or research appointments.

War Work

My wife and I spent our Summer holidays during these years usually in mountain-climbing in Switzerland, thus qualifying me later for membership of the Alpine Club, and I amused myself with masonic activities and with organizing professional orchestral concerts in Cambridge. When the Great War came in August, 1914, I tried vainly to continue the work in which I was then engaged, of studying the unique records of Australian music which the late Professor Baldwin Spencer had presented to the large collection of phonographic musical records which I had gathered together from all parts of the uncivilized world. I was then 41 years of age and, on applying to the British War Office for service in France, I was informed that no medically qualified volunteer who was over 40 years old could be accepted. A few weeks after the outbreak of war, I resolved to journey to Paris *in mufti* and succeeded in persuading the Commandant of the Duchess of Westminster's Hospital, which was about to open at Le Touquet, to appoint me as Hospital Registrar. Early in 1915 I was given a commission in the Royal

Army Medical Corps in France, and received the welcome news of my election into the Royal Society of London, into which Professors C. Spearman and F. C. Bartlett have since followed me. In March of that year I was instructed to proceed to Boulogne and to supervise the treatment of functional nervous and mental disorders occurring in the British Expeditionary Force. In 1916 I moved to General Headquarters at St. Omer, where I was appointed Consultant Psychologist to the British Armies in France and had to visit the special wards for "shell shock" and mental cases, both in the many base hospitals and in the casualty clearing stations nearer the front, which had by this time been established.

I must have been, I suppose, the first to recognize, in the British cases of "shell shock" in France, the essentially psychological nature of this condition and to apply psychotherapeutic measures, chiefly by obtaining persuasively the recall of repressed memories, with or without the aid of light hypnosis. The first successful results of such treatment were published by me in the *Lancet* during 1915 and 1916. During 1916, I also visited various field hospitals and certain advanced dressing stations immediately behind the firing line where I created opportunities of examining cases from their very outset, e.g., testing their first urine for sugar in relation to possible adrenal overstimulation by emotional shock. With psychotic disorders I had had virtually no experience, but my psychological and medical training was probably sufficient to justify my frequent appearance as witness in court-martial cases concerning a soldier's degree of responsibility for desertion or for other serious infractions of discipline. By 1917, when I was quartered at Abbeville, I had quite a large staff of psychotherapeutic specialists under my supervision, and the British armies had grown so vast that my duties became necessarily confined to one half of the total zone which they covered. During that year, I had the opportunity of visiting and reporting on the methods of segregation and treatment of psychoneurotic and psychotic cases practiced by the French Army.

Throughout my work in France I had to meet no little opposition from the Army Medical Service and the Adjutant General there. Indeed I doubt if even at the end of the War their original attitude was wholly changed that the "shell-shocked" soldier was necessarily a coward and that a deserter must be either a certifiable lunatic or a criminal deserving only of being shot. Hardly any of the administrative army medical staff recognized the value of the therapeutic work so devotedly and assiduously carried out morning, afternoon, and often evening by the excellent temporary medical officers who acted under my supervision. And when after the Armistice I had the courage to complain to the Director General of Medical Services at the War Office concerning the studied neglect to award these officers any honor for their wonderful services, the only success I achieved was the award to myself of a C.B.E., which, in the circumstances, I declined to accept until ultimately, without any application on my part, I received in 1919 the King's command to attend one of the investitures.

It is not surprising, therefore, that, when in France, I was only partially successful in getting my various recommendations accepted, and that by the end of 1917, at my own request, I was recalled to England, there to act during the rest of the War as assistant to Dr. (Colonel) W. Aldren Turner through whom I had received my original appointment in France. My duties now consisted in inspecting military shell shock hospitals throughout England and Scotland for the War Office, and in endeavoring to bring harmony among a body of dissatisfied home specialists. This last phase of my army service I began by residence at Dr. Rows's successful hospital for "shell shock" cases at Maghull, Lancashire. Here I reached the definite conclusion that I could never owe allegiance to any one of the various schools of psychoanalysis or of psychotherapy, preferring to recognize the undoubted partial truths in each and to refuse acceptance of their wild and mutually antagonistic generalizations. Here, too, owing to the chance remarks of an old pupil whom I found there, Professor T. A. Pear, I first came into touch with industrial psychology. He drew my attention to a book on the subject recently written by a Cambridge pupil, subsequently my demonstrator, the late Professor B. Muscio.

During the last year of the War I spent most of my leisure time devising tests, and supervising their application, for the better selection of men suited to hydrophone work, in which they had to listen in order to locate enemy submarines. This I carried out at the request of Captain (now Admiral) W. W. Fisher, Chief of the Anti-Submarine Department of the Admiralty.

On demobilization I returned to Cambridge, fired with the desire to apply psychology to medicine, industry, and education and becoming increasingly disgusted, after my very practical experience during the War, with the old academic atmosphere of conservatism and opposition to psychology. I found that the wild rise of psychoanalysis had estranged the Regius Professor of Physic; I received little encouragement from the Professor of Physiology; and the Professor of Mental Philosophy, to my surprise, publicly opposed the suggested exclusion of the word "experimental" in the title, now about to be conferred on me by the University, of Reader in Experimental Psychology. Thus medicine, physiology, and philosophy had little use then at Cambridge for the experimental psychologist. About this time I had obtained another academic distinction (which I should easily have gained in any other subject), but only by declining otherwise to return to Cambridge. And I lost two of my ablest research workers there owing to their outstanding merits' not being recognized by a Government Research Body on whose grants they were dependent for their work. On the other hand, a school for high-grade mental defectives had been established near Cambridge, and here an able research student, Miss L. G. Fildes, came to work under my supervision. Thus I was brought into close touch with various Bodies concerned with mental deficiency and mental hygiene.

INDUSTRIAL PSYCHOLOGY IN LONDON

In 1918 I gave two lectures to the Royal Institution which were subsequently published in a booklet under the title of *Present-Day Applications of Psychology*. This led to my contact with Mr. H. J. Welch and to our joint successful efforts to found in London the National Institute of Industrial Psychology. Towards the end of 1918 I obtained a year's leave of absence from Cambridge mainly in order to reflect on my situation, during which I wrote my first book on industrial psychology, entitled *Mind and Work*. In 1921, when this book appeared, the new Institute became finally incorporated, with Mr. H. J. Welch as Chairman and myself as Director (later Principal); and by the following year I had realized the physical impossibility of developing simultaneously the Institute's work in London and that of the Psychological Laboratory at Cambridge.

It was no easy measure to decide which work to abandon. I had spent most of my life from 1891 to 1922 at Cambridge. I had secured what would have been practically a life-long University appointment and a College Fellowship. My wife was devoted to Cambridge and hated the conditions of London life. But she left the decision entirely to me, and, influenced, I suppose, by the applied psychological work which I had been doing during the War, I resolved to desert academic life and, as my less friendly critics have said, to plunge into the business world—in imitation, if they but knew it, of my forbears. But, deeply as I loved and continue to love Cambridge, I have never had cause to regret my decision.

From 1922 onwards, therefore, I have given most of my available time to the development of the National Institute of Industrial Psychology. My able assistant and pupil, F. C. Bartlett, succeeded me as Reader at Cambridge, finally being promoted to a University Professorship in the subject. In 1932, jointly with Mr. Welch, I published a history of the first decade (1921-1930) of my Institute's work under the title of *Ten Years of Industrial Psychology,* from which I hope I may be permitted to quote here the following passages.

> On its incorporation the Institute started with two rooms. Its premises in Holborn were three times extended during its eight years' occupation of them—until 1928, by which time congestion and consequent interference with effective work had become so serious that it was forced to move to ampler offices, which it found in Aldwych House, Aldwych, W.C.2. . . . The latter comprise twenty-six rooms, and include well-equipped laboratories, library, lecture room, research rooms, rooms for vocational guidance, clerical offices, staff room, etc. In 1920 the staff consisted only of the present Principal and Director—Dr. Myers and Dr. Miles. By 1930 it numbered about fifty persons, including some thirty-five investigators, research workers, departmental heads and their assistants—practically all of them university graduates.
>
> The general scope of the Institute's work was planned on lines similar to those of a hospital medical school; the Institute would engage in practical work, research, and teaching, none of which could be effectively carried out singly by an organized body, apart from the two others. The practical work was to consist in undertaking investigations into the improvement of the human factor in factories, etc., in introducing better methods of selecting the workers best fitted for vacant positions, and in advising young people as to the careers for which they were most suited. The research work was to include the study of the human conditions necessary to give optimal output, the con-

ditions of mental and muscular fatigue and boredom, and the devising of tests and other methods for better vocational selection and guidance. The teaching was to include the establishment of a library, propaganda work among employers and employed, training courses, and university and other lectures.

The fees received by the Institute for its investigations (charged at cost) now amount to about £20,000 annually. They relate to practically the whole domain of industry. Membership has grown to nearly 1600. A considerable body of research work carried out under my supervision has been published—on tests of mechanical ability, the measurement of manual dexterities, performance tests as a measure of general intelligence, problems of attention and of perseveration, vocational guidance, etc. Courses of University and public lectures have been given and published on muscular work, incentives, accidents, rationalization, etc.

From 1918 onwards, for more than ten years, I was also closely connected with the early work of the Industrial Fatigue (later called Industrial Health) Research Board, being a member of this Government Body, serving on several of its Committees, and giving much time to its initial organization and to the supervision of its investigators' reports. One of the Board's first reports, published in 1918, I wrote myself on movement study in an iron foundry; for another report, describing an experimental inquiry into the effects of the menstrual period on muscular and mental efficiency, I was largely responsible.

THE BRITISH PSYCHOLOGICAL SOCIETY

In 1919 I was mainly instrumental in changing the constitution of the British Psychological Society, which had been founded in 1901 and of which I had been the Secretary from 1906-1910. Henceforth it was divided into sections (now) comprising the general, medical, educational, industrial, and aesthetic sections, each with its own officers, the first three of these publishing separate journals. Henceforth, too, membership was no longer confined to those who had made signal contributions to the advance of the subject. By these changes, general interest in psychology was widely extended and the enormously increased membership of the Society provided adequate funds for the publication of its sectional journals. These advantages, it is generally agreed, have outweighed any disadvantages which have arisen from throwing open the Society's meetings to non-experts. In mitigation of the latter, special meetings have recently been arranged which are attended almost solely by professed psychologists. In 1920 I was elected the first President of the newly constituted Society.

OTHER WORK

In 1922, at a few weeks' notice, I was asked to preside over the Psychology Section of the British Association, owing to the sudden death of Dr. Rivers who had been previously appointed to this office. I chose as my subject the contributions made by my old teacher to the advancement of psychology. Few could realize, so fully as I, all that he had done to promote the scientific status and recognition of the subject in Great Britain. He and I remained the closest of friends until his death. Not a year passed (save when he was engaged on anthropological research in the field) without his spending some part of his vacations with me and my family, despite the fact that I found it impossible to agree with some of the views which he so freely published after the War. It always seemed to me that his earlier laboratory work, carried out when he was far more diffident and cautious than later, was of immensely greater value and reliability. To him I owe the great importance which, as I have already said, I have come to attach to a strict training of the experimental psychologist in the psychophysical methods. To him I owe, too, the great interest I have always taken in the study of individual mental differences and the balance which I have striven to hold between the value of the results obtained from each individual and the value of the blurred, often meaningless, though statistically reliable, data obtained from large masses of individuals.

In 1922-1923, I was engaged in organizing the first International Congress in Psychology, held at Oxford, after the War. I was elected President of the Congress, and a difficult and delicate task it was to bring members of nations so recently hostile to one another to an amicable scientific meeting. An almost simultaneous International Congress in Physiology was being organized, but, whereas the French physiologists refused to come to this country to meet their German colleagues, the French psychologists showed every willingness to do so. Indeed such opposition as there was came from a handful of psychologists in Germany. Largely no doubt owing to their abstention, the Congress was an undoubted scientific success, and it helped to renew many interrupted friendships. I recall a letter which I received at the time from the Marquess Curzon, then Secretary for Foreign Affairs, who wrote that in his opinion the organizers of the Congress were doing more than his Department towards the establishment of peace conditions. It was found possible to raise funds privately in Great Britain for assisting Austrian, German, Hungarian, and certain other foreign psychologists from impoverished countries to pay their expenses of attending the Congress.

In 1924, I was invited to give a course of lectures on Industrial Psychology at Columbia University, New York. These were published in the following year under the title, *Industrial Psychology in Great Britain*. In 1929, I gave six lectures on the human factor in business organization as Muirhead Lecturer in Social Psychology at Birmingham University. In the same year I gave the Herbert Spencer Lecture at Oxford on "Psychological Conceptions in Other Sciences."

In 1931, I filled for a second time the position of President of the Psychology Section of the British Association at its Centenary Meeting in London, devoting my presidential address first to an outline of the progressive development of psychology in the Association (with which I had been for more than 20 years closely concerned), but mainly to a consideration of The Nature of Mind.

In 1932 I gave a course of three lectures in London on the dangers and advantages of *Business Rationalization*, considered from the social and psychological standpoints, and I delivered the second Hobhouse Memorial Lecture on the *Absurdity of Any Mind-Body Relation*. Both of these have since been published. In the latter I tried to establish the view that the differences between mind and matter are not those commonly supposed to distinguish spirit from substance, but that the essence both of mind and matter consists in activity— dead matter in blindly mechanical activity, living matter in "a unique combination of certain unique mechanical activities with non-mechanical directive activities." Mental activity and living bodily activity are identical; conscious activity is distinct from cerebral activity because "the former is only known to us individually and personally, whereas the behaviour (i.e. the activity) of the latter consists of public properties amenable to scientific treatment and partly common to the properties of non-living matter."

A more detailed presentation of these views would be out of place in this autobiography. But the foregoing sentences may serve to indicate the views which I have come to hold on the nature of mind. Their developn.ent has been by no means easy in a life largely spent in organizing and administrative work. My interests and talents in the latter direction are related probably to my ancestors' business careers. Many of my scientific colleagues in this country considered that I had taken a retrograde step by "going into business," when I gave up a secure academic position at Cambridge for the development of an institute in industrial psychology. It was a hard task to combine the reticence of a man of science with the necessity for a certain publicity in order to develop popular interest in the subject of my later work. My Institute was wholly unendowed. Funds had to be collected for research and for educational work. My tendency to supervise younger people's research work rather than to engage in it myself arose doubtless from my wide interests in various subjects and in my fellowmen, my love of novelty, and my consequent difficulties in concentrating attention on any one small sphere of work. But, in thus following my early inclinations and natural bent, I have probably served psychology better than I could have done in other, more usual, ways.

E. W. SCRIPTURE

How am I to respond to an invitation to write the history of my psychological life without committing more indiscretions than anybody would care to be responsible for? And how am I to tell the truth without revealing much that I would prefer to keep to myself? And what will come out if I once begin? I must either try to proceed logically, chronologically, restrainedly, and most uninterestingly to state the facts as I would wish them known or I must let myself go and say whatever comes into my head. The former method would produce a few dry facts of no interest or value to anybody; the other may lead to anything. G. Bernard Shaw says that he starts his plays with no definite plan and that he never knows beforehand what the characters will say or do.

I do not know why I became interested in psychology during the last year in college and foolishly refused an offer from my father to send me through a medical school. Foolishly, I repeat. Twenty years later I actually took up the study of medicine and found it to be a revelation and an inspiration such as I had never received before. No one can have the faintest idea of the action of the human soul unless he learns to understand human beings inside and outside, in health and disease. After twenty-five years of active service as a physician I cannot read the usual book on psychology without being bored.

Entering Wundt's Psychological Laboratory in Leipzig in 1888 I learned to listen to little ivory balls striking a board and to say whether I perceived a difference between two sounds or not. I also learned to press a button when the bell rang. As a result of such pursuits I grasped the fact that psychic measurements could be made. This understanding developed into a belief that can be best expressed in the words of Lord Kelvin:

> When you . . . can express what you are speaking about in numbers, you know something about it; but when you cannot express it in numbers, your knowledge is of a meagre and unsatisfactory kind; it may be the beginning of knowledge, but you have scarcely in your thoughts advanced to the stage of science. (Thompson: *Popular Lectures and Addresses.* London, 1889, 1, 73.)

The logical conclusion is: *only statements based on measurements are reliable.* The corollary is: statements without measurements are not worth listening to. The belief is strengthened by the fact that wherever measurements are introduced most previous statements are shown to consist of illusions and delusions or to be quite meaningless.

I must now make a jump over forty years ahead to the next advance in this line of thought. Like many another person I have had great difficulty in trying to understand the work of Einstein. I have finally got far enough to grasp the idea that the universe consists solely of numbers arrived at by measurement. According to earlier conceptions, measurements referred to properties of things; according to the new ones, the indicator numbers derived from measurements are themselves the things—the only things—that exist. Space of ordinary experience consists of indicator numbers obtained by the use of the meter rod. Space among the fixed stars consists of indicator numbers established by using the greatest attainable velocity, called a light year. Space within an atom is a queer thing whose unit is the quantum jump. Space within a spinning electron seems to be some kind of magnetic affair. There are as many kinds of space as there are systems of indicator numbers bearing that term. There is often no more possibility of comparing different kinds of space than of expressing a sour taste in wave-lengths of the spectrum. In a similar way the various kinds of time, mass, energy, etc., are established. As parts of the universe, *consciousness, the unconscious, emotions, thoughts, impulses, and all the rest are solely systems of indicator numbers.* Any further meaning that may be given to them we put there ourselves.

"Gott hat die Zahlen geschaffen; alles andere ist Menschenwerk."
(after Kronecker)

Publications on psychological topics that do not treat of mental phenomena in the form of indicator numbers have no meaning and no value. No exception can be made for psychoanalysis. Its revelations are the beginning of knowledge but it can become a science only when it presents its results in the form of indicator numbers established by measurements. Social psychology, habit psychology, and all the rest can be nothing but vague, erroneous guesswork until numbers are introduced. Faust was dissatisfied with the statement: "In the beginning was the Word" and proposed to substitute: "In the beginning was the Deed." This is not good enough. Modern science teaches; numbers are the beginning, the essence, and the end of all things.

In Leipzig I began my independent work with a research on the association of ideas. One set of experiments led to a strange result, namely, that the associations were influenced by ideas that did not appear in consciousness till later or not at all. In one case, for example, the word "pride" brought the association "Niagara." Immediately thereafter the person associated the proverb, "Pride goeth before a fall." Where was this proverb while it was controlling the association and actually producing an unintentional pun? The Leipzig laboratory was—like all the laboratories even today—an institution for the study of consciousness. We had no concepts that would enable us to deal with such a result and we could go no further than to say that consciousness might be influenced by an unknown factor outside of itself. We did not like to say that it was the brain and we did not believe in the Unconscious. That mind was an entity—a system of indicator numbers—of which consciousness is a quite subordinate part was a thought that had not yet arisen. Experiments of this kind, however, established the fact that *mind has at least four dimensions, namely, time, positive-negative consciousness, intensity, and quality.*

In Leipzig I learned to treat mental facts as mental facts and not to represent thoughts and emotions as nerve cells tickling one another. With the knowledge of neurology acquired at a later date such psychophysiological *Phantasterei* became so repulsive that I now throw aside every book on psychology the moment I see a picture of the brain in it. There is not a word of truth in any statement ever made concerning the *nature* of the activity of the brain; the indicator numbers have never been found. For the nature of mind-action the indicator numbers are still very few. When a psychologist attempts to explain mental activity in terms of nerve cells and nerve currents he is merely trying to cloak psychological ignorance with neurological foolishness.

During my student days in Germany I learned from physics and chemistry not only that everything must be measured but also that the results must be expressed in laws. People used to ridicule Herbart because he claimed, for example, that when two ideas try to enter consciousness they act against each other with a certain force. He tried to give mathematical formulas for such forces.

The attempt failed necessarily because he had no measurements from which to derive the formulas. The idea, however, was correct and the chief business of experimental psychology should have been to establish such laws by making measurements. One must express surprise that this did not occur more generally and that the work of experimental psychology even today usually stops with making measurements and does not go on to establishing laws. The reason is probably that the experimental psychologist of today is not a fully trained man. Experimental psychology can never rise above a rather amateurish level till the leaders can handle vectors, Hamiltonians, and potentials as well as the representatives of the physical sciences can. An experimental psychologist may not ordinarily think of his wife as a compound of differential equations and she may not care to be considered in such a mathematical light, but he cannot understand how her mind works until he knows the equations that express its action.

At Clark University in 1891 I carried on some work on the least perceptible change. About 1870 Pflüger's *Archiv für die gesammte Physiologie* contained an account of some experiments in which the temperature of a vessel of water containing a frog was raised very gradually—without any sign of perception by the frog!—to such a degree that the frog was found to have been boiled without knowing it. This suggested that there may be such a mental quantity as the greatest imperceptible or least perceptible change, and indicated that this depended on the rate of change. Let $\Delta\xi$ indicate the greatest imperceptible (least perceptible) change of the stimulus x. The dependence on the rate of change is expressed by $\Delta\xi = f(dx/dt)$. If the change is accelerated or retarded beyond a certain amount, it is noticed. The greatest imperceptible (least perceptible) change depends therefore on the acceleration, and we write $\Delta\xi = f_a\ (dx^2/dt^2)$. We find, moreover, that it depends on the amount of the stimulus itself, that is, $\Delta\xi = f_s(x)$. As a complete expression for the dependence we have

$$\Delta\xi = F(x, \frac{dx}{dt}, \frac{d^2x}{dt^2}).\qquad(1)$$

These relations must be of very fundamental importance in psychology. It is a mistake to treat sensation as depending on any one of the properties of the stimulus alone.

At Yale University in 1892 I undertook the task of developing a laboratory and conducting investigations. The results of ten years' work were published in the *Studies from the Yale Psychological Laboratory.* The research work consisted in making measurements and attempting to express the results in laws. Two such laws may be mentioned here.

In connection with the experiments of Miyake on tapping with the finger, the following facts were established. When a person is told to repeat an act continuously with no specification of the interval between the acts, he unconsciously selects an average interval; this we will call the natural interval. The successive individual intervals are never exactly alike; they vary around the average. If we now ask the person to repeat the action with smaller or larger intervals, we find that the average variation from the newly chosen interval increases with the amount of difference from the natural interval. Denoting the natural interval by T, any other chosen interval by τ, the average percentual variation for the natural interval by R and the average percentual variation for the chosen interval by r, we find the relation to be

$$r = R\left(1 + c\frac{(\tau - T)^2}{-\tau}\right), \qquad (2)$$

in which c is a constant depending on the particular person, the form of the act, and the occasion. This equation enables us to realize what we have found out. The average percentual variation is a measure of the difficulty of the action. The relation in equation (2) shows us that the natural interval is the least difficult and that any other interval, whether smaller or larger, is more difficult. From the equation it is possible to determine what intervals are 2, 3, . . . times as difficult. Such an equation serves three purposes. In the first place it makes us realize clearly as a whole what appears in only detailed form in our table of results. It also serves as an interpolation formula, from which we get such results as those just mentioned. Finally it presents a view of the inner nature of rhythmic action that connects it with other factors of science.

In an investigation carried out by Seashore it was found that a difference in size between two equal lifted weights influenced the judgment as to their weight in a definite way. From Seashore's results it was found possible to deduce the general law

$$I = \frac{k}{s+c} - d, \qquad (3)$$

where I is the amount of the illusion, s is the difference in size acting as a suggestion, c the diameter of the blocks of constant size, and d the weight of the blocks of constant weight; k is a constant depending on the person and the nature of the experiment.

Various other experiments were made on illusions and delusions. It was found to be a regular thing that a group of students holding a wire between the fingers would feel the wire become warm as soon as they thought they saw it connected to a battery, although it was secretly disconnected. If they happened to expect it, they would see a white bead on a black circle or hear a tone in a telephone when no bead or tone was present. In fact even skeptical students would hear, see, or think anything if they only expected to do so. A more striking demonstration of the completely illusory character of introspective psychology could hardly be found.

An important feature of the work of the Yale Laboratory was the work on reaction time. The method was ultimately developed into a form that presents the results directly to the eye. In one arrangement a rotating cylinder produced a stimulus, e.g., a click, at a certain point of its revolution and at the same time registered a dot by an electric spark on a covering of smoked paper. The person experimented upon was required to respond as quickly as possible by releasing a key that produced a second spark record. The experiment was repeated at each rotation of the cylinder. A specimen record is reproduced in Figure 1. The time from the first dot to the second one in each line gives the reaction time. The line of reaction dots reveals at once the variations among the results. The variation is greater at the beginning than in the middle, and the average time is somewhat longer. This is an illustration of one of the most fundamental processes of all nature that may be termed "fitting-in," or adaptability. The "steady-going" of the middle portion of the record also corresponds to a universal factor. The lengthening and the increased irregularity toward the end represent what may be called a "condition of fatigue"—again a fundamental factor. Persons with different characters furnish different dot curves. The dot curves differ characteristically with different emotions, different nerve diseases, etc. Such dot curves can be expressed in the form of laws mathematically defined. Laws of training-in are laws of habit formation. Habit psychology, social psychology, national and racial psychology built upon such laws would become quantitative and acquire scientific value.

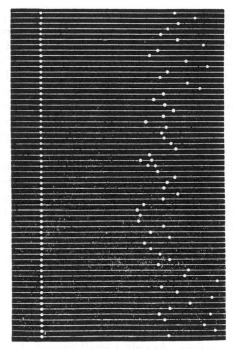

FIGURE 1
SERIES OF REACTION TIMES

For one of the exercises in a course of psychological measurements at Yale I developed a disc with series of dots illuminated by a radiant tube that responded to the vibrations of the voice. This was the first step in the development of the strobilion for making the pitch of the voice visible to the eye. The method has been applied to training the deaf to speak melodiously. There are indications that this method can be developed into a means of recording the pitch curve directly.

At the meetings of classical societies continual clashes occurred between a professor of Greek at Harvard and another at Yale concerning the nature of Greek verse. One asserted that it must have been quantitative (that is, consisting of long and short syllables) "just as in English." The other asserted that it must necessarily have consisted of differences in stress, "just as in English." Each appealed to the audiences for opinions on English verse as they heard it. Some of them heard it one way, some heard it the other way; others gave the matter up as undecided. The Yale professor appealed to me to do something with apparatus. I thereupon traced off the curve of speech from a gramophone record of the nursery rime "Cock Robin." The results were unexpected. The characteristics of English speech that produced the rhythm were found to be five, namely, change in speed (long and short), change in intensity (stress), change in pitch, change in quality, and change in precision of enunciation. The only persons in the controversy who were right were those who had said they did not know.

The most astounding result was that the curves contradicted every one of the prevailing notions concerning metrics. The metrists assume that English verse is based on four typical forms, the iambus, the trochee, the anapest, and the dactyl. These are only four out of more than fifty forms in classical Greek verse. Why the metrists selected only these four forms and how they got them all wrong owing to ignorance of classical verse are matters of no importance. Important is the way in which they have deluded people and maltreated the poets. For example, blank verse is the verse that Shakespeare wrote. The metrist, however, says that blank verse is "iambic pentameter." This is a form that never existed and never could exist in any language. He draws up a scheme into which he tries to fit Shakespeare's lines. As only a small portion of the lines can be forced into the scheme he proceeds to give Shakespeare "licenses" for innumerable deviations. Even these will not suffice, and he actually dares to alter the text. Shakespeare never wrote and no actor ever spoke many of the lines that appear in the standard editions. One metrist, for example, claims that Shakespeare intended the words, "Plainly conceive, I love you" (*Measure for Measure,* 2, 4, 142), to be spoken as, "Plain 'ceive I lo'y." All English verse was treated on the basis of the erroneous Greek forms. When a line did not fit any of these forms, the metrists said that the poet had used a "license" to cut off a head or a tail or to use the form backward. A line like

"Towered cities please us then"
Milton, L'Allegro

has the vowel scheme

$$\overset{\prime}{:} \cdot \overset{\prime}{:} \cdot \overset{\prime}{:} \cdot \overset{\prime}{:}$$

This is one of the commonest forms in English verse. Whole poems have been composed in it. Since it does not fit the metrical man's notions that it must be iambic or trochaic he calls this line "akephalic iambic" or "catalectic trochaic," that is, he considers that it has lost a head or a tail. But it never had any head or tail. An ordinary man would assume that the poet meant the line as he wrote it. The metrical man knows better. He thinks that it ought to read, "The towered cities please us then" or "Towered cities please us then, O!" and that Milton left something out. One metrist, v. Schlegel, went so far as to advise Goethe to send his verse to a Swedish expert for metrical revision before publication. Goethe even tried to write according to v. Schlegel's rules but gave up the attempt.

> Der Takt kommt aus der poetischen Stimmung, wie unbewusst. Wollte man darüber denken, wenn man ein Gedicht macht, man würde verrückt und brachte überhaupt nichts Gescheites zu Stande (Eckermann: *Gespräche mit Goethe,* 6, 4, 29).

The work on verse has been continued down to the present. Hundreds of records of spoken verse have been analyzed, and a science of metrics has been created. Of the older metrics, that fantastic fabric of fancy without the faintest foundation in fact, not a trace exists. There is not a word of truth in the whole library of books on metrics, and their only fit destination is the waste-paper basket. Curiously enough the greatest authority on ancient Greek verse, Wilamowitz-Moellendorff, has pronounced the same judgment not only on all modern publications on Greek verse but also on the works of Aristoxenos and Hephaistion.

The science of metrics could not begin until indicator numbers could be obtained. This was not possible until speech could be registered in a measurable form. The science started with a quarrel between two American professors, and Cock Robin's indicator numbers knocked them both out in the first bout. Hundreds of records of spoken English and German verse have since been analyzed. Some of the general results may be briefly summarized as follows.

Spoken verse consists of a stream of psychic speech power. The German term *Sprachleistung* is better because the term power is often misunderstood; power is the rate of doing work. In verse the power fluctuates with more or less regularity. These fluctuations produce an effect of repetition. For many purposes the power may just as well be treated as contained in a series of points that correspond to centers of gravity or centroids of force. In verse the intervals of time between successive centroids are approximately equal. In English and German the centroids occur nearly always within a long vowel or next to a short one. Such a vowel is termed a centroid vowel. The other vowels are termed twixt-vowels, fore-vowels, and after-vowels according to their positions. The number of centroids to a line may be anything from one ("Sleep!"— Shelley: *A Century of Roundels,* No. 77) upward. The number of twixt-vowels may vary from zero ["Tu-whit-tu-whoo" (:′ :′ :′ :′) —Coleridge: *Christabel*] up to five ["I'll carry him to his grave" (:′ . . . . . :′)—*Cock Robin*]. It usually varies within a line [I shall find time, Cassius, I shall find time" (..:′ :′ :′.. :′ :′)—*Julius Caesar,* 5, 3, 103]. With some poets the number of twixt-vowels varies constantly from zero to three. Sometimes, particularly in German verse, the number of twixt-vowels is rigidly constant.

After this work had continued for many years it occurred to me to do what I ought to have done at the start, namely, to ask the poets what they think about the matter. I sent out a series of questions to the most prominent poets of England and Germany. I will quote three English replies.

> With me a poem arises out of a couple of lines or so of rhythmic words that come into my head spontaneously; they dictate the measure and mood of the rest. I never could attempt to explain how the rhythm or thoughts of a poem come to me—they just spring into my mind, and that's all about it.
>
> John Galsworthy
>
> In respect of the questions I regret to say that I am unable to answer them, and can only suggest in a general way that I write poems because I cannot help it.
>
> Thomas Hardy
>
> Attitude towards the versification? Anything from friendliness to open hostility.
>
> How the verse form comes? It comes like the income tax form; I do not have to apply for it.
>
> Do I settle the meter beforehand? No. It is an accident for which I disclaim all responsibility.
>
> Do I think of the forms of iambus and so forth? No. I strive to keep my mind on pleasant subjects.
>
> Do I settle the number of stressed and unstressed syllables? I never thought of it, but it is an idea.

The number of stressed syllables alone? That would certainly
seem to be simpler.
  Why do I write poems? Ah! If I knew that, I might be
able to break myself of the habit.

Claude Burton

To the question: Where does your verse form come from?—all the
poets reply to the same effect as one of them, "God knows, I don't."
All the poets, past and present, are agreed; their poems come to them,
finished in form and content, from some source outside consciousness.
The verse factory is situated in the Unconscious. Metrics is a
department of psychology and its value lies in furnishing indicator
numbers for the Unconscious. The collection of replies from English
poets is to be found in my *Grundzüge der englischen Verswissenschaft*
and that of replies from German poets in an article, "Aeusserung
deutscher Dichter über ihre Verskunst (*Archiv f. d. ges. Psychol.*,
1928, **56**, 216).

  With the establishment of the principles of spoken verse, the fog
and the phantasms that concealed the beauties of Beowulf and other
Anglo-Saxon verse have been swept away. Applied to Greek verse
they reveal a grandeur and beauty of psychological expression in
the fundamental rhythms of speech that is hardly equalled in any
other language. Just these fundamental rhythms are found also
in English verse. The adoneus, the choriambus, the hemiepes, the
rising ionic, and the third epitrite are forms used by Galsworthy in
his *Devon to Me!* (compare Janvrin: "Analyse von zwei durch John
Galsworthy gesprochenen Gedichten," *Zsch. f Experimental-Phonetik*,
1930-1932, **1**, 147). A hemiepes occurs in "Hickory, dickory, dock," a
dochmius in "Gems of a master's art" (Bridges), a hypodochmius in
"Now that April's there" (Browning), a lekytheion in "Here a
little child I stand" (Herrick), a glykoneus in "Drunk with idolatry,
drunk with wine" (Milton), etc., etc.

  While at Yale I wrote a popular book, *Thinking, Feeling, Doing*,
in which I showed that knowledge of mental life could be obtained
only by making experiments and that the productions of the arm-
chair psychology had no more value than medieval speculations
concerning how many angels could dance on the point of a needle. The
abuse that was heaped upon this book can be imagined. Socrates, as
Bernard Shaw has pointed out, could not understand the cause of the
feeling against him. Even at his trial he argued that his teachings

were good ones. He failed to understand that he was to be condemned because he had shown up so many other people as incompetent or worse.

> Ich sag' es dir: ein Kerl, der spekuliert,
> Ist wie ein Tier auf dürrer Heide
> Von einem bösen Geist herum geführt,
> Und rings umher liegt schöne grüne Weide.

A second book, *The New Psychology,* was an exposition of the
psychology of consciousness from a strictly experimental point of
view. A third book, *Elements of Experimental Phonetics,* was a
systematic treatise on this science in which I aimed to include
everything that had been done in the experimental investigation of
speech. My work on speech at Yale was essentially psychological;
my book on experimental phonetics might just as well have been
designated as one on the experimental psychology of speech. This
line of work aroused much interest at the time; my pupil, assistant,
and friend, Seashore, with his group in Iowa, has continued it in
his brilliant investigations of speech and vocal music. I have never
been able to understand why experimental psychology never attempts
to use the methods of experimental phonetics for investigating the
most complete form of expression that the mind possesses.

Once again I was to suffer the fate of Socrates—all but the hem-
lock. After many years of work I published a systematic treatise on
English verse, *Grundzüge der englischen Verswissenschaft.* It was
the first book to give indicator numbers for verse. Metrics instead
of consisting of nonsensical speculation was to become a science. I
naïvely expected the German teachers of English to throw away their
antiquated textbooks and introduce mine. They didn't do so on
demand, and perhaps they never will. The lead still lies with the
professors who had already written books on metrics. The reaction was natural. A lifelong friend, a professor in one of the
most prominent German universities, sent me a letter enclosing a
copy of what he called a "rather queer review" that had slipped
from his pen, he "did not just know how" and expressed the
hope that this would not injure our friendship. The review consisted
entirely of personal attacks. I replied, "This review reminds me of
the solicitor who gave the following instruction to his barrister for
procedure at a trial: 'We have no case; abuse the plaintiff's attorney!' "

The most important results of an exploration are usually some for which the explorer himself was not looking. The tracings from the *Cock Robin* record contained the first good curves of the vowels. They were of such an unexpected nature that the Carnegie Institution of Washington made me a grant that enabled me to work for four years on this problem. I promptly transferred my activities to Germany. It was an unexpected thing to do; perhaps it was a mistake, but I do not think so. My scientific methods of thought were and still are specifically German. With freedom to do my work where I wished and with the contacts of a German university always at hand, I had an opportunity that I could not have found elsewhere. Parts of the results have been published in my *Study of Speech Curves (Carnegie Institution Publ.,* No. 44). The work on the vowels has been continued down to the present time. The latest results have been published in the *Zeitschrift für Experimental-Phonetik,* 1930-1932, 1, 16, 115, and *Nature,* 1932, 30, 275. They may be summarized as follows.

A vowel is produced by a series of sharp puffs of air ejected from the glottis into the vocal cavity. Each puff dies away immediately outside the mouth. It is not propagated and cannot be heard. Each puff sets the air in the vocal cavity in vibration. The vibrations are propagated and may be heard or received by a microphone. Speech curves register these vibrations. Pieces of some film curves of German vowels are reproduced in Figures 2 and 3.

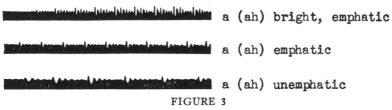

FIGURE 2

FILM CURVE OF A SNAP VOWEL

a (ah) bright, emphatic

a (ah) emphatic

a (ah) unemphatic

FIGURE 3

FILM CURVES OF VARIOUS VOWELS

The following facts are at once evident in the curves. (1) A vowel is made up of a series of adjacent vibration profiles. (2) The profiles differ in length, amplitude, and form. (3) Each profile begins strong and becomes steadily weaker. (4) Each profile shows various systems of inner repetition. (5) Different vowels show systematic differences of profile. Measurements reveal several additional facts, as follows: (6) The frequencies of the inner repetitions change within each profile. (7) The rate of weakening changes within each profile. These facts lead to the following conclusions. (1) A vibration profile in a vowel is initiated by a sharp impulse that does not appear in the profile itself. (2) The vibration profile consists of a more or less rapidly fading free vibration of complicated form.

The numerous systems of inner repetition suggest that the free vibration constituting the profile may be considered as the sum of a series of free vibrations. Let us make this supposition and indicate the radian frequencies of these inner vibrations by ω_1, ω_2, ω_3, ... Analyses of the curves show that all the frequencies from 0 to ∞ are present to a greater or less degree. The profile is therefore not the sum of a few discrete vibrations as ordinarily supposed but is really the sum of an infinite number of such vibrations differing infinitely little from each other, that is, the profile is an integration over $d\omega$ between 0 and ∞. Each element of the free vibration has a decremental index, p. The analyses show that the decremental indices are infinitely variable and that not one or a few but an infinite number of decremental factors between 0 and ∞ may be present. The extent of each inner vibration at each moment determines its contribution to the profile. Assuming a cosine form for the component vibrations and obtaining their amplitudes by an integration over the duration of the profile, a, β, we obtain as an expression for the profile

$$y = f(t) = \frac{1}{\pi} \int_0^\infty d\omega \int_0^\infty dp \int_a^\beta f(t') e^{-\omega p t'} \cos \omega \, (t'-t) \, dt'.$$

$$(4)$$

The change of the radian frequency and the factor of decrement within the profile require the additional equations

$$\omega = f_\omega \, (t'), \quad p = f_p \, (t'). \tag{5}$$

Equations (4) and (5) represent exactly what occurs in the vocal cavity. This cavity does not consist of a set of cavities connected by orifices but of one cavity of complicated form that cannot be divided into separate cavities. A sharp blow arouses a vibration that has every possible frequecy between 0 and ∞. Just how strong each one of the infinitely numerous ones is depends on the shape of the cavity. The factor of decrement depends upon the softness and moisture of the walls of the cavity. These may have any values; they are always changing according to the varying muscular tension and the action of the glands of the mucous membrane. The shape of the vocal cavity and the condition of its walls are under the control of the various nerve centers that act in response to the psychic speech impulse. The factors of the registered vowel profile refer ultimately to an *inner psychic profile*.

The view that the nature of a vowel is determined by the shape of the profiles and not by fixed frequencies has received striking confirmation from a recent experiment. With a gramophone record of speech in connection with a loud speaker various regions of frequency were filtered out as follows: (1) all frequencies above 1350, (2) all frequencies below 750, (3) all frequencies above 1350 and all below 750, (4) all frequencies between 750 and 1350. The musical character of the speech changed with every alteration, but the vowels were not changed in the least degree (!). The vowel characters do not depend on any special frequencies. Any region of frequency may be taken away without altering the vowel except in regard to its musical character. Moreover a small region of frequency anywhere is sufficient to give the vowel character. The conclusion cannot be avoided that the vowel character depends on the specific form of the vibration profile and that any frequencies of any kind suffice provided they give the specific form. This would explain how a magpie with extremely small vocal organs of a kind different from the human ones can imitate a human voice successfully.

We have now to consider the puff that arouses the cavity vibration. It consists of a sudden jet of air released at the glottis. It is produced by the muscles of breathing and the larynx under the same nervous and psychic control as the vocal cavity. From this fact we might expect that there must be special action of the larynx and the breathing apparatus for each vowel profile. I suggested this as a hypothesis many years ago; it has been confirmed recently by some photographs by Russell. The glottal puff must therefore receive as complete a mathematical expression as the cavity vibration. We write therefore

$$y = f(t) = \frac{1}{\pi} \int_{0}^{\infty} d\psi \int_{0}^{\infty} dq \int_{\gamma}^{\delta} f(t') \; e^{-\psi q t'} \cos \psi (t' - t) \, dt', (6)$$

$$\psi = f_\psi (t'), \qquad q = f_q (t'). \tag{7}$$

The puff theory of Willis was accepted by Helmholtz and established by Hermann. The theory stated here differs from the Willis-Hermann theory by assuming a frequency profile instead of one or two discrete frequencies and by introducing the variable inner frequencies and decrements. The greatest difference, however, lies in the treatment of a vowel profile as an expression of psychic activity rather than as a physical condition.

Equations (4) and (5) will express everything in a vowel profile, if the correct indicator numbers can be found. From an adequate analysis we can expect information concerning the language content, the mental and bodily condition, the character, etc. All depends on getting the indicator numbers. Up to the present the only method of obtaining indicator numbers from such curves has been the Fourier harmonic analysis. This makes the supposition that $p = 0$ and that only those values of ω are present that belong to the series 1, 2, ... As p is *never* 0 and values of ω outside the series 1, 2, ... are *always* present, the indicator numbers found by the harmonic analysis are always wrong ones. All vowel analyses made up to the present must be rejected as being erroneous. Some years ago I made an investigation in applying the harmonic analysis to curves whose indicator numbers I knew beforehand. One of the positive results was that, when the harmonic analysis said that a fundamental sine element or a harmonic was lacking, it actually was lacking. This is exactly what the harmonic analyses of vowel curves made by Miller and Crandall say. That is, the harmonic analyses made by such investigators declare to these investigators that the theory on which they are applying the method is mistaken.

The situation has recently become acute. Through the courtesy of a film company I have obtained sound tracks of a large number of English sounds. To treat them by the old methods would simply produce more nonsense, and no new method suggested itself. Finally I adopted the attitude recommended by Eddington (see below) that these curves represent something that appears to me merely as "Jabberwocky" and and that my job is to find numbers in it. The result is an entirely new method for analyzing vowel curves. It does not bear the slightest resemblance to the Fourier analysis or anything else. I cannot describe the method here beyond saying that it provides for all values of ω and p and that it derives the values of ω from the intervals between the centers of gravity of the successive inner pulsations and those for p from the successive decrease of amplitude.

For thirty years I applied the graphic method of making speech inscriptions (point recording on a moving smoked surface) with a receiver held closely over the mouth to problems of various kinds. One day I realized that I did not know the nature of what I was recording. This led to an understanding that physical speech consists of two parts. The familiar one that we hear consists of the waves that are propagated outward from the speaker. These consist of minute vibrations of the air particles, and they may be appropriately termed the *microphonic factors of speech*. The other part consists of the currents and puffs of air that issue from the mouth and nose and die away immediately in front of the face. These mass movements of air constitute the *macrophonic factors of speech*. They produce the microphonic speech. Macrophonic speech is what is registered by the graphic method of Rousselot. This method gives valuable information that can be obtained in no other way. It is the basis of most of the work done in experimental phonetics.

The director of a Russian Institute for the Rationalization of Work visited the Phonetic Institute in Vienna with an inquiry as to the possibility of using inscriptions of speech for the purpose of studying character. Inscriptions of the word *da* were made by four persons. Each one had a special form that corresponded to the type of character of the person who spoke. For types of character we have at present only vague terms. This experiment points the way to obtaining indicator numbers for them. The work is now being attempted by means of sound tracks. In the speech heard from film curves we recognize not only the intellectual content but also the emotional expression and much of the character of the speaker. These elements lie before the eye in measurable form in the curves themselves. A film curve is not only a curve of speech; it is a curve of emotion and character. The problem for the investigator is to unravel the various elements and measure those for character.

While on a visit to Zürich I first met Carl Jung. One day he handed me a book with the remark, "You are a pupil of Wundt; I wonder what you will say to this." I returned it after a few days with the comment that any fool could write a better book on dreams than that one. It was Freud's *Traumdeutung*. A couple of years later I formed the habit of carrying one of the monographs of the series founded by Freud to read in leisure moments. It is not difficult to imagine what a shock each of them gave a Wundtian psychologist. Over and over again I threw such a monograph down with the exclamation, "Either Freud is a fool or I am." I gradually became converted and at a later date I underwent treatment by one of Vienna's specialists. The dream analysis revealed a world of indescribable fascination and led to a complete revision of my psychological views. References to the immediate past in dreams are used as a convenient method for the appearance in consciousness of a soul-life that would otherwise remain unknown to it. Only by using admissible forms as symbolic expressions can the Unconscious reveal itself in consciousness. In my dreams I find myself acting as Coriolanus, Caesar Borgia, Sir John Franklin, Alice in Wonderland, a white-robed priest, the devil himself—but this is revealing too much. The usual interpretation of dreams refers to the person's individual past. This view, however, I have found inadequate to explain my dreams. A suggestion may be derived from the functions of the *corpus striatum*. The ganglia in this portion of the brain are of early appearance in the history of the development of the nervous system. They preserve the mechanisms of automatic movement from the very earliest stages of animal life. The swinging of the arms, for example, is a survival from the time when our ancestors went on all fours; it takes place now because this movement is not inhibited by the cortical centers. The ganglia contain the mechanisms for a host of other automatic movements held in suppression and coming out only when the inhibition from the cortical centers is lessened, as, for example, in hemiplegia. There is no reason to believe that only automatic mechanisms of movement are preserved. We would expect that similar automatisms of sensation, thought, and emotion would be kept. In sleep the sensations from the outer world are greatly diminished in intensity and the automatisms may come into the foreground. I do not say that they enter consciousness because I believe that they are present in waking also and that we do

not attend to them because we are kept busy otherwise. Dreams
are to be interpreted in reference to the entire past. An identification with mother-governed Coriolanus does not refer merely to a
mother-complex arising in my childhood or even to one acquired
when my ancesters lived in caves; all my mammalian ancestors had
mothers. The note of fear in my dreams certainly does not arise
merely or mainly from a personal birth trauma; all my ancestors
were born. Moreover, fear was a ruling emotion when my ancestors
crept stealthily among the ferns of the primeval swamps or hid
from aquatic monsters in the depths of the pristine seas. The trait
of sadism that produced a passion for anatomy was less attributable
to anything in my childlife than to an inheritance from my human
ancestors who killed and ate their enemies and from my animal
ones who preyed in the prehistoric jungles. The Unconscious is a
very ancient organ and its content must comprise a summary of the
whole history of one's ancestry back to the primeval organisms. Psychology must recognize the fact that *all forms of human activity are
based upon and controlled by inherited mechanisms present in the
Unconscious.*

While at work in my laboratory in Munich I attended a clinic
in laryngology and became so interested in learning about human
beings anatomically, physiologically, and pathologically that I took
up the systematic study of medicine. This brought me into contact with new types of men and new methods. At one time, while
I was making a study of speech by the graphic method, Professor
Kraepelin, the psychiatrist, suggested that this method might be
useful in the study of nervous and mental diseases. I made records of some cases of progressive general paralysis and hysteria in
his Institute but proceeded no further at the time.

Returning to America in 1906, I took up practical work in
neurology in the Vanderbilt Clinic, Columbia University. A laboratory of speech neurology—the first of its kind—was founded. The
first published results concerned thirteen cases of idiopathic epilepsy.
From measurements of the voice waves in the inscriptions, plots of
voice melody were computed. They showed that, although the
voice rises and falls in speech in a general way just as a normal
voice does, the finer fluctuations are absent. The original curves
are now inaccessible; specimen examples from a later study by
Janvrin (*Zeitschrift für Experimental-Phonetik,* 1930-32, 1, 56) are

reproduced in Figure 4. The melody plot marked N is from a normal person. The other melody-plot records are from epileptics not having attacks. The epileptic plots show a lack of the fine fluctuations that are present in the normal melody plot. This work has been continued down to the present. Hundreds of epileptic

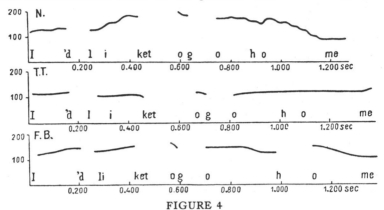

FIGURE 4

NORMAL AND EPILEPTIC MELODIES

melody plots show the lack of the finer fluctuation with preservation of the normal general melody. This occurs in no other disease and cannot be imitated by a normal person. This sign is the only certain basis for a diagnosis of epilepsy. The epileptic peculiarity has no connection with attacks. We must conclude that epilepsy is a constitutional condition. An epileptic can be taught to speak normally in a few minutes, but he relapses as soon as he forgets to think about it. The conclusion is unavoidable that epilepsy does not depend on a structural or histological alteration in the brain. The presence of the peculiarity at all times indicates that epilepsy represents some general condition such as an abnormal hormone balance, a special form of metabolism, an autointoxication, or a psychic peculiarity. Careful studies of the early and family histories of epileptics indicate that the condition is congenital. The finer fluctuations in the melody plots of normal speech are lessened when the speaker takes an attitude of resistance. The rather expressionless face, the frequent awkwardness in action, and the history of difficulty in nursery adaptation in cases of epilepsy point to the conclusion that the lack of fine fluctuation is due to lesser adaptability to environment. Epilepsy might be defined as a congenital constitution of which one characteristic is lessened adaptability to environment.

Inscriptions of speech in general progressive paralysis show a peculiarity that has not been found in any other disease and cannot be imitated. When, for example, the syllable *pa-pa-pa*... is repeatedly spoken, each of the elements, such as the stop-time of the *p*, varies around an average. The amount of deviation from the average is measured and the average of the deviations is computed and expressed as a percentage of the average itself. For normal persons the average deviation in such a case is about 7 per cent to 10 per cent. Paralytics, even in the earliest stages, show average deviations amounting to 50 per cent to 200 per cent. The increased average deviations are indications of a loss of the power of conformity to acquired type. This is exactly the psychic factor that is most prominent in the development of this disease.

In 1912 I transferred my work to London and founded a laboratory of speech neurology at the West End Hospital for Nervous Diseases. This is still continued under another administration. Work has been carried on for twenty years in the various hospitals in London and in the clinic of Wagner-Jauregg in Vienna. For quite a number of nervous diseases specific curves have been found. This makes it possible to diagnose a disease by comparison of a record with the classified collection of curves. It becomes possible for the physician to send the patient to some central laboratory and receive the report just as in a case of diabetes or nephritis. The methods used in speech neurology have been described in detail in my *Anwendung der graphischen Methode auf Sprache und Gesang*. The advent of the sound film has changed the outlook. At the moment of writing, Janvrin has had film records made of several nerve diseases under my direction. Such records may be obtained by a concealed microphone or even over the telephone from a distant hospital.

This line of work has a value in quite another direction. The results obtained in the study of epilepsy suggest the general hypothesis that the finer flexibility in activity of all kinds is an expression of the trait of adaptability. A clearer understanding of what we mean may be obtained by a statement in mathematical form. Let $y = f(t)$ indicate the curve of any form of expression, for example, the course of pitch in a speech record. If we smooth out all the fluctuations we get a smooth curve $y_m = f_j(t)$ that rises and falls. This we term the fundamental melody. We indicate its general character by M. The fluctuations in the pitch curve may be considered to be imposed on the fundamental melody. We distinguish two kinds: coarser fluctuations that depend on emotional conditions and finer ones that depend on the adaptability of character. As we cannot yet furnish indicator numbers for these fluctuations, we express them roughly by $y_e = f_e(t) = a_e \sin \phi t$ and $y_c = f_c(t) = a_c \sin \psi t$. For the general character of the coarser fluctuations we use the designation V and for that of the finer ones, P. Since the fundamental melody is the result of the speech impulse, S, the larger fluctuations that of the emotional state, E, and the smaller ones that of characteristic of adaptability, A, we have the causal relations

$$M \longleftarrow S, \qquad V \longleftarrow E, \qquad P \longleftarrow A. \qquad (8)$$

The next steps are not difficult. With an accurate pitch curve a Mader analyzer will furnish the amplitudes and frequencies of the fluctuation curves. We then have indicator numbers for S, E, and A. In a similar manner we attribute the degree of agreement with standard types of action to an impulse to conformity to rule. If we indicate the percentual divergence by d we can use the reciprocal value $B = 1/d$ as a measure of the agreement. Attributing B to an inner impulse to conformity H we get

$$B \longleftarrow H. \qquad (9)$$

Observations on paralytics tempt one to term H the factor of conscience or social ethics. The indicator numbers for such studies are easily obtained by the graphic method.

The importance of such investigations for the study of language cannot be overestimated. The French, German, and Austrian governments—and probably many others—are investing vast sums in the study of the dialects in their respective countries. The investigators proceed by noting down in sets of letters what they think they hear. Of what value are their results? James Whitcomb Riley's lines:

> "They aint no style about 'em
> An' they're sort o' pale an' faded"

are supposed to give an idea of how the Hoosier dialect differs from— what? What is indicated by *There* and what by *They?* And wherein does the difference lie? Until the indicator numbers are furnished for *There* and for *They*, we remain in total ignorance of what we are talking about. We cannot refer to writers of the usual books on phonetics for information concerning *There* and *They* or anything else because experimental phonetics has already shown that there is not a word of truth in any of their accounts. Dialect investigators at the present time use alphabetical symbols, of which they do not know the meaning, to record sounds of which they have no perception. The conclusions they draw are fantastic beyond the ravings of lunacy. A sound shift from sonants to surds is regarded by one writer as a result of the manlier character of the inhabitants —the shift occurred in his own country. Another attributes it to the bracing influence of mountain air—although it occurs just as frequently in the lowlands. Other sound shifts are attributed to an element termed economy for one's own country and laziness for other countries. And so on. Praiseworthy is the attempt to record dialects and praiseworthy also is the impulse to seek for the causes. Blameworthy is the neglect of the methods of registration that Rousselot introduced fifty years ago. The experimental phonetician can give the elements out of which the sounds are composed and can specify in numbers exactly the differences between a sound in one dialect and in another. Furthermore he can trace geographically just how the changes develop in passing from one locality to another (Rousselot's first proposition). Or he can give in measurements how the sounds in one locality change as time passes (Rousselot's second proposition). The discovery of the causes awaits the activity of the psychologists. I have shown above how some suggestions can be obtained from pathology. I would suggest that such character-elements as adaptability and persistence in type are important factors governing sound changes. Modern English is mainly Anglo-Saxon in character not merely because the Anglo-Saxons were more numerous than the Normans but also because their stubbornness in regard to adaptability and their persistence in keeping to the same type of mental activity were strong national traits that appear in their entire mental life under the name of "conservatism." The dialect studies would, if properly carried out, become studies of national character. The methods for dialect studies have been outlined in my *Anwendung der graphischen Methode auf Sprache und Gesang*.

In 1923 I was called to the professorship of experimental phonetics in the University of Vienna. Here I developed a laboratory on the model of the laboratory of Rousselot at the Collège de France. That is, it was essentially a laboratory of linguistic phonetics. A strong psychological tendency was present. It was located in the Physical Institute, and the contact favored strict methods of thought.

The usual linguistic phonetics consists solely of the study of printed letters and guesswork on the basis of what is supposed to be heard by the ear and felt in the mouth. The results of this method are sometimes astonishing. One distinguished authority declared that he could hear (!) that the Arabic sound *ain* was produced by a constriction below the glottis. He did not know that such a constriction would have broken a cartridge ring and caused death by suffocation. Linguists of the present day believe that speech consists of little speech blocks, termed "speech sounds," held together by little slides of cement, termed "glides." A single speech record is sufficient to destroy the delusion. There are no speech blocks and no little slides. An actually spoken piece of speech consists of a continuously changing speech gesture. We can divide this continuous flow into small parts that appear homogeneous; such a small part we may call a speech bit. When we now try to group the speech bits into speech sounds, we meet with a surprising result. A speech bit often belongs to two or even three neighboring speech sounds. If we insist on a grouping into speech sounds, we must partly superimpose the speech sounds. This cannot occur physically; we cannot speak several speech sounds and afterwards put them over one another. If such speech sounds exist, the superposition must have occurred before they were spoken. As the speaker knows nothing about the matter, it must have occurred in the Unconscious. The instinct of the linguist was correct in assuming that speech is made up of speech sounds; the mistake occurred in identifying them with printed letters. To avoid confusion let us apply the term *phonom* to a speech sound. The superposition of phonoms may be illustrated by the study of the Russian speech sound *šts* published in the *Zeitschrift für Experimental-Phonetik*, 1930-1932, 1, 164. Consider now what must be the nature of a phonom. It contains not only all the elements that have gone to building up the conception of the sound during the lifetime of the individual but also a summary of the condition of the individual himself and of his past individual and phylogenetic development. It must therefore contain a vast number of elements. Have we in a phonom a kind of psychic molecule composed of psychatoms and more elementary psychons?

All forms of activity consist of the transfer of energy from one system to another. A person in conversation receives impulses from without, and, after working them over, responds by impulses from within. An entrance transformer, T_E, comprising the air in the outer ear, the ear itself, the nervous mechanism, the brain, and the psychic mechanism of entrance arouse an amount of entrance activity, L_E, in the psychic center. How much activity enters depends on the capacity for receiving it, C. An inner activity, L_I, results in outwardly directed activity, L_A, in an exit transformer, T_A. In doing this it has to overcome such inner resistance, R, as may be present. The entrance activity, I_E, the inner activity, L_I, and the outward activity, L_A, use up some of the energy delivered to the system; the capacity, C, favors the acceptance. The difference between the capacity and the use by activity, termed the reactance, is expressed by $X=C—L_E+L_I+_A$. The total amount of energy used up in the system is expressed as the impedance, $Z=X+R$. The amount of energy developed in the system in response to the impressed amount E is given by $I=E/Z$.

This method of treating the transfer of energy has become fundamental in physics and technology; it should be equally fruitful in psychology. Even where measurements cannot be made, such definite expressions help to make things less vague. As an example we may take the conflict among the words *porc, swin,* and *pigge* in Middle English. The word *porc* received its energy from the Norman conquerors. Against it was the resistance of the Anglo-Saxon people and the inner mechanism of the English language. The necessity for communication produced a capacity for its use. In use on the land where the Normans were few the impedance was great and the word *porc* possessed almost no power to enter the language when applied to the animal as he existed on the land. In the castles of the conquerors, however, the capacity for the word was very large owing to the necessity for understanding on the part of the dependents. For the same reason the inner work and the resistance were less. The impedance was therefore small and the word impressed itself on the language for the animal as it was known in the castles, namely, as food. For analogous reasons, the word *swin* prevailed as the designation for the living animal. In competition with *swin* there was the word *pigge* of unknown origin. The word *swin* is the same in the singular and the plural, a fact that produced a resistance to it.   The details of how *pigge* won for the singular and *swin* for the plural are unknown.   Ultimately the animal was *pork* when prepared for eating, *pig* in the singular and when there are only few of him, and *swine* when present in numbers.   Lately the term *pigs* has almost completely supplanted *swine*.

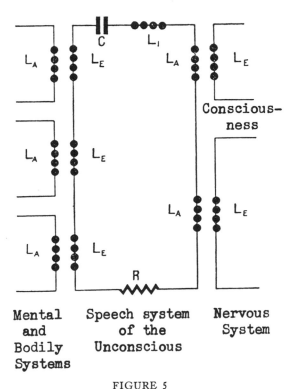

FIGURE 5

<small>SYSTEM OF ACTIVITY IN CONNECTION WITH THE SYSTEM OF THE UNCONSCIOUS</small>

The diagram in Figure 5 gives an outline of the relations of the psychic speech system to the systems that impress it and those that express its activities.   The diagram in Figure 6 indicates the many series of systems, each of its own peculiar kind, involved in a speech communication.   A speech impulse in the psychic center of the speaker undergoes at least ten transmutations of utterly different natures before it reaches the psychic center of the hearer. Each system has its own mechanism of transmission with more or less distortion. The reduction of the distortion within acceptable limits is the result of speech experience and education.

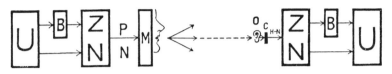

FIGURE 6

SPEECH SYSTEMS

U, the Unconscious; B, Consciousness; ZN, Central Nervous System; PN, Peripheral Nervous System; M, Muscular System; O, Ear; HN, Acoustic Nerve.

In my psychological life I have undergone four stages of mental development. In the enthusiasm of my college days I bought a big book by Descartes. "I think, therefore I am," wrote Descartes when he started to solve the problem of the universe. He ended by placing the soul in the pineal gland because the soul is indivisible and this gland is the only single organ in the brain—psychological nonsense located in an anatomical mistake. This type of thought went out of physics with the thud of the cannon balls at the base of the Tower of Pisa. Little ivory balls dropping on an ebony board in the Leipzig laboratory knocked it out of me, and I came to regard non-experimental psychology as talk-talk-talk and nothing but talk.

The second stage was a Fechner-Wundt phase. Modern psychology began with the attempt of Herbart to introduce mathematical methods. It was advanced by the introduction of experimental methods by Weber. Both methods were combined by Fechner to produce laws. Wundt collected the various currents into a systematic science.

Under the influence of Freud I passed into a third stage in which consciousness was treated as a quite subordinate element of mind. The mind itself became the Great Unknown and the object of psychology was the investigation of this Unknown by experiment and measurement. The Great Unknown included both the consciousness of the old psychology and the Unconscious of Freud. The general attitude was that expressed in Freud's *Das Ich und das Es.*

The fourth stage began with a shock. Everything that I had ever believed in was swept away as soon as I managed to get some understanding of relativity. Where were the Kantagories of space and time on which I had based all my work? What of matter and mind, causality and identity, and all the rest? Gone with the indivisible atoms and the wave theory of light into the limbo of outworn delusions. The physicists of the world have reacted to this shock by revising their notions entirely; it is evident that psychologists must do likewise. I am now trying to revise my psychological and phonetic notions to accord with the new mode of thought. I take a kind of malicious pleasure in thinking that my fellow psychologists must undergo a like shock and struggle.

The shock came in this way. The fundamental law of all activity in the universe is

$$pq-qp=i\ [p,q]. \tag{10}$$

Here $i=\sqrt{-1}$ is a device for introducing complex numbers, and $[p,q]$ is a relation between operators known as a Poisson bracket expression. According to modern physics the action of pq is not continuous but proceeds by jumps, each jump being known as a quantum. A quantum is of the value of $h/2\pi$, where $h=6.588 \times 10^{-27}$ erg sec. (Planck's universal constant). It is a unit of work. We therefore replace the bracket expression by that for the quantum and write

$$pq-qp=i\ \frac{h}{2\pi}. \tag{11}$$

It has been assumed in physics that p and q act on systems of the nature of the linear harmonic oscillator. The result is in each case the number h multipled by another number v. This number is the radian frequency of the oscillation. For an elementary account of the conclusions to be drawn, I must refer to the charming presentation in Eddington's *Nature of the Physical World*. The important point here is that they give a picture of the structure of the universe out of atoms and that the conclusions are verified step by step by the spectrum lines. We must recognize that there are no cavities in the universe where the action of p and q are suspended; they do not act up to the inner ends of the nerves leading to the brain and then hand over the job to something else that acts in a cavity filled with mind. The harmonic oscillator, however, is an assumption justified only for the physical world by the lines in the spectrum; we do not need to assume its existence for the mind. It is quite possible that we may ultimately do so; in that case mind and the rest of the universe become the same thing. This seems to be Eddington's notion. What we perceive in consciousness is the inner side of what happens in the material world.

Nothing could be more instructive than the following delightful quotation from Eddington:

> *Something is doing we don't know what*—that is what our theory amounts to. It does not sound a particularly illuminating theory. I have read something like it elsewhere—
>
> . . . . The slithy toves
> Did gyre and gimble in the wabe.
>
> There is the same suggestion of activity. There is the same indefiniteness as to the nature of activity and of what is acting. And yet from so unpromising a beginning we really do get somewhere. We bring into order a host of apparently unrelated phenomena; we make predictions, and our predictions come off. The reason—the sole reason—for this progress is that our description is not limited to unknown agents executing unknown activities, but *numbers* are scattered freely in the description. To contemplate electrons circulating in an atom carries us no further; but by contemplating eight circulating electrons in one atom and seven circulating electrons in another we begin to realise the difference between oxygen and nitrogen. Eight slithy toves gyre and gimble in the oxygen wabe; seven in the nitrogen. By admitting a few numbers even "Jabberwocky" may become scientific. It would not be a bad reminder of the unknowableness of the fundamental entities of physics to translate it into "Jabberwocky"; provided all numbers—all metrical attributes—are unchanged, it does not suffer in the least. Out of the numbers proceeds that harmony of natural law which it is the aim of science to disclose. We can catch the tune but not the player. Trinculo might have been referring to modern physics in the words:
>
> This is the tune of my catch played by the picture of Nobody.

The player we can identify as pq but the scale troubles us. Again a quotation from Eddington:

> Nowadays whenever enthusiasts meet together to discuss theoretical physics the talk sooner or later turns in certain directions. You leave them conversing on their special problems or

the latest discoveries; but return after an hour and it is any
odds that they will have reached an all-engrossing topic—the
desperate state of their ignorance. This is not a pose. It is not
even scientific modesty, because the attitude is often one of naïve
surprise that Nature should have hidden her fundamental
secret successfully from such powerful intellects as ours. It
is simply that we have turned a corner in the path of progress
and our ignorance stands revealed before us, appalling and
insistent. There is something radically wrong with the present
conceptions of physics and we do not see how to set it right.
The cause of the trouble is a little thing called h which crops
up continually.

The psychologist cannot hope to escape the fate of the physicist
who has found that his fundamental space and time have disappeared,
that an atom of iron has no more substance than six mosquitos
buzzing about in a railway station, that the mosquitos themselves
are merely knots in the ether, that even the ether consists of nothing
more substantial than differential equations, and finally that everything has turned into a lot of numbers scattered about in "Jabberwocky." One might suggest that the reality is a fundamental fog
in which the only things visible are the illuminated numbers on
the tramlines of the space-time universe, with the peculiarity that
the trams do not run continuously but proceed by jerks. Or shall
we say that the numbers belong to the airplanes of the Unknowable
that light up only at the end of each hop?

Of the new psychology that is just beginning in this way we can
already get some faint notions. The factor of time in mind is not
given by anything resembling physical timeclocks but by entropy
clocks (Eddington). In the physical world entropy is the measure
of the increase of the random element. In the mind it is the measure
of becoming. As it appears in consciousness we call it time. Entropy
can never change backward from more randomness to less randomness.
Entropy's arrow has only one direction. In consciousness it appears
as time's arrow. The sharp end is termed the future and the blunt
end the past. The time of consciousness can never be turned backward. This is not true of physical time. Every physical event can
be reversed in time like a picture reel run backward. Physical entropy,
however, cannot be reversed (second law of thermodynamics). Our
entropy clocks are not in consciousness, for we know nothing about
them. Eddington assigns them to the brain and remarks that they

are not very good timekeepers. This is not fair. The entropy clocks belong to the Great Unknown. What they indicate is the standard. Time in consciousness may or may not correspond accurately to the entropy clocks but that is a matter of perception and not of the clocks. We may "forget the time" in reading an interesting book, but, when we wake up, our entropy clocks warn us of how much of life we have spent. Even if the warning does not come into consciousness clearly or correctly, it is there in the Great Unknown.

The coming generation of psychologists is faced with the task of developing this new psychology. They must discover the needed methods of measurement and must be able to handle the results mathematically. Difficulties must be overcome and criticism disregarded. At all times they should bear in mind the motto of Boltzmann:

Tue, was wahr ist; sage, was klar ist; fichte, bis es dar ist.

*   *   *

I notice a paucity of personal details in my account. I have forgotten most of them and I am not interested in the rest; I do not think the reader would be interested either. In order to be dated and placed I have to state that I was born in 1864 in a village in New Hampshire, U. S. A.

EDWARD LEE THORNDIKE

I have no memory of having heard or seen the word psychology until in my junior year at Wesleyan University (1893-1894), when I took a required course in it. The textbook, Sully's *Psychology,* aroused no notable interest, nor did the excellent lectures of Professor A. C. Armstrong, though I appreciated and enjoyed the dignity and clarity of his presentation and admired his skill in discrimination and argument. These discriminations and arguments stimulated me very little, however, and this was later true also of the writings of James, Ward, and Stout. There is evidently some lack in my equipment which makes me intolerant of critical studies unless fortified by new facts or decorated by a captivating style.

The candidates in a prize examination were required to read also certain chapters from James's *Principles.* These were stimulating, more so than any book that I had read before, and possibly more so than any read since. The evidence is threefold. I bought the two volumes (the only book outside the field of literature that I voluntarily bought during the four years of college) and read all save parts of the most technical chapters. Though not, I hope, more impertinent than the average collegian, I reproached Professor Armstrong for not having given us James in place of Sully as our text. When a year later, circumstances permitted me to study at Harvard, I eagerly registered for the course available under James.

During the first semester at Harvard (1896-1897) my program was half English, one-fourth psychology, and one-fourth philosophy, the last at the suggestion or requirement of Professor Royce. The subtlety and dexterity of Royce's mind aroused admiration tinged with irritation and amusement. Most of the students saw him as a prophet, but to me then he seemed too much a performer. Under no circumstances, probably, could I have been able or willing to make philosophy my business. Its stars shone brightly at Harvard in those years (1895-1897); Royce and Santayana were at or near their full glory, and Palmer was, as ever, the perfect expositor, but what I heard from them or about them did not attract me. Later I read the *Life of Reason* with extraordinary interest and profit, and learned to value the integrity and sincerity and impartiality of Dewey's writings on philosophy as well as on psychology and education; but in general my acquaintance with philosophy has been superficial and casual. Work in English was dropped in favor of psychology in the course of the first graduate year, and, by the Fall of 1897, I thought of myself as a student of psychology and a candidate for the Ph.D degree.

Münsterberg was in Germany from the Fall of 1895 to the Fall of 1897. During the second half of 1895-1896, Mr. Hackett and I had made experiments in a course under the direction of Professor Delabarre, who had charge of the laboratory. During 1896-1897 I first attempted to measure the responsiveness of young children (3-6) to facial expressions or movements made unconsciously as in mind-reading experiments. I would think of one of a set of numbers, letters, or objects (I cannot now recall which or how many). The child, facing me across a small table, would look at me and guess which. If he guessed right, he received a small bit of candy. The children enjoyed the experiments, but the authorities in control of the institution would not permit me to continue them. I then suggested experiments with the instinctive and intelligent behavior of chickens as a topic, and this was accepted. I kept these animals and conducted the experiments in my room until the landlady's protests were imperative. James tried to get the few square feet required for me in the laboratory, and then in the Agassiz Museum. He was refused, and with his habitual kindness and devotion to underdogs and eccentric aspects of science, harbored my chickens in the cellar of his own home for the rest of the year. The nuisance to Mrs. James was, I hope, somewhat mitigated by the entertainment to the two youngest children.

During the two years of study at Harvard, I had supported myself by acting as tutor to a boy. We roomed together, and the incessant companionship and responsibility was burdensome, though he was cheerful, cooperative, and fonder of me than I deserved, and though I learned much practical psychology and pedagogy from the experience. A year free from such labor seemed desirable, so I applied for a fellowship at Columbia. I received the appointment, and upon inquiry was informed by Professor Cattell that an extension of my work on the mental life of animals would be suitable for a doctor's thesis. So I continued these experiments with chickens at my parents' home during the summer. I tried white rats also, but I was stupid in handling them and the family objected to the smell, so I let them go.

I came to New York, bringing in a basket my two most educated chickens, from whom I then expected in due time to breed, and so test the influence of acquired mental traits upon inherited capacity, a foolish project in view of the slow breeding rate of fowls. I also expected to test the permanence of their learning over a long interval, but never did, the first of a regrettable list of enterprises left incomplete.

Cattell was not only kind, but highly efficient, providing a room in the attic which was ample for my purpose, and giving, as always, sound advice. The freedom from work and worry for money was a great boon. The present policy of universities is to reduce grants for scholarships and fellowships relatively to the number of students, replacing them by loan funds, and this may be wise. But, so far as I can judge, scholarships at Harvard and a fellowship at Columbia increased my productive work in science by at least two years and probably improved its quality.

The motive for my first investigations of animal intelligence was chiefly to satisfy requirements for courses and degrees. Any other topic would probably have served me as well. I certainly had no special interest in animals and had never taken a course in biology until my last year of graduate work, when I worked hard at it and completed a minor for the doctor's degree. The work with monkeys, done in 1899-1901, was done from the mixture of duty, interest, and desire for good repute which motivates most scientific work. The extension of the fruitful experimental method to representative primates was obviously important. I would have gladly continued the work with the higher apes, but could not afford to buy or maintain them.

In the Spring of 1898, I was offered two positions, one as a teacher of psychology in a normal school, the other at a much lower salary as a teacher of education in the College for Women of Western Reserve University. I chose the latter, partly because my brother expected to go there and partly because of the repute of Western Reserve. I spent the summer in reading the facts and important theories about education and teaching. This could then be done if the history of educational practices was omitted. After a year at Cleveland, I was given a trial at teaching psychology and child study at Teachers College, and there I have spent the past thirty-one years.

I have recorded my beginning as a psychologist in detail because it illustrates what is perhaps the most general fact about my entire career as a psychologist later, namely, its responsiveness to outer pressure or opportunity rather than to inner needs. Within certain limits set by capacity and interest I did in those early years and have done since what the occasion seemed to demand. Thus for various courses taught at Teachers College I wrote the *Elements of Psychology, Notes on Child Study, Educational Psychology* (in three editions, from 1903 to 1914), *An Introduction to the Theory of Mental and Social Measurements,* and *The Psychology of Arithmetic.* It has always seemed to me better for an instructor to present his contributions in black and white than to require the labor and risk the errors of note-taking. Thus I have made somewhat laborious researches on mental inheritance, individual and sex differences, memory, work, fatigue, interest, the interrelations of abilities, the organization of intellect, and other topics in educational psychology, because in each case the matter seemed important for theory or practice or both. Thus I planned and directed the psychological work of the New York State Commission on Ventilation, prepared tests for the selection of clerical employees, and served on the Committee on Classification of Personnel in the Army and in various other enterprises because I was told by persons in whom I had confidence that it was in the line of duty. Thus I have written textbooks for children to show that psychology does apply in detail to the work of the classroom. Thus, in 1919, at the request of the faculty of Columbia College, I undertook the responsibility of preparing annually an intelligence examination suitable for use in the selection and placement of freshmen; and in 1922, at the request of Justice Stone, then Dean of the Columbia Law School, I conducted a three-year investigation which resulted in the Capacity Test adopted in 1928 as a part of the system of selection of entrants to the Columbia Law School.

Obviously I have not "carried out my career," as the biographers say. Rather it has been a conglomerate, amassed under the pressure of varied opportunities and demands. Probably it would have been wiser to plan a more consistent and unified life-work in accord with interest and capacity, but I am not sure. Even in the case of great men, there is considerable evidence that the man's own interests and plans may not cause a better output than his responses to demands from outside. So James wrote the *Principles* with wailing and gnashing of teeth to fulfill a contract with a publishing firm. *Pragmatism* and *The Will to Believe* were done when he was free to choose. An ordinary man of science has probably less reason to put his own plans above those which the world makes for him. So I do not complain of the restrictions imposed by the necessity of earning a living by various drudgeries to which I have been assigned. And I reproach myself only moderately for not having looked and thought longer before leaping to this, that, and the other job.

In the last dozen years I have been enabled by grants from the Carnegie Corporation to carry on two investigations which I did choose and plan, one on the fundamentals of measurement of intellect and capacity, the results of which appeared as *The Measurement of Intelligence,* the other on the fundamentals of learning, the results of which have appeared in *The Fundamentals of Learning* and in *The Psychology of Wants, Interests, and Attitudes.* These do seem to me by far the best work that I have done and I cannot help wondering what would have happened if similar support had been available in 1905 or 1915.

The impetuosity to which I have referred has influenced my work in detail. I often have to do corrective and supplementary experiments and discard work because in its course a better way is found.

Another weakness has been an extreme ineptitude and distaste for using machinery and physical instruments. Presumably my work would have been better, and certainly it would have seemed better, if I had been at home with apparatus for exposing, timing, registering, and the like.

The training which I have most keenly missed has been a systematic course in the use of standard physiological and psychological apparatus and extended training in mathematics. Perhaps the first would not have profited much in view of my extreme incapacity. I did not lack capacity for mathematics and tried to remedy the second deficiency by private study, but something else always seemed more important. I managed to learn the essentials of statistical method somehow, and have handled some fairly intricate quantitative problems without, I think, making more than one mistake (which I was able to correct promptly at the suggestion of Dr. T. L. Kelley). But I feel incompetent and insecure in the abstract algebraic treatment of a quantitative problem and am helpless when the calculus is necessary.

Young psychologists who share one or more of my disabilities may take comfort in the fact that, after all, I have done useful experiments without mechanical ability or training and have investigated quantitative relations with very meager knowledge of mathematics.

As personal features on the other side of the ledger I may put intelligence, good health, strong eyes, the interest in work and achievement which Veblen has called the instinct of workmanship, impartiality, and industry. As environmental features I may note home life with parents of superior intelligence and idealism, many profitable courses in Wesleyan, Harvard, and Columbia, especially those in abnormal psychology with James, statistical methods with Boas, and neurology with Strong, university colleagues eminent in psychology and other fields, and the great body of published work in science.

The last is of course the most important. Though an investigator rather than a scholar, I have probably spent well over 20,000 hours in reading and studying scientific books and journals.

I have tried to make two lists, one of authors all or nearly all of whose writings I have read, and another of authors not included in the above to whom I owe valuable facts or suggestions. But the first list of thirty or so names grades off into the names of many more, much of whose writing I have read, and the second list, which is very long, cannot be accurate because of faults of memory. So I may note only that the writings of James and Galton have influenced me most, and that factual material seems to benefit me more than what is commonly called discussion and criticism. Although, as has been stated, my tendency is to say "Yes" to persons, my tendency seems to have been to say "No" to ideas. So I have been stimulated to study problems, to which Romanes, Wesley Mills, Stanley Hall, Alexander Bain, Kraepelin, Spearman, and others seemed to me to give wrong answers, more often than to verify and extend work which seemed sound. Of late years this negative or critical tendency seems to have weakened and given place to an interest in questions to which the answers are conflicting or inadequate, and in questions which have not even been faced.

Up till the War I was able to keep fairly well informed of the findings of psychologists in respect to animal psychology, individual psychology, and educational psychology, but since 1917 I have been able only to follow specially important work and that which I had to know about in connection with my own researches. In spite of the saving of time due to the *Psychological Abstracts,* my reading is now less and less adequate each year.

I have a suspicion that our scientific code, which demands that an investigator should acquaint himself with everything, good, bad, and indifferent, that has been done on the problem which he is investigating, should be somewhat relaxed. Personally I seem to have profited more from reading important books outside of the topics I had to investigate, and even outside of psychology, than from some of the monographs and articles on animal learning, intelligence tests, and the like, which our code required me to read.

We are especially urged in these psychological autobiographies to describe our methods of work, but I seem to have little or nothing useful to say in this regard. In the actual work of advancing knowledge of human nature we may use three methods. We may observe and think about the facts that come our way; we may deliberately gather by observation or experiment facts which we see can be got and which seem likely to be instructive; we may put a question that we know is important and then do our best to get facts to answer it. I have done all three; most often the last. The most fruitful methods often come to mind late in the course of an investigation. When one does everything that he can think of, the doing often makes him think of something else. So the idea of the delayed-reaction experiment (which has proved the most valuable of my methods of studying animal mentality) came to me after two years of work with animals. So the idea that the difficulty of a task for intellect (or any other ability) can be measured only in the case of a task composed of enough elements to involve all of intellect (or of the ability, whatever it may be), and nothing but it, came only after 30 years of study of intellect, and over a year of special investigation of means of measuring difficulty for intellect.

Concerning conditions favorable and unfavorable to scholarly and productive work in science, I have little or nothing instructive to report. Peaceful successful work without worry has rarely tired me, though if I drop below a certain minimum amount of sleep, a headache results. Noise does not disturb me unless it is evidence of distress, as of a person or animal in pain. Surety of freedom from interruption is of course beneficial. Social intercourse except with intimate friends is fatiguing, and all forms of personal conflict, as in bargaining, persuading, or rebuking, are trebly so. Physical exercise is enjoyable, but not, so far as I know, beneficial. A general background of freedom from regret and worry is almost imperative, and I early decided to spend so little and earn so much as to keep free from financial worries. In order to reduce one cause for worry, it has been my custom to fulfill my contractual obligations as a professor before doing anything else. The good opinion of others, especially those whom I esteem, has been a very great stimulus, though I have come in later years to require also the approval of my own judgment.

Since my own history is so barren of interest and instruction I may add a few notes of general observation. Excellent work in psychology can surely be done by men widely different in nature or training or both. James and Hall were essentially literary men, one with an extraordinary sense of fact, the other with extraordinary imagination and prophetic zeal. On the other hand, some of our present leaders were first trained in physics or engineering.

Excellent work can surely be done by men with widely different notions of what psychology is and should be, the best work of all perhaps being done by men such as Galton, who gave little or no thought to what it is or should be.

Excellent results have come from the successive widenings of the field of observation to include the insane, infants, and animals, and from the correlation of mental events with physiological changes. Should we not extend our observations to include, for example, history, anthropology, economics, linguistics, and the fine arts, and connect them with biochemistry and biophysics?

JOHN BROADUS WATSON

I was born near Greenville, South Carolina, in 1878. I was married in 1903 to Mary Ickes. Two children came from this marriage —Polly and John. I was divorced in 1920 and was married immediately to Rosalie Rayner, of Baltimore. We have two children, Billy, now fifteen, and Jimmy, now twelve.

My earliest academic memories relate themselves to district schools in areas in South Carolina called Reedy River, White Horse, and Travelers Rest. From the age of six, I trudged two miles to one or another of these places. At nine years of age I was handling tools, half-soling shoes, and milking cows. At 12 I was a pretty fair carpenter. This manual skill has never lost its charm, and in the Summers of 1909 and 1910 I built a ten-room house from blue prints. At 54, I built a stucco garage, and at 55, on weekends, I built a 31' x 61' barn of stucco with copper roof.

In 1890, when I was 12 years of age my family moved to Greenville, South Carolina, a village of 20,000 souls where I entered the public schools, passing through grammar school and high school. I have few pleasant memories of these years. I was lazy, somewhat insubordinate, and, so far as I know, I never made above a passing grade. I used to have a friend by the name of Joe Leech with whom I boxed every time my teacher left the room, boxed until one or the other drew blood. "Nigger" fighting was one of our favorite going-home activities. Twice I was arrested, once for "nigger" fighting, and the second time for shooting off firearms inside the city limits.

I entered Furman University in 1894 at the age of 16, as a sub-freshman, and stayed there five years, taking an A.M. instead of an A.B. I earned my way for two years in the chemical laboratory as an assistant. Little of my college life interested me. In my first year, I fell in love with one of the three coeds in the University and I joined the Kappa Alpha fraternity. I was unsocial and had few close friends. The only real friend I had during my high school and college days was George Buist, late Professor of Chemistry in Furman University. I studied Greek for five years and Latin for five years. In my senior year, I was the only man who passed the final Greek exam. I did it only because I went to my room at two o'clock the afternoon before the exam, took with me one quart of Coca-Cola syrup, and sat in my chair and crammed until time for

271

the exam next day. Today I could not read Xenophon's *Anabasis* or Caesar's *Commentaries*. I couldn't to save my life write the Greek alphabet or conjugate a verb or decline a noun in Latin. My mathematics is equally poor. I went through plane geometry, trigonometry, statics and dynamics, integral and differential calculus. I would never have passed in any one, if Professor Wilton Earle, still Professor of Mathematics in Furman, and Love Durham, now Professor of Latin in Cornell, had not practically written my exam papers for me.

In philosophy and psychology I fared better. There I had Professor Gordon B. Moore. Under him I devoured Bowne's *Metaphysics,* Davis' *Psychology,* Weber's *History of Philosophy,* and considerable collateral reading including some of Wundt. I don't know how many of my colleagues have accused me of not having any philosophy. It always amuses me because my milk teeth were practically cut upon metaphysics. Moore, who was a philosopher and a clergyman at the same time, gave us his best. It was the progress I made in these fields that led me into psychology. A funny incident apparently made me decide to become a Ph.D. in psychology and philosophy. Professor Moore, during my junior year, had gone on a sabbatical to the University of Chicago to study psychology. I took my final year with him. One day in class he said that, if a man ever handed in a paper backwards, he would flunk him. Although I had been an honor student the whole year, by some strange streak of luck, I handed in my final paper of sixteen pages in Civics backwards. He kept his word. He flunked me and I had to stay another year, taking an A.M. and not an A.B. I made an adolescent resolve then to the effect that I'd make him seek me out for research some day. Imagine my surprise and real sorrow during the second year of my stay at Hopkins, when I received a letter from him asking to come to me as a research student. Before we could arrange it, his eyesight failed, and he died a few years later.

This failure of college to mean anything to me in the way of an education gave me most of my slants against college. Those years made me bitter, made me feel that college only weakens the vocational slants and leads to softness and laziness and a prolongation of infancy with a killing of all vocational bents. Only with the years have I reached a point of view to the effect that, until college becomes a place where daily living can be taught, we must look

tolerantly upon college as a place for boys and girls to be penned
up in until they reach majority—then let the world sift them out.

Where to go to a university? My old philosophy professor, G. B.
Moore, had gone to the University of Chicago. He told me of
Dewey. I was more interested in philosophy than psychology at
that time. I had heard of Baldwin at Princeton and I wrote him
first, asking him about Greek and Latin. He replied they still insisted on a reading knowledge. That settled it, and I went to the
University of Chicago with $50 in my pocket. I met Dewey, I met
Angell, and I met John Manly, my brother's brother-in-law. I
entered then, and felt at once that I had come to the right place.
Mr. Angell's erudition, quickness of thought, and facility with words
early captured my somewhat backward leaning towards psychology.
I spent three years and three Summers taking my Ph.D. They were
frightfully busy years. I had to earn my living, which I did serving
as a kind of assistant janitor. For two years I used to dust Mr.
Angell's desk and clean the apparatus. I delivered books for an
instructors' circulating library for $1.00 per Saturday. I
waited on table for my board for two years at a $2.50 per week
students' boarding house. One year later when I met Professor
H. H. Donaldson, he asked me to keep his white rats for him, a
job which helped me greatly on the financial side. Mr. Angell
steered me into experimental psychology as a major, philosophy as
a first minor under Dewey, Tufts, and Moore, and into neurology
under Donaldson as my second minor. In connection with neurology
I took biology, and then physiology under Loeb. Loeb wanted me to
do my research under him upon the physiology of the dog's brain.
Neither Angell nor Donaldson in those days felt that Loeb was
a very "safe" man for a green Ph.D. candidate, so I took my research jointly under Donaldson and Angell on the correlation between increasing complexity of the behavior in the white rat and
the growth of medullation in the central nervous system. Incidentally, it cost me $350.00 to publish my thesis, a sum which Professor
Donaldson lent me, and which I could not repay until I had been
in business two years.

I enjoyed the years in neurology and physiology and my research
on the rats. I worked night and day and established work habits
that have persisted the rest of my life. My debt to Angell, Donaldson, and Loeb can never be repaid except by gratitude.

On the philosophy side, progress was slower. I had two courses under Dewey, Kant under Tufts (I took this course twice), British philosophers under Moore, Greek philosophy under Tufts, two courses in the movement of thought under Tufts, private reading in Wundt under Tufts, a course under Ames, and other odds and ends. God knows I took enough philosophy to know something about it. But it wouldn't take hold. I passed my exams but the spark was not there. I got something out of the British School of Philosophers—mainly out of Hume, a little out of Locke, a bit out of Hartley, nothing out of Kant, and, strange to say, least of all out of John Dewey. I never knew what he was talking about then, and, unfortunately for me, I still don't know. Tufts and Moore were patient with me and I attach no blame to them for my failing to flower in philosophy. I took courses and seminars with Mead. I didn't understand him in the classroom, but for years Mead took a great interest in my animal experimentation, and many a Sunday he and I spent in the laboratory watching my rats and monkeys. On these comradely exhibitions and at his home I understood him. A kinder, finer man I never met.

In the Fall of the year before I was graduated, I had a breakdown—sleepless nights for weeks—a typical Angst. Getting up at three A.M. to walk eight and ten miles—then off for my first vacation in three years with my friends, the Van Pelts, in Norwood, Michigan. A month there during which, for three weeks, I went to sleep only with a light turned on. A sudden recovery and back to work. This, in a way, was one of my best experiences in my university course. It taught me to watch my step and in a way prepared me to accept a large part of Freud, when I first began to get really acquainted with him around 1910.

Finally I got my degree. I believe I was at that time the youngest Ph.D. turned out by that institution. I got my first deep-seated inferiority at the same time. I received my degree Magna Cum Laude and was told, almost immediately, by Dewey and Angell that my exam was much inferior to that of Miss Helen Thompson who had graduated two years before with a Summa Cum Laude. I wondered then if anybody could ever equal her record. That jealousy existed for years. Next, to get a job. Donaldson offered me an assistantship in neurology—I am proud of that to this day. Then the University of Cincinnati offered me an instructorship in psychology. I was on the point of accepting it when Dewey asked me to stay on in experimental psychology because Mr. Angell, who was teaching at the University of California that Summer, began to pay the penalty for ten years of overwork. I stayed on as his assistant for two years and was then made an instructor. In 1904, I spent a Summer at the Johns Hopkins Hospital under Dr. William Howell, working up an operative technique on animals. There I renewed my acquaintanceship with Professor J. M. Baldwin. We grew to be friends. In the Fall of 1907 Stratton left Johns Hopkins and Baldwin offered me the job as Associate Professor at $2500. I hesitated. He next invited me to come to Hopkins as Professor at $3500. During this moment of hesitancy, the University of Chicago had raised me from Instructor to Assistant Professor Elect. I felt when the offer of the chair came from Hopkins I was foolish not to go. I was then 29. I hated to leave the University of Chicago laboratory and Mr. Angell. I am sure I would have not gone had they offered me even an associate professorship. I had several researches going. I had wired the lab with my own hands, built partitions, animal yards, and much apparatus on vision, in which both Professors Milliken and Gale assisted me.

On the whole, my Chicago experience was most satisfactory. I think the only fly in the ointment was my inability, for financial reasons, to finish with my medical education. I never wanted to practice medicine. I wanted it only as a means of working with medical men and to save me from a little of the insolence of the youthful and inferior members of that profession when I had to come in contact with them. I learned my James under Angell, patience and exactness in research under Donaldson, and from Loeb the fact that all research need not be uninteresting. I learned also under Angell how to lecture and express my thinking in words simply chosen. Indeed, he worked daily with me on every sentence I wrote on my thesis, "Animal Education." He taught me rhetoric as well as psychology, and, if he failed me on logic, it was not his fault. The students in these years with whom I came into closest friendship were Miss Allen (now Mrs. Charters), Harvey Carr, who succeeded me, Clara Jean Weidensall, Florence Richardson (now Mrs. Robinson), C. S. Yoakum, and Mr. and Mrs. J. W. Hayes. Carr and I have remained close friends notwithstanding our difference in point of view and the distance and time that have separated us.

He is one of the most careful students I ever worked with. It was with him in the translation of a good deal of Wundt that I learned to get about in German psychology. The research he and I did together on the lengthened and shortened maze still brings a bit of a kick when I think of it. Besides my thesis, "Animal Education," and the work I did with Carr, I did at least one major piece of work before I left for Hopkins. This was my maze work on normal, blind, and anosmic rats. My thesis work on its behavior side was more or less a following of the technique of Small, Thorndike, and Lloyd Morgan. On its neurological side I was guided at every moment by Professor Donaldson. On the maze work I felt a certain independence. There I utilized the operative technique I had learned under Dr. Howell at Johns Hopkins in 1904. While at Chicago, I got well started on my work on animal vision, using monkeys as subjects, and upon my work on the noddy and sooty terns in the Dry Tortugas, carried out at the invitation of Dr. Alfred G. Mayer of the Marine Biological Station of the Carnegie Institution of Washington, D. C.

At Chicago, I first began a tentative formulation of my later point of view. I never wanted to use human subjects. I hated to serve as a subject. I didn't like the stuffy, artificial instructions given to subjects. I always was uncomfortable and acted unnaturally. With animals I was at home. I felt that, in studying them, I was keeping close to biology with my feet on the ground. More and more the thought presented itself: Can't I find out by watching their behavior everything that the other students are finding out by using O's? As I have said elsewhere, I broached this to my colleagues, as early as 1904, but received little encouragement.

In the Fall of 1908 I went to Hopkins—met Baldwin, Jennings, Dunlap, Lovejoy, and Dr. Adolf Meyer. The whole tenor of my life was changed. I tasted freedom in work without supervision. I was lost in and happy in my work. The late Dr. Remsen and Dr. Joseph Ames, later President of Hopkins, did everything in their power to make my work successful—money and apparatus were provided amply. Soon I had all the facilities I had at Chicago and more. As soon as possible, I began work with Jennings, taking his courses in evolution and his lab work on the behavior of lower organisms.

For two years at Hopkins I taught a modified James type of

general psychology, using Titchener's experimental manuals in my experimental courses. But my research continued in the animal field. I began to work upon more elaborate apparatus for the study of vision. Professor R. W. Wood of the Physics Department gave me great help, and Dr. A. H. Pfund of the Physics Department taught me the use of the selenium cell for equating the energy of light beams. Robert Yerkes came in 1909 to work upon the conditional glandular response in dogs at the Medical School. We began to collaborate upon visual apparatus and finally published a monograph together—"Methods of Studying Vision in Animals." This monograph involved a colossal amount of work on both of our parts, and on the part of our mechanician, Charley Childs.

About this time I began to perfect my point of view about behaviorism. To Dunlap I owe much. In his own biography in this series he has probably stated my indebtedness to him better than I can express it myself. I only want to add that what he says is true. Lashley, who came to me a well-trained biologist from Jennings, contributed to my point of view more than his own modesty will allow him to say. A large part of the material I sketched in my 1915 address as President of the American Psychological Association was contributed by him. I am sure I remember that he first used the term *conditioned emotional reflex* in one of my seminars.

The War played havoc with my work for the time being. I tried to get in as a line officer but failed on account of my eyes. I went on my vacation to Canada for the summer as usual In August, I was sent for by the Committee on Personnel in the Army and left for Washington. I was soon given charge of organizing and running the aviation examining boards. This work was complex and I worked night and day. In all, some 70 boards were established. This work held my interest until Colonel Bingham, now ex-Senator Bingham of Connecticut, was put in charge. His egotism and self-seeking soon made every one in the personnel section of aviation understand why it is that some officers fail to return from expeditions even when not engaged by enemy troops. After enough men were accepted for training, I was sent to Lake Charles and to San Antonio to work on the release of homing pigeons in planes and balloons and to study travelling military codes. I sent in a report on this which amounted to nothing, for by that time radio had forever put the pigeon out as a factor in war. I was ordered back to Washington and asked to go overseas carrying a trunk filled with Thorndike's questionnaires to be filled out by British aviators. Thorndike hoped to gather information that might guide us in the selection of aviators in the United States. I reported at once to General Foullois at Tours and there awaited orders to go to the Marne front. I received my orders, went to Paris, and was met by a courier telling me my orders were cancelled because of the reverses the British were meeting. I proceeded next under Colonel Von Horn's orders to Colombes Les Belles, near Nancy. There I first saw a little of action, was under fire for the first time. No real work for me being at hand, I asked for orders home after three months of overseas service. I happened to be in Paris the day the big gun opened up, was there in several Boche air raids and in London in an air raid. Sailed home on the Rochambeau and saw a torpedo cross our stern. So much for overseas.

I returned to Washington and was transferred to the Aviation Medical Corps to work under Colonel Crabtree on oxygen deprivation. Did some work of an unsatisfactory nature, got into trouble because my own Corps asked me to write them, directly and not through military channels, what I thought of the famous "Rotation Test." I was nearly court-martialled for doing so. I was returned by Colonel Crabtree to Aviation with the notation "that he be not allowed to serve his country in his scientific capacity, but be sent to the line"; in other words, the wish was implied that I be killed speedily. I was then transferred to the General Staff to train for overseas work on positive military intelligence (where I was sure to be killed). Bentley and I did considerable work on commonsense tests for the selection of men for night scouting. I was awaiting overseas orders when the Armistice was signed. I got into mufti as soon as possible. The whole army experience is a nightmare to me. Never have I seen such incompetence, such extravagance, such a group of overbearing, inferior men. Talk of putting a Negro in uniform! It is nothing to making a Major or Lieutenant Colonel of most of the Rotary Club men who went in as officers in the American Army (West Point and Naval Academy men excepted). The French and British officers were such a superior set of gentlemen that the contrast was pitiful; I can liken it only to a fanciful situation of a group of Yankee drummers dining at the Court of St. James.

Back again in November, 1918, to pick up the threads of my laboratory work at the Phipps Psychiatric Clinic. I began work upon infants and to formulate my book, *Psychology from the Standpoint of a Behaviorist*. The names of three medical men stand out here who helped me, Dr. Adolf Meyer, Dr. John Howland, and Dr. J. Whitridge Williams. They made possible my work on infants.

Dr. Meyer was kind enough to have his whole staff meet in my laboratory once each week and let me read my manuscript on *Psychology from the Standpoint of a Behaviorist* chapter by chapter. The kindly criticisms I received were very helpful. This book was published in 1919 by Lippincott. Dr. Karl Lashley, who was working in the department as Johnston Scholar at the time, Dr. Leslie B. Hohman, then resident psychiatrist at Phipps, and Dr. Curt Paul Richter stand out as my advisers, intellectual and emotional, during these years, 1919 being my last full year at Hopkins.

At this time, my infant work was in full swing, as well as extensive work on learning—learning and performance under hypnosis, alcohol, and drugs. All of this work came abruptly to a close with my divorce in 1920. I was asked to resign.

Upon resigning, I went to New York, stranded economically and to some extent emotionally. I lived the Summer and Fall out with William I. Thomas. What I should have done without his understanding counsel and his helpfulness on the economic side, I do not know. I was a product of schools and colleges. I knew nothing of life outside the walls of a university. He saw to it that I met people in business, and it was through him that I got my first business tryout with the J. Walter Thompson Company. His friends, Miss Alice Boughton and Miss Mildred Bennett, were employed at the J. Walter Thompson Company. I was introduced to the President, Mr. Stanley Resor, who sent me on a temporary investigation job, studying the rubber boot market on each side of the Mississippi River from Cairo to New Orleans. I was green and shy, but soon learned to pull doorbells and stop wagons in order to ask what brand of rubber boots was worn by the family. This took the Fall of 1920, the whole of the trying time when I was front-page news in Baltimore. On January 1, 1921, I was taken over permanently at the Thompson Company and was sent out immediately to sell Yuban Coffee to retailers and wholesalers in Pittsburg, Cleveland, and Erie.

I carried my pack for over two months. This job was just what I needed to rub off the academic. When I returned to the agency, I went through every department, media, research, and copy. I felt one distinct need. I knew little about the great advertising god, the consumer. Accordingly, I made private arrangements to clerk in Macy's Department Store for two months during the Summer of 1921. It took me a little more than a year to find myself in the agency. I began to learn that it can be just as thrilling to watch the growth of a sales curve of a new product as to watch the learning curve of animals or men. I was made a Vice-President of the J. Walter Thompson Company in 1924, in which capacity I served the agency until I resigned in 1936 to become Vice-President of William Esty and Company.

Leaving Hopkins did not mean a complete giving up of intellectual activity. After Beard and Robinson left the New School I was invited to lecture there and did so for several years. I enjoyed my lectures there very much. It satisfied a side of me that would have been starved if I had not had this outlet. I owe this opportunity to Horace Kallen, Leo Wallman, and Alvin Johnson.

Very shortly after leaving Johns Hopkins, W. W. Norton, then a struggling but now a flourishing publisher, got hold of me and practically forced me to write up a course of lectures I was giving for Everett D. Martin at the Cooper Institute. As rapidly as I could write a lecture, Norton published it in a pamphlet form called "Lectures in Print." This was a strictly rush job. My lectures were taken down in shorthand and then I looked over them and rushed them to Norton. Later they were rewritten as *Behaviorism*. This book still shows its hasty origin. I polished it still more in the second edition, finished in 1930.

Psychological Care of Infant and Child was another book I feel sorry about—not because of its sketchy form, but because I did not know enough to write the book I wanted to write. I feel that I had a right to publish this, sketchy as it is, since I planned never to go back into academic work.

From 1922 on I wrote popular articles for *Harper's Magazine* (thanks to Wells and Lee Hartman), *McCall's Magazine, Liberty, Collier's,* and *Cosmopolitan.* I received pay for them—generous pay. I had learned how to write what the public would read, and, since there was no longer opportunity for me to publish in technical journals, I saw no reason why I should not go to the public with my wares. Yet these articles have brought criticism greater than the offense, I believe, from no less a person than President Angell of Yale. His Commencement Address at Dartmouth some years ago left me with no bitterness but rather with a poignant sadness. I just wonder whether he or other of my colleagues confronted with my situation would not have sold himself to the public.

I have reached the end of my psychological career. I have even given up courses of lectures upon psychological subjects. I write an occasional popular article upon some general topic with a psychological background and an occasional radio talk. My life is taken up with business, my family, and my farm. I sometimes think I regret that I could not have a group of infant farms where I could have brought up thirty pure-blooded Negroes on one, thirty "pure"-blooded Anglo-Saxons on another, and thirty Chinese on a third—all under similar conditions. Some day it will be done, but by a younger man.

I still believe as firmly as ever in the general behavioristic position I took overtly in 1912. I think it has influenced psychology. Strangely enough, I think it has temporarily slowed down psychology because the older instructors would not accept it wholeheartedly, and consequently they failed to present it convincingly to their classes. The youngsters did not get a fair presentation, hence they are not embarking wholeheartedly upon a behavioristic career, and yet they will no longer accept the teachings of James, Titchener, and Angell. I honestly think that psychology has been sterile for several years. We need younger instructors who will teach objective psychology with no reference to the mythology most of us present-day psychologists have been brought up upon. When this day comes, psychology will have a renaissance greater than that which occurred in science in the Middle Ages. I believe as firmly as ever in the future of behaviorism—behaviorism as a companion of zoölogy, physiology, psychiatry, and physical chemistry.

WILHELM WIRTH*

I. University Study until Graduation (1894-1897)

In a rather long study in developmental psychology which I published under the title, "How I Came to Philosophy and Psychology,"[1] I have already explained the prehistory of my very early resolution to make university teaching in philosophy and psychology my life career, and therefore to major in these subjects right from the beginning. As the leader of my academic study I chose Theodor Lipps, whose *Grundzüge der Logik* I had already read in the senior class of preparatory school, and had found to agree in principle with the method of philosophizing on a psychological basis, and with the view of life so gained, which I had taken over from my father. Therefore, in the Fall of 1894 I entered the University of Munich to which Theodor Lipps had been called a short time before.

In his unusually stimulating lectures on psychology in the Winter Semester of 1894-1895 I found an abundance of new problems in the framework of a firmly integrated system which I strove to understand better and better through an intensive study of his principal work, *Grundtatsachen des Seelenlebens,* which my father gave me that Christmas. Its methodical foundation delimited psychology (very fittingly for that time) as an independent field of knowledge, particularly from brain physiology, with which it was often confused since the introduction of experiment. For this purpose Lipps gave a clear concept of the nature of its object, psychic life, whose phenomena are revealed to us only in the self-observation of our conscious ideas, feelings, and strivings, however much we may refine the exploration of its conditions through experiment. For the scientific understanding of these phenomena we must, however, in thoughtful digestion of such observations of consciousness, make deductions about subconscious processes, which are fundamental, which are the true psychic reality in the homogeneous whole of our "personality," i.e., of our "Psyche." These are, indeed, in close relation to the material processes of the brain, but are in no wise deducible from the observation of the brain.

---

*Submitted in German and translated for the Clark University Press by Harold S. Jantz.

[1] Wie ich zur Philosophie und Psychologie kam. *Archiv für die gesamte Psychologie,* Volume 80, pp. 452-510.

Lipps emphasized at every opportunity that the separate subconscious processes may not be regarded, as in Herbart's *Mechanics of Imagination,* as independent entities, but that their relation to the Psyche as the consistent basis of all action always comes into consideration for their manner of operation. He had already set forth his ideas in opposition to Herbart's in his inaugural dissertation. The formulation which he gave, from this point of view of uniformity, to the fundamental problem of *psycho-energetics,* above all of the so-called "constriction of consciousness," made an especially lasting impression on me. He said that the presupposition of a mutual inhibition between concepts considered relatively independent was not enough, but that the real question referred to that point under dispute, namely, to the uniform "psychic power" which is absorbed to a greater or lesser extent by the separate psychic processes.

The first service which I was allowed to perform in experimental psychology, to my considerable gratification, was the assembling of a reaction apparatus for this lecture with the Hipp chronoscope and accessories once procured by Stumpf, which I at once used with success after Lipps's reference to Wundt's *Grundzüge der physiologischen Psychologie* and its familiar procedure. This success encouraged me, as early as the following year, to begin with a problem of my own along with independent experiment, according to the above-mentioned line of thought of my teacher.

I also received many unforgettable impressions from the chapters on general psychological optics, and they have had just as stimulating an effect on my whole future. In reference to the doctrine of the perception of space they were considerably supplemented and deepened through the exercises of this semester in the psychological seminar in which Lipps, during separate reports of the participants, dealt with the geometric-optic illusions and their source in "aesthetic factors of space perception." After I, in applying for admission to this course, had spoken to him about the plan of my life and about my philosophical and psychological preparatory study, he took me immediately without hesitation into his seminar during my first semester. From among the small number of intellectually active fellow-students in the psychological seminar I am most deeply indebted to my friend, Alexander Pfänder, seven years my senior, who at that time had already studied a semester with Lipps and had found in him an equally well-wishing furtherer of his identical goals.

Almost daily a part of our stay in the reading-room of the seminar, and soon also many a walk together, was spent in discussion on definite questions, in which we laid the greatest stress upon methodical sharpness and sequence. Thus in the course of time we attained an ever broader basis for a fruitful understanding of fundamental problems of psychology, in which the mutual enthusiastic worship of our teacher formed the most important basis. Alongside these scientific studies, however, social life and the enjoyment of the glorious art treasures of Munich and its beautiful surroundings were not neglected.

As early as the first Easter vacation, in my home in Bayreuth in 1895, a short paper on the psychological contrast phenomena resulted from the recapitulation of my impressions of the lectures. This formed the basis of my later dissertation on the contrast of image and feeling. As a student of jurisprudence and philosophy I attended juridical and economic lectures just as regularly during my first semester. From the third semester onward, however, on the advice of Lipps, I changed the subject of my state examination from jurisprudence to mathematics and physics which could at the same time be minors for the doctoral examination.

My philosophic education in the following semester received its most important addition from the lectures of Lipps on general aesthetics, which he introduced with a comprehensive history of aesthetics with special reference to the work of Lotze on the dispute between the aesthetics of form and of content. In addition, I attended the lectures of Baron von Hertling, later our Bavarian Prime Minister and German Imperial Chancellor, on the history of modern philosophy, with which I was already acquainted in school through reading Falckenberg's book. To this there were added studies in the natural sciences, the lectures on experimental physics by Lommel, and on anthropology by Johannes Ranke, the nephew of the celebrated historian, who was on the medical faculty and introduced the students of the philosophical faculty into biology. The greatest event of my first Munich Summer, however, was the establishment of the Academic Psychological Society under the auspices of Lipps, in which we assembled on one evening every week for a paper by a member, with free discussion following. I was elected Treasurer among the charter officers, together with Endell, later the Director of the Breslau Academy of Art, as first President, and Felix Krüger as Secretary. The latter had entered Lipps's seminar this semester and soon belonged to that select circle of fellow-students who discussed all the questions of the day together; he had already studied philosophy in Berlin and in Strassburg, and in Munich did not attach himself at all so closely to Lipps as did Pfänder and I, but rather to H. Cornelius. Cornelius had begun his teaching career in Munich before Lipps was called there and stood in a certain antagonism to him. I also now became acquainted with him personally, since he, like Lipps, came regularly to our Society and took an active part in the discussions. These, in consequence, rather frequently became a contest between the two; this, however, was of advantage in that it trained all of us more and more to a sharp critical examination of the methodical and empirical presuppositions of the points of view which we received. On the advice of Lipps I chose as my first paper for the Society a theme of general interest, a critical report on Lombroso's book, *The Man of Genius.* In this forty-seven page paper I strove manfully to sever as much as possible the close relation of genius and insanity, even though I had the greatest respect for the factual material of this scientist from the reading of his other equally well-known work, *The Criminal,* which I had read on the recommendation of my uncle, Dr. Oscar Wirth, a well-known criminologist.

I now also attended lectures of Cornelius, and in all subsequent semesters in Munich I participated industriously in his pro-seminars with reports. If I now sought more and more carefully for the empirical foundation in self-observation of Theodor Lipps's theories of psychic activity, then I owe this more independent attitude above all to the sagacious stimulation of H. Cornelius, even though I at first practiced a very critical reserve toward his theses.

In the first academic Autumn vacation of 1895, I studied a book in Bayreuth, the great importance of which for the development of general psychology Theodor Lipps had pointed out again and again: David Hume's *A Treatise of Human Nature.* Lipps himself had at the time of my entrance to his seminar issued this in German translation with annotations, since he considered Hume much more appropriate as an introduction to philosophy than an immediate study of Kant. At that time Lipps defended with energy Hume's point of view that all philosophy was, in the final analysis, psychology, and that even in epistemology one must understand the psychological mechanism of association, through which originate the logical feelings of the consciousness of reality for facts not immediately perceived, and the logical feeling of the necessity of purely empirical conformance to law. Over against Hume's skepticism, however, Lipps put the psychological analysis of general validity in the tenets of the normative philosophical disciplines, which he considered the true *psychological* kernel in the Kantian continuation of Hume's critique of dogmatism, therein following his teacher and father-in-law, Jürgen Bona Meyer, of Bonn, with his psychological reinterpretation of the Kantian critique. Especially against the disintegration of the incomparable uniformity and constancy in the concept of the ego through Hume's critique of the perception of identity did he strive by referring to the immediate experience of the unity of consciousness; in this he also referred to Hermann Lotze, whose *Medical Psychology* he valued in spite of all adverse criticism. In the Winter Semester of 1895-1896, at the instigation of Lipps, I translated a large part of Hume's *Passions* into German. The first result of my studies in Hume, however, came earlier, in the second part of the Autumn vacation of 1895: a sixty-one page treatise on the "feelings for logic"; this indeed was merely an independent presentation of that which I, on the basis of the *Logics* and the *Fundamental Facts* of Lipps, considered the true understanding of Hume's rich data on my theme.

I devoted special care to the working out of an emotional resultant of the uniformity in all complexes which stand out through their qualitative correspondence in contrast to a background of another nature. This is, of course, an important factor of the present-day phenomenology of the concept of configuration. With this I understood that uniformity itself is a centripetal feeling, which however is experienced as a completely "partial" or "local" one motivated only in this psychic "surface" or "periphery" of sense perception, or, in the relations of its parts to one another and to the environment, The consciousness of inequality is interpreted as a specific transitional feeling which rests upon the "tendency to inertia" of every concept. According to the psychic signification of similar or different elements in the complexes compared, the same things can call forth feelings of similarity or difference, in other words, just as was postulated in my later application of the comparative method in the measurement of grades of consciousness at the different places of

the field of consciousness, only with this difference: that I at that
time also conceded such an influence on the comparative judgment to
subconscious stimulations, whereas, in the development of my threshold method for analysis of clarity after 1898, I considered just this
influence as a specific criterion of the *consciousness* of the factors.
In connection with Hume's description of the constancy of transition which is experienced when one perceives a walking man concealed momentarily by a wall, and always fills in the gap with an
intuitive imagination, I also paid especial attention from that time
on to the consciousness of identity in these feelings of relation, and
soon recognized the psychological constancy in stroboscopy as the
summation of a multitude of fine processes of this kind. However,
in that paper on the logical feelings, I did not yet especially emphasize
this in connection with the feeling of identity, but carried it out
more completely only later in my lectures on psychology. The
first main division of this paper, entitled "The Consciousness of
Reality," I delivered in our Society in the following Winter Semester of 1895-1896.

My interest in psychomechanical hypotheses for the explanation
of emotional experiences of uniformity and differentiation in the
production of configurative concepts was kept very much alive in
the new special lectures of Lipps on the "aesthetics of the plastic
arts," since Lipps here developed more and more in detail his
"aesthetic factors of spatial perception" with the aid of extensive
material in tectonic and architectonic profiles, and finally actually
stimulated one to attempt a mathematical representation of the
dynamic expression of every configuration as a formative law according to the principle of analytical mechanics. However, there is no
success to be noted in this problem. It was not quite clear to me
whether the representatation of the lines by means of the Fourier
series as suggested by Lipps was really the best way to the goal
(for the relation of these to the periodicity of wave motion is relatively remote from the aesthetic forces empathic in the *gefässformen)*,
or whether the beginning should not rather be accommodated immediately to such powers aş here come into consideration. So much,
however, remains certain for me, that the perception of movement
according to a purely psychological principle releases psychic tendencies which raise the perception of all forms, contours, surfaces, and
solids far above a mere juxtaposition of the same kind of optical im-

pressions, circumstances which the new Gestalt psychology, as is known, has translated into neuropsychological "cross-processes."

When Lipps in his lectures on psychology, which I attended for the second time that semester, came again to the reaction experiments, the thought occurred to me whether one could not perhaps also demonstrate experimentally these subjective tendencies of movement in the perception of figures, since, in the observation of an actual change of form in the *direction* of such a tendency, the time of reaction must prove to be shorter than in the reaction to a change running *contrary* to this aesthetic tendency.[2] This led me to the first attempt at an independent experimental investigation, for which my teacher set at my disposal his office in the seminar and all the apparatus, and my friend Pfänder was helpful to me in the construction of the chronoscope circuit. I chose the experimental subjects from among Franconian student friends and relatives who were as unfamiliar as possible with the psychological theory to be tested. Since Lipps specifically explained the geometric-optic illusion from these subordinate concepts, I chose the especially striking contrast of the Müller-Lyer illusion, in which the figure with the outer shanks seems to stretch, and the figure with the inner shanks, on the contrary, seems to shrink together. Up to the Summer Semester of 1896 I made preliminary experiments with a self-made apparatus, longed, however, for more exact aids, and make a sketch for a similar arrangement in metal. During the Psychological Congress in the Summer of 1896, Lipps introduced me to F. Schumann, who at that time was still Stumpf's assistant, and at the request of Lipps kindly explained to me the whole exhibition of apparatus at the Congress, thus giving me a kind of summary introduction to experimental psychology. Among other things, I here saw for the first time Marbe's new color circles, the sectors of which could be changed during rotation. Later, during the work on my inaugural dissertation, this did me good service in the measurement of negative afterimages. Schumann also introduced me to the mechanic, Petzold, who then on Lipps's order had the apparatus ready by Autumn. I found it again during the Munich Psychological Congress of 1925, at the Institute there. A vertical line, on both sides of which inner and outer shanks are to be put, can be lengthened or shortened on both

---

[2]Lipps had expressed earlier an analogous expectation for consonant tone sequences (in contrast to dissonant).

sides, whereby exactly at the beginning of the movement a circuit is broken. The experiments carried through with the apparatus during the afternoons of the whole Winter Semester of 1896-1897 did not, however, result in any unequivocal difference of the median times of reaction on the extension and contraction of the figures. However, I did not allow this to discourage me in the attempt at experimental demonstration that the perception of a change of form in a certain direction is psychically favored; but I attempted it with experimental facilitation of immediate self-observation of such tendencies whose increase I expected from such factual changes of the figures. For the further heightening of this effect, I constructed two strips for an ordinary stroboscopic drum such as is purchasable as a toy (road of life) ; these by stroboscopic effect showed one of the two Müller-Lyer figures extending or contracting according to the direction of rotation. Through this iterative summation of harmony or disharmony between the tendency to movement lying in the figure itself and the movement actually perceived, I hoped to make more striking the feeling for form which is already experienced in the quiescent form. But here also no decisive effect of an inner relation of the actual direction of movement to the genuine tendencies of the figure was recognizable, manifestly because into the moving figure new tendencies at once enter empathically as a uniform harmonious whole, tendencies which in turn seem to belong to the figure as its own direction without inner contradiction. With all this, these experiments even at that time allowed me to recognize in the stroboscope the apparatus with which one can study experimentally and quantitatively the logical feelings for relations, above all, naturally, the experience of the identity of an object in motion.[3] The strong stroboscopic impression, which is caused by a rapid change between the outer and inner shanks of the two Müller-Lyer figures, also became clear to me long before its description and theoretic employment by another person, when, on the request of Professor Wundt in the Summer of 1902, I prepared projection pictures for his lectures. In these the direction of the shanks of the two figures could be changed through a quick movement of the hand, whereby the two lines seem alternately to contract or expand.

Although no supports for the special theories of my teacher re-

---

[3]Cf. p. 9.

sulted from this, the latter followed my independent experimental attempts with the greatest pleasure and interest, and promised me to do everything to obtain for Munich an Institute for Experimental Psychology. In this I should then as his assistant be able to pursue independently this new branch of our subject, after I had received academic training in it at other places. The Third International Psychological Congress in Munich, in which I participated with Pfänder and Krüger on the local committee, gave new impetus to these wishes, since I was then privileged to listen to and to become personally acquainted with not only philosophical psychologists, like Franz Brentano, and the neurologists and psychiatrists in close contact with psychology, such as Flechsig, von Strümpell, Vogt, Richet, Janet, and others, but many men who had already made a name for themselves in experimental psychology, such as Stumpf, Ebbinghaus, Münsterberg, Külpe, Martius, R. Sommer, Betzold, the ear specialist, and others. Above all, however, Lipps's own lecture was of the greatest value to me, since he demonstrated as clearly and emphatically as never before that it was necessary to derive explanatory terms for subconscious conditions in a purely psychological manner. Also the lecture of Cornelius, "Psychophysische Prinzipienfragen" led me to the deliberations I expressed in my treatise, "Experimentelle Analyse der Bewusstseinsphänomene," p. 155. However clearly the problem of psychology as an independent empirical science was circumscribed by these two investigators at that time and in their regular lectures, and however much its systematic development in purely psychological explanatory hypotheses was demanded, especially by Lipps, we nevertheless noticed in lectures like that of Flechsig on his epoch-making discovery of association centers in the human brain, there demonstrated with splendid specimens, how little this independent pure psychology was for the time being recognized in the great scientific world; and we felt that in defending it in the future many a warm dispute was before us, such as we experienced in the discussion after Flechsig's lecture.

A short time earlier, however, we had seen the uniformity of such a scientific pursuit of psychology, in Lipps's sense of the term, threatened from an entirely different side, namely, by its philosophic representatives, who even at that time wanted to separate empiric psychology as an independent science from philosophy and philosophic psychology and thereby deprive it again of the position meanwhile attained in the professorships of the philosophic faculty. Güttler, then lecturer in Munich, in his paper, "Psychology and Philosophy," directed such an attack against Lipps's connection of philosophic problems with those of the separate sciences and also defended his point of view in our Society; whereupon F. Krüger answered with his rebuttal, "Ist Psychologie ohne Philosophie möglich?"[4] In my own educational career later on I, too, always retained the ideal of fitting the whole field of psychology into the academic teaching of philosophy, since I believed that philosophic thinking must not only be fructified by the exact observation of material nature, but above all by an understanding of psychic laws supported by experimental methods, and also that it must be brought back from unscientific postulates. Therefore I myself, in my increasing emphasis on the precision necessary in carrying on psychology in the service of general philosophy, had to suffer most from that philosophic countercurrent which unfortunately through Dilthey and his school in Prussia gained a more and more exclusive influence on the filling of philosophic professorships. Dilthey, who also received Güttler's paper favorably, at that time himself brought up very valuable methodological proof for the possibility of an independent pure psychology, in his well-known academy paper, "Ideen über eine beschreibende und zergliedernde Psychologie,"[5] proof which could be enlisted against the absorption of psychology by the brain physiologists with their localization hypotheses, which were very dubious in many details. In spite of this fact he and his disciples did not recognize that his correct methodological points of view were most strictly followed precisely by individual *experimental* psychologists. Of course, an independent theoretic psychology in our sense of the word can never come into conflict with somatic physiology, but must work hand in hand with it, as I have always attempted to do in all my experimental psychological work and particularly as a psychological collaborator on physiological manuals.

The strongest bond of personal solidarity between Lipps and his pupils, however, was to be his lecture course at that time, "Ethick und philosophische Voraussetzung der Gesellschaftslehre," the funda-

---

[4]Munich, 1896. Cf. also my treatise, "Zur Wiederlegung der Behauptung von Krisen in der modernen Psychologie." *Viertelj. f. Psychol. u. Medezin,* Volume II, No. 2, p. 100 (103).
[5]Cf. *Arch. f. d. ges. Psychol.,* 1922, **43**, p. 77 (Jasper's review).

mental thoughts of which were soon to be published in his *Ethische Grundfagen*. His Society lectures at that time were also concerned with ethical themes. The new thing here for me was how the good kernel of the Nietzschean ethics was fitted into the system under the point of view of the ethical worth of the strong, inwardly rich personality, and was separated from the pathological exaggerations.

My own production, however, was for the time being concentrated on general psychology, and that first sketch on contrasting phenomena done during the Easter vacation of 1895 was formed into a more comprehensive treatise after I had first lectured on it in the seminar and in the Society. Most of all a self-observation of my own encouraged me in this work, and through it the chief problem became clear, as to just how the contrast illusion of apparent changes of familiar objects perceived everyday results from the perception in the interim of analogous objects of different size. On one of the first walks after the return to my Bayreuth home, at Easter, 1896, we walked past the equestrian statue of Markgrave Christian Ernst before the new palace. This statue now suddenly appeared to me as though it had shrunk together. The impression was so strong and surprising that I immediately took thought, and then it became clear to me, even before I had traversed the palace square, that the image of the much larger equestrian statute of Ludwig I hovered before me, since I had passed it almost daily and, what is more, very closely during my walks in Munich. Thus, at the renewed sight of the Bayreuth equestrian statue in our immediate vicinity, this remembrance from the daily life of Munich stood absolutely in the place of the remembrance of its earlier perception, and through its size (even more impressive because of the angle of vision) generated that impression of a real change in the figure of the Bayreuth Markgrave. This explanation of the illusion from a completely concrete single perception which, however darkly, is nevertheless consciously present and is demonstrable in introspection as the basis of comparison[6] represented something quite new over against Lipps's explanation, which took the roundabout way over a completely general association of the feeling of contrast with definite departures from normal size, something new in which indeed I still regarded as possible the assistance of the process described by Lipps. In con-

---

[6] Cf. *Zsch. f. Psychol.*, 1898, **18**, pp. 65 ff.

sequence of a certain shyness of all too personal communication, I omitted, by the way, a concrete description of this own decisive experience in my dissertation and used only the well-known examples of everyday life.

From my interpretation of this contrast illusion I later derived a completely general theory of all geometric-optical illusions, after I had see from Schumann's analyses of the same how here, too, a person always compares a length or an angle with something other than that with which he really wants to compare it and mistakenly thinks he is comparing it. In this way I also understood the results of Benussi, according to which the illusion, during concentration of attention on the magnitudes really to be compared, recedes under certain conditions. In my book, *Experimental Analysis of Phenomena of Consciousness,* I have carried through these theories in detail and have also come back to them in my discussion of the Sander's illusion.[7]   The dissertation of F. Hermann also had reference to it.[8]

Above all, however, this work on contrast contained the germ for my later optical investigation on the successive contrast or negative after-images as such.   For, in differentiating that psychological contrast of perception from the physiological-optical contrast of brightness and color, I was already applying myself intensively to Hering's *Lehre vom Lichtsinn.*   With this I had at first carried on independent research only on simultaneous contrast in order to check Wundt's observation, according to which this illusion is supposed to be minimized through the introduction of a transitional strip between the differently induced fields.   After my negative results I held to Hering's purely sensory physiological explanation, which Lipps also had maintained in his lectures, and from that time on I studied Hering's writings more and more intensively.   Thus I began my literary activity in the experimental field with a very definite opposition to an observation and theory of Wundt.[9]   Later, on the occasion of the preparation of his new (5th) edition of *Physiological Psychology,* when I had been a lecturer and his assistant for some time, Wundt tried to convince me of his point of view through the renewed presentation of the same material of observation.   This was

---

[7]*Archiv f. d. ges. Psychol.,* Volume 70, pp. 427 ff.
[8]*Ibid.,* Volume 41, p. 1.
[9]*Zsch. f. Psychol.,* Volume 18, pp. 56-58.

of course in vain, but this renewal of differences of point of view, which was known to him from my dissertation when I entered his Institute, did not bring with it any serious ill-feeling.

The greater part of my work, however, which unfortunately remained unpublished when my dissertation was accepted by the *Zeitschrift für Psychologie und Physiologie der Sinnesorgane,* was a detailed exposition of Lipps's theory for the explanation of contrast of feeling and dulling of feeling through habit.[10] The degree of consciousness of the image (or the "height of consciousness," as Lipps said because of his polemic against the "degree of consciousness") formed according to this a chief factor of the intensity of its emotional effect. This degree, however, becomes less and less in habituation through the effluent tendency, which allows the "psychic power" (cf. above, page 284) to flow faster and faster toward other interests because of the manifold associations to everyday life. Only the interruption of the usual result through the loss of attributes possessed till now allows the full attention to be turned to this once more through a "damming up" of the psychic power at this point of vital continuity, and then, on the basis of the consciousness of value corresponding to this attention, allows it to experience a stronger pain. With this, therefore, association is never thought of as "atomistic" (as I said, employing the catchword of Dilthey's academy treatise), but active *in the full breadth of consciousness.* To quote from page 147 of the manuscript:

> Psychic life is at every moment an indivisible entity in which each [part] is active only as a factor in the whole and can only be understood as such. Every extraction of a single thing from this whole is indeed a necessary abstraction, in which, however, the consideration of the necessary connection of the separate parts may never be forgotten. If, therefore, in a definite environment a perception occurs persistently, this means that it is connected in a very firm unity with a definite environment of space and time. If psychic stimulation goes further from here to something else, then it has not gone over to something else from one part of the environment alone, for instance, from that most regarded and striven for, but from the entity of the whole contemporaneous condition of consciousness. Thus, an association never really exists between two single perceptions, but only between the whole psychic conditions of two

---

[10] Pp. 85-207 of the manuscript accepted by the faculty.

moments of time. Thus for a later time, too, the preliminary condition for the continuation to the other contents of psychic life does not consist in a single perception, but in the simultaneous appearance of the entire content of that time. Single associations are at first something secondary. They originate because definite factors in several complexes are always to be found again in varying surroundings. Only through this general formulation of association is it explicable how the disappearance of objects in themselves negligible, to which one has accustomed oneself in a definite environment, can under circumstances be felt as a very unpleasant disturbance (the torn-off button of the student in Kant's lecture course).

I do not believe that the present-day integral psychology can add anything to that, and, if Ebbinghaus had not rejected this second part of my dissertation as too extensive, these expositions could be cited by the representatives of integral psychology as one of the oldest expositions of their fundamental principle.

After Lipps had looked through my manuscript, he requested that I be admitted to graduation even before the completion of the *triennium,* whereupon on July 17, 1897, not quite twenty-one years of age, I passed the doctoral examination, Summa Cum Laude; in time between A. Pfänder and F. Krüger.

Meanwhile, in the Winter Semester of 1896-1897, after finishing differential and integral calculus with seminar work under Lindemann and experimental psychics under Lommel, I had ventured to take the course in analytical mechanics under Grätz, and was attending lectures in inorganic chemistry with Beyer. In the Summer Semester of 1897 I also took a laboratory course in physics, and then for the first time felt the full intellectual joy in exact measurement, which since then has never again left me in experimental psychology and in my own construction of new apparatus. For the latter, the careful practical introduction to descriptive geometry with Döhlemann was of advantage to me.

Immediately after the doctoral examination, I passed the first state examination in mathematics, which at that time in Bavaria had to be taken in two divisions separated by at least a year: a general written and oral preliminary examination, and a special oral examination, for the latter of which a special mathematical or physical paper was to be handed in. However, since within a year after turning to experimental psychology, in the Summer Semester of 1899, I was offered by Wundt an assistantship in his Institute, and with it at the same time had prospects for an immediate admission to the philosophical faculty, I refrained on Wundt's counsel from the continuation of my mathematical studies. For Wundt believed quite correctly that the second part of that state examination could in case of necessity just as well be taken later, whereas such favorable prospects for my academic career would not so soon return. No doubt my inaugural dissertation, with its psychophysical character, would perhaps at the request of Grätz have been counted as the examination paper, but for the special oral examination I would nevertheless have had to devote myself exclusively to mathematical-physical studies, through which my teaching career in philosophy would have been materially delayed.

The Winter Semester of 1897-1898 was in part still devoted to theoretical physics, since I took Grätz's course in the theory of electricity and magnetism, which was of great importance to me for natural philosophy. Above all, my aesthetic interests, furthered in that semester by work under Cornelius on the problem of form in Adolf Hildebrandt, brought me to a more thorough study of art history, for which I attended the popular general lectures of Furtwängler on ancient art and particularly those of Wiese on the history of the Renaissance. Under the latter, I also participated in a very stimulating pro-seminar in the same field. Also, in the Society I spoke on the aesthetic theme, "Representation and the Represented Object," in which I combatted a naturalism in artistic representation which went too far, and which endangered the boundaries between reality and the world of imagination. I sought in general to work against a mere evaluation of the representational form as such, and maintained that the stimulus of an ideal artistic world of the imagination was the real goal of artistic endeavor. The strongest effect on my work that followed, nevertheless, came again from the lectures of Lipps, who had just at that time been strongly impelled through the phenomenology of the Brentano school to combat "psychologism"; he now expressed his chief thoughts in a lecture course on "Special Psychology." These lectures were soon thereafter published in his well-known papers, "Fühlen Wollen und Denken" and "Einheiten und Relationen," as well as in his *Leitfaden*. The ideas of this lecture I developed critically in the next semester; from them plus the experimental experience of the next semester there resulted a fruitful synthesis, out of which the formulation of my investigations in psycho-energy first came forth.

The decision was also made this semester as to the place of my contemplated education in experimental psychology. The choice had narrowed down to Leipzig and Würzburg. Külpe of Würzburg had immediately answered very cordially when I sent him my dissertation. He agreed with Lipps among other things in the rejection of Wundt's theory of eye motion for spatial vision as well as in his aesthetic interests. However, in consequence of his rejection of the theory of empathy there were also the seeds for differences here. In any case, Lipps finally decided to advise me to study under Wundt as the founder of experimental psychology, and so for the Summer Semester of 1898 I went to Leipzig for the first time. F. Krüger had already arrived there at the beginning of the Winter Semester of 1898 and also intended to remain further.

II. PREPARATION FOR ADMISSION TO THE FACULTY IN LEIPZIG (1898-1900)

Since I had studied Wundt's *Grundzüge der physiologischen Psychologie* and his *Grundriss der Psychologie* industriously in Munich, the new thing for me in his lectures, aside from the direct impression of his personality, was above all the demonstration of experiments, which from that time on became for me the model for my own "Lectures in Psychology with Experimental Demonstrations." In the Psychological Institute the introduction was in the hands of the assistant, Mentz, who indeed did not strive for any completeness of survey, but that which he offered he explained thoroughly. Also in my independent work under Wundt's eye I could immediately utilize my experience in the technique of reaction experiments by helping to construct the procedure for the well-known work of Alechsieff on reactions in transition observations. Otherwise also I cooperated as an experimental subject in almost all the other investigations. Along with this I attended the lectures on the brain by Flechsig, to whose clinic I came repeatedly for observation of demonstrations with patients, and the lectures on the psychopathology of emotional life by Störring, whose emphasis on the pathological method for general psychology indeed temporarily contradicted my views brought along from Lipps in regard to the foundation of psychology on self-observation of the normal, but on the other hand widened my horizon all the more surely and stimulated me to an exact study of his work on the same subject which appeared two years later. In addition, I attended the sensory-physiological lectures of Hering, in which on occasion his assistant demonstrated to me for the first time the oscillatory course of after-images according to the Kries-Hess method of successive pictures. In the field of the humanities I attended Lamprecht's lectures on the history of German historical science and historiography, since his method at that time occupied the center of discussion among historians, and I participated in Heinze's philosophical seminar on ethical theories.

Along with this reception of material rich in new facts and points of view, there was carried out a renewed industrious production in three main directions which had been indicated in the renewed concern with the themes of the three dissertations of our Munich trio of the Summer Semester of 1897 and in my notebooks on Lipps's lectures on special psychology. From my own dissertation there were two groups of principles considered there which I pursued quite independently of one another: the successive contrast or the so-called "negative after-images," and then the distribution of the psychic powers over the separate contents. Concerning negative after-images, I now found for the first time in the *Beiträge zur Philosophie und Psychologie* quantitative experiments by Lipps's friend, Götz Martius, with whom I had already spoken at the Munich Congress. The experimental method indeed was based on Martius' special theory as to the nature of these after-images. He considered them independent subsidiary processes which only temporarily under special circumstances are mingled with the act of seeing, to be specific, either as a darkening after-image after the fixation of bright surfaces on a dark background, or in a reverse situation as a brightening after-image; in color contrasts the after-image approximates the colors to those of their surroundings. Alongside this (according to this theory) the *normal* perception of brightness of color kept on existing and was only temporarily diminished through intense fixation and special observation of the after-images. My own observations, on the contrary, had convinced me as to how easily one could overlook really extant differences of stimulation in the field of vision, in the normal process of glancing over objects; normally, simply the differences of *objects* outside the eye interest us, and the purely subjectively conditioned differences of adjacent colors and degrees of brightness, changing with the glance, certainly cannot be considered as such. Therefore, Martius' presentation aroused my sharpest contradiction, and I immediately resolved to show with new measurements that the negative after-images are changes in stimulation which with a definite time interval continuously participate in the ocular image. Along with this it occurred to me immediately that the rotation apparatus once shown to me in Munich by Schumann with its change of sectors during rotation was the correct instrument for such measurement, since the difference of neighboring stimuli can herewith, through a very quick adjustment, be measured for subjective equality in a certain stage without change of the causal fixation of the original contrast in brightness. The objective difference in the direction of the primary contrast, which is necessary for this subjective equality, is the measure of the after-image, as I later described it in detail in my inaugural dissertation.[11] Even at that time I sketched a complete plan for such measurements of negative after-images, according to which I first sought to define in a purely empirical manner the concept of a definite change in stimulation on all the different "reacting" degrees of color and brightness through such a measurement of the after-image. In Helmholtz, *Physiologische Optik,* which I carefully read at that time, I found the theoretic concept formulated as a definite factor of stimulation, whereas the factual material gathered together in it had never yet been empirically controlled. During this preliminary work I became acquainted with the mechanic, E. Zimmermann, with whom I later worked so much.

The second problem, however, which I followed up after my work on contrast, dealt with the laws for the formation of the grades of consciousness. This now came into a completely new light through the critique of a fundamental thesis of Lipps's psychology which he had once more particularly emphasized in a special lecture course. With the intent of putting these laws, too, upon a strictly empirical basis, I sought for a *fundamental principle of phenomenology* (in the simple sense of the description of the actual phenomena of consciousness, out of which, of course, the laws of dispositional, unconscious processes must be derived, if they are not to be physiological but indeed purely psychological explanatory concepts). I found this

---

[11] *Phil. Stud.,* Volume 16.

principle in this: that everything which founds a conscious relation of equality, similarity, or *difference on a comparative judgment must also itself be a decisive part of a content of consciousness.* Lipps, on the contrary, had regarded the comparative judgment also as the means toward the direct derivation of similarities and differences in *subconscious* excitements, to which no correlate of consciousness corresponded. The phenomenological principle, which I then worked out for myself in contrast to this thesis of Lipps, was thus the thought which lay at the basis of my later measurements of the relations of clearness on the basis of a definite distribution of attention in the field of vision and in other sensory regions. I set down all this preliminary thought in the exchange of letters with my friend Pfänder, through whom I, in Leipzig, remained in very close contact with Munich. I have already referred to this correspondence in my treatise, "Zur Wiederlegung der Behauptung von Krisen in der modernen Psychologie,"[12] and cited several especially important passages (May 4, June 12, and September 1, 1898) on this phenomenological principle, which I then for the first time published in my contribution to the Wundt Commemorative Volume, *Zur Theorie des Bewusstseinsumfanges und seiner Messung* (pp. 556 ff.). This scientific correspondence, which was continued up to Pfänder's own vacation trip to Leipzig, comprised from my side over one hundred closely written pages in 1898 and again about the same amount in 1899, and the answers from Pfänder were not much shorter. Since he, some twenty years ago, sent me back my own original letters for the perusal of their content, I can survey the whole rich exchange of thought, especially on those fundamental phenomenological problems. From the second letter (June 12, 1898) onward, everything was put under definite headings, for instance, under this date:

    I. Is There a Consciousness of Similarity without a Definite Foundation? (Pages 1-14.)
    II. The Foundation of Uniformity. (Pages 14-18.)
    III. The Special Cases of the Relation of the Ego to the Content. (Pages 18-32.)

Under III, I relegated various degrees of intimacy of the said relations to the degrees of consciousness of the content, however, with

---

[12] Cf. note 4, above, pp. 122 ff.

the warning against identifying this gradation of "the most general fact of consciousness," "the having of any content at all," with the degrees of activity of the ego, which usually stand only in causal relation to it. Thus with this, much of the point of view is anticipated from which I later combated "logical egoism" in my book, *Zur Orientierung der Philosophie am Bewusstseinsbegriff* (Munich, 1919). This "logical egoism" I later also called "phenomenological egoism."[13] In "uniformity," too, I also saw at that time a "contentual"[14] characteristic clinging to the uniform concept of form itself. Further, at that time the problem of the maximum "extent of consciousness" began to be of interest to me, since every increase in the complex lowers the degree of consciousness of the separate parts. The difficulty that first occurred to me here was the "determination of contemporaneity," which, so to speak, takes a temporal cross section from the course of consciousness. But even if this problem could be solved, the extent could never be indicated in an absolute "number of contents" (because of the different forms of the distribution of clearness), as it had been attempted by Wundt and Dietze. This would not be so different from an attempt at "counting the waves of the sea." In the methodological foundation of such psycho-energetic analyses in my contribution to the Wundt Commemorative Volume, it thus formed later (1901) a special problem as to how one could at least derive for the extent of the so-called "immediate retention" (called by me "extent of new comprehension") an absolute number (perhaps 4-6) as universally valid. I also worked with especial intensity in the Summer of 1898 in Leipzig on the *ethical problems of the psychology of values,* in which I had always been interested ever since my philosophic studies in preparatory school, and which, after the study of F. Krüger's dissertation, *Der Begriff des absolut Wertvollen als Grundbegriff der Moralphilosophie,* now stimulated me again to a completely matured but unfortunately unpublished treatise of 52 pages, "Das Wertbewusstsein." I gave it to my fellow-student to read and he supplied it with detailed marginal notes. However, the main content, quite independent of Krüger's dissertation, consisted of an exposition as to how I myself thought of experience and the dispositional

---

[13]*Psychologie und Medizin,* Volume II, No. 2, p. 124.

[14]With "content" in the narrower sense, I meant at that time, as Meinong did, the content of consciousness in reference to objects. Cf. below.

basis of ethical evaluation on the basis of my new point of view in
regard to the phenomenology of consciousness. This evaluation, I
maintained, was, *even as a content of consciousness, something more
general* than the special feelings of satisfaction, of striving, and of
displeasure, which with the same abstract content of consciousness of
a definite "evaluation" can appear as the different embodiments of
this evaluation, depending upon whether the possession of this same
valued good is envisaged as safe, or only striven for, or threatened.
Krüger also had, in the first part of his excellent dissertation on the
psychology of the will, differentiated evaluation from all separate conscious processes of actual desire, and had also not identified it, for
instance, with a *single* subconscious process, as this had been relegated
by Lipps to every process of consciousness in the same way as a single
concrete physiological nerve process was by the parallelists. Evaluation is, according to Krüger,[15] rather the constant disposition, which
under corresponding subsidiary conditions leads to the actual separate
experiences of evaluation in consciousness or subconsciousness; this
was in the sense of Dilthey's concept of psychic disposition, which
is derived from the separate experiences as the principle which rules
them in the same manner as the concept of experience of a thing
is derived from single judgments of perception. In addition, he had,
just as I in my paper on the logical feelings,[16] already accepted even
in the separate actual evaluations Theodor Lipps's idea of an immediately experienced "quality of depth" on the basis of the various
"breadths and depths of personality" and had emphasized this against
the pleasure-displeasure theories of the emotions. The new thing
in my own concept of evaluation in contrast to Krüger's thus consisted above all in this: that I attributed a factor of consciousness to
the tendency toward evaluation, that indeed was for me the revealing criterion of its existence. I called it "the consciousness of
friendly or inimical attitude" or simply "positive" or "negative
evaluation." This idea had occurred to me in connection with my
dissertation on contrast while observing the modification of feelings
through habit. For I saw that in spite of the dulling of feeling
which occurs with a permanent possession of a good, there nevertheless remains preserved with every clear realization a definite
emotional coloring when the loss of the good really leads to a re-

---

[15]*Op. cit.,* p. 39.
[16]Cf. above.

newed intensive action of the emotions, and when the tendency toward evaluation has thus really been preserved. In setting up criteria
for the whole complex of feeling at any given time, this constant
factor of consciousness seemed to me to be the most likely carrier of
"depth," that dimension of feeling taken over from Lipps. For I
found that precisely this quality can belong in full measure to the
consciousness of value even with the blunting of feeling through
habit. This ascertainment even then belonged for me to the further
development of the phenomenology of the "peripheral" and the
"central," in which I also did more justice to, though I never accepted the one-sidedness of, the theories of emotion of C. Lange and
Wm. James, so much criticized by Lipps and by Pfänder, since they
pay attention only to the peripheral side of feeling with the sense
perception contained in it. I believe I came to understand their true
kernel particularly through the lectures of Störring. Also in my
letters to Pfänder on September 1, 1898, and July 24, 1899, these
thoughts were expressed, and were then carried out in greater detail
in my book, *Die experimentale Analyse der Bewusstseinsphänomene,*
in the third chapter on "the inner arrangement of consciousness and
the main types of its contents" (pages 10 ff.).

In that treatise, "The Consciousness of Value," the correct derivation of the psychological principle of evaluation from the description of consciousness continued further to be most important to me.
In this, I demanded again the consideration of the whole situation,
at any given time, of the content of consciousness, just as in that consideration on the "breadth of association" in my dissertation on contrast and in my later psycho-energetic investigations on the distribution of clearness in consciousness. As the really evaluated content,
the whole situation must in every case be considered, if one wishes
to come to truly unequivocal laws. Thus, for instance, many apparent contradictions could be explained from the change of mood
of the person evaluating, changes which belong to this whole situation just as much as the content of perception, which, independent
of this mood, remains approximately constant with a valuable outer
object. With such a concrete completion of our experiences of the
true psychological basis of our feelings of value one would indeed
then recognize that the basic *ethical* question in regard to the possibility of *absolute* evaluation is not yet solved if one, as in F. Krüger's
dissertation, simply formulates the concept of the constant lawful

tendency in contrast to the single actual evaluation. For, with the separate laws which lie at the basis of *every* evaluation, the relative constants would be self-evident and of no especial ethical value. Indeed, one cannot command any absolute constancy, but everything rather depends on a definite *development* of these evaluating tendencies. For this, even the purely quantitative principle of "as high an energy of evaluation as possible," which Krüger added, would not yet suffice. The really ethical point of view would really enter only through a new intrinsic foundation of values. It would consist of the evaluation of the uniform psychological basis of our separate evaluative experiences themselves, of the evaluation of our evaluating, volitional, and acting personality to which Lipps especially referred us again and again. In order, however, to realize this special evaluative point of view in our experience, one must fill one's total content of consciousness as completely as possible with it; that is, concentrate as much as possible on the personality to be judged. Such a concentration upon a more narrowly circumscribed circle of partial contents would be the characteristic formal attitude in all normative experiences as well in epistemological as in ethical and aesthetic respects; with this at the same time other disturbing partial contents must subside in consciousness. Thus there are here already essential points of the theory of a *relatively generally valid* evaluation, which I published much later in my *Grundfagen der Aesthetik* (1925) in the chapter on absolute aesthetic evaluation. I said, in opposition to Krüger's theory, that the deciding ethical factor was not at all that anything remains constant in the personality, *but that its volitional foundations are so transformed that they can be given a constantly positive evaluation.* According to this, constancy comes normatively into consideration only to the extent that it is contained in the concept of general validity.

At Easter, 1899, and especially on July 24, 1899, I carried out more explicitly the volitional psychological side of my phenomenology of the consciousness of value in two long letters to Pfänder, and I emphasized among other things that in considering the total situation at any one time, which is extraordinarily different individually and temporally in relation to the same kinds of values, one need no longer make any separation between "motivation" and "driving force" in Wundt's sense.

However much we missed, in Leipzig, an institution for scientific discussion similar to the Munich Academic Psychological Society, the Philosophic Society nevertheless offered us a certain substitute. It had originally been founded by Avenarius, and Vaihinger, Kraepelin, and other important men had once belonged to it. For it, I developed the ethical consequences of that treatise, "The Consciousness of Value," into a new manuscript entitled "Das Ethische Wertgefühle," finished November 4, 1899. It was the opening lecture of the Philosophic Society for the Winter Semester of 1899-1900, after Krüger had already gone to Kiel on Wundt's recommendation to be the assistant of G. Martius. In conclusion, I advanced six theses of which the first three brought into short formulae what I have already said. As an example of the general validity of evaluation of the evaluating personality, I further developed the ethical value of neighborly love which considers impartially the weal of the neighbor along with one's own, since just in this there had been frequent debate between Paul Barth, who ascribed to altruism an absolute ethical value, and Krüger, who represented the Nietzschean point of view. In the discussion after my lecture, Ernst Dürr especially took part; he was a few years younger than I, was a pupil of Külpe and Marbe, and had just come from Würzburg in order to take his doctoral examination here and later perhaps to be admitted to the faculty in our field. As Bavarian countrymen we soon formed a friendship and I found in him again a partner for daily psychological and philosophical discussion in Wundt's Institute and in walks together; during vacation he also visited us at home in Bayreuth.

It is perhaps not quite accidental that in the midst of these occupations with ethical theories, an evaluation especially important for life also took a practical turn, namely, the fulfillment of military service. Since my professional preparation was not completed, I could have had this postponed until after the doctoral and state examinations. But the function of the reserve officer was for me such an integral component part of the life of a citizen fit for military service that as soon as possible after the fulfillment of the preliminary conditions contingent upon my status as civilian I entered as a one-year volunteer into the Bayreuth Royal Bavarian 7th Infantry Regiment "Prince Leopold" on the first of October, 1898. To its officer corps there belonged four of my best school friends and numerous other acquaintances of preparatory school, who were at the same time pupils and friends of my father. This gladly offered sacrifice of time has been repaid for life through the strengthening of my whole psycho-physical organism, and was rewarded on the part of the military authorities by very careful watching over my health, as it was natur-ally only possible in peace with a superabundance of human material. On the very first day after an originally unconditional acceptance I was, to my grief, put down for monthly reexamination by the physician in service, who happened to be a heart specialist; I, how-ever, refused dismissal since I hoped to overcome through habit the slight excitability of my heart on bodily exertion; and so for the time being only some slight alleviation was prescribed for strenuous exer-cises. After the customary seven weeks' training I did full service for about two months with the old troops of the 9th Company, until the physicians declared it was absolutely essential that I sign a state-ment that I would refrain from claims for compensation in the case of a lasting organic heart attack, if I wished to remain further in service. At that time the interesting officers' training had already begun; however, I finally yielded to the counsel of my father now and allowed myself to be furloughed until the final disposition of the recruiting authorities, who then in Saxony declared me "perma-nently unfit for service." In all events, my health has sufficed till now for the uninterrupted practice of my academic career, so that in these more than thirty years of teaching I have missed only a very few lectures because of sickness. That subjectively maximum fulfillment of my duty also saved me in the World War, for in the naturally very careful reexaminations of the medical staff I was declared as "useful only for secretarial work at home." With my activity at the University I was not even drafted for this. As soon as I foresaw my dismissal from military service in January, 1899, I wrote immediately to Wundt concerning whether I might begin in his Institute an experimental investigation on the measurement of negative after-images, the program which I had already outlined in the Summer of 1898 and wished to use for my admission to the faculty in Munich. Wundt answered me by return post that I could resume my work in his Institute at once. No later than February I began the preliminary experimental work with an older model of Marbe's apparatus. In the measure in which the work progressed, Wundt, however, also put at my disposal all the means hitherto reserved for his lectures, above all a new model of Marbe's apparatus and the projection apparatus with its very constant differential arc lamp. I had from the beginning introduced the variations of the "reacting" stimuli according to Hering's principles, and this arc lamp now enabled me to attain them in as great a part of the field of vision as possible by means of the gelatine discs described in my inaugural dissertation,[17] which I allowed to rotate on the Marbe apparatus in place of the lantern slide of the projection lamp. In one phase of the experiments, with ocular adjustments to darkness, I used the most homogeneous possible gelatine combinations of Kirschmann in order to demonstrate the after-effect of the fixation of a contrast with any kind of homogeneous colors for the whole system of our color sensitivity, which in this always reacts as an organic unity.

Along with sensory physiology, however, I also continued energetically the study of general psychology and above all attended the lectures of Wundt on folk psychology, the first volumes of which were just then appearing, and also the philosophic seminar of Heinze. In addition I now came in to personal contact with the third full Professor of Philosophy in Leipzig, J. Volkelt, whose book, *Die Ästhetischen Zeitfragen,* I had already taken notes on in Munich, and whose lectures, "Ästhetik des Tragischen u. Komischen," I then attended.

Among my own productive work I must first mention again the correspondence with Pfänder, taken up once more in Bayreuth after my dismissal from military service, under the dates of January 24, February 26, and July 24, 1899. After the disposal of the comparative method, the motivation of volition above mentioned and then particularly *the conscious execution of the deed* now stood in the foreground of interest, since Pfänder was just studying various problems in this field for his work on the Frohschammer prize competition. I immediately emphasized that from mere striving in the phases of volition *before* the deed, one must sharply differentiate the real action, in which I was conscious of a special *quality of the exercise of strength;* I designated this as the content of consciousness of the "impulse" or the "innervation." Only one should not speak of the *perception of innervation,* since I do not observe the facts of the case passively, as in sensory perception, but rather feel

---

[17]Der Fechner-Helmholtz'sche Satz über negative Nachbilder und seine Analogieen. *Phil. Stud.,* Volumes 16, 17, 18.

myself active. It developed later that Pfänder was entirely of my opinion, and wished only to have the immediate experience of innervation designated in good German as *"Tätigkeitsbewusstsein"* (consciousness of activity). At that time it also became especially clear to me that the *contents of consciousness are not only a last powerless vestige in the psychophysical interdependency,* as it was considered by Lipps in the sentence, "Consciousness is a luxury," and as it was quite similarly considered in psychophysical parallelism, but that *reality in the full sense of cooperation in the psychophysical causal relation belongs to the contents of consciousness,* since they are not only conditioned but are at the same time conditions, as I later showed in the epistemological introduction of my book, *The Experimental Analysis of the Phenomena of Consciousness.* The differentiation at that time in mere introspection of different phases from mere readiness of will up to real action also guided me later when I tried to ascertain exactly by experiment the *temporal threshold* of this action proper by means of counter-commands in the various stages of the development of the will.[18] In the same direction lay further experimental knowledge with *ergographic* investigations, which Wundt's new assistant, Dr. Robert Müller, who replaced Mentz in the Winter Semester of 1899-1900, initiated with his critique of this method; in connection with Adolf Fick's well-known comparison of the two types of fatigue through voluntary impulses and through Faradayic impulses, he was able to bring about in me too, in addition to normal voluntary action, such involuntary weight lifting by means of direct electrical stimulation of the motor *nervus medianus* in the upper arm. This was indeed very painful but nevertheless instructive in so far as it enabled me to differentiate such passively received peripheral contractions from the conscious voluntary impulse according to my phenomenological method of direct comparison (cf. above).

Even earlier in the Summer vacation of 1899 I completed an extensive treatise on *psychic inhibition,* to which the new investigation of Heymans on the subject stimulated me; this was his friendly return gift for my dissertation which I had sent to him after becoming acquainted with him at the Munich Congress. As is well known, Heymans tried to understand by means of this concept of

---

[18]Cf. *Psychophysik*, 1912, pp. 490 ff.

psychic inhibition the threshold of discrimination for the adding of a color quality to white. As early as my contribution to the Wundt Commemorative Volume on the "extent of consciousness," I put the psychological interpretation of Weber's law completely under this concept of psychic inhibition.

For the time being, however, stimulations from an entirely different direction urged me to defend my *epistemological point of view*. First, in my study of Cornelius' *Psychologie als Erfahrungswissenschaft,* I took exception to his identification of the critically purified concept of the environment with an anticipation of sensory perception, since from the time of the reviews of my father I was immune to the subjective disintegration of the indispensable concept of an object independent of consciousness; and in spite of the frequent application of the "psychological method" I have never in my life been a follower of "psychologism," not even before I came to know this catchword from Husserl. As soon as I had once and for all attained clarity in regard to the nature of introspection as the contemplation of consciousness and its separate contents as such, I saw the fundamental epistemological mistake in Cornelius in the confusion of two different kinds of experience from which originate the concept of recognized environmental objects and the concepts of the contents of consciousness of the observer. But it was therefore just as clear to me from the beginning that only *one* of the two kinds of experiences, namely the *psychological* contemplation of consciousness itself, was capable of understanding this difference scientifically. After becoming acquainted with antipsychologism in the spirit of Husserl, I at once in my lectures and pro-seminars opposed just as decidedly his encroachment on the psychological foundation of normative philosophy. However, even before my acquaintance with Husserl's point of view, the final formulation of my epistemology in a lecture before the Society and in my trial lectures was stimulated particularly by the fact that every day I had to defend psychology as a science against the attacks which the above-mentioned Dr. R. Müller directed against it in all our scientific discussions.

Müller was an excellent physiologist, pupil, and worshipper of Hering; after a sensory-physiological experiment on spatial vision in the Psychological Institute and after his brilliant state medical examination he was chosen as Assistant by Wundt, especially because

Wundt wished very much, after A. Lehmann's results, to develop the investigation of the physiological methods of expression. However, Müller was little suited to positive work in this field, since even on undertaking this work he was convinced of the impossibility of getting even approximately positive correlation of such symptoms with the psychological facts of the case, and only aimed at refuting everything which up to now had been attempted in this direction. To be sure it was to his credit that he had dismissed many an uncritical thesis of Lehman and other psychologists by pointing to the purely physiologically conditioned variations of these symptoms, as he did, for instance, in his publication in regard to the physiological interpretation of the ergogram in the *Zeitschrift für Psychologie.* This whole negativism, however, was based upon the fact that he thoroughly despised psychology as a science having its source in introspection. The second assistant, Möbius, however, also had no liking any more for the experimental work of the Institute and was planning to leave at Easter, 1900. So it happened that at the end of that same Summer Semester, 1899, the departing assistant, Mentz, disclosed to me on departure to my great surprise and joy that Wundt would probably offer me the position of second assistant. During my vacation visit in Munich I could immediately ask Lipps for his opinion on this matter, and he advised me very much to accept such a fine offer as soon as Wundt should give me prospects of habilitation in Leipzig, inasmuch as the founding of an experimental institute in Munich was still in the distant future. Actually, at the beginning of the Winter Semester of 1899, on my visit, Wundt offered me that assistantship for April 1, 1900, and promised me at the same time to aid in every way my admission to the Leipzig faculty and my further academic career, and also to take into consideration as an inaugural dissertation my work already begun on negative after-images. At the same time he revealed to me that in order to facilitate our scientific work (in which he was generous as hardly another chief) he was going to alternate the introductory course from now on between the two assistants. He transferred this course to me for the first time in the Summer Semester of 1900, and thus according to the custom of the time, even before admission to the faculty, I was mentioned together with Wundt in the lecture program.

Müller naturally regarded all this as a setback to his own physiological tendency and was from now on energetically concerned to make it clear to me that I, without training in medicine, was scientifically inferior and that even Wundt was completely backward in his field. Since, however, he was in other ways a likeable, jolly colleague and indeed showed a certain respect for my technique of measuring after-images, I never had a personal quarrel with him, but on the contrary received many valuable suggestions from his physiological training, for which I indeed had great respect. Wundt advised me against going back and taking courses in anatomy and physiology, probably not least of all because of the unfavorable turn which Müller's relation to psychology had thereby taken. However, the uninterrupted examinations to which my colleague subjected me almost daily brought me to a very intensive self-study of the anatomy of the sense organs according to Schwalbe and of physiology according to Hering, Landois, Tigerstedt, Bernstein, and others, so that I gradually built a substructure of a general genetic and anatomic-physiological training under my knowledge of physiological psychology, as far as one can attain it in that way. The introductory course offered me immediately the best opportunity for proving my knowledge in this, especially in the explanation of experiments in sensory physiology and the symptomatics of expression. My knowledge of higher mathematics was also to my advantage now in the psychophysical methods of measuring.

My scientific, theoretic attitude as to the essence and problem of psychology was, however, not in the least shaken by R. Müller, but on the contrary there were formed from those lengthly discussions the foundations for a new treatise, "Die psychologische Betrachtungsweise," in which I for the first time formulated my *concept of consciousness as the individual self-contained totality of all contemporaneous contents of consciousness.* It must form the beginning of all psychology, since this condition is the uniform object of every self-observation. The attitude defined by Wundt as the "psychological attitude" thus had reference to an entirely different *object* than the attitude of natural science, which on its part is directed only toward the outer world. In the *naïve* attitude there is indeed not yet present a clear separation of the two concepts of objective, since direct sensory impression of the stimuli present at any time and other reproductive representatives of the outer world, which belong to the momentary condition of consciousness, are to a large extent originally identified with the environment and are not at all attributed to "consciousness" in that sense. The independent center of the object understood by introspection, about which only gradually the whole concept of consciousness is crystallized, is the immediately experienced ego of the *emotions and the acts of volition* together with the imagination of its future goal, as well as other free formations of imagination and representations of memory. Only when this subjective fundament of the conscious totality has become clear enough would one succeed in understanding clearly the connection of the *conscious relation* of the outer world to it. The scientifically exact content of the concept of the outer world itself was from that point on only an extra-conscious system of *conditions* of sensory perception (and even beyond the material sense organs), which can be *deduced* from sensory observation according to special methods of thought. The perceived environment only then appears clearly divided from the factual condition of consciousness by the whole psychophysical organism, which mediates centripetally and centrifugally, whereby the subconscious-psychic, in Lipps's sense, is causally closest to consciousness. With this, therefore, psychology has its clear independent object, which can be understood only according to its methods and can never be replaced conceptually by anything else, i.e., not by material causes or symptoms of expression. Psychology must clarify this object with all feasible aid of experiment in all directions and probe into its principles theoretically and systematically. In this, of course, the results of the physiological auxiliary sciences must also be drawn upon in addition to the hypothetical explanatory concepts of the psychic subconscious, since the biologic causal connection does not come to a stop at the border of the formation of purely psychological hypotheses. After I had delivered the first draft of this treatise at the Philosophic Society in February, 1900, at the close of the semester, I revised one part of it as the trial lecture for admission to the faculty; this was herewith attained on October 26, 1900. Everything essential on the epistemological point of view was later published in the introductory chapters of *The Experimental Analysis of the Phenomena of Consciousness,* and above all in my *Orientation of Philosophy on the Concept of Consciousness.* My above-mentioned inaugural dissertation on negative after-images I had at first called only "The Helmholtz Proposition in Regard to Negative After-Images," since Helmholtz and his school had already predicated theoretically this proposition, which was proved empirically by me. Since, however, in my final draft, which was finished at the beginning of the Summer Semester of 1900 and published in late Fall in Volume 16 of Wundt's *Philosophische Studien,* I referred at the same time to Fechner's parallel law as a theoretic employment of this proposition, Wundt correctly suggested, after I had handed in the paper to him, that I should call it "The Fechner-Helmholtz Proposition." I passed the "Colloquium" on July 16, 1900, that is, before the completion of my 24th year; Wundt, Volkelt, and H. Bruns were the examiners. R. Müller soon left now to practice medicine, whereupon Wundt, on April 1, 1901, made me first assistant and E. Dürr second assistant. When Dürr a few semesters later wished to return to Würzburg, I suggested to Wundt that F. Krüger be appointed as his successor, so that he too might work toward admission to the faculty, which at present seemed impossible at Kiel with Martius. With the promise of Wundt that he would also support Krüger's admission to the faculty I was able to bring the latter to accept the offer, which turned out happily for him.

III. My Teaching Career at Leipzig (1900-)

The proverb, *"Docendo discimus,"* has been well demonstrated in all the field of my lectures so early begun. An especial interest for the history of the sciences was to my good, since not only for the special lectures on the history of philosophy but also for every systematic lecture it made me pursue the historic development and more and more read philosophic and psychologic authors in the original.

My very first two-hour lecture course, which I began in November, 1900, dealt with the history of psychology. Later indeed I had to drop more and more of the historic introduction of the systematic lectures, the more its material accumulated. Up till now I have conducted altogether eleven specifically historical lecture courses on all periods of philosophy, most frequently on modern times, among which I devoted special lecture courses and pro-seminars to English epistemology and Kant.

Out of this interest resulted my memorial papers for Wundt, Kraepelin, G. Martius, and the short-lived W. Konrad in the *Archiv für die gesamte Psychologie,* as well as my speech on G. Th. Fechner at the dedication of a memorial tablet on his birthplace

in Grosssärchen in the Lausitz in 1929;[19] these actually developed
into small historic monographs through an extended study of the
work and personality of the person to be honored; and this study
was not even lacking in my newspaper articles for the jubilees of
Stumpf and Volkelt. With these belong the above-mentioned essay,
"In Refutation of the Assertion of Crises in Modern Psychology,"
and the exposition of the historic importance of my relative, L. Ph.
Thümmig, the friend of Christian Wolff, in my autobiographical
study in Volume 80 of our *Archiv*.[20] My independent production
in the history of philosophy, made during the War when the laboratories were less active, was a survey of the development of religious
scholarship, beginning with Luther and consisting of monographs on
Luther, Melanchthon, Giordano Bruno, Montaigne, Bacon, Herbert
of Cherbury, Hobbes, Descartes, Spinoza, Locke, Pascal, Pierre
Bayle, Shaftesbury, and Leibnitz; it has not yet been published. These
labors were made easier for me since R. Werner Schulte, who now
edits with us the quarterly founded by him, *Psychologie und Medizin*,
came to the laboratory and in 1914 became my personal assistant.
Through his great skill and independence he very quickly became
familiar with the experimental methods, and then as personal
assistant of Professor Wundt he took over a part of the duties of
the assistants who had gone to the War. Above all he assisted very
reliably in Wundt's lectures. In addition he had good philosophical
training and showed great interest and understanding for my work
in psychology and religious philosophy. The systematic second part of
my whole manuscript on religious philosophy, for which the above-
mentioned historic part was intended only as the introduction, is
the most extensive, and unfortunately also unpublished, part of my
philosophic work to date.

This renewed intensive occupation with the old problems of religious scholarship, from which my philosophizing in youth had
gone forth, was however by no means only begun with the War,
but had been standing on my program of work for a long time; the
completion of my two extensive psychological and psychophysical
works at the end of the year 1911 finally gave me the opportunity to
work at it. The founding of a family of my own in the Summer

---

[19]Published in the *Blätter des Geschichtsvereins in Forst in der Lausitz*,
December, 1929.
[20]Cf. above, p. 1.

of 1913 was also a motivation toward this, since I particularly hoped to be able to give my family just as firm and clear a foundation in this for the future as my father had offered tc me myself. Thus as early as the Summer Semester of 1913 I delivered a lecture course, "Die erkenntnistheoretischen und. ethischen Grundlagen des Glaubens," which was further developed in the above-mentioned manuscript. Also in the *Verein für Volkswohl* (Society for Social Welfare) in Leipzig, I delivered a long lecture on this theme in 1918, after I had lectured there on Wundt in 1917. After the War, in 1921, I then lectured for two evenings on the theme, "Die Berechtigung und Verpflichtung zum religiösen Glauben," in my church (St. Peter's) at the suggestion of my friend, Professor Paul Fiebig, the pastor there. The latter in collaboration with me published a review of the lectures in the *Leipziger Kirchenblatt,* No. 41-42 of the same year. Since then I have lectured seven times on religious philosophy.

Further stimulation to publication on my philosophic attitude toward life was offered to me in my contribution to the Commemorative Volume for Volkelt's 70th birthday, "Zur Orientierung der Philosophie am Bewusstseinsbegriff," 1919, which also appeared separately, as well as in my contribution, "Die Zeitwahrnehmung," to the second Volkelt Commemorative Volume, *Zwischen Kunst und Philosophie,* on the occasion of the 50th anniversary of his career as a teacher; in this I took a critical position toward Einstein's theory of relativity and among other things found a parallel between the physical difficulties of a uniform determination of world time and the psychological time shifts of disparate sense impressions of the individual inner world. My occupation with the philosophy of Volkelt, with which I had many points of contact, permitted me then to return to my *aesthetic* interests, out of which resulted, as early as the Summer Semester of 1903, a lecture course, "Psychologische Grundfragen der Aesthetik," and later a pro-seminar on "Aesthetische Einfühlung." Then, in 1925, in connection with the reading of Volkelt's work, *Das ästhetische Bewusstsein,* I completed my book, *Grundfragen der Asthetik,* in which I tried out new points of view even in the most general arrangement of consciousness, especially in the mental visualization of other persons, and also differentiated among the different kinds of empathy.

Even though I must speak briefly in regard to these philosophic works because we are dealing here with psychology, I should like to survey my *further psychological investigations,* classifying them into several groups of problems, for precisely on these I can everywhere refer to publications at hand. Besides, I hope soon to finish a short treatise on the chief phenomena of psychic life under the title, "Grundfragen der Psychologie." Since, as assistant and as co-director of Wundt's Institute, and from 1917 as independent director of the psychophysical seminar of the University of Leipzig, I was continually stimulating and directing doctoral theses; I shall also have to refer frequently to these.

I have not yet gathered together in a monograph my work on the problems of sensory physiology, which could be solved by means of subjective methods, even though these had become one of my special fields since the measurement of after-images in my inaugural dissertation. The second installment of that investigation, which extended to the dependence of colored after-images on the reacting stimuli, led deep into the dispute on color theory still acute at that time. In criticizing these controversies in the third and final part,[21] I took impartially from all sides all that was valuable in observations and theories and put into the center of discussion von Kries's proposition on the persistence of color compromise in any color adaptations appertaining uniformly to the whole area of comparison; this is most simply explained in my hypothesis of admixture. My work stimulated a new concern with the problem of negative after-images in the school of von Kries as well as in that of Hering, whereby, indeed, my results were at first not carefully considered. A. Tschzermak, as the first, gave a correct exposition of it in his contribution to Bethe's *Handbuch der Physiologie,* after I had taken a stand against those misconceptions in the Commemorative Volume for Martius.[22] Here, as well as in my most recent paper in regard to this, in the Commemorative Volume for Kiesow, I indicated also the means by which the especially large after-image value in the very first stage immediately after fixation of contrast (ca. 0.1/sec.) can be measured. Most recently G. E. Müller has devoted a passage in acknowledgment to several chief results of my thirty-year-old work in his psychophysical investigations on color perception.[23] I should be especially glad if the working circle of

[21] *Philosophische Studien,* Volume 18.
[22] *Archiv,* Volume 45.
[23] *Zeitschrift für Psychologie,* supplementary Volumes 17, 18.

Jaensch, in the testing of individual differences in the phenomena of after-images, would also make use of my quantitative methods which eliminate the large individual differences in the *recognition* of actually present after-images of perception, since my method of investigation is completely independent of this apperception (so difficult for many people) of the after-image changing with the glance. The Fechner-Helmholtz proposition, by the way, also stood the test in a recent dissertation of E. Hummel, which came from my seminar, on the adaptation of the temperature sense to the fatigue components found by Goldscheiter, an adaptation which always in the same way weakens the perception of coldness and warmth.

Since my cooperation on E. Dürr's dissertation on the increase of retinal stimulation, which had been suggested by his teacher, Marbe, I was especially interested in this *rising* branch of the curve of activity of a contrast suddenly occurring and fixed through a variable time, *t,* up to the maximum, whereas the times of fixation used for the above-mentioned measurement of after-images all lie in the *descending* branch. The very first effect proportional at time *t* of very short stimuli I then used particularly for my perimetric determination of the influence of different distributions of attention (the degrees of clearness) on the thresholds of point-like illumination in the different regions of the field of vision.[24] The extension of those investigations of the increase of excitability to the various sensory regions, in which we were interested also psychologically because of the "tachistophonic" and "tachistotypical" analogies to the tachistoscopic analysis of attention, led to the dissertations of Büchner, Kafka, B. Berliner, and G. F. Arps. Also, in regard to the mixture of adaptive influences of periodically changing and longer lasting stimuli, I suggested at that time to C. Schneider an investigation in Volume 7 of the *Psychologische Studien.* In an investigation by Mitscherling on color mixtures with the same brightness of components, I attempted to make useful for the mixing of real and virtual images the principle of my mirror tachistoscope by means of a rotation apparatus with a mirror surface variable in the width of its sectors. Numerous prelimary experiments of the lapse of time in simultaneous contrasts, in which even during the War I had interested Theodoridis, at present Professor at Saloniki, reached a certain conclusion with the dissertation of B. Striegler. In

---

[24]*Psychologische Studien,* Volume 2.

my contribution to the Commemorative Volume for Kirschmann,[25] I discussed further the result (at first surprising) that the usual measure of contrasts remains essentially constant at fixation up to twenty seconds, when, in addition to the inducing and induced field of stimulation, there is also present in the field of vision a surface of comparison as free of contrast as possible.

An especially comprehensive survey of the many groups of normal and pathological phenomena of visual perception and their mutual relations I gained at the time I prepared for our *Archiv* collective reviews on the progress in the field of psychophysics, on the perception of light and color. Wundt had particularly desired these from the time of the founding of the *Archiv für die gesamte Psychologie*. At that time the single phases of excitation, especially with the phenomena of a moving strip and a fixed glance, were studied by the Helmholtz school as well as by the Hering school, and by McDougall and others; this later brought W. Frölich to his theory on the immediate determinability of the perception time between the stimulus and its effect in consciousness. However, I believed that I had to interpret his observations otherwise; nor could I confirm the results of Hazelhoff and of Heleen Wiersma in regard to the much more complicated phenomena of a moving strip with the following glance.[26]

Along with this far larger number of subjective observations of optical phenomena, objective anthropological observations, the material for which I was gathering ever since 1900, enabled me in time to claim a correlation of outward, visible, constitutional signs of facial coloring to cases of color-blindness. These signs were perhaps related to the anomalies of the papillary bodies and anomalies of pigment later discovered by Walter Jaensch. This correlation could at times even be used positively in diagnosis, although an unvarying relation can in no wise be asserted, at least as far as the signs described till now are concerned.

Among the elementary facts of perception of space, I was not only occupied with the threshold of space and the thresholds of difference of position investigated with Katzenellenbogen and with Poschoga but above all with the perception of depth. In this I measured with Arwed Pfeifer a theoretically interesting illusion, namely, an ap-

---

[25]F. Krüger's *Neue psychologische Studien*, Volume 6, p. 269.
[26]Cf. Bethe's *Handbuch*, Volume 10, p. 598 f.

proximately fivefold overestimate of the distance of objects lying behind the point of fixation, measured from this point; this is also present
monocularly and can therefore probably be traced back to conditions
of accommodation and therefore has little to do with the disparate
double image present at this same time. Also, for the location in
depth of *moving* objects, whose two half-images are through shielding
never simultaneously perceptible, and therefore also do not permit of
any disparity's being perceived immediately, I attempted a new theoretic
explanation after their rediscovery by O. Klemm (independent of
Dvorčak's earlier observation). I discussed it in the colloquium of
Krüger's Institute at the beginning of the Winter Semester of 1931,
and I indicated the graphic completion of the phases not perceived
according to the principle of the stroboscope. In a little-noticed review
of Theodor Lipps's *Psychologischen Studien* I dealt with the problems
of the *development of space perception* and offered among other
things a theory of the gradual gauging of regions of the field of vision
or touch, spatially less well ordered, by means of others already
better ordered, on the basis of the movement of the organs.[27]

The works on the *psycho-energetic group* began in 1900, after the
above-mentioned theoretical preparation, with the tachistoscopic investigations for my large contribution to the Commemorative Volume for Wundt, and continued with the perimetric measurements of
the distribution of clearness in the sense areas which now have been
tested again by Guratzasch, Schatz, and Truöl. After I had then
worked through the whole psychological literature on the confines
of consciousness, I attempted in my book, *The Experimental Analysis
of the Phenomena of Consciousness,* 1908, to place a whole psychology
under this central point of view, the understanding of which in all
its separate problems of actual recognition, feeling, and volition,
as well as of its dispositions, brings to light the phenomenological
and functional uniformity of psychic life as hardly any other point
of view.

Even in correspondence with O. Külpe around 1900 about the
Commemorative Volume for Wundt, I had especially pointed to the
significance of the independent variability of the grades of consciousness of *abstract characteristics of configuration,* and showed
that I was from the philosophic point of departure of my psychological
investigation myself independently investigating this point of view

---

[27] *Archiv für die gesamte Psychologie,* Volume 14.

which was kept in mind in the *experimental psychology of thinking* of the Würzburg school. With Mittenzwey I then demonstrated the influence of such an *abstracting* attitude toward the thresholds for observed and unobserved characteristics of two complexes of comparison, and with Lohnert I showed by means of my right-angle variator, already constructed in 1909, that in the comparison of two right angles the consciousness of *similarity,* which is based upon the correspondence of form, can put an absolute amount of simultaneous change of length *and* breadth below the threshold; this same amount with isolated change of length *or* breadth leads much sooner to a clear consciousness of *difference,* because of the simultaneous change of *form.* C. Bühler has confirmed this independently of us.

The increase of difficulty of perception for several simultaneous stimuli *below* the maximal boundary of extent of the new tachistoscopic interpretation was measured in various directions by J. Lorenz and later by W. Schlegel, likewise by means of thresholds of differentiation and stimulus. With a purposeful later development of Schlegel's procedure, Unger, whose rich material has not yet been published, tested the *influence of the intensity of stimulus on the learning and retention* of stimuli consisting of simple combinations of points. This influence is probably conditioned by a *general* influence of intensity of the "eidetically" persevering after-images of memory; for this the celebrated work of E. Jaensch attempted at once to understand the *individual* differences. The comparative method, which is able to bring out much weaker tendencies than the method of free reproduction, I recommended for the investigation of memory in the work of F. Reuther,[28] for which I constructed my memory apparatus. Also the dissertations of Bucholz and Rüsche belong to this application of the comparative method to the testing of tendencies of memory.

In regard to the course of *fluctuations* of attention, for the phenomenology of which I made advantageous use especially of the dissertation of Hugo Eckener as early as 1908, O. Klemm has continued my formulation of the problem experimentally in an independent manner. Our first collaboration at a time when he was still a student of mine extended to his investigations of the time shifts between disparate sense impressions by means of Wundt's pendulum according to the method of self-regulation. Even earlier in the ex-

---

[28]*Psychologische Studien,* Volume 1.

periments with the "complication clock" of M. Geiger, in whom experimental psychology has given an especially well-equipped worker to general philosophy, I helped technically and as an observer. The apparatus used by him, plus similar additions of devices as with Klemm's experiments, I later had K. Heyde use for the investigation of time shifts for several hands to be observed at the same time. In Moede's measurement of the time shift, however, we substituted for the separate stimuli of short duration the more sharply determinable beginnings and endings of *lasting* disparate sense impressions. On Wundt's special wish and likewise stimulated by Ach's lecture on his reaction experiments at the first founding Congress of the German *Gesellschaft für experimentelle Psychologie* in Giessen in 1904,[29] I turned in the same year to correlating my demonstration of the distribution of clearness in the field of vision by means of the thresholds for brief illumination over against analogous tables of the *times of reactions* upon such additional point stimuli, without however regarding these times as an equivalent measure of clearness, as it was occasionally misunderstood.   In taking up these reaction experiments again I now put the chief emphasis upon the control of the dependence of the volitional impulse by the prescribed motive of stimulation, which control corresponds to the general principles of the induction of such a dependence.   Thus I came to the development of my *systematic control of reaction,* through which the differentiation, which was at that time still considered important, between putting emphasis on the muscular and sensorial on the one hand, and on individual types on the other, yielded place for me to the question as to the optimum of participation of all those three components of every reaction achievement (namely, the recognition of motive, the addition of the impulse, and the carrying out of it), which were worked out by L. Lange and Martius.   These three components can be most clearly differentiated in the most complicated achievement of the so-called choice reaction with disjunctive additions of several impulses to just as many possibilities of stimulus, but they are already present in the simplest reaction as such, which is really conditioned only by the stimulus.   Through the consideration of these, all the reaction achievements can be classified in an ascending order of difficulty, as I attempted it in my monograph, "Die Reaktions-

---

[29] I also attended all the subsequent Congresses except one in 1908, and always read papers at them, in part with experimental demonstrations.

zeiten" in Bethe's *Handbuch der normalen und pathologischen Physiologie,* 1927, Volume 10, p. 524. But *only with constant control of the correctness of retention of a definite motivation of action can a corresponding ascending order of reaction times be expected.* These controls also proved their validity for the training of the correct attitudes particularly with extensive *preparation* of the reaction (which otherwise threatens to take possession of the unequivocal *motivation* of the impulse), as with *transit reactions* in the manner of the astronomical ones in which F. Günther for the first time trained pure reactions by means of such controls, or in rhythmic preparation (Bertha Paulssen, E. Kühnert), further in the case of the previous agreement on general or special criteria of stimulation as the deciding motivation (Deuchler, Kraskowsky, Westphal, Handrick), in simultaneous reaction with two hands (Salow), in the succession of two simple reactions independent of one another (Topciu), and others. In addition I also paid especial attention to the anticipating release of the impulse which as a so-called "synchronization" takes place here *simultaneously,* i.e., with a positive or negative error in time, with a procedure which can be anticipated because of its regularity. I have already spoken above of the threshold method of determining the time of the impulse in such experiments. In synchronizing thoroughgoing registrations this was attempted for the first time by A. Hammer, whereas P. Müller controlled both this "synchronization" and also the actual reacting release of the impulse according to this time-threshold method. H. Rey, now in my seminar, used a variable preliminary signal with such synchronizations just as in the choice reactions, and thus each time commanded anew the type of impulse wanted; he found that the time of this signal, which just suffices for correct synchronization, was in harmony with the time of the choice reaction, if there were the same number of disjunctions. We have also carried out such experiments on children and adolescents. In the anticipating release of the impulses, by the way, one quickly accommodates oneself to short "dead times" between the impulse and an end goal brought about by an intervening mechanism, as A. Kleber and E. Schulze showed. Through my friend, E. Grossman, Professor of Astronomy in Munich, previously at the Leipzig Observatory, I also came upon the idea of analyzing psychophysically the newest psychologically conditioned determination of time of astronomers by means of Repsold's passage-micrometer; I had a model built for this according to the conditions of operation on the Munich apparatus, which I had there examined in 1912 for that purpose. Naturally it appeared that here also there remain inexactnesses of temporal correlation of impulses to regular perceptions, even though they may be much smaller than with the one-time registration according to the old graphic method.

In addition we sought to develop physiological graphics above all in *phonetics,* for which there was special interest in Wundt's Institute because of the speech-melodic researches of our celebrated Leipzig phonetician, Eduard Sievers, who later also introduced us to Rutz's typology. So I invented at that time my guttural sound recorder for the direct reception of the change of vocal tone in speech melody. F. Krüger, who at that time had been assigned by Wundt to this investigation of speech melody, then modified the principle of this apparatus for his own experiments and published a paper on it in collaboration with me.

The energy with which the method of reaction and the symptomatology of expression were then carried on by the psychologists must show the representatives of an "objective psychology" or of "Behaviorism" how the careful study of the overt behavior need never come into conflict with our chief problem as to the correlation of these expressions to the course of consciousness and to psychic tendencies. Also in another respect, this symptomatology was exemplary for me since it showed how purely physical figures of measurement of these symptoms come in a *psychically mediated* relation of dependence to just as commensurable objective conditions of stimulation. For I also saw the same thing realized where physical measurements come into lawful relation to one another through *comparative judgments,* as for instance in the proportion of the barely noticeable differences in stimulation to the strength of the compared stimuli, or through arbitrary impulses, as in the dependence of reaction time upon strength of stimulus. Through this I came to my concept of *"psychophysics in the narrower sense,"* which deals only with such relations between *physical measures,* which are all exactly determinable but are nevertheless *transmitted throughout in a purely psychic manner.* I formulated this position in my *Psychophysics* of 1911 and have in recent times repeatedly come back to it as, for instance, at the Congress in New Haven and most explicitly till now in my treatise, "Das Wesen der psychophysischen gesetzmässigkeit" (*Archiv,* Volume 60). I believe I have thereby demonstrated that particularly the concepts of apperceptive accomplishments, feared as being especially controversial, and above all the concept of "attention," defined more particularly by me as the clarification of present sense perception, are objectively strictly controllable.

I first came to independent work on the mathematical foundation of the psychophysical measurement when I undertook the section on psychophysics for Tigerstedt's *Handbuch der physiologischen Methodik,* which had been offered to me by the editor on Wundt's suggestion; but this could be undertaken only after the completion of my book on the phenomena of consciousness, which had delayed me longer than I had anticipated because of the necessity of abridging it to one volume from the two volumes to which it had grown. In this I wanted to bring to recognition above all the principle of the arithmetical means for the so-called immediate procedure, as it can be of value particularly for "complete rows" of the constants method (now simply called by me "method of statistical judgment"), and I found after a few experiments in this direction that Spearman had already accomplished everything necessary for the utilization of this. I had to add only the general development under the assumption of constant collective objects by means of integral calculus, whereby the employment of finite extremes, criticized in such a friendly way by Urbam, was decisive. I was given the first stimulus for the formulae of the measures of distribution because of their necessity for the work of Lohnert mentioned above. In regard to the "treatment by means of formula," F. M. Urbam's excellent exposition in Volumes 14 and 15 of our *Archiv* had helped me materially, and with him I had since then remained in constant contact renewed through several visits in Leipzig. Among these investigations into the method of measurement since then instigated by me in Leipzig, that of Stephanowitsch on the graphic analysis of the manner of regulation in the method of production (method of median errors) in part was still able to come to recognition in my *Psychophysics* completed in the Fall of 1911. On the other hand, I was not able to take cognizance of the material which Herfurth had accumulated according to the "proposition of correspondence" for the equivalent value (on the change of level of stimulation), which I treated purely theoretically in the *Psychophysics* and which in more recent times was expanded by Nagel[30]

---

[30]*Archiv,* Volume 47.

in part with logarithmic transformation of the stimulus values, and also not the derivation of a uniform measure of dispersion and an equivalent value belonging with it, until I wrote my second treatise on the methods of measurement, "Die speciellen psychophysischen Massmethoden."[31] Up to the time of planning these, a few polemic airings of differences with Urbam and G. F. Lipps in Volumes 21, 24, and 27 of the *Archiv* came to a certain conclusion. The first main part of this work, however, is devoted to the calculation of correlations, in the theory of which I did not become deeply absorbed until 1918 after a more intensive occupation with the requirements of applied psychology, especially of psychotechnics. This was stimulated by my invitation in the Easter vacation of that year to a lecture cycle, arranged on higher commission by Stumpf and his pupils together with W. Moede, for the introduction of military physicians into the psychotechnical test of fitness.

In the occupation with the calculation of correlation I gained above all a definite answer to the question about its relation to the method of least squares, which I already had in mind before knowing of the Bravais-Pearson and the Yule derivation of correlation coefficients as the problem of a medial function of dependency, i.e., one symmetrical for the coordinates X and Y. I put this problem into the center of the whole theory of correlation. Then the old master of statistics, E. Czuber, became vitally interested because of the relation of my medial function to his earlier deduced "main axes" of the body of dispersion; in addition to his treatises for our *Archiv*,[32] he sent me several valuable letters. In this whole field Spearman's derivation of a rank correlation coefficient seemed to me the most important achievement for our psychological practice, and I have ever since been active in attaining for it more general recognition.

In my seminar newly founded in 1917, the works chiefly on methods of measurement naturally form an important part. At times I was also supported by Kraepelin and Kiesow in that they put at my disposal rich and valuable material for statistical analysis. The problems of the seminar, however, extend under this point of view of a method made to be as exact as possible to all the problems of psychology which can be clarified through the determination of thresholds and errors in any kind of objectively tangible performance,

---

[31] In Abderhalden's *Handbuch der biologischen Arbeitsmethoden*, Part 4.
[32] *Archiv*, Volumes 41, 44.

and through measuring of reaction-times and of energies of symptoms of expression. In these, in recent times, we have occasionally also utilized children and adolescents as subjects. My four-hour lecture course on general psychology with demonstrations, which I have already conducted eighteen times and have worked out for free delivery in a continuously amended manuscript of about one thousand pages, naturally serves a far larger circle of students and excludes no group of problems hitherto handled with success from any point of view, wherein also the biological auxiliary sciences come to justice. Since I here do not sacrifice old problems, it does not mean that they are also dealt with by old methods, as many an all too ambitious scientist likes to reproach others. The now generally recognized mistakes of the beginnings of our experimental psychology, through the manifold foundations of my point of view, I have recognized at least just as early and have tried to avoid just as much as those who today raise themselves all too loudly over the old times. We know, however, that we are still standing at the beginning of the insight into psychophysical laws attainable by us human beings, to the extension of which our teachers have given us the best example.